Grafting Helen

GRAFTING HELEN

The Abduction of the Classical Past

Matthew Gumpert

THE UNIVERSITY OF WISCONSIN PRESS

The University of Wisconsin Press
1930 Monroe Street
Madison, Wisconsin 53711

www.wisc.edu/wisconsinpress/

3 Henrietta Street
London WC2E 8LU, England

5   4   3   2   1

Printed in the United States of America

Library of Congress Cataloging-in-Publication Data
Gumpert, Matthew.
      Grafting Helen: the abduction of the classical past / Matthew Gumpert.
      352 pp.   cm.
      Includes bibliographical references and index.
      ISBN 0-299-17120-5 (alk. paper)
      ISBN 0-299-17124-8 (pbk.: alk. paper)
      1. Classical literature—History and criticism.   2. Helen of Troy (Greek
mythology) in literature.   3. Civilization, Western—Classical influences.
4. French literature—Classical influences.   5. Trojan War—Literature and
the war.   6. Influence (Literary, artistic, etc.)   7. Beauty, Personal, in
literature.   I. Title.
      PA3015.R5 H374   2001
      880′.09—dc21   00-010615

Publication of this volume has been made possible in large part
through the generous support and enduring vision of Warren G. Moon.

Sırmaya

Immitant les meilleurs aucteurs Grecz, se transformant en eux, les devorant, & apres les avoir bien digerez, les convertissant en sang & nouriture, se proposant, chacun selon son naturel & l'argument qu'il vouloit elire, le meilleur aucteur, dont ilz observoint diligemment toutes les plus rares & exquises vertuz, & icelles comme grephes, ainsi que j'ay dict devant, entoint & apliquoint à leur Langue. Cela faisant (dy-je) les Romains ont baty tous ces beaux ecriz, que nous louons & admirons si fort.

[Imitating the best Greek authors, transforming themselves into them, devouring them, and after having fully digested them, converting them into blood and sustenance, they selected, each according to his natural inclination and the theme he wanted to treat, the best author, whose rarest and finest virtues he had diligently observed, and as if these virtues were grafts, as I said before, they grafted and applied them to their Language. By doing this (I say) the Romans built all of those beautiful writings which we praise and so greatly admire.] (Trans. author)

La donq', Françoys, marchez couraigeusement vers cete superbe cité Romaine: & des serves depouilles d'elle (comme vous avez fait plus d'une fois) ornez voz temples & autelz. . . . Donnez en cete Grece menteresse, & y semez encor' un coup la fameuse nation des Gallogrecz.

[And so, Frenchmen, march bravely toward that proud Roman city: and with her spoils (just as you have done on more than one occasion), adorn your temples and altars. . . . Take Greece, that impostor, and sow there once again the great city of the Gallo-Greeks.] (Trans. author)

—Joachim du Bellay, *La deffence et illustration de la langue françoyse*

Contents

Preface

In Book 3 of the *Iliad,* Greeks and Trojans have laid down their arms while Paris and Menelaus prepare to fight for Helen. At that moment Helen herself appears upon the city walls, in a passage (3.154–60) traditionally referred to as the *teichoskopia* (the Look-Out on the Wall or the View from the Battlements). Priam and his counselors marvel at Helen's beauty, but their admiration is troubled:

> And these, as they saw Helen along the tower approaching,
> murmuring softly to each other uttered their winged words:
> "Surely there is no blame on Trojans and strong-greaved Achaians
> if for long time they suffer hardship for a woman like this one.
> Terrible is the likeness of her face to immortal goddesses.
> Still, though she be such, let her go away in the ships, lest
> she be left behind, a grief to us and our children."
>
> (Trans. Lattimore 1951)

Helen has been uprooted from her native Sparta and transplanted to a foreign country. The Trojan elders, so receptive to her charms, cannot forget that she does not really belong. It is the premise of this study that the history of Western literature is a *teichoskopia,* perpetually reenacted. *Grafting Helen* reads the abduction—or flight—of Helen as a figure for the cultural appropriation of Homer. It tells the story of how the West has labored to make Helen belong or make the past at home in the present.

Grafting Helen explores the myth of Helen, first in Greek poetry from the archaic to the classical period, and then in French writings, medieval to modern. This division allows me to explore how Homer is adopted and adapted in classical antiquity and, at the same time, to extrapolate my findings to the larger field of classical humanism.[1] The trajectory from Greece to France is my way of traversing that field; it has no pretensions to being the only way. In moving from Greece to France, *Grafting Helen* becomes a study both of a particular figure in a particular tradition and of tradition itself.[2] By *tradition* I mean the familiar tale Western culture has always told about its relation to the past, the tale of seamless continuity. My objective is to bring the seam to light and show that continuity is always grafted. Continuity, in other words, is a trope or, more specifically, a *catachresis,* a metaphor whose metaphoricity has long ago been forgotten.[3] This makes *Grafting Helen* an unusual kind of literary history. If literary history is always a narrative that links past to present, it is that link itself which is the object of study here.[4] Graft is thus not only the subject of this book but also its shape. Part 1, "Helen in Greece," is to part 2, "Helen in France," as stock is to scion, or scion to stock (the later poet or culture can assume the role of the stock, the principal body warding off foreign infection, impurity, corruption). In the middle is a seam, the sign of an elision of some two thousand years separating Greek antiquity from European modernity. Elision itself is a form of graft.

So is desire. Helen's appearance upon the walls has always been read as her debut entrance, not only upon the Trojan stage, but upon that of Western literature.[5] That makes it a good place to begin any study of Helen.[6] But there is another reason why the *teichoskopia* is *Grafting Helen*'s point of departure and recurrent point of return: it is a scene about desire as critical reading. Gazing upon Helen, dazzled and distracted by beauty they cannot possess, longing to embrace and plotting to expel her, the elders are the archetypal lovers and poets of this study. Reading Helen is indeed critical for them in all senses of the term. *Grafting Helen* is a history of this critical reading. Its chapters are all *teichoskopias,* its protagonist-poets all elders, dazzled and daunted by the spectacle of the past. Chapters are not organized by chronology or genre; rather, each focuses on a particular strategy for reading the past into the present. Mimesis, Anamnesis, Supplement, Speculation, Epideixis, and Deixis in part 1 and Idolatry, Translation, Genealogy, Cosmetics, Miscegenation, and Prostitution in part 2 are all variations on graft, strategies for recuperating the past and for concealing that act of recuperation.[7] What these chapters tell is a story about coveting the past, stealing it, and covering it up (the past and its theft). Not only are erotic and imitative gestures (embracing, rejecting, coveting from afar) figures for each other here, but both are forms of graft.

Why privilege this particular term? Both in the organic sense of an artificial union brought about between distinct bodies and in the economic sense of embezzlement, *graft* is ideally suited to represent both poetic and erotic possession. The first definition of the word in *Webster's Third New International Dictionary* already weds the natural and the artificial: "an individual resulting from the union of scion and stock: a grafted plant" (Gove 1963). The second definition complicates matters: "the act of grafting or of joining one thing to another *as if* by grafting" (my italics). So we can use the term in a figurative as well as a literal sense to refer to any act of joining disparate entities. But to use *graft* figuratively is already, in effect, tó graft it to a context in which, literally speaking, it does not belong. There is, in fact, no way of using the term properly. By definition graft is always improper, an illicit union. Every graft can be resolved into its *scion* and its *stock,* but that resolves little, since each of these constituent elements is already a graft of distinct meanings: commercial, botanical, genealogical, racial, linguistic.[8] Searching for an original meaning also proves futile. *Graft* comes from the Greek *graphein,* to write, from "the resemblance of the scion inserted at an angle in the tree to a stylus poised for writing." It is not correct to say, then, that in this study I use graft simply as a metaphor for writing; from the beginning, writing is a metaphor for graft. If graft is always a metaphor, metaphor itself—artificial union of distinct conceptual bodies, like and unlike—is defined as early as Aristotle as a form of graft, as language coerced and corrupted.

Transported from Sparta to Troy, and from Troy back to Sparta, Helen's own story literalizes the metaphor implicit, etymologically, in all metaphor (from the Greek *metaphorein,* to carry over, to transfer). Metaphor is always a journey across an epistemological space, a cognitive wandering, a way of being led astray. Helen is led astray, just as those who gaze upon her are. The Trojan elders, for example, cannot decide who or what she is, or which side she is on, and vacillate instead within the uncertainty of resemblance: "Terrible is the likeness of her face to immortal goddesses" (3.158). This vacillation is the back-and-forth of all graft. It is Helen's identifying feature, and precisely that which makes her impossible to identify. Helen as a subject is always elusive. She is always a graft, more than one thing at a time.

To say, then, that Helen of Troy is the subject of this study is to state the problem with which it is concerned. To take Helen herself as a subject of writing, I would argue, is to confront writing itself as an always disrupted subject. This makes *Grafting Helen* very different from other recent works about Helen, works which have nevertheless all played an important role in the formulation of my own project, in particular Linda Lee Clader's *Helen: The Evolution from Divine to Heroic in Greek Epic Tradition* (1976), Mihoko Suzuki's *Metamorphoses of Helen: Authority, Difference and the Epic* (1989), and, most recently, Norman Austin's *Helen of Troy and Her Shameless Phantom* (1994).[9] All of these are specialized in ways that make them very distinct from this present study; only Suzuki's is a comparative study, and her focus is the epic genre. More important, in each Helen is approached as an intensely ambivalent figure, mediating between specific antithetical values: between ritual and secularity in Clader, between feminine passivity and male authority in Suzuki, between honor and shame in Austin. Helen remains ambivalent in *Grafting Helen,* but with a crucial difference. Here, Helen does not mediate between designated antitheses; she is a figure for mediation itself. Here, Helen is not any given ambivalence between an *a* or a *b:* she is, rather, an emblem of ambivalence itself, a sign for self-difference, something close to what Jacques Derrida attempts to capture in a term like *différance.* In this respect my work builds on Froma Zeitlin's insights in her essay "Travesties of Gender and Genre in Aristophanes' *Thesmophoriazousae*" in *Playing the Other: Gender and Society in Classical Greek Literature* (1996); this and Austin's volume seem to me by far the most powerful pieces of writing on Helen in recent years. To a large extent, in fact, *Grafting Helen* is the scion of Derrida's early reflections on writing. Playing on the etymology to which I referred above, Derrida writes: "Ecrire veut dire greffer. C'est le même mot" ("To write means to graft. It's the same word" [1972a:395]). That assertion stems from a reading of a text by Mallarmé that, for Derrida, challenges the Platonic view of writing as a simple reference to something prior (speech, presence, truth):

se passant de tout prétexte extérieur, *Mimique* est aussi hantée par le fantôme d'un autre texte ou entée sur l'arborescence d'un autre texte. . . . Il faudrait explorer systématiquement ce qui se donne comme simple unité étymologique de la greffe et du graphie . . . mais aussi l'analogie entre les formes de greffe textuelle et les greffes dites végétales. . . . élaborer un traité systématique de la greffe textuelle. (1972a:230)

[doing without any external pretext, *Mimique* is also haunted by the ghost or grafted onto the arborescence of another text. . . . One ought to explore systematically not only what appears to be a simple etymological coincidence uniting the graft and the graph . . . but also the analogy between the forms of textual grafting and so-called vegetal grafting . . . one must elaborate a systematic treatise on the textual graft.] (Johnson 1981:202)

Grafting Helen is just such a treatise on "la greffe textuelle" ("textual graft").[10] As a study of Helen and a study of imitation, *Grafting Helen* is an exploration of the way one text is "haunted by the ghost or grafted onto the arborescence of another text." Elsewhere Derrida insists upon the "possibilité de prélèvement et de greffe citationnelle qui appartient à la structure de toute marque. . . . Tout signe . . . peut être cité . . . par là il peut rompre avec tout contexte donné" ("possibility of removal and citational graft which belongs to every mark. . . . Every sign . . . can be cited . . . by which it can break from any given context" [1972b:381]). What *Grafting Helen* suggests is that *prélèvement* (removal) is always *enlèvement* (abduction).[11] Homer's fate is like Helen's: to be forever abducted, torn from one context, and grafted to another.

Part 1

Helen in Greece

1

Mimesis

Introduction: *Teichoskopia*

Helen's beauty fractures her, making her epistemologically (who is she?), ontologically (*is* she?), and ethically (whose is she?) undecidable: a Helen-graft.[1]
This undecidability is precisely what Plato will come to fear in all mimesis. In
this chapter I argue that Helen in the *Iliad* is always tied to questions of representation and referentiality. In the next chapter I focus on Helen in the *Odyssey* as a
reader and writer of representations (for example, her preternatural mimicry of
the wives of the Achaean heroes as they wait inside the Trojan horse, recounted
by Menelaus at *Odyssey* 4.265–89). To be seduced by the face of Helen of Troy,
I am suggesting, is to be drawn into what Plato will understand as the error of
mimesis.

The issue is complicated by the fact that the Homeric Helen can never be
said to have attained the status of an official or orthodox figure, even if Homer's
remains the overwhelmingly authoritative version that post-Homeric authors
cannot help but follow or reject. There is no definitive myth of Helen, then,
but a host of Helen myths, all posing as the truth. Thus the "alternative" tradition of the *eidolon* or phantom Helen, about which I will have much to say, is
only a more explicit version of the "standard" or Homeric myth. Homeric epic,
which attained its own "official" status through a long process of selection and
synthesis,[2] is very good at "splitting the difference" when it comes to Helen.
Rather than telling one version of the tale, Homer grafts several. The *Iliad* and
the *Odyssey* form another graft, each implicitly acknowledging the existence of
the other. The Iliadic Helen is always haunted, as it were, by the Odyssean, and
vice versa. In the first part of this chapter I consider the Iliadic Helen; in the
second I turn to Plato's prosecution of Homer in the *Republic*. Plato's references

3

to Helen in *Republic* 10, we will see, suggest the extent to which her banishment is also poetry's. Even the allegory of the cave in *Republic* 7 can be read as another *teichoskopia,* Homer's Trojan elders refigured in Socrates' captives, enslaved by beautiful deceptions.

Who *is* Helen? ask the citizens of Troy. It is a question Helen renders unanswerable at the very moment that she makes it most urgent. Helen, we will see, unsettles the very status of that *is,* disturbing the line between appearance and reality, original and facsimile, replacing the equations of the copula with the approximations of analogy. The elders look upon the face of Helen of Troy, exclaiming, "Terrible is the likeness of her face to immortal goddesses" (αἰνῶς ἀθανάτῃσι θεῇς εἰς ὦπα ἔοικεν [3.158]). They cannot say who she is; they can only say what she is *like.* Helen resists our attempts to identify her, to fix her, to name her; she forces us to speak in metaphors and riddles, contradictions at once seductive and disturbing.[3] Hence the elders' αἰνῶς (terribly, strangely), as in αἴνιγμα (riddle or enigma).[4] The elders are (mis)led into error, an error they long to embrace ("Surely there is no blame on Trojans and strong-greaved Achaians / if for long time they suffer hardship for a woman like this one" [3.156–57]), and yet fear ("Still, though she be such, let her go away in the ships" [3.159]) to commit (trans. Lattimore 1951).[5] The stakes are high. Upon their decision, which, in fact, they are powerless to make, rests the fate of a city.

Where Helen is present—and that, in itself, is never clear—there is this sentimental wavering, this cognitive movement back and forth. The elders waver between admiration and fear, love and hatred, idolatry and the longing to possess. Helen herself is a shimmering figure: now woman, now goddess; now real, now illusory; now here, now there (where? Sparta? Troy? Egypt?); now Greek, now Trojan; now guilty, now innocent; now subject, now object. This epistemological, ontological, and ethical indeterminacy, teasing us, moving us back and forth, from *on the one hand* to *on the other,* is the painful and seductive crisis (from the Greek *krinein,* to separate, to distinguish) of mimesis, and the recurrent crisis of this study. In the *Cratylus* (439d) Plato calls this indeterminacy the *flow* or *flux* (ῥεῖν, from 'ῥέω, to flow) of beauty. I call it *graft.* Graft, I want to emphasize, is not simply a metaphor for imitation: it is constitutive of metaphor itself. Aristotle, we will see, defines metaphor as a dubious displacement of the word, an illegitimate yoking of like and unlike. Thus Aristotle's conception of metaphor suggests a scenario of language in crisis, a story told in terms of exile and abduction: the story of Helen of Troy.

Différance in Homer

Helen's entrance upon the Trojan proscenium in *Iliad* 3 is traditionally viewed as her textual debut. But are there really beginnings as such in Homeric epic? From Helen's first appearance Homer's narrative betrays the possibility of its own belatedness. At *Iliad* 3.121 Iris the messenger is sent to inform Helen of the duel that Menelaus and Paris are about to fight in her name: "She came on Helen in the chamber; she was weaving a great web, / a red folding robe, and working into it the numerous struggles / of Trojans, breakers of horses, and bronze-armoured Achaians, / struggles that they endured for her sake at the hands of the war god" (3.125–28). What is Helen weaving here? To this question many critics have answered: the *Iliad*.[6] In this, Helen's "first" representation in Western literature, Helen has already represented herself, and in convincingly Homeric fashion. Comparing *Iliad* 3.125–28 with 1.1–7 suggests how closely Helen's "authorship" is modeled on Homer's: both passages introduce the broad "matter" of the work as a whole, both stress the sufferings of the Achaeans and the role of the gods in those sufferings, and both, finally, point to an essential division, either between Achaeans and Trojans or between Achilles and Agamemnon.

Weaving regularly appears in ancient literature as a form of feminine writing substituting for the voice that has been silenced,[7] and this has significance in a text such as the *Iliad,* which, at least in some phase of its evolution, has been orally composed and performed.[8] A moment later, in what is generally considered the *teichoskopia* "proper," Helen's own viewing of the Achaean hosts from the wall—I will use the term to refer to the Trojans' viewing of Helen—Helen introduces the star Achaean players of the Homeric drama in a dialogue with Priam.[9] Helen begins in Homer, then, as a narrator of beginnings, both written (woven) and oral. Note that Iris's first words to Helen, an exhortation to leave her work and witness the duel, are a citation from Helen's own woven narrative: "Come with me, dear girl, to behold the marvelous things done / by Trojans, breakers of horses, and bronze-armoured Achaians" (Τρώων θ'ἱπποδάμων καὶ Ἀχαιῶν χαλκοχιτώνων [3.127 and 131]). Positioned at this moment in Homer's narrative, Iris's speech sounds strangely like a reading of Helen's previously written text.

Ann Bergren links the motif of Helen's weaving to the obvious and oft-remarked anachronism of the *teichoskopia:*

> The art of the *Iliad* is the art of the tableau. The two conventions of realistic narration and temporal suspension produce a verbal version of what we would see in Helen's tapestry, i.e., the action of struggle in stasis, both movement in time and metatemporal permanence, both at once. These paradoxical poetics are also those of the Teichoskopia as a whole. Not in spite of but because it is a stock scene of the epic tradition, used here anachronistically, the Teichoskopia becomes part of a design to show beginnings in ends and by that transcendence of linear time, to show simultaneously both something that happened once and what there is in that "something" that ever "recurs." (1979:23)

The anachronistic back-and-forth of Homeric temporality is, I submit, another form of graft. It is a central principle driving narrative forward in the *Iliad* and the *Odyssey.* Thus the plot of the *Iliad* appears to represent this kind of temporal graft in spatial terms. Hector's advance to and retreat from the ditch built by the Greeks "reproduces," according to Bergren, "the forth and back and forth of battle in a period of suspended time" (24).

Bergren's notion of anachronism in the *Iliad* suggests a conflation, however, not only of the past and the present, but of the general and the specific. Thus Paolo Vivante writes concerning the *Iliad:* "Each moment here overflows with its silent contents; and each occurrence, as it is portrayed, becomes a theme— a supreme instance rather than a fact" (1970:146). One might compare these discussions of Homeric temporality to Erich Auerbach's famous statement on the *Odyssey* in *Mimesis:* "Homer . . . knows no background. What he narrates is for the time being the only present. . . . One might think that the many inter- polations, the frequent moving back and forth, would create a sort of perspec- tive in time and place; but the Homeric style never gives any such impression" (1953:4–7).[10] Auerbach is right, I think, but not for the reasons he cites. The Homeric texts are everywhere interested, in fact, in collapsing perspective. Per- spective is an opening up of vistas upon the past, something that suggests the distances and disconnections of history. Homeric epic, however, offers a past made repeatedly present. Temporal graft or anachronism represents the collaps- ing of perspective in Homeric epic. (One is tempted to argue here that Auerbach is guilty in *Mimesis* of the very conflations he sees at work in Homer, as he gathers together and revives the dead and disparate figures of literary history.) Thus the *teichoskopia* is everywhere marked by the irruption of the *already written,* by the echoes and intimations of other scenes, present *in absentia.* At the center of this textual rupture, this *dehiscence*—a term, like *trace, fold,* or *graft,* sometimes favored by Derrida to suggest the way writing is split open by contradictions and anterior voices [11]—this *différance,* is Helen.

Derrida regularly employs the term *différance*—which can mean both "differ- ence" and "differing"—to suggest the way meaning in language always differs from itself and defers all efforts to fix it. That *difference* (ordinarily spelled with an *e*) and *differing* (with an *a*) *sound* the same in French is also Derrida's way of making *writing* the critical factor. Speaking the word fails to communicate meaning as something undivided: speech is already undermined, then, by the distinctions and divergences traditionally associated with writing. The implica- tions of Derrida's use of *différance* are potentially enormous for an understand- ing of Homeric poetry and its readings, especially when we understand that poetry as the end-product of parallel or intersecting oral and written traditions.

In fact, *différance* has long been a central notion of Homeric criticism, even if it is rarely referred to explicitly. In *Heroic Poetry* Cecil Bowra presents the the- matic anachronism of heroic poetry, its preservation of details from an archaic age combined with contemporary customs, as an inevitable consequence of the oral transmission of that poetry (1952:396). Bowra's vision of heroic poetry's "conservativism," its importation and retention of themes from alien cultures and prior periods, is remarkably close to more recent and more "radical" models of "intertextuality" (403). This is something we have already touched upon with regard to anachronism and temporality in Homer.

Cedric Whitman's structural analysis of the *Iliad* in *Homer and the Heroic Tradition* suggests that Homeric poetry is traversed by self-difference internally as well as externally. Whitman is a self-named unitarian when it comes to the Homeric question, but his discussion repeatedly shows how the unity of the Homeric poem is fractured or compromised by formulaic repetition, ring composition, *hysteron proteron,* and repeated themes. Whitman recalls Milman Parry's warning against making too much of recurrent scenes, but goes on to argue that Homer controls what he calls "echoes" better than anyone (1958:249–50). Homer's exploitation of the echo makes the *Iliad* into a text that is continually affirming its own self-identity as it establishes its own self-difference: "even as ring composition balances by similarity or identity the idea of inversion in *hysteron proteron* is simply a form of balance by opposites. Probably all aspects of formal symmetry depend ultimately upon these two categories of similarity and opposition, as Plato seemed to know when in the *Timaeus* he finished off his cosmology with the two spheres of Sameness and Difference, which revolve in opposite directions" (254).

Iliad 3: "Did this ever happen?"

Who is Helen? That is precisely the question the duel in *Iliad* 3 is meant to resolve. Helen is she for whom, in the words of Iris, "Menelaos the warlike and Alexandros will fight / with long spears" (136–37). Asking who Helen is means asking who possesses her. The Helen Iris addresses, then, is an inchoate and divided Helen: "You shall be called beloved wife of the man who wins you" (138).[12] At precisely this point Helen remembers another Helen, a Helen who once was, and is no more: the result is a hybrid Helen:

> Speaking so the goddess left in her heart sweet longing
> after her husband of time before, and her city and parents.
> And at once, wrapping herself about in shimmering garments,
> she went forth from the chamber, letting fall a light tear;
> not by herself, since two handmaidens went to attend her,
> Aithre, Pittheus' daughter, and Klymene of the ox eyes.
> Rapidly they came to the place where the Skaian gates stood.
>
> (3.139–45)

Helen's simple identity as Menelaus's wife is undermined by her marriages, in various mythic traditions, to Paris, Deiphobus, and even Achilles. Her parentage is similarly a matter of debate. Is she the daughter of Zeus and Leda? In the *Cypria,* part of the post-Homeric epic cycle that supplemented the *Iliad* and *Odyssey,* Helen is said to be the child of Zeus and Nemesis (Allen 1912: fr. 8.499).

On the other hand, in the Archaic *Catalogue of Women,* ascribed to Hesiod, Fr. 66,[13] a scholiast's note referring to Pindar's *Nemean* 10.150a reads intriguingly: "Hesiod, however, makes Helen the child neither of Leda nor Nemesis, but of a daughter of Ocean and Zeus" (trans. Evelyn-White 1914:191).[14] And Classical tragedy, which generally looks less kindly upon Helen than Homer does, is replete with alternative myths of genealogy suggesting more ignominious origins for her.

Helen, who in the *Iliad* is represented as a reader and a writer of her own mythic tradition, collaborates with this project of mythic heterogeneity. Helen as an interior subject revealed to Homer's listeners/readers suggests a dramatic representation of schizophrenia. Helen rushes from her chamber to see the latest news, and yet it is a vision of the far away and the long ago that moves her. A vision, too, of the future to come, for the mention of husband, city, and parents points to a very different Helen, a Helen to be — and yet, from the perspective of epic performer and listener, a Helen that already *is* — the Helen of *Odyssey* 4 (explored in the following chapter). Helen is torn by the contradictions of *eros,* by the "sweet longing," γλυκὺν ἵμερον (3.139), that Aphrodite has instilled in her. Stranger in a strange land, Helen mourns that which she has lost, and longs to return to Sparta.

And yet it is in Paris's arms that Helen lies in the aftermath of the duel in the *Iliad.*[15] Here we do not see Helen as the elders do, in theophanic fashion — although there is less difference between the two scenes than this contrast would suggest — but as Paris does: a woman of flesh and blood: "Come, then, rather let us go to bed and turn to love-making" (441). In the dialogue with Aphrodite that precedes, Helen is again torn by contradictory desires: "my heart," she says, "is confused with sorrows" (412). "Confused sorrows" is Lattimore's translation of ἄχε᾽ ἄκριτα; it may be rendered more literally as "sorrows which are disordered," or "not to be distinguished"; ἄκριτα, I note, derives again from κρίνω (to distinguish, separate, interpret, estimate). At first Helen resists Aphrodite's entreaty to comfort the rescued Paris, conjuring up an image of still more abductions: "Will you carry me further yet somewhere among cities / fairly settled? In Phrygia or in lovely Maionia?" (400–401). The goddess puts Helen in the middle of a squeeze play:[16] "Wretched girl, do not tease me lest in anger I forsake you / and grow to hate you as much as now I terribly love you, / lest I encompass you in hard hate, caught between both sides, / Danaans and Trojans alike, and you wretchedly perish" (414–17). Eros as contradiction — hate grafted to love — defines Helen.[17]

This contradiction has its ethical considerations. Should Helen be blamed? Priam does not seem to think so: "I am not blaming you," he tells her: "to me the gods are blameworthy / who drove upon me this sorrowful war against the Achaians" (164–65). What does Helen herself have to say on the matter? Her self-recriminations (as when at 3.180 she calls herself a "slut," literally a κυνῶπις, "dog-eyed woman" or "dog-faced woman") admit her guilt at the same time that they render her endearing, and even innocent. If we look at the context in which Helen indicts herself, the connections between the ethical and the ontological are more apparent. Upon the wall with Helen beside him, Priam points to the figure of Agamemnon and asks Helen to identify him:

> Always to me, beloved father, you are feared and respected;
> and I wish bitter death had been what I wanted, when I came hither
> following your son, forsaking my chamber, my kinsmen,
> my grown child, and the loveliness of girls my own age.
> It did not happen that way: and now I am worn with weeping.
> This now I will tell you in answer to the question you asked me.
> That man is Atreus' son Agamemnon, widely powerful,
> at the same time a good king and a strong spearfighter,
> once my kinsman, slut that I am. Did this ever happen?
>
> (172–80)

Helen's own relationship with Priam, given the circumstances of her status in the city, is understandably ambiguous. Once again, as for Priam's counselors, love is mixed with terror: φίλε ἑκυρέ, δεινός τε, literally "[you are] beloved, and dreadful" (3.172). Helen's greeting to Priam is followed by a different sort of confusion: the irruption of the possible (what could have been) into the actual. Helen turns to the past, rewriting it as a set of new scenes and new narratives. As she lapses into self-incrimination, she retreats to the safety of skepticism, casting doubt not only upon her own experience but upon that of Homer's audience, wondering εἴ ποτ᾽ ἔην γε, "Did this ever happen?"

It is a good question. The text of the *teichoskopia* is haunted by the specter of competing and contradictory Helens. Which Helen is the right one? Which Helen is the first one? Which Helen is the real one? Helen's own abduction is marked *from the beginning* as repetition. In Fr. 11 of the *Cypria*, Paris's act has a precedent: "For Helen had been previously carried off by Theseus." The trace of the Theseus saga remains detectible, however, in the *teichoskopia*, like a clue left casually at the scene of a crime by someone who wants to be caught. After her first abduction Helen is cared for by Theseus's mother Aethra, the same figure, apparently, who accompanies Helen as her handmaiden at the Skaian gates in *Iliad* 3. Plutarch, who includes the story of Theseus's abduction of Helen in *Theseus* 34.1,[18] cites the *teichoskopia* and suggests that Aethra, too, had once been abducted: "It is also said that Aethra, Theseus's mother . . .was carried off to Sparta and from there later to Troy, and Homer confirms this when he says that Helen was attended by 'Aethra, the daughter of Pittheus, and ox-eyed Clymene'" (trans. Scott-Kilvert 1960:34).[19] The "shadow" of Theseus in the *Iliad* has been explained alternatively as a vestige of an earlier cultic Helen more recently secularized.[20] Martin Nilsson argues that the story of Helen's abduction represents the literary secularization of what had once been sacred myth, a variant on the story of the Kore. Theseus's abduction of Helen suggests the links to that myth. As Nilsson explains: "In the myth of Theseus . . . there is an apparent doublet; he and his friend Peirithous try to carry off Persephone, who is identified with Kore. That may be better understood if there was a reminiscence that Helen was originally akin to Kore-Persephone" (1932:75). Just as Peirithous helps Theseus rape Helen, Theseus would help Peirithous rape Persephone. The trace of one myth in the other, as in *Iliad* 3, would seem to be another example of grafting at work. Nilsson puts it more delicately: "the friendship of Theseus and Peirithous serves as a means to harmonize two parallel myths which else would seem to be incompatible" (174).

Beginnings, when it comes to Helen, are problematic, and not just in Homer. Greece, it is regularly claimed by Classical authors, *begins* with Helen. Her abduction is how the Greeks define their coming-into-being as a nation. As Isocrates puts it in the *Encomium on Helen:* "because of her . . . the Greeks became united . . . and organized a common expedition against the barbarians" (trans. van Hook 1945:67–68). In Herodotus's *History* 1.5, however, Paris's abduction of Helen is both a primordial event—it is to the retaliatory expedition against Troy that the Persians, according to Herodotus, trace "their ancient enmity toward the Greeks" (trans. Rawlinson 1942) [21]—and merely the last in a series, a reenactment of other abductions (Io, Europa, Medea). Even the fall of Troy is a repetition. The chorus in Euripides' *Trojan Women* lament the destruction of their city, but also recall "King Telamon, / Who once, as ally and friend of the mighty Heracles / Came with an army to Ilion, Came long ago to plunder and burn our city of Ilion" (trans. Vellacott 1954:116). The Trojan past recollected by the chorus in Euripides' play is a series of abductions: Ganymede, son of King Laomedon (or King Tros), abducted by Zeus, and Tithonus, son of King Laomedon, abducted by Eos. [22]

With Helen it is hard to know, then, where to begin, or where to end. Helen has always *already* been abducted; she is always to be abducted again. It is also possible that she was never abducted at all. There is no "original" or "real" Helen: only a perspective of innumerable Helens receding backward into the past and forward into the future. We may turn to Homer for a glimpse of the original or real Helen, only to find that this Helen herself unsettles our faith in origins and realities. To look at Helen is always to see more, or less, than we bargained for, to see Helen and something else (other Helens). This is true not only because Homeric epic engages in a dialogue with traditions external to epic, but also, as has been suggested, because epic itself is internally divided or fractured.

One could begin with the most obvious binary division between the two Homeric epics. The Iliadic Helen is Paris's concubine and Aphrodite's reluctant whore (among other things); the Odyssean Helen, on the other hand, is the very image of domestic happiness, at home in sunny Sparta with her husband Mene-laus. The difference between these two Helens—a difference, we have begun to see, which already inhabits each of them—is not simply a question of before and after. Epic does not work that way: the *Odyssey* is not the *Iliad*'s sequel, but its competitor or companion (the same could be said for the *Iliad* in relation to the *Odyssey*). I cite Monro's law here: the *Odyssey* "never repeats or refers to any incident in the *Iliad*" (1901:325). Gregory Nagy notes that critics have applied this law in antithetical ways, depending on their critical bias or goal. Denys Page (1955a) for example, uses it to demonstrate, ostensibly, that the two Homeric epics are absolutely disconnected (Nagy 1979:158). Here I side with Nagy, who argues, against Page, that "the traditions of the *Iliad* and the *Odyssey* constitute a totality with the complementary distribution of their narratives" (Nagy 1979:21).[23] I would go even further and posit that each Homeric epic is not so much the other's *complement* as its *supplement:* each posing as an addi-tion or extension to the other and, at the same time, threatening to replace it. A few words of explanation are in order here. The problem with Monro's law, as it is formulated, lies in the ambiguity of the term *refer.* I would restate the law as follows: *each Homeric epic refers at every moment to the other.* As Nagy himself points out, it is difficult to explain how an epic as monumental and syn-thetic as the *Odyssey* could fail to refer explicitly to the *Iliad* unless it were at every moment cognizant, as it were, of the borders of the territory belonging exclusively to the latter's tradition.

Again, the relation between the *Odyssey* and the *Iliad* suggests *différance* in the Derridean sense, for if the *Odyssey* is always and everywhere distinct from the *Iliad,* it is also always present proleptically in the *Iliad* itself, deferred that is, just as the *Odyssey* is everywhere disrupted by the shadows of an *Iliad* that refuses to be remembered simply as the past. Recollection as the central motif of the *Odyssey* is the subject of the next chapter. The *différance* between the *Odyssey* and *Iliad* is thus the very image of Helen's own self-difference. To the question "Who is Helen?" one might respond: "*Which* Helen?" Her origins, parentage, marriage, her very identity are all subjects of speculation and in-determinacy. The *Laconia* 11–21 and *Messenia* 26–27 of Pausanias suggest the extent to which the Helen myth was appreciated, even in antiquity, as a collec-tion of competing and contradictory myths. It is true that to a certain extent all Greek myths are really sets of competing submyths, but Helen is particularly undecidable. More than that, undecidability, paradoxically enough, is perhaps Helen's essential feature.

"Did this ever happen?" Helen herself articulates this undecidability. From the perspective of Helen as a character in Homer's narrative, these words are Helen's way of questioning her own identity. From the perspective of Homer as an authoritative poetic tradition, these words are that tradition's way of question-ing its own authenticity or authority. From the perspective of the post-Homeric tradition, these words seem to confirm the validity of competing and alternative traditions, most notably that of the *eidolon*. The *eidolon* is the phantom Helen fashioned by the gods to provoke the Trojan war—a copy, that is, of the real Helen, who, depending on the text and the particular version of the story, may have spent the war in Egypt, or who may never have left Sparta at all.[24] This alternative tradition, supposedly inaugurated by Stesichorus in the sixth century[25] in his *Palinode* (Recantation), cited by Plato in the *Phaedrus,* and later dramatized by Euripides in the *Helen,* is itself a supplement to the Homeric tradition, a tradition which it joins but which it threatens to replace. In fact a host of phantom Helens circulate throughout Greek lore. Pausanius 3.19.11 recounts the legend that the ghosts of Helen and Achilles are regularly heard to hold revelry on the Isle of Leuce in the Black Sea, where it is said they were married. In Tztetzes' *On Lycophron* Achilles makes love with Helen in a dream, before marrying her (as a shade or ghost). In Pausanius 4.27.1 a Messenian named Aristomenes attempts to attack Sparta at night, only to be repelled by the phantoms of Helen and her brothers, the Dioscuri. Finally, according to Isocrates, the Homeridae, the hereditary clan of rhapsodes who claimed descent from Homer, recount that Homer himself was visited by an image of Helen bidding him to celebrate the sack of Troy. In Euripides' hands the story of the *eidolon* grows into something like a treatise on the nature of the real and the illusory. But even within the corpus of Euripides, the "real" Helen of the *Helen,* chaste and faithful in her exile in Egypt, must compete with the culpable and vain Helens of *Orestes, Trojan Women,* and *Andromache* (which makes the *Helen,* in effect, Euripides's own palinode). The figure of the *eidolon* is, we will see, only the most explicit image of an ontological and epistemological instability already constitutive of the "standard," Iliadic Helen.

Helen always and everywhere unleashes this instability. It is precisely because she refuses any definitive predication that she provokes endless predications, and endless contradictions. In every text that deals even incidentally with Helen, she is an enigma to be interpreted and reinterpreted. In Aeschylus's *Agamemnon,* for example, when the chorus learns that Troy has fallen and that Menelaus is lost at sea, their first act is to try to make Helen's name refer, etymologically (681–87): "Who is he that named you so / fatally in every way? / Could it be some mind unseen / in divination of your destiny / shaping to the lips that name / for the bride of spears and blood, / Helen, which is death" (trans. Lattimore 1947).[26] This effort to fix Helen's identity only generates more names and more images: "And that which first came to the city of Ilium, / call it a dream of calm / and the wind dying, / the loveliness and luxury of much gold, / the melting shafts of the eyes' glances, / the blossom that breaks the heart with longing" (737–42). Helen always refracts assertion in this way, transforming simple predication into lists, analogies, and names. In fact the Helen ode in the *Agamemnon* is explicitly about the effort to categorize or name ("Who is he that named you," "call it a dream") that which is uncategorizable or unnameable ("a dream of calm," "a wind dying," the bright and superficial beauty of "gold"). Helen is here a figure for the dangerous, alluring, and deceptive world of appearances. This is what Helen is, the Chorus in *Agamemnon* tells us, at least *on the one hand.*

On the other hand . . . In the very next line the same chorus tells us what it means to be deceived. Abruptly, without warning, the wind changes direction: dream turns to nightmare; beauty turns to death; blossom turns to blight. The structure is that of the pivot or the flux or the graft, the preeminent sign of Helen: "But she turned in mid-step of her course to make / bitter the consummation, / whirling on Priam's people / to blight with her touch and nearness." [27] Helen, in all her mythic manifestations, is always the site and agency of this whirling, this turning in mid-step, this grafting. To gaze upon her beauty is to experience epistemological, ontological, and linguistic contradiction—we no longer know what *is,* or what to *call* it. This is the *aporia* of the Trojan elders, caught between terror and rapture.[28]

"Then let us seek the true beauty, not asking whether a face is fair"

Helen is something that repeatedly eludes us, a presence that recedes into other presences. To look upon her is to find ourselves whirling back and forth between competing likenesses, phantom Helens, phantom narratives. We are led astray, maddened. Helen, too, has been maddened, and led astray, as she reminds us in the tale she tells about Odysseus in *Odyssey* 4.261–63: "and I grieved for the madness that Aphrodite / bestowed when she led me there away from my own dear country, / forsaking my own daughter, my bedchamber, and my husband" (trans. Lattimore 1965).[29] This would be a way of summing up Helen's career: exile, displacement, possession, and dispossession. Helen is she who always comes from afar, who does not belong, who is never completely *at home*—not in Troy, not in Sparta, not in Egypt. In the next chapter I focus on the paradox of a Helen at home, and yet in exile, possessed by memories of Troy. To look upon Helen, likewise, is to find ourselves—ethically, ontologically, epistemologically—*homeless.*

Helen's career, I want to suggest, acts out or is a figure for Plato's understanding of mimesis. When Plato speaks of mimesis, he tends to frame what he has to say as a narrative. More often than not, this will be a narrative, like Helen's, about seduction and desire. If we consider that mimesis as a literary strategy—what medieval and early modern poets will refer to as *imitatio*—is the essential poetic act being explored throughout this book, then we can begin to appreciate how Plato's story is reenacted, in a broader sense, in the history of poetry itself. This is a story, as I suggested in the preface, not of simple continuity, but of erotic seductions and rejections and conquests. The belated poet of post-antiquity resembles nothing so much as a lover. What I want to suggest here is that this repeated erotic scenario is central to Plato's work—not just a figure for it. Plato's notion of imitation is metaphorical from the very beginning, and the story of Helen is as much the *literal* shape of Plato's argument as its *figure*.[30] Here is Plato in the *Cratylus* (439d): "Then let us seek the true beauty, not asking whether a face is fair, or anything of the sort, for all such things appear to be in a flux [καὶ δοκεῖ ταῦτα πάντα ῥεῖν], but let us ask whether the true beauty is not always beautiful." [31] If any face is fair, it is Helen's, by definition. And if sensible beauty, the beauty of appearance, is dangerously misleading, then Helen is most dangerous of all. Let us take a closer look at the Platonic story of seduction, this tale of the dangerous flux of beauty, and let us see how Helen appears to inhabit that tale from the beginning.

Without attempting to summarize Platonic thought on mimesis (something that would be futile, in any case), let me offer just a few passages useful for our discussion here. In the *Seventh Letter* (342a–b), Plato writes:

For everything that exists there are three classes of objects through which knowledge about it must come; the knowledge itself is a fourth, and we must put as a fifth entity the actual object of knowledge which is the true reality. We have then, first, a name, second, a description, third, an image, and fourth, a knowledge of the object. (Trans. Post 1925)

The name, ὄνομα; the description, λόγος; the image, εἴδωλον: what these terms share is a common difference from and relation to the object of which they are all in some sense a likeness. This relation is what Plato refers to as *mimesis, μίμησις*. Richard McKeon puts it most succinctly in "Literary Criticism and the Concept of Imitation in Antiquity": "In its expansion and contraction, the word 'imitation' indicates the lesser term of the proportion of being to appearance" (1936:9). The true versus the false, knowledge versus opinion, good versus bad—all these distinctions operate along the same Platonic axis, pitting *being* against *appearance*. The very difficulty of defining Plato's use of *mimesis* is precisely what gives the term its versatility and power in the dialogues. As McKeon suggests, "imitation, in its broadest sense, was a *metaphor* to which Plato resorted, with evident dissatisfaction, to explain the relation of the world of sense to the world of ideas" (5n11; my italics).[32] Imitation is a metaphor, then, to explain a metaphorical relation, as in any relation of likeness. This is why Plato can speak in exactly the same terms of the appearance of a face, the image in a painting, or the words in a play.[33] In *Republic* 2 (377e), Plato calls the Homeric epics the work of "a painter whose portraits bear no resemblance to his models" (trans. Shorey 1953).[34] Plato is thinking, of course, of what he sees as Homer's theological errors. Homer's fictions, Plato asserts, pose as truths: therefore they deceive or seduce the listener.

Plato's concern in such passages is clearly ethical, not technical. Plato only reluctantly accords artistic creation a technical or systematic status of any kind (the *Ion* brings this out most comically and crudely). Not surprisingly, then, there is a general instability at work in Plato's discussion of representation and in the terms used to describe the representational relation. The imitation is sometimes called $\mu\acute{\iota}\mu\eta\sigma\iota\varsigma$ or mimesis, sometimes $\dot{\alpha}\pi\epsilon\iota\kappa\alpha\sigma\acute{\iota}$ or representation, sometimes $\epsilon\dot{\iota}\kappa\alpha\sigma\tau\acute{\eta}$ or copy. In *Sophist* 266b, Plato describes the art of imitation as an art of production, and suggests that production itself can be divided into the making of "originals" or "actual things" and the making of "images" or "likenesses" (trans. Cornford 1931).[35] The products of human labor belong to the latter category; those of divine labor, to the former. Note that Plato is not speaking of artistic labor alone, but of all human industry, as an "image-making art," $\epsilon\dot{\iota}\delta\omega\lambda o\pi o\iota\kappa\grave{\eta}$ $\tau\acute{\epsilon}\chi\nu\eta$. Thus the figure of the carpenter producing beds in *Republic* 10 is not as distant as it might appear from that of the poet. In fact the word Plato uses here is $\tau\acute{\epsilon}\kappa\tau\omega\nu$, referring either to a carpenter/joiner or to any craftsman/maker. We might imagine that for Plato and his audience the word would still betray its associations with the activity of poetry. In *Republic* 10 the imitator or $\mu\iota\mu\eta\tau\acute{\eta}\varsigma$ is a maker of images, $\epsilon\dot{\iota}\delta\acute{\omega}\lambda o\upsilon$ $\pi o\iota\eta\tau\acute{\eta}\varsigma$, as opposed to a maker of realities (601c). Finally, Plato's taxonomy in the *Republic* is unstable, breaking apart into subcategories: images are of two species, either "likenesses," or "semblances." In likenesses, which are a product of "copy-making art," $\epsilon\dot{\iota}\kappa\alpha\sigma\tau\iota\kappa\acute{\eta}$, there is a resemblance between the imitation and the model; in semblances, the result of "fantastic art" or $\phi\alpha\nu\tau\alpha\sigma\tau\iota\kappa\acute{\eta}$, no attempt is made to adhere truthfully to a model. The products of fantastic art are labeled $\phi\acute{\alpha}\nu\tau\alpha\sigma\mu\alpha$. While it is true that the $\epsilon\dot{\iota}\kappa\acute{\omega}\nu$ refers to an imitation that is like its object and a $\phi\acute{\alpha}\nu\tau\alpha\sigma\mu\alpha$ to one that is unlike its object, both are likenesses, and, as McKeon says, "a copy, to be correct, must not reproduce all the qualities of that which it copies" (1936:11).

It is clear that the precise nature of the imitation in Plato is profoundly undecidable. This is not because Plato is imprecise, but because undecidability is part of the nature of the imitation. Which is the imitation, then? This is a question as problematic as asking: "Who is Helen?" [36] The analogy here is not merely incidental: it is my contention here that to a very large extent the two questions are the same. With Helen, after all, we are never quite sure what we are dealing with: phantoms or realities. And so we waver, moving from likeness to likeness, $\epsilon\dot{\iota}\delta\omega\lambda o\nu$ to $\epsilon\dot{\iota}\delta\omega\lambda o\nu$. Helen's mythic tradition is always, fundamentally, an image-making art, an art of phantom-making, an $\epsilon\dot{\iota}\delta\omega\lambda o\pi o\iota\kappa\grave{\eta}$ $\tau\acute{\epsilon}\chi\nu\eta$.

Republic 7.514: Plato's Troglodytes as Homer's Elders

Plato's discussion of imitation in *Republic* 7 and 10 is articulated as a series of metaphors and allegories about deception and seduction. Book 7 opens with the conceit of the cave as the allegorical dwelling place of the ignorant, those who do not strive for real knowledge (governed by reason), but live benighted amid opinions and delusions and the illusions of the senses (514a). The scene Plato paints for us—prisoners gazing fixedly at a wall upon which shadows are cast by a procession of men and objects—is essentially, I would argue, a theater (514b). We should be reminded here of another wall toward which another captive audience is turned: the wall of Troy, upon which Helen walks. The analogy between Plato's allegory of the cave and Homer's *teichoskopia* has a special relevance, I would argue, in the context of the *Republic,* a work devoted to the theoretical elaboration of the ideal city, and a work that draws, as many a critic has noted, explicit parallels between the human soul and the polis.[37]

Plato's benighted troglodytes "deem reality to be nothing else than . . . shadows" (515c). It is therefore the duty of the philosopher, Plato tells Glaucon, to deliver them from the darkness. To do that the philosopher himself must descend into the cave and grow accustomed to the darkness. Philosophical rescue thus demands a certain complicity with delusion:

Down you must go then . . . and accustom yourselves to the observation of the obscure things there. For once habituated you will discern them infinitely better than the dwellers there, and you will know what each of the "idols" is and whereof it is a semblance, because you have seen the reality of the beautiful, the just and the good. (520c)

Helen is the ultimate *idol* of Troy, and her appearance upon the walls of Troy in just this fashion turns its citizens into prisoners. But who are the Trojan elders in Plato's allegory of the cave? Are they the shackled captives, ignorant that the shadows that delight them are mere phantoms, empty delusions, or are they the philosophers, striving to separate the real from the phantasmic? Is Helen a puppet, or the shadow that puppet casts? The task of the philosopher is not going to be easy, if the example of the elders is any kind of lesson: for Helen, or the semblance thereof, has a way of challenging the "reality of the beautiful, the just and the good."

In *Republic* 10 the space of the cave is both diminished and expanded: here Plato is interested in both the individual space of the human soul and the larger arena of the polis itself. I will not repeat Plato's theory of mimesis here, except to say that Plato's interest in the ethical makes an easy passage from one space to the other. Plato's point is that the powers of the senses are inferior to reason in the pursuit of true knowledge, and that imitation, as W. C. Greene puts it, "appeals to the faculty that is deceived by the illusions of sense," illusions which "appeal especially to a promiscuous crowd" (1918:54). Book 10 begins with Plato stating that imitative poetry "seems to be a corruption of the mind of its listeners who do not possess as an antidote a knowledge of its real nature" (595a–b). As in Book 7 the philosopher is there to administer the cure—the *antidote* [φάρμακον]—for this corruption. The antidote will return in the form of the "countercharm" that Plato urges us to sing in Book 10 as a defense against the seductive siren song of poetry.

Plato's notion of corruption here is unambiguously erotic. Poetic mimesis, which produces only "phantoms [φαντάσματα], not realities" (599a) is "inferior in respect of reality." It therefore appeals, in turn, to our baser appetites, "the inferior elements of the soul" (603a–b), and collaborates with them. Representation, here as in the *Ion,* is a form of erotic contagion in which the image and the individual at which it is directed are grafted (think of Socrates' image of muse, poet, rhapsode, and audience as links in a chain of magnets). This kind of contagion is typical of Helen, who, we have seen, is simultaneously a figure for violent displacement and doubling and the agent of such a displacement and doubling in those who look upon her. As Plato goes on to describe the nature of this contagion, erotic discourse is joined to political discourse. The poet "sets up in each individual soul a vicious constitution [πολιτείαν] by fashioning phantoms [εἴδωλα] far removed from reality, and by currying favor with the senseless element that cannot distinguish the greater from the less, but calls the same thing now one, now the other" (605c). Plato's diagnosis would seem to match the epidemic unleashed in Homer's Troy, where the elders, gazing upon Helen, struggle to distinguish the real from the fantastic, calling *the same thing now one, now the other.* And, as in Plato, Homer's hallucinating elders are the mirrors of a citywide disturbance. Plato's reference to a "vicious constitution" leaves no doubt about the analogy he wants to draw: both the polis and its denizens are on the brink of civil war.

Plato has identified poetry as the illness; what, then, is the cure? What Plato proposes for his republic is very much what the elders decide upon for Troy: the agent of infection must be expelled from the city. Like Plato's poetry, Helen is a foreign agent who does not belong in Troy; she has entered the city from without, she has undermined its defenses from within, she must be returned to the place whence she came. Putting Homer on trial is Plato's way of curing the city; it is also a way of reminding us that when Plato talks about poetry, Helen should never be far from our minds. The problem, here and in Homer, is that it is not clear that the city wants to be cured. Like the elders who recognize that Troy will surely fall if Helen stays, Plato only reluctantly casts out Homer—reluctantly because all too "conscious of her [Homer's poetry's] spell" (607d).

Thus Plato defers poetry's expulsion from the city, just as he allows his philosophers in Book 7 a brief sojourn in the cave. Poetry must be allowed her defense. Those who plead her cause will be not poets but "lovers of poetry." And yet Plato puts us on guard against the seductions this defense may hold for those who listen, in a warning that sounds very much like Euripides' Hecuba in *Trojan Women,* cautioning Menelaus against Helen's persuasive powers:

even as men who have fallen in love, if they think that the love is not good for them, hard though it be, nevertheless refrain, so we, owing to the love of this kind of poetry inbred in us by our education in these fine polities of ours, will gladly have the best possible case made out for her goodness and truth, but so long as she is unable to make good her defense we shall chant over to ourselves as we listen the reasons that we have given as a countercharm to her spell, to preserve us from slipping back into childish loves of the multitude, for we have come to see that we must not take poetry seriously as a serious thing that lays hold on truth, but that he who lends an ear to it must be on his guard fearing for the polity in his soul. (608a–b)

This is Plato's vision of the soul: the city of Troy, crowded with the multitudes, men who have fallen in love, wavering between embrace and expulsion, on guard against phantoms, fearing for the polity, calling the same thing now one, now the other (605c), chanting countercharms. To continue the medical terminology we have been employing, Plato's defense against poetry—his antidote—is a vaccine made out of poetry. What Plato recommends here is a kind of homeopathic poetics, in which the cure looks uncannily like the disease. Thus in chapter 2 we will watch Helen administer just such an antidote in *Odyssey* 4, a narcotic that defends Telemachus and Menelaus against the emotional impact of the stories they are sharing but does so only by anesthetizing them into a state of indifference. Derrida has analyzed this recurrent homeopathic structure in "La pharmacie de Platon" (1972a) in the image of the city that preserves its purity and health only by repeatedly and ritually casting out a poisonous body it repeatedly and ritually discovers within.

As we will later (in chapter 3) see in the *Phaedrus,* Plato's gift of the countercharm casts him in the role of a new Stesichorus. For what is the *Palinode,* after all, but a countercharm to Homer? "I spoke nonsense and I begin again: / The story is not true. / You never sailed on a benched ship. / You never entered the city of Troy" (trans. Barnstone 1962). Stesichorus, in the Platonic version of the tale, writes a poem indicting Helen in the Homeric manner; as a result the gods strike him blind, just as they did Homer for composing the *Iliad.* Writing the *Palinode* is Stesichorus's homeopathic antidote, and it gives him back his sight.[38] It is not clear, however, that either Stesichorus or Plato or the elders of Troy leave us much better than we were before: sometimes the cure is worse than the disease. Who is to say that one day we will not need a countercharm to Plato's countercharm, or Stesichorus's? And, indeed, the whole history of Helen's myth, its transplantation from one text to another, one culture to another—the entire arc of the present study—is a history of countercharms, each warding off the power of the one that came before, each inevitably repeating it. And looking back, back to Homer and to the possibility of a "original" or "real" or "definitive" Helen, what Plato's remedy suggests is that Homer's Helen is already a counter-Helen, and the *Iliad* already a countercharm. In this history we are always protagonists inside Stesichorus's *Palinode,* mistaking the phantom for the real thing.

Ultimately (as the story of Stesichorus shows), failure to distinguish the real from the false is inevitable. It is a failure that leads straight from Sparta to Troy. Discussing what he calls the "life of the multitude," Socrates asks in Book 9 of the *Republic:*

are not the pleasures with which they dwell inevitably commingled with pains, phantoms of true pleasure, illusions of scene painting, so colored by contrary juxtaposition as to seem intense in either kind, and to beget mad loves of themselves in senseless souls, and to be fought for, as Stesichorus says the wraith of Helen was fought for at Troy through ignorance of the truth? (586b–c)

The story of Helen stands for Socrates as a figure for the dangers of all mimesis.

Helen as Metaphor

Who is Helen? We can begin to appreciate, by now, why that question is so difficult to answer. Our answers will always be misreadings—*palinodes.* Like Stesichorus, like Plato's ignorant multitudes, like Homer's Trojan elders ("Terrible is the likeness of her face to immortal goddesses"), we can only call *the same thing now one, now the other (Republic* 10.605c). Helen, as I have been suggesting, forces us to speak the language of likeness; she sets into motion an inexorable and irrepressible metaphoricity. Her virtue—and her vice—is thus to mediate between or graft disparate terms. In other words, Helen is a figure— a metaphor—for metaphor.

One might think of Helen as the heroine in the drama of the metaphor sketched out by Richard Klein in "Straight Lines and Arabesques: Metaphors of Metaphor":

Metaphors of metaphors are figures that allude to their own allusiveness, signify their power of signifying. . . . They are tautologies,—but not happy ones. As with all tautologies, the first term must lose itself in a second term in order to find the bliss of identity with itself: for A to equal A, A must first be not-A. But with metaphor of metaphor, that initial loss, in passing from one term to another, is the beginning of an endless and futile effort to recover itself—a recovery which is, nevertheless, its whole aim. The drama of the metaphor is thus its spiraling movement to rejoin itself, to signify its signifying, and thereby to halt the movement, to silence the text it has become—or rather, that it has always been. For the center towards which it tends has been from the beginning its spinning periphery: the *signifié* of this kind of metaphor is the signifying of the *signifiant.* It means its meaning, understood as the *metaphorein,* the transferring, the carrying of one term across an equal sign to another—its very movement. It has no choice but to continue spinning itself out, to lose itself in the movement from one figure to another. Such figures "rise up in the void" (Maurice Scève), execute "prestigious pirouettes" (Baudelaire), plot a text, weave a plot, institute a place, a stage—a drama (Mallarmé). (1970:64)

Helen's story is just such a drama of *metaphorein,* a drama in which Helen, carried back and forth from shore to foreign shore, is never quite able to re-join herself or recover herself. Helen, too, is an unhappy tautology; for Helen to equal Helen, Helen must first be not-Helen. Klein's metaphoric arabesques— *spiraling, spin, weaving,* Scève's *rise,* Baudelaire's *pirouettes*—are all variations upon (and figures for) the fluctuating indeterminacy of *graft* that is the subject of this study.

Klein's allegory of futile tautologies is an extended metaphor not only for the mythic career of Helen of Troy, but also for the whole saga of Western *imitatio,* the effort by the belated poet to lose himself or herself in antiquity in order to find the bliss of identity with himself or herself. That is the subject of part 2. Klein's *spiral,* like the back-and-forth of graft, conspires to proclaim the illusion of stability, to articulate a perfect and unchanging meaning. All graft, similarly, conceals its own catastrophic instability:

> But in order to continue to spin, in order to go on signifying, the metaphor of metaphor must forever create the fiction of its repose. . . . The metaphor of metaphor must pretend to forget its real aim, which is to signify its own movement, by seeming to aim at a lit-eral term which appears to be its truth. It creates the fiction of its happy repose as the condition for continuing to spin. (1970:65)

In precisely this manner the figure of graft promotes as it disguises the trope of organic stability and unity that Western culture cherishes, the fiction of its uninterrupted continuity, the myth of untroubled repose. Meanwhile the "real aim" of culture is the perpetual signification of its own movement, the eternal effort to recover itself—at whatever cost to the past it seeks to rejoin. I would thus agree with Paul de Man when he argues that literary history may itself be a figure, the product of a rhetorical genre.[39]

Is Helen's transit a figure for metaphoric passage, or vice versa? This unde-cidability, this reversibility of figure and ground, vehicle and tenor, is a crucial feature of all structures of grafting, as we will come to see. When we attempt to define metaphor literally, we find ourselves always already enmeshed in meta-phor. This is de Man's point in his reading, in "The Epistemology of Metaphor," of Locke on metaphor. Locke insists on the importance of defining basic terms, but the Cartesian definition of *motion* which he cites, a "passage from one place to another," fails to define and is simply another *translation.* De Man comments:

> Locke's own "passage" is bound to continue this perpetual motion that never moves be-yond tautology; motion is a passage and passage is a translation; translation, once again, means motion, piles motion upon motion. It is no mere play of words that "translate" is translated in German as *"übersetzen"* which itself translates the Greek *"metaphorein"* or metaphor. Metaphor gives itself the totality which it then claims to define, but it is in fact the tautology of its own position. The discourse of simple ideas is figural discourse or translation and, as such, creates the fallacious illusion of definition. (1978:17)

To say that Helen is a metaphor, then, is not just a metaphor. Let us go back to Aristotle here. Compare Helen—transferred, for example, from Theseus to Menelaus to Paris to Deiphobus and back to Menelaus, or conveyed illicitly across an ocean, from Sparta to Troy, from Troy back to Sparta—with Aristotle's definition of metaphor in the *Poetics* (21.1457b18): "Metaphor is the transference of a name from the object to which it has a natural application" (trans. Golden 1981).[40] I want to show here that metaphor, for Aristotle, is defined at the start in terms of exile, error, and abduction, and that the pleasures Aristotle ascribes to metaphor are the same Helen offers: pleasures dangerous, misleading, and seductive.[41] They are the pleasures of poetry against which Plato urges us to sing a countercharm.

Helen does not belong in Egypt any more than she does in Sparta, or Troy. It is Helen's fate always to be the Stranger, grafted to a culture where she belongs and yet does not belong. Helen's presence in Troy—familiar yet foreign, beautiful yet strange—suggests the language of metaphor as characterized in Aristotle's *Rhetoric* and *Poetics,* something suspect and improper, a species of linguistic transference and exile, an aberrant and exotic verbal creature. In fact the whole *Rhetoric* can be read as a guide to linguistic graft, that is to say, a lesson in how to *make the most* out of language. We will have to wait until chapter 4 to fully appreciate just how profitable this linguistic subterfuge can be.

Helen the Stranger

Egypt is not just an *in-between-land;* it is a land *outside,* geographically and epistemologically. Euripides' fairy tale treatment of the Egyptian Helen myth is also a story of exile and abduction. The first word of the *Helen* is Νείλου, "[streams of the] Nile." "My home country," Helen informs us in the prologue, "is a place of some note—Sparta" (trans. Vellacott 1954), whereupon she proceeds to narrate the tale of the Rape of Leda. Upon the reefs of this kingdom of the castaways arrive Teucer ("I have been driven out of my father's land," he tells Helen by way of an introduction, "I am an exile" [87]) and Menelaus. In every case, exile is linked to an unsettling kind of schizophrenia, where identities and names and faces multiply comically and yet horrifyingly. Menelaus cries out to Helen: "How did you steal from home that day?" (660). Teucer curses what he takes to be the real Helen: "I pray she may never reach home" (162). Helen is fated never to be *at home,* even when at home. Herodotus begins his discussion of Helen's sojourn in Egypt as follows:

Within the enclosure stands a temple, which is called that of Aphrodite the Stranger. I conjecture the building to have been erected to Helen, the daughter of Tyndarus; first, because she, as I have heard say, passed some time at the court of Proteus; and secondly, because the temple is dedicated to Aphrodite the Stranger; for among all the many temples of Aphrodite there is no other where the goddess bears this title. (2.112)

Herodotus's discussion of Helen begins, perhaps not surprisingly, with a mis-named temple. The name itself is significant. Helen is always a figure come from afar, a figure transferred from shore to shore, perpetually in exile, even (as we will see in chapter 2) in sunny Sparta: *Helen the Stranger.* The word Herodotus employs in 2.16 for "stranger" is ξείνης—an Ionian form of ξένος, meaning anything strange or foreign. Once again geographic displacement—stories of exile, abduction, journeys between shores—seems to be an acting out of metaphorical displacement: forced transfers of meaning, illegitimate acts of grafting.

Compare Helen the Stranger in Herodotus with Aristotle's description, *Rhetoric* 3.2, of the style of speech appropriate to the orator's task:

> Of nouns and verbs it is the proper ones that make style perspicuous; all the others which have been spoken of in the *Poetics* elevate and make it ornate; for departure from the ordinary makes it appear more dignified. In this respect men feel the same in regard to style as in regard to foreigners and fellow-citizens. Wherefore one should give our language a "foreign" air; for men admire what is remote, and that which excites admiration is pleasant. (1404b2–3)[42]

The remote and the foreign can also excite terror and dark misgivings. In "La mythologie blanche: La métaphore dans le texte philosophique," Derrida emphasizes the potential danger always present for Aristotle in the metaphor, where "the meaning of a name, instead of designating the thing that name ordinarily designates, moves elsewhere" ("le sens d'un nom au lieu de désigner la chose que le nom doit désigner habituellement, se porte ailleurs" [1972b:247–324]). For Aristotle the metaphor is, quite literally, the *exile* of the name from its proper object, its home. It is the Word become strange, or Stranger. The third chapter of the *Rhetoric,* which appears to be strictly concerned with technical matters, is often omitted from critical studies and translations.[43] And yet Aristotle's discussion of metaphor, we can see, is always highly metaphorical, and always in the same manner. At 1405a8, Aristotle declares: "It is metaphor above all that gives perspicuity, pleasure, and a foreign air" (trans. Freese 1926); at 1405b13 he asserts: "Metaphor is a kind of enigma, so that it is clear that the transference is clever"; at 1410b10–12: "All words which make us learn something are pleasant. Now we do not know the meaning of strange words, and proper terms we know already. It is metaphor, therefore, that above all produces this effect"; and, finally, at 1412a: "Most smart sayings are derived from metaphor, and also from misleading the hearer beforehand."

Helen, I have said, does not belong in Troy. Familiar yet foreign, her presence in the city is a figure for, and is figured by, the language of metaphor in Aristotle's *Rhetoric*—a dubious instrument, halfway between the commonplace and the unintelligible. In the *Poetics,* similarly, metaphor has its proper place, but is nevertheless a departure from "ordinary modes of speech," grouped along with "strange words," "lengthened forms," and "the ornamental equivalent." A language made out of pure metaphor, "an impossible combination of words," is a *riddle* (1458a24–25). This should remind us of Aristotle's dictum (1460a81–82): "The use of impossible probabilities is preferable to that of unpersuasive possibilities" (Golden and Hardison 1981). In support of this claim, Aristotle cites the painter Zeuxis, celebrated for his portrait of Helen (the *locus classicus* for this story is Cicero's *De inventione* 2.1–2, trans. Hubbell 1993). Zeuxis, we are told, made his Helen by combining the features of the five most beautiful women of Croton—an emblem of artistic *techne* as graft. Zeuxis will make an appearance in many of the chapters that follow in this study.

Helen's seductive beauty is always half-familiar, a riddle that must be solved; her face demands recognition or completion. This act of completion—solving the riddle, or constructing the metaphor—suggests the basic operation of the Aristotelian syllogism.[44] Consider the pronouncement of the Trojan elders: *Terrible is the likeness of her face to immortal goddesses.* In other words: (*a*) The divinely beautiful is immortal; (*b*) Helen is divinely beautiful; (*c*) therefore Helen is immortal. Helen's beauty in itself, which gets us from (*a*) to (*c*), is a means to an end. It is in the nature of the middle term, the minor premise, to exhaust itself in its conclusion. In fact, this kind of metaphorical syllogism has a technical name: it is an *abduction* (from the Latin *abductio*, a translation of the Greek ἀπαγωγή, *apagoge*, a leading away): that is, a syllogism in which the major premise (let us say, the vehicle, or model) is evident but the minor premise (the tenor, or imitation) and therefore the conclusion (that *this is that*, οὗτος ἐκεῖνος) only probable. Metaphor is constituted from the beginning, we see again, by the language of exile and abduction.

Aristotle's conceit in the *Rhetoric* of the polis opening its gates to the foreign or the exotic (just as Troy opened its gates to Helen and to the Horse) returns us to Plato's republic, the city of the soul corrupted by a strange and seductive importation. Helen's long career of abductions and transmigrations has always been a story of foreign importation and exportation. To speak of Helen in this sense is to speak of graft as *illicit trade*. If the story of Helen is the story of all metaphor, then graft is perhaps the essence of the plot. Here is de Man again paraphrasing Locke, whose criticism of metaphor's violation of epistemological boundaries is Aristotelian: "We have no way of defining, of policing, the boundaries that separate the name of one entity from the name of another; tropes are not just travellers, they tend to be smugglers and probably smugglers of stolen goods at that" (de Man 1978:19). A glance at some of the chapters devoted to style in the *Rhetoric* clearly reveals the extent to which the allure of Helen is akin to the allure of metaphor in that both are objects and agents of economic grafting and graft: both allow ill-gotten gains, with profitable, pleasurable, and potentially disastrous results.

2

Anamnesis

Introduction: From *Mimesis* to *Anamnesis*

Mimetic pleasure depends upon a kind of cognitive slippage or graft: a structure of misreading or metaphorical displacement. For Aristotle that pleasure is the sign that we are learning something. What mimesis teaches us, however, and how it teaches us remain, even in Aristotle, relational: functions of linguistic displacement or pivoting (from this thing to that thing, from the specific to the universal, from an object to a class of objects). The Aristotelian conception of mimesis closely resembles the moment of dramatic recognition in tragedy, described by Aristotle as a crisis of sudden reversal. This is a moment much like that experienced by the elders of Troy as they gaze, in the *teichoskopia,* upon the face of Helen of Troy.

This crisis of reversal, I am suggesting, is also a crisis of memory, or what I will be calling *anamnesis.* To seek to know who Helen is, in other words, is to confront that of which she reminds us. Knowing in this sense remains a form of perceptual or epistemological displacement or division, and the object of our knowledge remains a grafted entity, present receding to past, past always pointing to present. I have suggested that Homeric epic is always divided in this sense from itself, or doubled upon itself. In fact, epic represents itself self-dividing or doubling in precisely in this fashion, as an act of recollection in which the past is retrieved and resituated in the present. The invocation to the Muses (daughters, in the *Theogony,* of Mnemosune or Memory) is the rhetorical gesture representing that retrieval. Thus the poet in the second invocation in the *Iliad* (2.484–93) tells us that he himself could never hope to list the names of those who fought at Troy, "not unless the Muses of Olympia, daughters / of Zeus of the aegis, remembered [μνησαίαθ'] all those who came beneath Ilion" (491–92). The verb *mimnesko* here, Marcel Detienne has argued, suggests that the Muses do not merely remind the poet but, more precisely, put the poet in connection with the past. The epic poet is the figure, then, who has the power to shuttle back and forth between the present and the past (1973:20).

This chapter focuses on Helen as an emblem for the back-and-forth of *anamnesis* in the *Odyssey*. Much of the rhetorical power of the *Odyssey*, after all, lies in its obsessive referring *back* to Troy. The here-and-now of the *Iliad* is always pointing toward a future that has always already happened; its narrative is a present tense always threatening to become a future perfect. Helen *will* return to Sparta; Achilles *will* perish at Troy; Troy itself *will* one day be no more. These things have not yet happened in the *Iliad*, and yet, paradoxically, they have already receded into a future that is already past. The *Odyssey*, too, is fractured by this kind of temporal instability, but in the opposite direction: this epic is dominated everywhere by the dynamic of memory. The *Iliad*, as Nagy writes, "makes the painful death of Achilles ever present by allusion inside the *Iliad*, even though the actual death scene lies in the future, outside the *Iliad*. The future for the *Iliad* is a suitable past for the *Odyssey*" (1979:21). In the *Odyssey* Troy has already happened; Troy is past: that is the single, great, unforgettable fact. At the same time, Troy continues to live on. Troy will not recede into the past: no one can forget it; it everywhere threatens to undo the primacy and coherence of the present. The *Odyssey* owes its particular poignancy to the way in which it gestures toward the past while refusing to acknowledge it—as something past. One could put that another way: on the one hand the *Odyssey* indulges its audience in the fiction that it *follows* the *Iliad;* at the same time, on the other hand, it ties itself at every moment to an ongoing *Iliad*, the one narrative sutured to the other.

The Scar of Odysseus

If we look at the *Odyssey* in these terms, we discover a poem very different from the one Auerbach describes in the first chapter of *Mimesis*, "Odysseus' Scar" (1953:3–23). For Auerbach's famous observation that "Homer . . . knows no background" (4) could have very different implications than those Auerbach affirms. He argues essentially that Homeric epic is an eternal present without temporal perspective; what I have tried to suggest is that Homeric epic is an eternal present that is achieved only by virtue of a temporal perspective that is repeatedly collapsed but to which it repeatedly alludes. A few more words on Auerbach's essay are relevant to the subject of this chapter.

Everything in Homeric epic, Auerbach asserts, is driven by the "need for an externalization of phenomena in terms perceptible to the senses" (1953:6). Homeric narrative is essentially a "procession" of such "phenomena," one that "takes place in the foreground" (7); thus, "despite much going back and forth, it yet causes what is momentarily being narrated to give the impression that it is the only present, pure and without perspective" (12). Auerbach's case in point is Eurykleia's discovery of Odysseus's scar at *Odyssey* 19.392–468. The story of Odysseus and the boar (*Odyssey* 19.393–466), which explains the origins of the scar, is an interpolation framed by the nurse's discovery. But it does not refer to the frame outside it, nor is it referred to by the narrative that frames it. Odysseus, for example, does not "remember" the scene, which would have been an obvious way of justifying its inclusion. No, says Auerbach, "any such subjectivist-perspectivist procedure, creating a foreground and background, resulting in the present lying open to the past, is entirely foreign to the Homeric style" (7).

I would certainly agree with Auerbach that there is no explicit reference here, either in the interpolation to the frame or in the frame to the interpolation. Nevertheless, the fact remains: the interpolation is there. It is not there as background, or as memory, that is true; the only connection to the frame outside it is, as Auerbach points out, syntactical. But it is precisely the way Homer's narrative refuses to position the story "in relation to" a dominant or neutral narrative plane that makes the passage stand out *as an interpolation.* That Auerbach classifies it as such, and feels compelled to "explain" it, suggests that Homer has done his job: the interpolation is something aberrant, a moment of dislocation, and effectively signaled as such by the text itself. The story of Odysseus and the boar is not a memory, but it is a story from the past. That Homer's narrative here refuses to treat it any differently than the present is precisely what we are meant to see. Past here is grafted almost seamlessly to present. But in that "almost" lies all the difference: for the seam is visible and gives the passage its particular force. What this means is that it is not true that Homeric narrative is without perspective: on the contrary, it is strategically and unambiguously antiperspectival, and, by that very fact, everywhere intimates the possibility of perspective. We have seen traces of those perspectives—seams, as it were—in chapter 1 in the figure of Helen in *Iliad* 3, where the narrative refers, by not referring, to other Helens and other narratives. Let us now look at the passage from the *Odyssey* a little more closely.

It would have been easy, Auerbach asserts, to have introduced the story of Odysseus and the boar with perspective in mind. Instead, the connection between the anecdote and the larger narrative is almost mechanically syntactical:

The way in which any impression of perspective is avoided can be clearly observed in the procedure for introducing episodes, a syntactical construction with which every reader of Homer is familiar; it is used in the passage we are considering, but can also be found in cases when the episodes are much shorter. To the word scar (v. 393) there is first attached a relative clause ("which once long ago a boar . . ."), which enlarges into a voluminous syntactical parenthesis; into this an independent sentence unexpectedly intrudes (v. 396: "A god himself gave him . . ."). (1953:7)

Despite Auerbach's claims that Homeric narrative is a "uniformly illuminated, uniformly objective present" with "never a lacuna, never a gap, never a glimpse of unplumbed depths" (1953:7), syntactically speaking Homeric narrative is a shifting and hazardous landscape. Hypotaxis competes with parataxis; attached clauses and parenthetical digressions derail the audience off the straight and narrow path of linear narrative; asyndeton and unexpected intrusions put road-blocks or false paths in the way.[1] All of these linguistic features are evidence of severe repression and condensation—perspectives upon the past, yes, but perspectives closed off to view. All of them are seams, then: traces of graft.

Other seams are also visible in Homeric narrative. Auerbach, as has already been mentioned, notes that Homer could have made Odysseus the subject of this interpolation by having him remember it. The focus in Auerbach's essay is on Odysseus. But what if the real subject here is Eurykleia? This is something Auerbach implies when he first describes the location of the interpolation: "The interruption, which comes just at the point when the housekeeper recognizes the scar—that is, at the moment of crisis—describes the origin of the scar" (1953:4). The interpolation is indeed framed on both sides by the moment of Eurykleia's recognition: "She came up and washed her lord, and at once she recognized / that scar" (392–93). "The old woman, holding him in the palm of her hands, recognized / this scar as she handled it" (467–68). This is indeed a classic recognition scene: a moment, as we will see it is in Aristotle, of epistemological and perspectival crisis. It is a dangerous moment for Aristotle, but delightful precisely because of that danger. It is the crisis of mimesis, the moment in which, faced with a sign, a representation, an image, we understand "that this particular object is that kind of object" (*Poetics* 1448b16–20). We could easily add the scar itself to the examples of such objects mentioned by Aristotle: "the forms of the most despised animals and of corpses." The scar, moreover, is mentioned specifically by Aristotle in the *Poetics* as belonging to the larger category of recognition or *anagnorismos:* the kind prompted by external signs, and accompanied by a "reversal of action" (1454b19).

The transition to *Odyssey* 19.393–466 is motivated by more, it would appear, than syntax. As a moment of syntactical dislocation, the interpolation is, I would argue, the structural equivalent of Eurykleia's recognition—a moment of epistemological and temporal dislocation. Consider the exchange between Eurykleia and Odysseus that directly precedes the moment of recognition: it is a conversation about the disturbances of mimesis. Upon seeing Odysseus, Eurykleia remarks: "There have been many hard-traveling strangers who came here, / but I say I have never seen one as like as you are / to Odysseus, both as to your feet, and voice and appearance" (379–81). To which Odysseus replies: "So all say, old dame, who with their eyes have looked on / the two of us. They say we two are very similar / each to each" (383–85). And so the *Odyssey* provides us with the spectacle of Eurykleia, and Odysseus himself, agreeing that Odysseus looks uncannily like—Odysseus. The result is a vertiginous opening up of perspectives, a splitting of the text: two Odysseuses, each like the other, and yet now torn asunder. Similarly, in the interpolation that follows, this Odysseus (an Odysseus in the here-and-now) confronts that Odysseus (a distant Odysseus, an Odysseus then), and present gives way to past. The point at which these Odysseuses meet is the scar itself: the very literalization of the seam or the trace, an emblem of all graft. Perhaps the lesson of *Odyssey* 19.393–466 is that all textuality is a form of scar tissue.

Aristotle on Mimesis

Aristotle's *Poetics* begins as a discussion of the imitative arts (1447a–b), the "arts of making" ($\pi o i \eta \sigma \iota s$), which are "imitations" ($\mu \iota \mu \acute{\eta} \sigma \epsilon \iota s$) in Leon Golden's version (1981). In chapter 4 of the *Poetics,* Aristotle speculates as to the "general origin" of these arts and suggests that their source must lie in the pleasure of learning:

> The proof of this point is what actually happens in life. For there are some things that distress us when we see them in reality, but the most accurate representations of the same things we view with pleasure—as, for example, the forms of the most despised animals and of corpses. The cause of this is that the act of learning is not only the most pleasant to philosophers but, in a similar way, to other men as well, only they have an abbreviated share in this pleasure. Thus men find pleasure in viewing representations because it turns out that they learn and infer what each thing is—for example, that this particular object is that kind of object; since, if one has not happened to see the object previously, he will not find any pleasure in the imitation qua imitation but rather in the workmanship or coloring or something similar. (1448b10–20)

This passage plays a central role in this chapter. It is, when looked at closely enough, a strange and elusive passage. A number of observations are in order. First, Aristotle's paradigm of mimesis is a dramatic scenario: a specular confrontation—that is, a moment of theater. A viewer, faced with a visual tableau, responds, and it is in that response that the pleasure of mimesis is located. It is, we should remember, the scenario of a crowd taking pleasure in the theater that Socrates employs in *Republic* 10 to convince his interlocutor of the dangers of mimetic representations (604e–606c). The theater, for Plato, is a place of moral dissolution: the theater-goer, Socrates complains, praises that which in real life he would condemn (605e). That the audience can do this at all belies Socrates' own attempts to prove the morally corrosive deceptiveness of artistic representation. The audience of a play recognizes that this is precisely what is being watched: a representation. The parallels with Aristotle's passage are important. Here, too, the pleasure of the viewer stems from an implicit awareness that what is being looked at is, in fact, a likeness, and not the real thing. The delicate yet crucial boundary separating pleasure from horror in the mimetic moment is manifest in the macabre and repugnant nature of the "real thing" Aristotle employs as an example: "despised animals and corpses." There is pleasure, but there is also the possibility of fear and disgust. Everything depends on distinguishing the likeness from the original: on understanding, that is, what one is looking at.

This leads to a second observation. The pleasure afforded the viewer by the representation is contingent upon an act of pivoting, perceptually speaking. We move, that is, from a percept to a concept: from one entity (the image), which we can see, to a second entity (the original, or the general category), with which what we can see is identified, or in which it is classified: *"Thus men find pleasure in viewing representations because it turns out that they learn and infer what each thing is—for example, that this particular object is that kind of object."* The real drama of this movement or pivoting between this *on the one hand . . .* and that *on the other . . .* has not been fully appreciated. Commentators have generally treated b16–20 as a description of an intellectual step forward in knowledge. A great deal of commentary has attempted to ascertain the meaning of the phrase italicized above. What is it, exactly, that the viewer learns from the imitation? I give the original here: διὰ γὰρ τοῦτο χαίρουσι τὰς εἰκόνας ὁρῶντες, ὅτι συμβαίνει θεωροῦντας μανθάνειν καὶ συλλογίζεσθαι τί ἕκαστον, οἷον ὅτι οὗτος ἐκεῖνο[ς]. Generally, the knowledge obtained by the viewer is considered to be that of classification. One recognizes, in other words, that the object depicted is a certain kind or class of object, and by recognizing this one has, in effect, identified what thing it is. Gerald Else translates the key phrase, οὗτος ἐκεῖνο[ς], as: "this individual is a so-and-so."[2] This notion is perfectly consonant with the idea, expressed in the course of the *Poetics,* that what tragedy imitates is a universal action, not a specific one. This movement from the specific to the universal as a displacement or pivoting suggests connections with Aristotle's conception of metaphor. Those connections are more clearly visible if we ignore the emendation usually made of ἐκεῖνο[ς] and read ἐκεῖνο, as Samuel Butcher does, who translates b16–20 as: "Thus the reason why men enjoy seeing a likeness is, that in contemplating it they find themselves learning or inferring, and saying perhaps, 'Ah, that is he' " (1932). Here the dramatic force of mimesis as a recognition of likenesses, and as something perilously close to misreading, is much stronger.

Third, and most important for our purposes here, as Aristotle takes pains to point out in the last sentence of the passage above, the pleasure in the kind of cognitive pivoting sketched out above also moves from past to present: "if one has not happened to see the object previously, he will not find any pleasure in the imitation qua imitation but rather in the workmanship or coloring or something similar." Aristotle's theory of mimesis is also a theory of memory: a theory of *anamnesis*. Here I disagree with Hardison's reading of the second half of lines 17–20 (Golden and Hardison 1981:95). Hardison argues that Aristotle's reference to workmanship or coloring is *not* a way of saying, "True imitative pleasure comes from comparing the copy to the original; but if you can't do that you still have the consolation prizes of workmanship and coloring." Precisely the opposite, Hardison insists; Aristotle is saying that "the pleasure of imitation comes from learning, not from comparison to the original; that the proof of this is that we get the pleasure even if we have not seen the original; and that the learning and pleasure are caused by the artist's skill (his mastery of his *techne* and his materials)." But what Hardison does *not* say here is that, in this last case, the pleasure in question is not imitative in nature, and the imitation is not appreciated as an imitation at all. There is simply no other way to read the passage in question. By rejecting a reading that would turn Aristotle into a Platonist (defining imitation as a copy of an original), Hardison falls into a trap, it seems to me, of his own making. The imitation for Aristotle is not a copy referring back to an original, that is true; it remains an object, nonetheless, that must refer. Hardison wants to make the object refer forward only — that is, from the specific to the universal. But that kind of reference forward cannot occur without repetition, without our understanding that in what is presented to us something is being re-presented. Imitative pleasure, in other words, is both a referring forward (inference) and a referring backward (recognition or anamnesis). This fits with Nagy's definition of mimesis as the "reenactment, through ritual, of the events of myth" (1990:42) and, by extension, "the present reenacting of previous reenactments" (43). Such a definition yields a reading of Aristotle 1448b7 consistent with my analysis:

> the represented "that" identified with the representing "this" can be perceived not only as the previous experience but also as the sum total of previous experiences. "This," then, is particular, the experience in the here and now, whereas "that" is potentially universal, a cumulative synthesis of all previous experience. (1990:44)

For Nagy this would make Aristotle's οὗτος ἐκεῖνο[ς] parallel to the formulation *hoc illud* as a formal statement of affirmation, a way of declaring: *that's the way it was* (1990:44n132).

From Aristotle to Euripides: Mimesis, Recognition, Displacement

I want to further explore the specular or theatrical nature of Aristotelian mimesis, and the pivoting pleasure felt by the audience therein, before moving on to the role anamnesis plays in that pleasure. Hardison's reading of *Poetics* 1448b10–20, we have already seen, follows Else's emendation and emphasizes the thrust of the passage as a perception of universals in specifics. Aristotle, Hardison insists, is here offering a different understanding of imitation than the Platonic one. The example Hardison uses to illustrate Aristotle's understanding of mimesis is that of a photograph of an acquaintance (an example which, it should be said, is very different in its dramatic value from that which Aristotle himself employs). To say: "That photograph is a fine likeness of John" is not, according to Hardison, what Aristotle has in mind here; but rather: "That photograph is a fine likeness of John; it catches his character beautifully; and he should use it for the application form" (Golden and Hardison 1981:93). The example is one, however, that unwittingly underscores a subtle ambiguity in the role Aristotle gives to the imitation. The photograph that captures the generic John, after all, in its use on the application form, can thereby also *substitute for* John. The photograph, in other words, as an imitation of its model, can also be its supplement. In the following chapter I will pursue this point further, arguing that Helen herself may be said to be constituted by the logic of supplementarity. For now, I would emphasize the following: the possibility that the imitation can replace and supersede the model is precisely one of its dangers in Plato's eyes, and remains, I would argue, an implicit threat in Aristotle 1448b16–20. Hardison is, it is true, one of the few commentators to recognize to any extent the peculiarly dramatic paradox of Aristotle 1448b16–20, but he does not pursue this recognition any further than Plato himself did in *Republic* 10: "Aristotle's examples [of ugly animals and dead bodies] may have been chosen simply because they are striking and extreme, but it should be noted that both involve a paradox that is closely related to tragedy—the paradox of pleasure resulting from things that would be painful if experienced or witnessed in real life" (92). It is precisely the way the same paradox appears to structure both mimesis and tragedy in Aristotle that I would like to pursue further.

At first glance, nothing would appear to be more different from Aristotle's scenario of imitative pleasure than the moment where we "recognize" Helen of Troy. What could Helen possibly have in common with "representations" of "despised animals" and "corpses"? What gives Aristotle's mimetic moment its dramatic piquancy is the necessity of perceiving the representation *as* representation. But the possibility remains that we may hesitate, in that moment, if only for an instant, and hover between what we think we see and what we end up seeing. To gaze upon the face of Helen, I have already suggested, is *always* to hover in this fashion between percept and concept. We can never be sure, with Helen, that we are not in error. This is a truth that becomes comically explicit in Euripides' treatment of the myth of the phantom Helen. For we are never certain, when gazing upon the face of Helen (phantom or real thing), if we are gazing upon an original or upon a likeness, a specific or a universal.[3] This makes her a kind of monster, something far more frightening to behold than a corpse. The reaction of the Trojan elders in the *teichoskopia*—something close to nausea—begins to make more sense. Learning, in the *teichoskopia* as in Aristotle's archetypal mimetic moment, is a form of dislocation or graft: it takes place in the seam between categories, or in the movement back and forth between them. That, in turn, should remind us again of Aristotle's definition of metaphor in the *Poetics* 1457b5–10: "Metaphor is the transference of a name." For metaphors, too, are a form of recognition, a grafting of specifics to universals. The uneasy pleasure of the elders as they marvel at the face of Helen lies in understanding what kind of face it is, which is to say, what kind of face it is like. Meanwhile, the face itself begins to flicker and fade in the course of the very recognition that it provokes and frustrates. And so the elders play the role of Socrates in the *Cratylus,* asking: "Can we rightly speak of a beauty which is always passing away, and is first this and then that?" (439e). Mimetic pleasure for Aristotle, similarly, lies in the displacements of graft, in a sliding or a leap back and forth between one thing and another. In both cases the pleasure of recognition is founded on the flaws and fissures that make recognition, ultimately, impossible, or forever deferred. All of which makes the pleasure of mimesis a risky proposition. This is more explicit in another passage on learning in the *Rhetoric,* one that itself cites *Poetics* 48b14–16. The question with which Aristotle is grappling in the *Rhetoric* is that of the pleasure caused by changes or encounters with the new. Learning, Aristotle suggests, is just such an encounter:

it follows that such things as acts of imitation must be pleasant . . . and every product of skillful imitation; this latter, even if the object imitated is not itself pleasant; for it is not the object itself which here gives delight; the spectator draws inferences ("That is a so-and-so") and thus learns something fresh. Dramatic turns of fortune and hairbreadth escapes from perils are pleasant, because we feel all such things are wonderful. (1371b4–11)

Recognition in this passage is not a simple and comfortable advance in intellectual knowledge, but a rather perilous moment, hovering as on the brink of disaster. Pleasure is inseparable from peril in the wisdom we secure from mimesis.

What W. R. Roberts translates in the above passage as "dramatic turns of fortune" is περιπέτειαι — the same term employed by Aristotle in the *Poetics* to describe those moments of dramatic reversal and recognition crucial to the ideal tragedy. They are also, I would argue, the dramatic epistemological turns that accompany Helen of Troy wherever she goes. At 1452a22–b3, Aristotle defines the terms *peripety* and *recognition,* both of which he understands as a form of dramatic reversal or change (μεταβολή, a22). Recognition itself (ἀναγνώρισις) is defined as follows: " 'recognition' . . . is a shift [μεταβολή] from ignorance to awareness, pointing either to a state of close natural ties (blood relationship) or to one of enmity" (52a30–32). Recognitions and reversals, Aristotle asserts, are always accompanied by "pity or fear . . . and furthermore happiness or unhappiness" (38b1–b3). This second clause is, Else argues, dependent on the first; the recognition that points to "close natural ties" (εἰς φιλίαν) will generate pity (ἔλεον) in the audience, and that which points to "enmity" (εἰς ἔχθραν), fear (φόβον). But Else hastens to add, "Actually, of course, the two situations are reciprocal: each puts one of the tragic emotions to the fore while the other is kept in the background" (1957:351n21).

For Aristotle, then, tragic recognition, like mimesis, is a moment of dramatic reversal, a change from ignorance to knowledge. In both cases the subject exclaims: οὗτος ἐκεῖνο[ς]. *This is (like) that. That is a so-and-so. Ah, that is he!* That which is recognized, by virtue of being recognized, is made unrecognizable, fissured, doubled, divided into likenesses and translated into metaphors. The moment when we recognize Helen of Troy is the moment when we are unable to say who or what she is; it is a moment both dangerous and delightful, full of pity and fear. It is the moment of crisis, for example, in Euripides' *Helen* when, faced with what appears to be his wife, Menelaus is ready to mistake the real thing for a phantom, and the phantom for the real thing. "Who are you?" says the astonished Menelaus. "Whose face am I looking at?" And a moment later: "To me you appear to be exactly like Helen! . . . In appearance you are the same; but the mystery of it baffles me." Unable to defeat his incredulity, Helen asks her husband, "Will you leave me, and go away with your phantom wife?" To which Menelaus responds: "Yes, you are too much like Helen; so good-bye!" (557–91). Much is at stake in our ability to recognize the real Helen. As the Messenger who enters the scene says: "What? All our sweat and blood—spent for a ghost?" (706). Thus Menelaus's confrontation with Helen is a perfectly Aristotelian moment, a moment of terrifying and seductive uncertainty.

Perhaps what the Aristotelian subject exclaims as he enjoys the moment of mimetic learning is not: "Ah, that is he," but rather: "Ah, that *was* he," or: "That *is* what he *was* like." We do not fully understand Aristotle's conception of mimesis if we do not appreciate the extent to which he approaches it as reenactment of a ritual nature. This returns us to Nagy's reading of Aristotle 1448b10–20 as the affirmation of a mythic truth, a truth thereby reenacted, in which οὗτος or *this* would refer to a specific act in the here and now, while ἐκεῖνο[ς] or *that* would refer to the sum of all previous reenactments.

Odyssey 4.112ff.: "I never saw such a likeness"

Menelaus's recognition of Helen in Egypt turns all of his most cherished mimetic assumptions upside down, in a perfect instance of Aristotelian reversal. At the same time it threatens the very relation he has taken for granted between past and present. One could suggest that the same sort of reversal takes place on an intertextual level as well. In other words, Menelaus's encounter with Helen is also, necessarily, Euripides' encounter with Homer, a referring back to or revising of Homer. And yet, as is suggested in chapter 1, Homer has already engineered his own revisions. The Helen of the *Iliad* is already phantasmic, already indeterminate, already a likeness of herself. The Helen who stands upon the Skaian gates in the *teichoskopia* and recalls her life before Troy already refers forward to another Helen, the Helen of the *Odyssey,* at home in Sparta with her husband Menelaus, remembering Troy. It is time we turned to this Odyssean Helen: an openly nostalgic Helen, a Helen haunted—and thus bisected— by the memory of Troy. Revisionism and "rewriting," we have seen, are dominant poetic strategies in both Homeric epics; in the *Odyssey* they become explicit features of the plot. Everyone in the *Odyssey*—Odysseus, Telemachus, Phemios, Demodokus, Penelope, and Helen—is recalling, reciting, and revising the *Iliad*. In Euripides' *Helen,* and to a certain extent in the *Iliad,* Helen was a figure to be recognized; in the *Odyssey,* however, she is a figure who recognizes, who remembers, and reproduces the past (herself included).

The scene from the *Odyssey* on which I want to focus here is Homer's portrait of Helen in Sparta. Here is Helen at "home," then; and yet she is strangely absent at the same time. Helen is here and elsewhere, at home and in exile. Even home Helen is undone by other Helens, the Helens recalled (by herself, by Menelaus) from the past. Back in Sparta (but haven't we always already been there, even in the *Iliad?*), at the palace of Menelaus, the young Telemachus arrives with his companion Peisistratus in search of news of his father. Menelaus does not recognize him but, without knowing why, succumbs to a sudden attack of nostalgia, recalling his wanderings back from Troy. He longs to see Odysseus, he tells Telemachus (112–13). It is at this point that Helen makes her entrance, as in a second *teichoskopia:* "Helen came out of her fragrant high-roofed bedchamber, / looking like Artemis of the golden distaff" (121–22). In both scenes Helen is said to have just left her bedroom (*Iliad* 3.142: "she went forth from the chamber," ὁρμᾶτ' ἐκ θαλάμοιο; *Odyssey* 4.121–22: "Helen came out of her ... bedchamber," ἐκ Ἑλένη θαλάμοιο [. . .] ἤλυθεν). In both scenes Helen has just been spinning or is about to start. In both scenes Helen is likened to a divinity (*Iliad* 3.158: "Terrible is the likeness of her face to immortal goddesses," αἰνῶς ἀθανάτῃσι θεῇς εἰς ὦπα ἔοικεν; *Odyssey* 4.122: "looking like Artemis of the golden distaff," ἤλυθεν Ἀρτέμιδι χρυσηλακάτῳ ἐϊκυῖα. ἐϊκυῖα is the feminine present participle of the verb ἔοικα, *to be like*—the same verb that appears in its active form in *Iliad* 3.158).

There are significant differences, of course. The *Iliad* leaves Helen's divinity nameless, whereas the *Odyssey* compares her to the goddess to whom we would least expect her to be compared. The comparison may be a way of introducing from the beginning of this scene a subtle and, perhaps, comic tension into the figure of Helen, a gap between what Helen appears to be (chaste as Artemis, a happy homemaker for Menelaus) and what we know her to be.[4]

In both of these would-be theophanies, Helen's entrance is the occasion for an intense confrontation with reminders of the past. In the *teichoskopia* Helen's appearance is inspired by a longing for her former husband and home in Sparta. Once upon the walls of Troy, she is busy pointing out her former kinsmen to Priam. Here, back home in Sparta, it is ironically Troy, and the absent Odysseus, that she recalls. Telemachus's resemblance to Odysseus is, of course, the pretext for these recollections. When Helen recognizes Telemachus, she is simultaneously remembering Odysseus. It is significant that it is Helen, not Menelaus, however, who first speaks this recognition out loud. This is one of the many signs of the Homeric Helen's acumen: Helen in Homer is a figure of considerable *metis,* a quality traditionally associated with Odysseus.[5] Helen's first words upon her entrance are these:

> Do we know, Menelaos beloved of Zeus, who these men
> announce themselves as being, who have come into our house now?
> Shall I be wrong, or am I speaking the truth? My heart tells me
> to speak, for I think I never saw such a likeness, neither
> in man nor woman, and wonder takes me as I look on him,
> as this man has a likeness to the son of great-hearted Odysseus,
> Telemachos, who was left behind in his house, a young child
> by that man when, for the sake of shameless me, the Achaians
> went beneath Troy, their hearts intent upon reckless warfare.

> (138–46)

Helen's recognition of the father's likeness in the son is again conveyed by the verb twice employed to establish her own resemblance to a divinity: οὐ γάρ πώ τινά φημι ἐοικότα ὧδε ἰδέσθαι [. . .] ὡς ὅδ' Ὀδυσσῆος μεγαλήτορος υἷϊ ἔοικε ("for I think I never saw such a likeness . . . as this man has a likeness to the son of great-hearted Odysseus" [141–43]). Helen's prefatory "Am I speaking the truth?" would indeed appear to make the question of resemblance and reference the central motif of this scene. The rest of what Helen and Menelaus have to say is all about resemblances and appearances: not so much what things are, but what they seem to be like. Note, too, how Helen's perception of Telemachus's identity immediately segues into narcissistic nostalgia. We would expect nothing less from Helen.

Menelaus's recognition turns Helen's into an explicit sequence of metaphorical structures, a series of one-to-one correspondences moving back and forth between father and son, grafting the stock and the scion:

> οὕτω· νῦν καὶ ἐγὼ νοέω, γύναι, ὡς σὺ ἐΐσκεις·
> κείνου γὰρ τοιοίδε πόδες τοιαίδε τε χεῖρες,
> ὀφθαλμῶν τε βολαὶ κεφαλή τ' ἐφύπερθέ τε χαῖται.
> καὶ νῦν ἦ τοι ἐγὼ μεμνημένος ἀμφ' Ὀδυσῆϊ
> μυθεόμην

> (148–52)

[I also see it thus, my wife, the way you compare them,
for Odysseus' feet were like this man's, his hands were like this,
and the glances of his eyes and his head and the hair growing.
Now too I was remembering things about Odysseus
and spoke of him.]

Menelaus's symmetrical correspondences—"feet of such kind are [like those]
of that man [Odysseus]," κείνου γὰρ τοιοίδε πόδες—seem to point ahead to
the Aristotelian model of mimesis as recognition. But Menelaus does something
more significant with Helen's recognition than extend it comically: he also filters
it through the melancholy of *memory* ("remembering," μεμνημένος, 4.151).
Telemachus is not just the likeness of Odysseus: he is a *reminder* of Odysseus.
Recognition here is recollection, the memory of that which is absent in space,
and distant in time. Menelaus, like Helen, moves in this fashion from recognition to recollection, lamenting Odysseus's absence. These recollections prove
contagious, and soon the whole party is besieged by memories of what they have
lost: "Thus did he speak, and his words set them all a-weeping. Helen wept,
Telemachus wept, and so did Menelaus, nor could Peisistratus keep his eyes
from filling, when he remembered his dear brother Antilochus, whom Memnon,
the son of bright Dawn, had killed." Weeping is, of course, a frequent event in
the *Odyssey.* In fact, Odysseus (whose name, etymologically, suggests *pain*—
pain for himself and for others) sheds more tears than anyone in the course of
the epic that bears his name. The lamentations of Helen, Menelaus, and Telemachus, and the stories of Odysseus and the Trojan horse that follow, should remind us of Odysseus's weeping as he remembers his own exploits, recounted by
Demodokus at the court of the Phaiakians (8.83), at a moment when the hero's
identity has not yet been revealed. Odysseus as master manipulator of identity
is a central theme of the *Odyssey*—another respect in which Helen suggests a
female counterpart to him.

   Weeping in both of these scenes, Nagy has suggested, is a sign of personal in-
volvement (designated by epic itself as *penthos,* or pain) in the "public" events
of epic poetry, the *kleos,* glory, conferred by epic upon the material it records
(1979:94–99). I would only want to add that to become "personally involved"
in an event is, in effect, to *remember* it. Nagy refers to the song of Phemios at
Odyssey 1.325–59, and to the different ways that song is received by Penelope
and Telemachus (97–98). The self-reflexivity of the scene has long been noted:
Phemios's subject, in an epic about the return of Odysseus, is the *nostos* or
homecoming of the Achaeans. His song, then, is easy to read as a paradigm of
all epic performance: including that of the *Odyssey* itself. For Penelope, who is
always remembering (μεμνημένη αἰεὶ) her husband (1.343), the song causes
πένθος ἄλαστον, "unforgettable grief" (1.342). Telemachus, on the other hand,
is not yet personally connected in the same way, and can only think of his father

in the most abstract terms. For Telemachus the subject chosen by Phemios is a fitting one, since it is the "latest [νεωτάτη] to circulate among the listeners" (1.352) and therefore the most popular. The irony here, as Nagy does not fail to point out, is that the song is the newest both for Telemachus, listening to Phemios, and for the audience, listening to Homer. At this point we may recall another moment of communal weeping linking fathers and sons: that shared by Achilles and Priam in *Iliad* 24: a son remembering a father, a father remembering a son, τὼ δὲ μνησαμένω ("and the two remembered," 24.509). Here, too, the heroic events recorded by epic (*kleos*) have been transmuted into private griefs (*penthos*) by those who remember them. Looking ahead to the scene we are about to describe, note that the *phármakon* Helen places in her audience's wine, which disengages them personally from the stories to which they are listening, is called νηπενθές, "without *penthos*" (4.221).

Odyssey 4.235ff.: Helen Remembers Helen

Helen and Menelaus now exchange recollections of Odysseus. The subject of their tales, however, is more precisely Helen than Odysseus.[6] In fact, things are more complicated than that, for one might also say that the subject of these tales is the status of the subject itself. If Helen is the subject, in other words, then who or what that subject is, is far from clear. Menelaus does not remember Helen, in any case, in the same way that Helen does. These Helens do not match; they are like and yet not like each other. This brings us to a crucial motif in both Menelaus's and Helen's stories: both are about the problem of *resemblance*.

Helen is the first to entertain her listeners with recollections of Troy:

> Son of Atreus, dear to Zeus, Menelaos: and you who
> are here, children of noble fathers; yet divine Zeus sometimes
> gives out good, or sometimes evil; he can do anything.
> Sit here now in the palace and take your dinner and listen
> to me and be entertained [literally, listen to stories].
> > What I will tell you is plausible.
>
> > > > > (235–39)

From the very beginning of her tale, the question of *authenticity* is raised. What I will tell you, says Helen, is "plausible": that is, ἐοικότα: likely, reasonable, probable. Helen promises to tell us that which seems to be true, not necessarily what is true. This ambiguity also appears in the term Helen employs when she refers to storytelling: listen to μύθοις, stories. On the one hand, a μῦθος is any speech or set of words; on the other hand, a μῦθος is a legend, a story, a fable, and conventionally opposed to λόγος, which implies truth or historical veracity. Even before she begins her tale proper, then, Helen situates her words in rela-

tion to, but with some distance from, the real, the true, the historical. Helen is
aiming for verisimilitude, she warns us, not veracity.

The tale Helen tells concerns itself, we should not be surprised to learn, with
disguise and recognition. Odysseus, after all, is a master of disguises. We will
find, however, that he has met his match in Helen. Odysseus has concealed his
identity in the garb of a beggar, just as he will do upon returning to his own
home in Ithaca. In both cases, his aim is to secure information from the enemy.
Here is Helen's description of Odysseus's infiltration into the city:

> οἰκῆϊ ἐοικώς,
> ἀνδρῶν δυσμενῶν κατέδυ πόλιν εὐρυάγυιαν·
> ἄλλῳ δ᾽ αὐτὸν φωτὶ κατακρύπτων ἤϊσκε
> δέκτῃ, ὃς οὐδὲν τοῖος ἔην ἐπὶ νηυσὶν Ἀχαιῶν.
> τῷ ἴκελος κατέδυ Τρώων πόλιν, οἱ δ᾽ ἀβάκησαν
> πάντες·
>
>   (245–50)

[He *looked like* a servant.
So he crept into the wide-wayed city of the men he was fighting,
disguising himself *in the likeness of* somebody else, a beggar,
one who was *unlike himself* beside the ships of the Achaians,
but *in his likeness* crept into the Trojans' city, and they all
were taken in.] (my italics)

The question of resemblance appears in almost every line. Helen, alone among
the inhabitants of Troy, can perceive these likenesses: "I alone recognized him
even in this form" (250). At least this is how Helen remembers it.

Helen's story, ostensibly a fond memory of the lost Odysseus, is more properly a bit of public relations for herself. She, not Odysseus, is the hero of her tale.
She could have turned Odysseus in, she tells us, but did not. She remained an
Achaean all the time, she tells us, despite appearances. This is a confession that
at some level undoes itself, serving only to betray the dangerous ambiguity that
is Helen's constant attribute. She could indeed have turned him in at any time—
that may be just the point. About Helen the Greeks were never sure. Odysseus
divulges his identity and the purpose of his mission only after Helen has sworn
"a great oath not to disclose [ἀναφῆναι, from ἀναφαίνω, to bring to light, to
show forth plainly] before the Trojans that this was Odysseus" (253–54). Helen,
it is to be feared, may be more of a liability than an asset to Odysseus; she may
well reveal *who he really is*.

Helen's story ends with the nostalgic recollection of a nostalgic recollection.
She recalls that seeing Odysseus in Troy, and recognizing who he was, made
her homesick for Sparta. She was happy to see Odysseus escape unscathed, she
tells us, for "my heart had changed by now and was for going back home again"
(260–61). Helen in Troy (that is, Helen in the *Iliad*) remembers her former life in

Sparta (in the last chapter we saw this Helen reminiscing on the walls of Troy). Helen in Sparta (Helen in the *Odyssey*) remembers her former life in Troy. That is: Helen of Sparta remembers Helen of Troy remembering the former (and future) life of Helen of Sparta. Wherever Helen figures in poetry, she tends to be accompanied by this dizzying multiplication of Helens. "My heart," Helen says literally, "had turned around": τέτραπτο, from τρέπω. Helen typically provokes this turning around, this swerving, now from Sparta back to Troy back to Sparta, and from present to past to present.

Odyssey 4.274ff.: Menelaus Remembers Helen

Like Helen, Menelaus begins his tale with Odysseus and ends it with Helen; like Helen, Menelaus deals with Helen's dangerous commerce in resemblances and reminders; in both tales, Helen's powers of recognition and recollection threaten the lives of her kinsmen. Menelaus's Helen, however, is a darker figure than Helen's Helen. Here we are much less certain about the answer to the question: which side is Helen on?

Menelaus's story of Odysseus is really a response to Helen. In fact the arrangement of the two tales, one in answer to the other, suggests the structure of the *agon* or rhetorical debate, later formalized in Attic tragedy and comedy (in chapter 5, "Epideixis," we will examine just such an *agon* between Helen and Menelaus in Euripides' *Trojan Women*). Or, recalling Plato's reading of Helen in the *Republic,* we might describe Menelaus's tale as a countercharm to Helen's insidiously charming speech (an image discussed in chapter 1, "Mimesis"). Or, if we look ahead to Socrates' "invention" of dialectic in the *Phaedrus* (treated in chapter 3, "Supplement"), Helen's and Menelaus's opposing speeches resemble those "opposing speeches" or *antilogoi* that Socrates sees as the fundamental method of rational debate. Finally, Menelaus's answer to Helen is also a palinode, like Stesichorus's answer to Homer[7] (examined more fully in chapter 3). All of these discursive structures are species of *graft*.

Menelaus chooses a different episode in the Trojan saga: the story of the Trojan horse. He begins, like Homer, *in medias res:* at the moment when, already inside the city, Menelaus, Odysseus, and the rest of the Achaeans await their opportunity to attack. More specifically, what Menelaus recalls is Helen's uncanny ventriloquism of the Achaean wives, an act of mimicry that brings his comrades and himself to the brink of destruction. The horse itself as an emblem of deception already prefigures the cruel mimicry that Menelaus recalls:

> Then you came there, Helen; you will have been moved by
> some divine spirit who wished to grant glory to the Trojans,
> and Deïphobus, a godlike man, was with you when you came.
> Three times you walked around the hollow ambush, feeling it,

and you called out, naming them by name, to the best of the Danaans,
and made your voice sound like the voice of the wife of each of the Argives.

(274–79)

Helen here is not so much she who recognizes likenesses as she who produces
them. Her mimicry, moreover, is perfect, impossible, demonic (Antiklos is
ready to cry out in answer to what he thinks is the voice of his wife).[8] Zeitlin calls
this Helen the "mistress of many voices, the mistress of mimesis" (1996:409),
and that is exactly what she is. Helen's imitations here are nothing less than
simulations in Baudrillard's sense of the term, or *supplements* in the Derridean
lexicon, representations of a nightmarish order in the Platonic system, imitations that pose as the real and threaten to take the place of the real. They are
also reminders: what Helen impersonates is what each of the Achaean heroes
remembers and longs for. Menelaus's gracious suggestion that some unknown
deity moved her to this strange caprice is not enough to erase our doubts. She
cannot be trusted, this Helen. Which Helen is this? She is the wife now, not of
Menelaus, nor of Paris, but of Deiphobus (we are late in the war). Which Helen is
this? Human, divine, demonic? Trojan or Achaean? Good or evil? Helen began
the evening's storytelling by reminding her audience that "Zeus sometimes /
gives out good, or sometimes evil" (236–37), a bit of wisdom fully borne out
by the matter of the tales told, and fully embodied in the figure of Helen herself.
In each case, moral undecidability (the line, wavering, between good and evil)
is intimately linked to ontological undecidability (the line, wavering, between
what is real and what is false, what is true and what is probable, what is present
and what is absent). With Helen, as with all mimesis, it is difficult to tell which
side of the line we are on.

Conclusion: Helen as *Pharmakon*

The question of undecidability looms larger when we take into account a bit of
subterfuge in which Helen has engaged prior to the telling of the tales. Homer
lets us see what Menelaus and Telemachus are unaware of: that their very power
as listeners to distinguish good from evil, likeness from reality, truth from fable,
μῦθος from λόγος, has been erased. They have been drugged, and by Helen:

Into the wine of which they were drinking she cast a medicine [φάρμακον]
of heartsease, free of gall, to make one forget all sorrows,
and whoever had drunk it down once it had been mixed in the wine bowl,
for the day that he drank it would have no tear roll down his face,
not if his mother died and his father died, not if men
murdered a brother or a beloved son in his presence
with the bronze, and he with his own eyes saw it.

(220–26)

Helen's *pharmakon* is a drug that cancels out all suffering—but only by abolishing memory. To lose one's ability to remember here is to lose the capacity to distinguish real from unreal.[9] If one can witness the murder of a loved one and laugh, then one has mistaken life for theater. To forget all sorrows, as the frightening image of familial slaughter played out before our eyes suggests, is also to lose all sense of ethical distinctions. Thus the virtues of Helen's *pharmakon* are highly ambiguous in a way that replays the anxieties spoken in the tales over what is real and what is illusory. This is an ambiguity essential to the term φάρμακον itself, which means either "remedy" or "poison."[10] This becomes even clearer in Homer's brief digression on the manner in which Helen has come to possess the drug:

> Such were
> the subtle medicines Zeus' daughter had in her possessions,
> good things, and given to her by the wife of Thon, Polydamna
> of Egypt, where the fertile earth produces the greatest number
> of medicines, many good in mixture, many malignant.
>
> (226–30)

Helen's drugs, the text insists, are "good things," ἐσθλά; and yet that designation is offset by the image of Egypt's dual crop, which is half "good," half "malignant": φάρμακα, πολλὰ μὲν ἐσθλὰ, "many good," πολλὰ δὲ λυγρά,"many baneful."

Behind this Helen of Sparta then, narrating the exploits of a Helen of Troy, there is still another Helen, a Helen of Egypt.[11] This Egyptian Helen is a sorceress Helen, a *pharmakeus* Helen. This figure appears elsewhere in the Helen tradition: in, for example, the "Eastern" and "sensual" Helen of Euripides' *Orestes*.[12] This orientalized Helen, a witch-doctor Helen—but whether a good or a bad witch is far from clear—deals in likenesses: that is, memories and reminders. The power of these reminders is always erotic, a power to seduce. One example, from Euripides' *Trojan Women,* serves to make this clear. Hecuba, upon handing over her grandson Astyanax to be murdered, turns to Menelaus and recommends that he do precisely the same with Helen. Menelaus agrees, but wants to see Helen first. Hecuba suggests that this would be a fatal error:

I commend you, Menelaus, for your intention to kill your wife. But flee the sight of her, lest she captivate you with longing. She captivates the eyes of men, she destroys cities, she sets homes aflame. Such are her witcheries. I know her; so do you and all her victims. (194)

Hecuba articulates more fully what the Trojan elders only intimate: that to look upon Helen is to fall prey to a sorcery that confounds. This sorcery is the seduction of beauty, a seduction that throws into dangerous disarray our notions of what is and what is not, of what is good and what is evil. But to look upon the face of Helen of Troy is never, despite what Hecuba says, to know her. Figure for all mimesis, Helen makes this kind of knowledge impossible. This is precisely what Menelaus's countercharm has already demonstrated. Menelaus's story, in a scene "ruled by the enchantment of the *pharmakon,*" as Zeitlin puts it, ruled, too, by the figure of the Egyptian Proteus, archetypal image of mimicry and illusion,

functions as a self-reflective comment on the nature of fiction and mimesis, which Helen embodies. Menelaos's story thus intimates that Helen's previous story may be a fiction and suggests in the process that Helen and storytelling may be one and the same: the imitation of many voices in the service of seduction and enchantment. . . . Only Odysseus, the master-storyteller himself, is capable of unmasking her disguise. (1996:410)

And only Helen, we might add, as she herself suggests in her own story, is capable of unmasking Odysseus's disguise. When it comes to grifters, it takes one to know one.

3

Supplement

Introduction: That Dangerous Supplement

In "La double scéance" (1972a:212–13), Derrida analyzes the Platonic model of mimesis. What is significant for our purposes about his reading of the *Philebus* is its suggestion that contradiction is built into the Platonic notion of imitation. Derrida points out that there are at least two simultaneous yet irreconcilable conceptualizations of imitation: (1) on the one hand, the imitation is devalued as an object in its own right, it is nothing in itself, it is an illusion, merely a double of its model, and whether it is good or bad depends on the goodness or badness of the model; (2) on the other hand, the imitation is undeniably something in its own right, it exists, and while it is a copy and therefore inferior to its model, at the same time it can sometimes replace that model and is therefore potentially superior to it. This contradictory movement is what Derrida calls the logic of *supplementarity*. Barbara Johnson, in the introduction to her translation of "La double scéance," describes that logic cogently: if *B* is the supplement to *A,* then *B* is added to *A and* replaces *A* (Derrida 1972a). Thus the imitation for Plato is a *supplement.* Not only is the supplement one of the most recurrent structures in deconstructive writing; it is also a powerful variation on the notion of graft. For Derrida it is a way of suggesting that the fundamental distinctions upon which Western culture rests—for example, between culture and nature, or speech and writing, or the original and the imitation—are inherently unstable and always potentially reversible. Each of the three distinctions just cited is also a hierarchy, a conventional axiology; in each the second member of the pair is marked as a supplement to the first. All of these hierarchical pairs can therefore be inverted (and are always already potentially inverted), so that what was originally the first element is now supplement to the second.

Derrida elaborates this structure most fully in his discussion of Rousseau's *Confessions* in *Of Grammatology*. The issue becomes explicit in Rousseau's attempt to define writing as a supplement to speech. Derrida argues that writing, for Rousseau,

> is dangerous from the moment that representation there claims to be presence and the sign of the thing itself. And there is a fatal necessity, inscribed in the very functioning of the sign, that the substitute make one forget the vicariousness of its own function and make itself pass for the plenitude of a speech whose deficiency and infirmity it nevertheless only *supplements*. For the concept of the supplement—which here determines that of the representative image—harbors within itself two significations whose cohabitation is as strange as it is necessary. The supplement adds itself, it is a surplus, a plenitude enriching another plenitude, the *fullest measure* of presence. . . . It is thus that art, technè, image, representation, convention, etc., come as supplements to nature. . . . This kind of supplementarity determines in a certain way all the conceptual oppositions within which Rousseau inscribes the notion of Nature to the extent that it *should* be self-sufficient.
>
> But the supplement supplements. It adds only to replace. It intervenes or insinuates itself *in-the-place-of;* if it fills, it is as if one fills a void. . . .
>
> This second signification of the supplement cannot be separated from the first. . . . But their common function is shown in this: whether it adds or substitutes itself, the supplement is exterior, outside of the positivity to which it is super-added, alien to that which, in order to be replaced by it, must be other than it. (Derrida 1967 = 1976:144–45)

Derrida's point, that the logic of the supplement is not restricted to the question of writing but somehow constitutes all binary categories and critical cultural distinctions, is borne out by the way the supplement structures Rousseau's condemnation of masturbation in a later passage in the *Confessions*. Masturbation is "that dangerous supplement" ("ce dangereux supplément" [1967 = 1976:150]) that gives Derrida the title of his chapter. If autosexuality substitutes a phantom love for the real thing, then, Rousseau demonstrates, so does "real" sexuality— which therefore can be defined as a subspecies of masturbation. Desire itself does not escape the logic of the supplement.

Neither does Helen: especially Helen. Even where Helen is "real," she remains phantasmic. Helen has always been a supplement, in other words, marked by its essential contradictory logic: on the one hand this, on the one hand that, both herself and something else, beauty "which is always passing away, and is first this and then that" as Socrates puts it in the *Cratylus* (439e). The most dramatic expression of this contradiction is the myth of Helen's phantom, the famous *eidolon,* which we have already encountered in Euripides' *Helen.* The *eidolon* is a copy Helen, a second or surplus Helen. But the supplement, Derrida points out, always threatens to replace that which it supplements, and thus the *eidolon* always poses as the real Helen and threatens to take her place. If the *eidolon* is the emblematic expression of a supplementary logic tied to the figure of Helen, perhaps it would be more accurate to say that Helen is in some sense *always* an *eidolon,* and that far from being an alternative tradition, the *eidolon* is the standard Helen myth in its starkest, most explicit form.[1]

Helen is essentially supplementary not only in an erotic sense, but in terms of literary history as well. Every Helen myth is a supplement/scion to the Helen "tradition," to the stock of Helen myths already in place. We have seen in chapter 1 that the Helen of the *Odyssey* is the supplement to the Helen of the *Iliad* (and vice versa). We should not be surprised, then, that Helen as *eidolon,* figured so explicitly in Euripides' *Helen,* has her counterpart in the poem that, at least as the tradition was understood in the classical period, gives birth to her: Stesichorus's *Palinode.* The *Palinode,* in other words, is a literary supplement. If Derrida's notion of the supplement is as pervasive a structure of discourse as he suggests, however, then we can perhaps go farther than that. Rather than treating Stesichorus's recantation as an exceptional act, one that resists the dominance of a hegemonic tradition, I would define it as a normative literary move. There are no entirely new moves in this game, no original texts: there are only *palinodes.* This chapter begins with Plato's *Phaedrus* and the crucial role that Stesichorus's Helen plays in that text, before returning to Euripides' *Helen* as the most elaborate dramatization or incarnation of Helen as supplement.

Being Seized by Fluency

From the beginning of the *Phaedrus,* language is linked to seduction, deception, violence, and supplementarity. At the start of the dialogue, Socrates and Phaedrus are discussing the rhetorical prowess of the famed Lysias as they stroll along the banks of a river outside the city walls.[2] Phaedrus has just come from hearing a speech or *logos* by Lysias on the subject of love (227c4). Socrates, who in Rowe's translation is "sick with passion for hearing people speak [$\pi\epsilon\rho\grave{\iota}$ $\lambda\acute{o}\gamma\omega\nu$]" (228b6–7) and a "lover of learning [$\phi\iota\lambda o\mu\alpha\theta\acute{\eta}s$]" (230d3), is all too eager to hear the speech that Phaedrus has brought with him in written form (trans. Rowe 1986).[3] Phaedrus is in fact concealing the speech "beneath his cloak," $\acute{\upsilon}\pi\grave{o}$ $\tau\hat{\wp}$ $\acute{\iota}\mu\alpha\tau\acute{\iota}\wp$ (228d7). This is the first of the many supplements that inhabit the *Phaedrus,* for much in this dialogue is concealed and deferred. Phaedrus's insistence that he has forgotten Lysias's oration is a tease, as Socrates knows full well (228b–c): Phaedrus "intended," he affirms, "to speak in the end, even if he had to do so forcibly," $\beta\acute{\iota}\alpha$, with or by means of force (228c3). Again and again in this dialogue the charm of seduction threatens to become the dangerous violence of abduction and possession.[4] The two friends find a picturesque venue for their recitations: a bit of shade beneath a plane tree along the banks of the Illisus. The shapes and smells of tree and river are seductive, but in the tranquil shade lurk shadows of violence;[5] the spot, Socrates remarks,

"seems to be sacred to some Nymphs and to Achelous" (230b1–10).[6] There
is something *unsettling* about the beauty of this place.[7] But the motif of being
unsettled is central to the whole *Phaedrus*. Our suspicions about this pastoral
setting should have already been alerted by a previous bit of small talk on the
subject of myth. Phaedrus asks Socrates, innocently enough, at 229b5: "Tell
me, Socrates, wasn't it from somewhere just here that Boreas is said to have
seized Oreithuia from the Illisus?" Discussing the figure of Theseus in Greek
mythology, Graves suggests: "Helen's abduction during a sacrifice recalls that
of Oreithyia by Boreas . . . and may have been deduced from the same icon." [8]
So this "fine stopping-place" by the banks of the Illisus is haunted, in fact, by
phantoms of abductions.

The pastoral setting of the *Phaedrus* is an unusual one for a Platonic dialogue. Socrates, we cannot help but feel, is out of his element here, in unknown
and (as Achelous, Orethuia, Boreas, the Centaurs and Chimaera, Gorgons, and
nymphs remind us) potentially dangerous territory. But Phaedrus has found the
way to make Socrates leave the city: "you seem to have found the prescription
[φάρμακον] to get me out. Just like people who lead [ἄγουσιν] hungry animals
on by shaking a branch or some vegetable in front of them, so you seem to be
capable of leading me round all Attica and wherever else you please by prof-
fering speeches [λόγους] in books in this way" (230d6–e1). Lysias's speech,
this exercise in pure rhetoric, is a *pharmakon*—a prescription, yes, but also a
drug or a poison, as Derrida reminds us in "La pharmacie de Platon." Socrates
has indeed been drugged and kidnapped, lured outside, *led* (this word and its
many variations, all derived from the stem verb ἄγω, to lead, will be of the utmost importance throughout the *Phaedrus*), from the straight and narrow path
of dialectic.

The true menace Socrates faces, as he well knows, comes from language, a
power perhaps prefigured in the name *Lysias,* which may remind us of λύσσα,
rabies or madness. And, indeed, the whole point of Lysias's speech, a λόγος [. . .]
ἐρωτικός (227c4–5), an "erotic speech," or a "speech on love," which Phaedrus proceeds to read, is that the lover is always mad (231d2–4).[9] The reading of
the speech, like Socrates' description of the effect of a rhapsodic performance
upon the innocent populace in the *Ion,* produces a contagion of possessions and
minds gone *astray* with erotic desire. After Phaedrus's reading, Socrates feigns
possession; he is, he says, "beside himself," ὥστε με ἐκπλαγῆναι (234d1).
Indeed, Socrates explains, his own amorous excitement is a reaction to the excitement felt by Phaedrus; Phaedrus's possession, like a disease, is infectious.
Rhetoric as contagion is a motif we will have occasion to return to in the course
of this study. It is the sight and sound of Phaedrus being carried away that carries
Socrates away; the latter follows the former's lead: ἡγούμενος [from ἄγω, to
lead] γὰρ σέ, "following you" (234d4). He was, he assures us, "in ecstasy,"
συνεβάκχευσα (d5).[10] Socrates even refers to his criticism of the speech as a

"teasing attack" upon Phaedrus's "darling" (236b5).[11] The motif of madness or possession—the idea of *being carried away somewhere*—is duplicated on the level of the complicated series of speech acts that are performed in the dialogue. In brief, Socrates seduces Phaedrus into reading Lysias's speech, a speech that is designed to enable an *erastes* (lover) to seduce and possess an *eromenos* (beloved), designed to persuade the beloved that the nonlover is to be preferred to the lover because the lover is possessed by madness. Next Phaedrus must persuade—or force—Socrates to pronounce a speech more seductive than the one made by Lysias ("I've got something to say," Phaedrus threatens, at 236d6–7, "which will pretty well force you to speak").[12] Socrates does, indeed, speak, and quickly finds himself *carried away*.

In his first speech (237b–241d), Socrates sets out, in good dialectical fashion, to define his topic formally. Love is understood to be a form of desire (237d3), and desire is paired with judgment, the two being forces that "rule and lead," and "which we follow wherever they lead" οἷν ἑπόμεθα ᾗ ἂν ἄγητον (237d7). The difference between the two is the *direction* in which they lead: judgment leading toward the good, desire toward "pleasure in beauty" (238c1). Desire is that which *misleads*. Now, midway in Socrates' own attempt at seduction, Phaedrus asserts: "you've been seized by a fluency greater than normal," τὸ εἰωθὸς εὔροιά τίς σε εἴληφεν (238c6–7); the verb here, λαμβάνω, means anything from "grasp" to "take by violence." This occurs just after a bit of "playful" (according to Rowe) etymologizing, in which Socrates links the word for love, ἔρως, with the word for force, ῥώμη (238c3–4).[13] To Phaedrus's assertion, Socrates replies, confirming the suspicions of 230b7–8: "Then hear me in silence. For the spot seems really to be a divine one, so that if perhaps I become possessed by nymphs [νυμφόληπτος], do not be surprised" (238d1).[14]

Socrates and Phaedrus are leading each other; but where is all this *leading* us?

The *Palinode*

To Helen, naturally. But getting there is never a straight line; we arrive at Helen only by moving back and forth. This is the image that Socrates employs, in his first speech, to describe the shift in the behavior of the once maddened lover when he falls out of love: "compelled to default, the former lover changes direction and launches himself into flight with the flip of the shard on to its other side; and the other is compelled to run after him" (241b4–7). Note the system of compulsions at work here: the lover compelled (ὑπ' ἀνάγκης) to flee, the beloved compelled to chase the fugitive. Note, too, the motif of reversals: the lover changing direction (μεταβαλών), like the flip of a shard (our *flip of the coin*).[15] Socrates, too, upon the completion of his first speech, is compelled to take flight and reverse direction. At 242d5 Socrates insists that it was Phaedrus who compelled him to utter his speech: ἐμέ τε ἠνάγκασας εἰπεῖν, "you forced me to speak." That speech is ended, quite abruptly, after Socrates' model condemnation of the lover. Socrates categorically refuses Phaedrus's exhortations to "complete" the speech and enter into the praise of the nonlover: "Do you know that I'll patently be possessed by the Nymphs to whom you deliberately exposed me? . . . I'm off across the river here before you force me into something worse" (241e3–242a1). Again the shadow of the nymphs looms.

Meanwhile Socrates has only half-finished his speech: "But I thought," says Phaedrus, at 241d4, "it was just in the middle," μεσοῦν. Dramatically, we seem here to be at a standstill, in some kind of moment held in temporary stasis: Socrates' speech is left hanging at its midpoint, and Socrates himself is ready to take flight. As Socrates is about to depart, Phaedrus remonstrates: "Don't go yet, Socrates; not until the heat of the day has passed. Don't you see that it's just midday, the time when we say everything comes to a stop? Let's wait and discuss what's been said, and then we'll go, when it's cooler" (242a3–6). And indeed, everything has come to a stop. We are at a midpoint, a seam. Something is going to happen.

At this precise moment, Socrates does an about-face. The *daimon*—that force which regularly turns Socrates back from saying or doing something—makes its presence felt (242b9). Socrates renounces the speech he has just made. He must make amends; he must reverse himself. It is here, at the joint of the graft, at the crucial moment where Socrates pivots, that the figure of Helen intervenes. Just as Socrates has blasphemed against Love (242e1), so Stesichorus once blasphemed against Helen, and Socrates, like Stesichorus, must now sing his own *palinode*. Plato now cites the only fragment left to us of Stesichorus's recantation (243a5–b1). Socrates makes it clear that in speaking his recantation, he will undergo his own purification (243a4); his καθαρμὸς. One might compare this ritual act of purification or *katharmos*, in the course of which Socrates recognizes *what Love really is* (or *who Helen really is*), with Aristotle's conception of tragic *catharsis*: a moment of recognition suspended between pity and fear. The same pleasures and the same perils are at stake, the same dangerous transaction of the space between one thing (οὗτος) and another (ἐκεῖνος), a transaction explored in detail in chapter 2. At 243e10, in fact, Socrates does indeed seem to be playing a role; he has *become* Stesichorus, and grafts his own story of Eros on to Stesichorus's tale of Helen. In his second speech on love, Socrates confesses the errors of his former rhetorical ways, and those of the eminent Lysias. He was misled, he tells us (it was the nymphs who made me do it, or Phaedrus), and so were we. Now Socrates, led by his *daimon*, is to lead us in a different direction. This, too, is how Socrates will define *eros*: as a force that leads us somewhere, in pursuit of supplements.

Not only is this second speech, which includes the Myth of the Charioteer (245c–249d), a supplement to the first, but it is essentially a theory of love as supplementarity. The beloved is only an image, after all—Socrates calls it a "reminder," ἀνάμνησις (249c2)—of the divinity that once upon a time accompanied the lover in the celestial realm.[16] Thus desire mediates between our mortal and immortal selves, our present and our past.[17] This mediation, a grafting of antitheses suspended in proximity, supplies the dominant motif in the Myth of the Charioteer—as in the image of the soul as a good horse coupled to a bad one, or the figure of *eros* as *daimon,* half-mortal and half-divine, half-rich and half-poor.[18] Note that the myth itself, cast in the form of an allegorical narrative, is itself characterized by Socrates as a supplement to "normal" philosophical discourse: "To say what kind of thing it is would require a long exposition, and one calling for utterly superhuman powers; to say what it resembles requires a shorter one, and within human capacities. So let us speak in the latter way" (246a2–8). Afterward Socrates apologizes for the lyricism of his palinode: "'This, dear god of love, is offered and paid to you as the finest and best palinode of which I am capable, especially given that I was forced to use somewhat poetical language because of Phaedrus" (257a4–6). This apology is significant: for from beginning to end the *Phaedrus* is also a defense of poetry (which Socrates will sometimes call dialectic, sometimes philosophy, sometimes rhetoric—good rhetoric, that is, as opposed to Lysian sophistry). This makes the whole of the *Phaedrus* a palinode: a rebuttal of the *Republic* and its censure of poetry.

I have suggested that one of the central images in the *Phaedrus* is that of leading and misleading. This motif of displacement—writ large in the image of the divine procession in the Myth of the Charioteer—is a function of the logic of the supplement. Neither the lover nor the philosopher gets what he wants here (love and truth, respectively); both must be content with the lure of asymptotes and the satisfaction of substitutes (the body, for example, for the lover; *logos* for the philosopher). Language itself, as in the *Cratylus* (e.g., 391e), is a supplement for truth, and thus what we call Love is only an approximation of its "real" name: "We mortals call him Mighty Love [῎Ερωτα], a winged power of great renown, Immortals call him Fledgeling Dove [Πτέρωτα]—since Eros' wings lack down [because of a wing-growing necessity]" (252b8). *Logos* can only approximate or resemble or remind us of the truth; hence it always leads us and misleads us at the same time.

The function of *logos,* Socrates asserts, "is to influence the soul." What Socrates actually says is that "the power of speech is a leading of the soul," Λόγου δύναμις τυγχάνει ψυχαγωγία οὖσα. At 261a8 Socrates defines rhetoric as a "leading of the soul by means of things said [*logoi*]," ψυχαγωγία τις διὰ λόγων. Leading is never far from misleading, as Socrates suggests the speeches in the *Phaedrus* show: "by some chance . . . the two speeches which were given do have in them an example of how someone who knows the truth can mislead [παράγοι] his audience by making play in what he says" (262d1–7). But how do we know we are not being misled now? It is true to the motif of the

recurrent backward and forward movement throughout the *Phaedrus* that Socrates is once again, here, leading us on, teasing us, being coy.[19] Later we will see
that παράγω, to mislead or lead aside, is the verb Sappho employs in Fr. 16 to
describe Helen's desertion of Sparta: "[the Cyprian goddess] led her from the
path," ἀλλὰ παράγαγ᾽ αὔταν.[20] To say that persuasion is like abduction may be
to do violence, as we say, to those terms, but it is a violence already constitutive
of those terms. Note, finally, that an *abductive syllogism,* in which persuasion
rests on probabilities as opposed to proofs, is also called an *apagoge — a leading
astray.* (For a discussion of the abductive syllogism, see "Helen the Stranger"
in chapter 1.)

Desire and Dialectic: Collections and Divisions

Supplementarity as a motif in the *Phaedrus* suggests a response to the many
readers of the dialogue who have complained of the difficulties in linking the
analysis of rhetoric that follows Socrates' second speech to the discussion of
love that precedes it. Various interpretive strategies have been adopted to overcome the apparent fissure dividing the *Phaedrus* in two. "The Eros speeches
in the first part," says Werner Jaeger in *Paideia: The Ideals of Greek Culture,*
"rising to a pitch of wild excitement, are hard to fit into a unity with the abstract theorizing on the nature of true eloquence which occupies the second
part" (1944:183). The *Phaedrus,* Jaeger decides, "derives its unity from its concern with the subject of rhetoric" (184). This statement in itself is difficult to
counter, but it has the distinct disadvantage of making the sections of the dialogue devoted to love purely contingent. Indeed, Jaeger goes so far as to say that
Lysias's speech on Eros was selected "mainly because it was a favorite theme
for such exercises in rhetorical schools" (186). But it should be clear by now
that more is at work here than the emulation or evaluation of rhetorical models.
The *Phaedrus,* I would agree with Carson, is a dialogue about rhetoric, and *also*
about love. This is what Jaeger expressly *forbids* us to think: "We must not be
led to think," he warns, "that Eros is the real subject of *Phaedrus,* by the fact
that Plato discusses it in such detail at the beginning" (186). Jaeger's admonition echoes Socrates' own cautionary statements on the tendency of rhetoric to
mislead us. Jaeger wants to control precisely what cannot be controlled, wants
to keep us on the straight and narrow path. But the *Phaedrus* is designed to lure
us off the path toward strange and forbidden vistas haunted by seductive and
dangerous nymphs. It is not simply a question of two subjects and one dialogue:
I would argue that the *Phaedrus* demonstrates that the two subjects are necessarily linked, and that the distinction between them is artificial. Both love and
rhetoric are conceptualized as supplements in the *Phaedrus.* "Eros and Logos,"
Carson writes, "are fitted together in the *Phaedrus* as closely as two halves of a
knucklebone" (1986:123).[21] That description is a perfect representation of the

structure of graft—a structure that, we have already seen, recurs within the dialogue itself.

This structure of graft is the key to Socrates' rehabilitation of rhetoric in the *Phaedrus*. We have seen that Socrates calls rhetoric, at 261a8–9, "a kind of leading of the soul by means of things said." But if the rhetor is to lead his listener in the right direction, Socrates claims, he must have knowledge of the truth: "he should get the truth first and then *seize hold of me* [λαμβάνειν]" (260d7–9). (Even when Socrates is at his most technical, his language betrays, as here, an undercurrent of physical violence.) Socrates' claim is based on the observation that rhetoric is in essence a mode of debate in which opposing arguments— *antilogoi* (261c5)—are exchanged. This is a good description not only of Socrates' first attempt to outdo Lysias, but also of his second speech, which contradicts the first. Thus the science of *antilogic,* meaning "words in opposition to each other," ἀντιλογική, as Socrates calls it (261d10), is the same as that of the palinode. *Antilogic* is ultimately the art of demonstrating resemblances: it is the "one science," Socrates insists, "in relation to everything that is said, by which a man will be able to make everything which is capable of being made to resemble something else resemble everything which it is capable of being made to resemble" (261e). It is the "business" of the *antilogician,* then, "to hunt down appearances" (262c2), to recognize likenesses, to expose differences and similarities. This is what it means to know the truth (262a9).[22] Lysias misleads us, Socrates asserts, because he never stops to *define* his subject, never distinguishes what love really is from what it is not or from what is misleadingly like it.[23]

Socrates insists that the science of antilogic is nothing less than a new philosophical method: that of the *dialectic.* What is dialectic? A classifying system, Socrates suggests, a system of what he calls *synagoge* or *collection* ("perceiving together and bringing into one form items that are scattered in many places" [265d4–5]) and *diaeresis* or *division* ("Being able to cut it up again, form by form, according to its natural joints, and not try to break any part into pieces, like an inexpert butcher" [265e1–3].[24] This method both defines the structure of the *Phaedrus* as a whole and, more specifically, suggests the shape of eroticism sketched out in this and other dialogues (most notably the *Symposium*). The winged soul in flight to rejoin that from which it has been divided reenacts this drama of collection and division. There is no question that Socrates' dialectical pursuit of knowledge is thus at the same time an erotic quest: "I am myself, Phaedrus, a lover of these divisions and collections" (266b4–8). Dialectic is erotic from the very start: it is the process of coming to know, of being led, or being seduced, toward the elusive truth.[25]

It has long been observed that the *Phaedrus* is a written work that condemns the written word.[26] But even this apparent irony or contradiction suggests the dialectical eroticism which is at work throughout the *Phaedrus* and which is its culminating theme.[27] Writing is represented by Socrates in the *Phaedrus* as a supplement. In the image of the Garden of Adonis (276d), for example, Socrates compares writing to an artificial garden, ephemeral, infertile, cosmetic, while living speech is like the true garden that produces fruit. For Mary Margaret Mackenzie the contradiction of a written dialogue condemning writing is simply one of the many antinomies that make this dialogue so frustrating and so seductive, a dialogue that is, she reminds us "about coming to know, not being in a state of knowledge." [28] Palinodes and paradoxes tease us: no wonder the reader "falls in love with them" and "follows their tracks" (Mackenzie 1982:72). Thus the *Phaedrus* is a dialogue that "leads us on."

So does Helen. Eros as dialectic helps to explain why Helen of Troy is at the center of the *Phaedrus*. For Helen is a dialectical heroine presiding over *synagoge* and *diaeresis* on a vast scale. These are the very terms, we will see, that Gorgias applies to Helen in the *Encomium:* her beauty, that speech will argue, gathers men together as it divides them in contention. In similar fashion, Isocrates and Herodotus alike see Helen as a dialectical force of national proportions: Helen defines Greece (makes it cohere) as she opposes it from what is distinct (pitting it against a common foe). What I have tried to show in the two previous chapters is that Helen's beauty always differs from itself, always functions as a system of collections and divisions, producing likenesses and resemblances that lead and mislead those who try to grasp it. Helen's beauty delights and diverts just as all graft does, and in the end dialectic is another name for graft: the projection of sameness upon difference.[29]

Euripides' *Helen:* "Will the real Helen please stand up?"

The projection of sameness upon difference is a recurrent motif in Euripides' *Helen,* which could be characterized as, in essence, a staging of Stesichorus's *Palinode.* En route from Troy, Menelaus and an ersatz Helen are shipwrecked in Egypt, where the real Helen has been a guest of Proteus for the duration of the war. Proteus, however, has recently died, and his son Theoclymenus now threatens to take Helen as his wife by force. The expected recognition scene reunites husband and wife, and is quickly followed by the disappearance of the phantom Helen. Recognition leads, as A. M. Dale puts it, to Stratagem (1967:xiv). Helped by the sister of Theoclymenus, the chaste prophetess Theonoe (a variation of Eidothea, daughter of Proteus in Menelaus's tale in *Odyssey* 4), Helen convinces Theoclymenus that Menelaus is a simple sailor, come to inform her that her husband has died. Helen agrees to marry Theoclymenus, but only after carrying out the funeral rites for her husband, rites that must be performed, conveniently, at sea. Menelaus and Helen sail off, and Theoclymenus is left empty-handed.

Helen's *eidolon* is also Helen's supplement, and Euripides' play shows us what happens when the logic of supplementarity is set in motion. The mimetic tension between the real and the copy is only *actualized* now in the figure of the *eidolon* (which is the very antithesis of the actual or the real). For that tension, we know by now, is constitutive of *all* representations of Helen. To look upon Helen is *always* to negotiate the treacherous distinctions between *what is* and *what only seems to be*.[30] The rupture between appearance and reality is an all-pervasive motif in the *Helen*. As Anne Pippin Burnett puts it: "The language, the plot, and the very form of the *Helen* all have been made to express this tension between what is and what only seems to be" (1960:152).[31] This tension is present from the moment Helen introduces herself in the prologue to the play: "There is . . . a legend which says that Zeus took the feathered form of a swan, and that being pursued by an eagle, and flying for refuge to the bosom of my mother, Leda, he used this deceit to accomplish his desire upon her. That is the story of my origin—if it is true. My name is Helen" (17–22). The problem of telling true from false will prove to be central to the rest of the play, and the role of the name will be crucial in the representation and resolution (to the extent that one exists) of that problem.[32] Helen now proceeds to tell us what *really* happened at Troy. Hera, vindictive after her recent humiliation by Aphrodite in the Judgment of Paris, "turned the substance of Aphrodite's promise into air. She gave the royal son of Priam for his bride—not me [$o\mathring{v}\kappa\ \mathring{\epsilon}\mu$'], but a living image compounded of ether in my likeness [$\mathring{a}\lambda\lambda$' $\mathring{o}\mu o\iota\mathring{\omega}\sigma a\sigma$' $\mathring{\epsilon}\mu o\grave{\iota}\ /\ \epsilon\mathring{\iota}\delta\omega\lambda o\nu$]" (32–48). What Paris possesses is in fact only an "emptiness," $\kappa\epsilon\nu\mathring{\eta}\nu$ (36), nothing more than a "name," $\mathring{o}\nu o\mu a$ (43).

The distinction between what is real and what is only illusory is crucial to the dramatic recognition scenes that immediately follow the prologue. The Achaean archer Teucer arrives, shipwrecked, at the tomb of Proteus and exclaims, upon seeing Helen: "What do I see? It is the accursed image! The murderess who blasted my life and ruined Greece! May the gods abhor you as the perfect copy of Helen!" Teucer's confrontation with this "copy," $\mu\mathring{\iota}\mu\eta\mu[a]$ (74), is, in Aristotelian terms, his moment of dramatic reversal, his hairbreadth escape from the peril implicit in mimesis. It is a scene that impresses upon us the instability of the line separating the real from the apparent. Faced with what is real, Teucer acknowledges it as such, only to retract his identification and decide, mistakenly, that it must be a copy. This instability is repeated and reinforced (as Burnett suggests) in almost every aspect of the play. Menelaus arrives in Egypt, his clothes tattered, looking less like the Trojan warrior he was than the humble sailor whose role he will later mime. When Theoclymenus gives his blessing to Helen and Menelaus as they board the Egyptian ship, the happy couple are, in effect, performing a mock funeral.

It is not difficult to read the *Helen* as a philosophical drama, structured in its entirety around certain philosophically authorized dichotomies.[33] Menelaus is the impetuous soldier, a kind of epic philosopher, his faith in the reliability of names, the trustworthiness of appearances, and the efficacy of action (possession, violence, murder) as yet unshaken. Theonoe, chaste, pure, impassive, on the other hand, would seem to emblematize the search for something beyond appearance, desire, and action: transcendent (Platonic?) reality. In this philosophical charade, Helen is exactly where we would expect her to be: *in between.* Hence the indecision, the hesitations, the vacillating sentiments, the wavering beliefs, the fluctuating conclusions that characterize both Teucer's and Menelaus's readings of her. How does one recognize something that cannot be identified to begin with?

Purity, Identity, and Genre: From Euripides to Aristophanes

Images of chastity or purity abound in the *Helen,* for Euripides' dramatic idyll allows us to imagine, if only intermittently, the possibility of a coherent, simple Helen, uncorrupted, undefiled by the traces of the past.[34] The essential premise at work in the play seems to be that what is pure must be real, and vice versa. The real Helen is ἀκέραιον (48), which is to say, chaste, pure, unmixed, uncontaminated. In the play's opening lines, Helen says, "This is Egypt; here flows the virgin river [καλλιπάρθενοι ῥοαί], the lovely Nile." The recent accession of Theoclymenus to the throne poses an immediate threat to Helen's carefully tended chastity. But the prologue concludes by moving from the distinction between fiction and fact, appearance and reality, name and body, to that between sexual purity and impurity. Helen intends to pray, she tells us, at the tomb of Proteus, "so that even if my name is reviled in Hellas, here in Egypt I may keep my body free from reproach" (66–67).

Burnett argues that through the phantom Helen, the real Helen is, by the end of the play, effectively vindicated, exonerated, purified: "The *eidolon,* like a scapegoat, has borne her sins away. It is actually made to speak words [ll. 608–15] which wash her clean of guilt" (1960:157; brackets are mine).[35] There is no question that the *Helen* at least offers the audience the conventional outlines of a triumph. Action does seem to achieve its ends. The Egyptians are defeated; the Greeks victorious. Menelaus's funeral becomes a celebration, not of the hero's death, but of his rebirth. Theoclymenus's threats of violation go unfulfilled. Miasma, or corruption, is repelled. Helen is cleansed, renewed, and returned to Greece with her "good name" intact.

All the same, ambiguities remain unresolved at the end of the play. If, as Charles Segal puts it, the final battle against the Egyptians "heals the split in her identity between *onoma* [name] and *pragma* [body, material, object] and is a final overcoming of her *Selbstentfremdung*" (1986:260; brackets my translation), it is also a renewal of the violence emblematic of Troy, and a potential corruption of Helen's inviolate rebirth. The end of this fairytale is particularly epic in tone and imagery; it is a blood sacrifice, a kind of Troy II, which Helen presides over, as she did (at least in name) over Troy I.

The conflict between purity and impurity as an ethical and an epistemological problem remains unresolved in the *Helen*. In a larger sense, it remains unresolved in Helen herself, and in modern as well as ancient treatments of her myth.[36] Thus "between the epistemological and the ethical themes, illusion and war," as Segal puts it (1986:227), which he sees as the play's defining issues, stands Helen. Segal sees the whole play as a meditation on those themes, a confrontation between opposing forces that centers upon the figure of Helen: on the one side "reality" (the real Helen, Zeus, Beauty as a good, Egypt, the *Odyssey*), on the other "appearance" (the phantom Helen, Hera, Beauty as a curse, Troy, the *Iliad*). This categorization is helpful: all the examples of "appearance" Segal lists (231) can also be termed *supplements* to their "real" counterparts. But supplements, we know, have a way of transforming the things they supplement into supplements themselves: thus "reality" in the *Helen* is always already undermined by "appearance" (just as *Iliad* 3, we have seen, is already marked by the "memory" of *Odyssey* 4). Helen is always a graft of the real and the illusory, is always a supplement of herself. This can be framed in ethical terms: there is no such thing as an entirely "pure" Helen; Helen is always "impure." In another sense, the new and improved Helen that emerges victorious at the end of the *Helen* is as insubstantial as the illusory *eidolon*. As Zeitlin puts it: "This new eros that Helen incarnates divides itself to establish another set of opposites—the false eidolon and the figure of the divine—which are now equally unattainable" (1996:407).

Finally Euripides' *Helen,* as a work of literature, is itself a supplement: one more version of the Helen myth, one more likeness of the truth. This raises the issue of how we are meant, as viewers or readers, to respond to this play. Is Euripides offering us philosophical argument, lighthearted fantasy, tragedy, comedy, or something in between? This kind of critical reading, collecting and dividing on the level of genre, again represents an effort to define something that resists definition. A glance at Aristophanes' reading of Euripides' *Helen* in the *Thesmophoriazousae* demonstrates this clearly. In "Travesties of Gender and Genre in Aristophanes' *Thesmophoriazousae*" (1996:375–416), Zeitlin shows that Aristophanes' parody of the *Helen* raises questions about the coherence not only of art, but of gender and identity as well. Aristophanes—like Euripides—gives us a false Helen and a false *Helen.* What both of them come to threaten is the notion of genre itself. Thus the figure of Mnesilochos, disguised as a woman and forced to impersonate Helen, elicits the following comment from Zeitlin: "The transvestite actor might succeed in concealing the tell-tale sign that marks him as an imitation with a difference, but parody, by its nature and definition, is the literary device that openly declares its status as an imitation with a difference." The problem, of course, is that Helen is always already her own parody. Already in the "real" *Helen* (as opposed to its parody in Aristophanes), as Zeitlin herself points out, Euripides has upset whatever distinctions we may have wanted to maintain between the real and the false, the original and the imitation. With regard to the *Thesmophoriazousae,* she concludes:

In satirizing Euripides' theatrical innovations in the *Helen* and in presenting a parody with metatheatrical dimensions, Aristophanes reaffirms, as it were, through the tradition that goes back to Stesichorus, the perennial utility of Helen as the figure upon whom can be focused the poetic problems of imitation itself. (407)

Zeitlin helps us to see why Euripides' play itself has for much of its history met with critical responses remarkably similar to those leveled at its heroine: confusion, skepticism, contempt. Is this a serious play, with serious ideas? Dale, commentator of the 1967 Oxford edition of the *Helen,* thinks critics like Segal and Burnett are essentially "reading into" the work:

it is hardly justified to claim as critics sometimes do that the *Helen* gains in profundity, or qualifies as "tragic" . . . because it concerns the interplay of illusion and reality. This is to allow oneself to be mesmerized by abstract nouns. There is much play with antitheses as σῶμα/ὄνομα, and flashes of irony from this source point the dialogue; but there is no metaphysical or psychological depth here. (1967:xvi)

Such criticism replays the very acts of dialectical classification and recognition that are the central motifs of the *Helen.* Dale is distinguishing between what is surface and what is depth, what is really here and what is merely superficially there, what is serious and what is play. When we turn critic in this fashion, we become one more Trojan elder, gazing at the face of Helen of Troy and offering the latest reading. But which is the real Helen, we might continue to ask, the Helen of Euripides or the Helen of Homer, Dale's Helen or Segal's?[37] This is, after all, what Euripides' play is about: competing readings or renditions of reality, each vying to persuade us. In the end Euripides does not really decide: the *Helen* ends up caught between versions, grafting incompatible readings. Euripides' *Helen* is a kind of fairytale romance situated nowhere, suspended, like Helen herself, between history and fiction.[38]

Conclusion: A Few Remarks on Helen in Herodotus

Or between Homer and Herodotus. For Euripides' romance also hovers between them: between history and epic. And if Herodotus situates Helen in Egypt, and Homer situates Helen in Troy, then Euripides' Helen is a grafting of the two. The Herodotean Helen, however, much like the Homeric Helen (as chapter 1 argues) is already a graft of pseudo-Helens. Herodotus devotes no fewer than nine chapters (112–20) of Book 2 to the story of Helen in Egypt. He does not represent himself, however, as entirely convinced that this is, in fact, what really happened. On the other hand, neither is Herodotus willing to accept the Homeric version at face value. "I made inquiry of the priests," he assures us

(2.118), "whether the story which the Greeks tell about Ilium is a fable, or no" (trans. Rawlinson 1942). Herodotus finds a middle ground, then, citing the references to Egypt in the Homeric epics as evidence that "Homer was acquainted with this story" (2.116).

In Herodotus as in Euripides, as in Homer, Egypt remains a privileged site for Helen's "alternative" adventures. Certainly Egypt, as early as Homer, is a standard Greek correlative for all that is exotic and mysterious, a sign for the non-Greek.[39] But Herodotus's representation of Egypt is complicated, and appears to have left its mark upon Euripides' *Helen*. Egypt at Herodotus 2.16 is certainly "mysterious," "picturesque," and "barbaric." But Herodotus goes further, setting up Egypt in binary opposition to Greece: Egypt is not simply "different," not simply "non-Greek": it is an anti-Greece, or a proto-Greece, or a supplement to Greece. This is borne out by Herodotus's efforts in Book 2 to fix the physical boundaries of Egypt (just the Delta or beyond the Delta) and graft it to a larger land mass (either Asia or Libya). This is, in effect, supplementary geography: Herodotus's Egypt is nowhere and everywhere, an in-between-land.[40] This makes it a perfect site for the sojourn of Helen, the ultimate in-between heroine.

Herodotus's Egypt is also significant as the kingdom of Proteus. We recall the figure of Proteus, recalled in turn by Menelaus in *Odyssey* 4, as the archetypal shape-shifter, an emblem of the instability of identity. No one can grasp who Proteus really is; he, too, is always in-between. Helen, then, is an essentially protean figure. We are never really sure if we have grasped the real Helen. And the central issue of Euripides' *Helen,* like that of Herodotus's *Histories,* may be the exquisite difficulty of deciding what something, or who someone, really is. Helen always forces us to ask that question, a question that she renders, at the same time, unanswerable.

4

Speculation

Introduction: *Caveat Emptor*

We have seen that Aristotle tends to regard metaphor with suspicion, as an instrument of linguistic profiteering. The Trojan elders in *Iliad* 3 are not simply admiring Helen; they are speculating on and about her. The acquisition of Helen by Troy has made this appraisal imperative. How much, the elders are asking, is Helen worth? Is she worth the sufferings endured by Trojans and Achaeans alike? Speculation of this kind depends on comparative thinking. Assigning Helen value, in other words, means comparing her to something else. But metaphor, here, is expensive. Ultimately, we know, the privilege of keeping Helen simply costs too much, and the elders pray for her return. Their pleas come too late, we know. The damage has already been done: Helen has bankrupted Troy.

Let the buyer beware, then, when it comes to Helen. Helen's beauty makes her the most appreciated of commodities, and it is in the nature of the commodity to circulate. The problem with Helen is that she will not stay put. Helen is fated, always, to be fought *for,* bargained *for,* paid *for;* never to be kept, and never to be owned. The *Catalogue of Women,* loosely ascribed to Hesiod, lists Helen's many suitors (an all-star cast including Philoctetes, Odysseus, Aias, and Teucer) and the gifts they offered for her hand (fr. 68). As suitors they are also bidders, and potential buyers. Menelaus prevails because he pays the highest price: "But warlike Menelaus, the son of Atreus, prevailed against them all together, because he gave the greatest gifts" (fr. 68.98–100). Helen is a valuable piece of property — but one that has a marked tendency, as we have seen, to change hands.

Helen's status as chattel—belonging now to Theseus, now to Menelaus, now to Paris, now to Deiphobus, now to Achilles—is emphasized in the recurrent Homeric formula, "Helen and her possessions," κτήματα. What Paris took from Menelaus was his material wealth (κτήματα), and Helen is simply the most valuable item in the inventory. And yet that formula, turning Helen into so much property, is always stated in terms that contest the ownership of that property: Menelaus and Paris are to fight "for the sake of Helen and all her possessions," ἀμφ᾿ Ἑλένῃ καὶ κτήμασι πᾶσι μάχεσθαι (3.70). This is the price one pays for appreciating Helen: always more than one thought. To look upon Helen or to speak of her is inevitably to find oneself trapped in an inflationary economy that is out of control. Think, again, of the elders at the Skaian gates, calculating the costs of Helen's sojourn in the city, suffering hardships "for a woman like this one" (157): τοιῇδ᾿ ἀμφὶ γυναικὶ. I want to isolate, for a moment, the force of that dative *for* that is so consistently tied to Helen. With perhaps no other preposition is Helen so regularly associated in Archaic and Classical Greek literature as this *for*—ἀμφί or περί—which calculates expense.[1] Helen's grammatical case by nature is the dative. And where Helen is concerned, the dative is always—no matter what other functions it serves—what the grammarians call the *dative of price*.[2]

That price is always too high. The economy Helen always sets in motion is unstable and illegitimate. Wherever Helen appears, speculation follows: appreciation, inflation, theft, hoarding—in a word, graft. It is time, now, to fully capitalize on the financial register of this term. In the *Politics* (1257b), Aristotle, we will see, distinguishes between *economics* (the natural distribution of goods fueled by demand) and *chrematistics* (the unnatural pursuit of profit driven by desire). This chapter argues that Helen always stimulates a chrematistic economy. This is illustrated in an emblematic way in Helen's role in the tradition of the Judgment of Paris, the "quarrel" (*neikos*) recounted in Homer (*Iliad* 24.25–63) and the *Cypria* (fr. 1.5). For the Judgment is represented as an archetypal beauty contest in which Helen is not simply Aphrodite's bribe but her surrogate, her likeness, her cash-equivalent. Chrematistics, Aristotle tells us, is an economy of metaphor, rooted in equivalences. "All things that are exchanged," says Aristotle in the *Nicomachean Ethics,* "must be somehow comparable" (1133a15–20, trans. Ross in McKeon 1941).[3] What makes comparison possible, according to Aristotle in this work, is a middle term (*meson*): in other words, money. Helen, I am arguing, always functions as this middle term. Helen's tendency to mediate makes her, in other words, as much a figure for money as for metaphor. I turn to Sappho's Fr. 16 as an example of Helen literature effectively promoting a chrematistic economy. For if Fr. 16 asks, "What is the most beautiful thing?" it answers, "That which you love." Helen is what makes both the question and the answer meaningful. What Sappho elaborates in Fr. 16 is nothing less than an entirely speculative economy, and its currency is Helen.

Aristotle: Helen as Money

Let us compare Aristotle's descriptions of metaphor and money as parallel figures for mediation. Aristotle, in his discussion of the "art of acquisition" in the *Politics,* distinguishes between the natural possession and barter of property, based on need, and the unnatural pursuit of wealth for its own sake, an abuse made possible by the invention of *money (nomisma)* and the exercise of *exchange.* For Aristotle, a *natural* economics, or *oikonomia,* refers to the equitable administration and management of property or goods. *Chrematismos,* identified with profiteering and the hoarding of money, on the other hand, is unnatural, a perversion of the natural economy.[4] Note that the field of application for both these concepts is, from the beginning, a broad one, encompassing not only explicitly financial dealings, but all social systems linked to distribution and value. Thus *oikonomia* is essentially a scheme of just governance, as much the law for the merchant as it should be for the playwright.[5]

Aristotle distrusts money in and of itself, calling it "a mere sham, a thing not natural, but conventional only" (trans. Jowett in McKeon 1941). An economy fueled by money is one based on exchange. Exchange is an essential mechanism, of course, in any economy; but when it is no longer driven by real need, but by *desire*—something self-serving and hence always unlimited—it becomes a chrematistic perversion. This is the economy Helen sets into motion: she is something always to be exchanged and never consumed. Her beauty, suspect, unnatural, is both agency and object of unlimited desire. Helen's beauty, never used, is ultimately useless: it does not satiate, it is not enjoyed. It is, instead, the coin that, always elusive, keeps chrematistics going: its function is continually to unsettle and destabilize, to set into motion unending contests of possession, dispossession, and repossession.

We should recall here Plato's exhortation at *Cratylus* 439d: "Then let us seek the true beauty, not asking whether a face is fair." Attempts have been made to link the origins of currency with the institutionalization of sacrificial rituals, as one scholar speculates: "the path that would lead from the first victim to its final substitute, the effigy engraved on a coin" ("le chemin qui conduirait de la victime première à son dernier substitut, l'effigie frappé au coin" [Will 1954:212]). But suppose this face of the coin is the face of Helen of Troy?[6] The *eidolon* of Euripides and Stesichorus is also a substitute, after all, for a sacrificial victim. Herodotus's history, reflecting on the myth of Helen, points back to an economy with its origins in abduction, the ritual sacrifice of Helen. From those violent origins emerges the phantom Helen, "a mere sham, a thing not natural," a substitute for the real thing.

If money (*nomisma*), as we are taught in the *Politics,* is "spurious" as an object in its own right, it is, on the other hand, essential as an instrument of exchange. This last notion is revised in the *Nicomachean Ethics,* and in the context of a discussion on social justice. Aristotle asks at 5.5.17–20: what is it that holds the city together? and answers: the equitable exchange of disparate goods. That means, in essence, setting up equivalences between them: "all things that are exchanged must be somehow comparable. It is for this end that money had been introduced, and . . . becomes . . . an intermediate [*meson*]; for it measures all things" (1133a15–20; trans. W. D. Ross 1941; bracketed term is mine).[7] Money, which permits comparison, makes evaluation possible. Exchange, then, is not entirely divorced from need, and thus money has its utility and its place in culture; money "has become by convention a sort of representative of demand; and this is why it has the name 'money' [*nomisma*] — because it exists not by nature but by law [*nomos*]." E. Laroche, in "Histoire de la racine 'nem-' en grec ancien," notes that in the earliest instances of *nemesis,* conventionally defined as *blame,* the term ıs always used to make a "value judgment" (1949:93), in both an ethical and an economic sense.[8] Both are central to the act of assessment at the walls of Troy, as the elders gaze upon the face of Helen (3.156): οὐ νέμεσις Τρῶας ("Surely there is no blame if Trojans . . ."). Helen is, indeed, a form of *vomos,* a powerful generator of equivalences, but ruthlessly pursued — like money — as a possession in her own right. This is chrematistics, not *oikonomia,* at work, an economy of the metaphor. Paraphrasing Aristotle, Marc Shell writes in *The Economy of Literature,* "To men such as Midas gold becomes everything, just as to some poets metaphor appears to be all" (1978:92). Helen is the golden metaphor.

Helen as nemesis suggests the financial abuses described by Aristotle in the *Politics:* she provokes an economy fueled entirely by *desire,* as opposed to *demand.* And the face of Helen is, to use Aristotle's definition of *nomos,* a "representative" of desire, instead of demand. It is worthwhile recalling at this point the long history of mythic traditions linking Helen to the figure of Nemesis. Thus Fr. 8 of the *Cypria* asserts: "Nemesis . . . gave her birth when she had been joined in love with Zeus . . . by harsh violence." Born in violence, brought in violence from Greece to Troy, making them distinct, defining them in relation to each other, drawing them into violent conflict and comparison, Helen is the archetypal intermediary of desire.

It is hardly surprising, then, that one of Helen's most familiar emblems is the *beauty contest* between Hera, Athena, and Aphrodite at the Judgment of Paris. That Helen is always the *contested* is one reason why her myth is so profitable a device for later poets striving, like Aphrodite, for the title "the Most Beautiful." The face that launched a thousand ships will bring forth just as many poems. What Helen does, for example, in the work of Sappho, as we will see, is to introduce an economy of *relative worth.* Helen is always the most beautiful, *comparatively speaking.* And to mention Helen is always to start speaking comparatively.

Currency of comparison, Helen is the end and the means of an economy of

desire or graft, a chrematistics. This is a currency that increases itself, reproduces itself, compounds itself, through metaphorical likenesses (*eidola*). That
this economy is an example of graft and grafting becomes clearer when we take
into account the standard genealogical metaphors employed in classical Greek
to talk about *profit*. Here is Shell on Aristotle's discussion of interest (*tokos*) in
Politics 1258b. The first meaning of *tokos* is offspring or scion; only metaphori-
cally does it come to stand for interest:

> In the Greek language after the development of money, words such as *tokos* come to
> refer not only to the biological generation of likenesses but also to monetary generation
> or interest. Aristotle objects to this easy metaphor from natural, animate, to nomic, in-
> animate things and writes that it is "natural [*kata physin*] to all . . . to draw provision
> [economically] from the fruits of the soil and from animals" but that usury or monetary
> generation draws not from nature [*physin*] but from money [*nomisma*]. (1978:93–94)

This is an important passage for our purposes. What Shell demonstrates is that
the cornucopia of metaphors inexorably generated by the introduction of Helen
into a system of warring desires is homologous to the usurious profit generated
by interest. Both biological and economic systems are, for Aristotle, essentially
corrupt, sterile, unnatural modes of reproduction, variations of graft. In fact,
the very metaphorization of the term *tokos* itself illustrates the mechanism of
graft in both senses of the term. That is, if *tokos* can mean first "scion" and then
"interest," it is because (1) language can compound itself, capitalize upon itself,
exceed its own "natural" worth through semantic speculation; and (2) language
can reproduce itself in illegitimate ways, can bring forth from itself a perverse
and foreign progeny.

Looking at Helen's mythic tradition, Shell's economic analysis appears con-
gruent with George Devereux's psychoanalytic discussion of Helen. What Devereux sees as central to the Helen myth is the motif of what he calls "aberrant"
reproduction. There are intimations of anal sex in the story of the "first" rape by
Theseus; suggestions of infertility in the convention of at most two children, and
more frequently a single daughter. Devereux writes: "I would also connect to
the sterility of Persephone the fact that, despite the number of her husbands and
lovers, Helen has only two children attested by the ancient tradition: a daughter
Hermione, a son Nikestratos" ("Je rapprocherai de la stérilité de Perséphone
. . . aussi le fait que, malgré le nombre de ses époux et amants, Hélène n'eut que
deux enfants attestés par la tradition ancienne: une fille Hermione, et un fils,
Nikestratos" [1982:38]).[9] Helen may be a sterile graft: her beauty does not bear
fruit.

The Judgment of Paris

Looked at through the perspective of Aristotle's theory of economy, the rape
of Helen appears to be a shady sort of financial operation indeed: a violation,

above all, of the "culture of gift exchange" (duBois 1995:115). The Trojan war, we have already seen, can be approached as a matter of trade gone awry.[10] In fact, the opening chapter of Herodotus's *Histories,* in which the abduction of Io leads to that of Europa, and that of Medea to that of Helen, is explicitly represented as a succession of trade violations.[11] When Herodotus recounts Helen's arrival in Egypt, he depicts King Proteus chastising the wayward Paris, not so much for abduction, or adultery, as for theft, and the violation of the guest–host relationship (2.115):

> You are a villain. You seduced your friend's wife, and as if that were not enough, persuaded her to escape with you. . . . Even that did not content you—but you must bring with you besides the treasure you have stolen from your host's house. But though I cannot punish a stranger with death, I will not allow you to take away your ill-gotten gains: I will keep this woman and the treasure. (Sélincourt 1954)

"I will not allow you to take away your ill-gotten gains: I will keep this woman and the treasure." The first phrase is not in the original; what Proteus actually says is limited to the second phrase, the familiar Homeric formula cited above.

Yet "ill-gotten gains" is a phrase the translator cannot resist, even where the text does not authorize it. It seems to be a way for the translator to reap his own gains, also ill-gotten. The very same phrase, I cannot help but note, is employed by Jonathan Culler in *On Deconstruction: Theory and Criticism after Structuralism,* in a passage defending Derrida's brash exploitation of what appear to be contingent etymological likenesses. Culler asks: "What is the status of such relations: the grafting on to one another of *pharmakon, pharmakeus,* and *pharmakos,* or the pun of *différance,* the play of *supplément?* Many might say that they are examples of *graft* in philosophy and that Derrida enjoys *ill-gotten gains*" (1982:144; my italics). The status of such relations is very much what is at stake in the career of Helen of Troy. We should hardly be surprised to hear Culler suggest that illicit profit is behind Derrida's paleonymics. For Derrida as etymologist is only playing by the rules of rhetoric—those described by Aristotle, chiefly in the *Rhetoric.* Helen of Troy has been compared to many things (that is her essential character, we have seen, to set comparisons in motion), but I think it is safe to say that she has never been compared to Derrida. What do Helen and Derrida have in common? Both of them owe much of their success (in love, in language) to an almost entirely speculative economy, what we have been calling chrematistics; both of them profit shamelessly (to use a word frequently associated with Helen)[12] from a system of value that has lost its stability, a system in which value is essentially determined (and must therefore be determined over and over again) by comparison, exchange, and the exploitation of metaphorical resemblance.

If this chrematistic economy has a founding myth, one could argue that it is to be found in the Judgment of Paris. Fruitless speculation, after all, is what spoils the Wedding of Peleus and Thetis. An apple marked *kallistei,* "for the most beautiful woman," is not an apple of "discord" if the designated recipient is not in doubt. Although the famous apple of discord does not figure explicitly in Greek literature until the second century A.D.—for example in Lucian's *Dialogues of the Sea-Gods* 5 and *Dialogues of the Gods* 20 (Fowler and Fowler 1905)—it appears much earlier in Greek art. What the apple proves is that beauty is not an absolute value. Thus the *neikos* or quarrel caused by Eris (strife) at the Wedding of Peleus and Thetis in *Cypria* 102.14–15 amounts to an inability to agree on value. That is what Paris is called upon to determine, and that is what he will fail to do—because Paris is bribed and the contest is rigged (the bribe, of course, is Helen). The instability of value as source of conflict or quarrel is repeated on every level of the Trojan saga. The entire war is called an *éris* or "conflict" in the *Cypria* (Allen 1912: fr. 1.5); the *Iliad* begins with the quarrel of Achilles and Agamemnon, a quarrel over the failure to respect Achilles' designated *time*—his socially acknowledged honor or value. Helen's abduction is also labeled *eris* in *Cypria* Fr. 1.5, and Helen herself explains in the *Iliad* that the Trojan war was fought εἵνεκ' ἐμῆς ἔριδος καὶ Ἀλεξάνδρου ἕνεκ' ἀρχῆς, "for the sake of this my quarrel since Alexandros began it" (3.100).[13] We have seen that Helen is fated always to generate conflict, to destabilize value, to provoke the acts of collecting and dividing that Socrates sees as central to *eros* and *logos*.

The Judgment itself is an *eris*. Paris, who is called upon to end the quarrel, only incites more speculation and more conflict. At the center of this quarrel is Helen. The only other reference to the Judgment in the *Iliad* reinforces the connection. In *Iliad* 24 only Hera and Poseidon maintain their hatred for Troy "because of the delusion of Paris / who insulted [νείκεσσε] the goddesses when they came to him in his courtyard / and favoured her who supplied the lust that led to disaster" (24.28–30). Implicit here is the suspicion that the contest has been perverted. Awarding the prize to Aphrodite ought to settle the question for good; but she has bribed the judge. The giving of the apple (real or figurative) marked "for the fairest" is supposed to be a definitive act, an act that closes off speculation and gives a determinate value. Instead, giving the apple to "the fairest" is contingent upon giving "the fairest" woman (real or figurative) to "the fairest" man (that is, Paris); it becomes another act of exchange, payment in return for another award, the beginning of another cycle of trade violations.

Later narrations of the Judgment tend to emphasize the way in which the contest was fixed. In Lucian's *Dialogues of the Gods* 20 (trans. Fowler and Fowler 1905:78–85), Aphrodite is unabashed about offering Helen as Paris's recompense for her victory. Moreover, Aphrodite's strategy here is closely linked to the seductive tactics associated with Helen: what we might call rhetorical persuasion.[14] In both a verbal and a visual sense, Aphrodite sets out to "con" her victim. Athena complains when she sees Aphrodite at work: "she has no right to come thus tricked out and painted—just like a courtesan! She ought to show herself unadorned" (82.9). It is in precisely the same terms, we will see in the next chapter, that Hecuba condemns Helen's persuasive techniques for regaining Menelaus's affection in *Trojan Women*.[15]

Sappho, Fr. 16: Poetics as Chrematistics

Sappho Fr. 16 is a poem that speculates, in more ways than one, on Helen. I discuss this poem in greater detail in chapter 6 as a system of demonstratives or deictics. Here I want to explore the way in which Fr. 16, and above all the first half of the poem, essentially *gambles* on or with Helen to elaborate an entirely chrematistic economy.

> Some [ο]ἰ μέν] say a host of horsemen, others of infantry, and others
>   of ships, is the most beautiful thing on the dark earth:
>   but I say [ἔγω δέ], it is what you love.
> Full easy it is to make this understood of one and all: for
>   she that far surpassed all mortals in beauty, Helen, her
>   most noble husband
> Deserted, and went sailing to Troy, with never a thought for
>   her daughter and dear parents. The [Cyprian goddess] led
>   her from the path . . .
>   . . . [Which] now has put me in mind of Anactoria far away:
> Her lovely way of walking, and the bright radiance of her
>   changing face, would I rather see than your Lydian
>   chariots and infantry full-armed.
>
> (Trans. Page 1955b:52–53)

Asking, in rather crude fashion, "What is this poem about?" is actually a good way to begin here. For Fr. 16 seems to have difficulty deciding exactly what its subject is. The poem begins, in effect, by throwing the apple of discord at us, still inscribed "for the fairest." Thus Fr. 16 revisits the Judgment of Paris. Sappho appears to be answering the same question Paris was called upon to answer, a question about absolute value: what is the most beautiful thing? Or, to put this in more economic terms, Fr. 16 is the lyrical version of Aristotle's *Nicomachean Ethics;* both poet and philosopher are seeking to define the "best," that which is most valuable.[16] In fact, the speaker wastes no time in making the very notion of the absolute unthinkable, at the same time that she forces us to think about it. There are unambiguous answers in the first two lines (all epic visuals, all collective entities: horsemen, infantry, ships): the problem is that there are too many of them. The poem's efforts to answer the question it poses only serve to make that question more insistent. The next two lines of the first stanza appear to be making amends. The poem would seek to offer a definitive answer, clearly meant to be distinguished from and preferred to (ἔγω δέ) the stock (epic) responses offered by others (ο]ἰ μέν). It is an answer that tells us everything and tells us nothing: "but I say, it is what you love." This is an answer that refuses to speak in absolute terms (since any one specific answer offered as absolute would violate the principle of the answer, which is that there is no one general answer, only specific answers).

It is at this point, in the second stanza, that Helen makes her appearance in the poem, and in a manner perfectly consistent with the authoritative assertion at the close of the first stanza. What is Helen doing in this poem? Helen is enlisted as an example to demonstrate the validity of that assertion; she is, therefore, both a specific subject in this poem and an abstract universal: an end and a means to an end. Her beauty, infinitely desirable and infinitely dangerous, makes the task of evaluation urgent. "Terrible is the likeness of her face to immortal goddesses," αἰνῶς ἀθανάτῃσι θεῇς εἰς ὦπα ἔοικεν exclaim the Trojan elders when Helen appears at the Skaian gates in the *teichoskopia* (3.158), while, below, Paris and Menelaus prepare to compete on the field of battle for her. Page duBois, in "Sappho and Helen," draws a connection between the act of evaluation at work in Sapphic verse and the appraisal, theft, exchange, and abduction of women—Helen being the primary model—in the Archaic period.[17] We have already seen Helen, in the *Catalogue of Women,* exchanged for a dowry commensurate with her value. The Trojan war was, we have suggested, a battle for economic stability, and it was Helen who made such stability urgent and, at the same time, impossible. Sappho Fr. 16 mounts a powerful argument *against* economic stability, an argument *for* chrematistics, and it relies on the figure of Helen to make this argument.

Let us look at the first two stanzas of the poem in greater detail. Fr. 16 opens with a literary commonplace, the *priamel,* which Elroy Bundy defines in *Studia Pindarica* as "a focusing or selecting device in which one or more terms serve as foil for the point of particular interest" (1986:5). Helen is, in traditional epic/lyric terms, what Bundy calls the *priamel cap*—the climax, the superlative in the series. Bundy even uses Fr. 16 as a model to illustrate the standard structural elements of the priamel:

A straightforward example is Sappho A.16 (L.-P.).1–4. . . . Here a host of cavalry, a host of foot, and a host of ships are foils for the writer's own choice, which she states in a general proposition. This proposition is then glossed by an exemplum (lines 5–14), which is, in turn, used as a foil for the introduction in line 15 of the poetess' favorite Anactoria. The concrete climax, Anactoria, fulfills the gnomic climax of lines 3f. introduced by ἔγω δέ. Such concrete climaxes, or caps, whether preceded or not by a gnomic climax, are often accompanied, as here in Sappho A.16 (L.-P.).15, by the adverb νῦν [now]. Typical also of climactic terms, whether gnomic or concrete, is Sappho's pronominal cap ἔγω δέ. The second and third personal pronouns are also used in capping terms. (1962:5–6)

What Bundy offers here is a lesson in chrematistic poetics. Approaching Fr. 16 as a structure of foils and priamels signaled by conventional markers suggests

a system of praise based on assertions of relative worth. Later (chapter 6) I return to these markers—νῦν ("now"), or ἔγω δὲ ("I, on the other hand")—as
indices of subjective positioning, or *deictics*. There are no such things as absolute priamels; superlatives, or caps, as Bundy calls them, can serve as climaxes
or be said to have specific value only in relation to foils.

But things may not be as clear as Bundy's analysis suggests. It is not always
obvious how to distinguish foils from climaxes. The foil is that which mediates, that which allows comparison to take place. Foils are the coins, then, of
Sappho's chrematistics. Helen begins as a foil, as Bundy suggests; she is merely
an exemplum. At the same time, Helen can never be just an example. In a poem
about beauty and desire, Helen is by definition the most beautiful and the most
desired. Helen functions as a foil here only because she is a universal cap or
climax. This is easy to demonstrate in terms of literary history and genre. To
speak of Helen is to adopt, necessarily, the lyric discourse of erotic superlatives
(Helen is surrounded by such superlatives in Fr. 16). But Helen's beauty is, at
the same time, of gravely epic consequence. To speak of Helen is thus to capitalize immediately, and equally necessarily, upon the rich "stock" of Homeric
myth available to the poet. The difference between the first set of answers in this
poem (clichés of collective battle) and the second (clichés of individual desire)
is not only that between the notion of an absolute, public value and that of vacillating, private values,[18] but also that between epic and lyric.[19] Helen, that is, is
not only Anactoria's foil, but the epic foil to the lyric genre itself.

DuBois encourages us to think of Fr. 16 in economic terms by contextualizing
it historically and culturally, linking its evaluative mechanisms to the invention
of coinage in Lydia. One cannot weigh one proposition against another, duBois
makes clear, without a way of mediating between the two, and she reminds us
that Aristotle's analysis of currency in the *Nicomachean Ethics* defines money
as the middle term, allowing exchange and comparison (see my discussion of
the *Nicomachean Ethics* above). For duBois, in conclusion, Fr. 16 imitates the
mechanism of money in order to function as a sustained exercise in abstract
thought:

the process of abstracting from objects their relative value, and conceiving of these in
relation to the third term, coins, resembles the process of logical definition. . . . Helen,
and Anaktoria, and ships, and chariots, and infantry are all equivalent to the abstract term
to kalliston, "the most beautiful." It may be that these two processes of abstraction enable each other, that the abstraction of the notion of "the most beautiful" coincides with
and allows for and profits from the invention of a mechanism for the measure of value.
(1995:113)

I agree with duBois's analysis here, but reach a rather different conclusion. I
would suggest that what Fr. 16 illustrates is not the possibility but the *impossibility* of abstract thought and logical thinking. Long before the poetry of Paul

Valéry, abstraction in Sappho's poem is continually threatening to solidify into flesh.[20] Can one really think of Helen of Troy entirely in the abstract? Can one think of currency in this way? The coin, as duBois herself notes earlier, is not an entirely abstract middle term; it is an object in its own right. Every coin, we might say, has a face. In Sappho Fr. 16, that face belongs to Helen. The middle term that mediates in the manner of a coin in Fr. 16 is not *to kalliston,* an abstract notion of beauty; it is, rather, Helen herself. The irony of this poem is that the example takes revenge on what it is supposed to be an example *of.* If Fr. 16 establishes any kind of system of value, it is a system that is highly unstable, relativistic, fetishistic: a chrematistics. No other form of economy is possible where Helen is concerned. This is a repetition, I would add, of the economy at work in the Judgment of Paris, where Helen begins as a means to an end (Venus's bribe). But the *eris* on Mount Ida leads straight to the *eris* at Troy—where Helen is the end of the whole affair.

Still, there is Anactoria, and a second half to this poem. By the logic of its own assertion in the first stanza, Fr. 16 must move from Helen—universal coin—to its own idiosyncratic currency of value. At least in formal or structural terms, it is Anactoria who seems to occupy the place of the true cap, not Helen. Is this the advent of a new and "modern" subjectivity, as many a critic has maintained?[21] This is the question I tackle, along with the second half of Sappho's poem, in chapter 6.

5

Epideixis

Introduction: An Allegory of Persuasion

In *Metamorphoses* 14, Ovid recounts the courtship of Pomona by Vertumnus. It is a tale about persuasion as a form of violence barely checked and barely concealed. Pomona is a wood-nymph or *hamadryas,* one of a class of nymphs, according to the *Oxford Companion to Classical Literature,* "whose lives were *co-terminous* with their trees" (Howatson 1989:259; my italics). More wood than nymph (*nympha* is the regular term for *bride*), the chaste Pomona spends her time cultivating her orchards, presiding over fertile unions that she herself conspicuously evades:

> She cared nothing for woods and rivers, but only for the fields and branches laden with delicious fruits. She carried no javelin in her hand, but the curved pruning-hook with which now she repressed the too luxuriant growth and cut back the branches spreading out on every side, and now, making an incision in the bark, would engraft a twig and give juices to an adopted bough. . . . This was her love; this was her chief desire; nor did she have any care for Venus; yet fearing some clownish violence, she shut herself up within her orchard. (Trans. Miller 1916:626–35)[1]

Pomona presides over a fecundity that is the displaced image of her own repressed sexuality. Her diligent acts of cultivation, pruning, and grafting are both defenses against and emblems of desire. The enemy arrives, sure enough, and only half-concealed. Vertumnus—whose name is linked to *vertere* (to turn) and who, as Roman god of fruit and cultivation, presides over the seasonal changes of the year[2]—approaches Pomona not as he *really* is, but in a succession of innocent guises. He is accompanied, however, with a succession of less than innocent accoutrements: as reaper (644: "And he was the perfect image of a reaper, too!"), leaf-gatherer, "with hook in hand" (649), soldier, "with a sword" (651), fisherman, "with a rod" (651). It is "in the disguise of an old woman" ("adsimulavit anum," 656) that Vertumnus prepares his final assault, making a speech about weddings that itself weds nymph-speech to orchard-speech, grafting one set of meanings upon another in a conceit that is itself about grafting:

> if that tree stood there unmated to the vine, it would have no value save for its leaves alone; and this vine, which clings to and rests safely on the elm, if it were not thus wedded, it would lie languishing, flat upon the ground. But you are not touched by the vine's example and you shun wedlock and do not desire to be joined to another. And I would that you did desire it! Then would you have more suitors than ever Helen had. (663–71)

In this exhortation to join with another, meaning is itself joined to meaning. Vertumnus speaks in metaphors, language that turns one way, now another, just as he adorns himself in disguises, appearing now as this, now as that. The spoken figures and vestiary disguises he employs are graftings that move back and forth between the figurative and the literal. They are bad figures and bad disguises, designed as much to reveal as to conceal. And Ovid's story ends in revelation and recognition: "When the god in the form of age had thus pleaded his cause in vain, he returned to his youthful form . . . and stood revealed to the maiden. . . . He was all ready to force her will, but no force was necessary" (765–71). Beneath the beautiful words and the comforting disguises lurks the possibility of violence; all too often in the *Metamorphoses,* of course, force *is* necessary to achieve the ends desired.[3] If Vertumnus does not need to resort to force, it is only because Pomona is already captive: "inque figura / capta dei nymphe est" ("the nymph is overpowered by the beauty of the god," 770–71: more literally, "by the *shape* or *image* of the god"). Another way of understanding this submission is as an Aristotelian scene of mimetic learning: for Pomona is overpowered, we might say, by the seductive knowledge of recognition. *This* (Vertumnus, old woman), Pomona comes to learn, is *that* (Vertumnus, a god).

In various guises, I would suggest, this is the scene we have seen played out over and over again, with Helen in the role of Vertumnus. In the place of Pomona: Menelaus, Teucer, and the Trojan elders, all stunned into submission, as they stand before Helen, her beauty *on display.* Put into these terms, Helen's beauty suggests the power of a rhetorical proof that is absolutely persuasive. This is the epideictic moment.

Enthymeme and Epideixis

Pomona does not infer that Vertumnus is a god; she knows it. The god revealed — "as the Sun breaks through the clouds" — stands as clear as a dialectical proof.[4] The god concealed, or half-concealed and half-revealed, suggests the mechanism of rhetorical persuasion at work. This is the source of Helen's power, as well. Helen's syllogism is an *abductive syllogism,* one based on probabilities and likenesses.

The abductive syllogism instructs, but because it *persuades* (that is, *seduces: suadere* can mean either persuade or seduce). Such an abductive syllogism is what Aristotle calls the *enthymeme,* defined, in the *Prior Analytics* (2.27.70a9–10) as a "syllogism starting from probabilities or signs," συλλογισμὸς ἐξ εἰκότων ἤ σημείων (trans. Jenkinson in McKeon 1941). The dialectical syllogism, on the other hand, is a deductive proof. R. C. Seaton distinguishes between the enthymeme and the dialectical syllogism in the following way: "The dialectical syllogism is a valid syllogism, the rhetorical syllogism or enthymeme is invalid . . . and this corresponds with the distinction between dialectic and rhetoric, the aim of the former being to demonstrate, of the latter to induce belief" (1914:114–15).[5] Inducing belief, we have already seen from our reading of Aristotle's *Rhetoric,* can be a dangerous and dubious business. It is also, to a large extent, Helen's vocation. In the last chapter we began to focus on Helen's mediation between disparate entities, her role as a middle term in metaphorical and probabilistic predications. That the enthymeme is traditionally labeled an *invalid* syllogism seems to confirm our suspicion that Helen's seductive power is somehow improper, a matter of coercion, or faith.[6]

The same suspicion is common in classical Greek writings about rhetoric. Aristotle calls rhetoric a dubious, hybrid, and improper language, halfway between clarity and impenetrability and made up of half-truths: metaphors and enthymemes. Aristotle, we have seen, essentially treats metaphor in the *Rhetoric* as a gamble. The entire *Rhetoric* may be called a guide to verbal graft, lessons in how to get ill-gotten gains out of language.

This chapter approaches Helen not only in but as rhetoric. Helen has always been she who persuades/seduces and who is persuaded/seduced. This makes Helen the perfect rhetorical subject: victim, practitioner, theme. My two principal texts in this chapter are Gorgias's *Encomium on Helen* (Diels and Kranz 1951) and Euripides' *Trojan Women.* Gorgias's defense of Helen rests on the assertion that persuasion by language (*logos*) and seduction by beauty (*opsis,* appearance, or *kallos,* beauty) are equivalent to coercion by force (*bia*). This argument owes much of its own persuasiveness to the exploitation of verbal appearances: paranomasia, word-play, repetition. The weapons Gorgias exposes are precisely the ones he wields against his audience, so that it is not clear if he is defending Helen or rhetoric itself. It is my contention that the two are necessarily one and the same. Helen mounts her own defense in *Trojan Women.* Not only does she maintain there that appearance always proves more powerful than reason (*logos*); her speech (*logos*), part of the *agon* against Hecuba in defense of her life, succeeds precisely to the extent that no one listens to it. Helen's most powerful argument, in other words, is her beauty. The premise of this argument is that we are too busy looking at Helen to listen to her.

If Helen is in essence rhetorical, then what kind of rhetoric are we talking about? The encomium of Helen became early on a standard *epideictic* theme in the rhetorical schools.[7] Without going into too much detail regarding the Aristotelian division of the rhetorical craft, suffice it to say that epideixis, as distinguished from deliberative and forensic modes of rhetorical speeches, refers to a speech of *demonstration*.[8] If deliberative oratory takes the form of exhortation or dehortation, aimed at political solutions to be implemented in the future, and forensic oratory assumes the mode of accusation or defense, seeking to reward acts of justice or redress acts of injustice committed in the past, epideictic oratory is a matter of praise or censure, attaching honor or disgrace to a present object.[9] *Epideixis* is often referred to as a rhetoric of *display,* an "empty show" of words, aiming only to praise or blame.[10] Gorgias's style in particular, Larue Van Hook notes, "was characterized by a plethora of words and a paucity of ideas" (1923:163). Epideixis is a rhetorical argument, in other words, that relies entirely on appearances. Perhaps we can begin to appreciate Helen's visible beauty not simply as a display, but as a demonstration.

Gorgias's *Encomium on Helen*

Gorgias of Leontini, *rhetor* from the second half of the fifth century, author of one of the first known handbooks on rhetoric, seems a fitting author for an *Encomium on Helen.* In the traditional narrative, Gorgias is a foreigner who comes to Athens and brings rhetoric with him. Like Helen in Troy, rhetoric is characterized in the Greek imagination as an importation, a foreign and improper sort of language. The trope of the foreign may remind us of Aristotle's descriptions of metaphorical language in the *Rhetoric,* half-xenophilic and half-xenophobic. Gorgias is also the founder, according to the tradition, of the epideictic mode of rhetoric, and in that sense he is the quintessentially rhetorical artist, the rhetorician's rhetorician.[11] Van Hook's description of Gorgias's particular style, cited just above, is tied to the invention of epideixis itself:

Gorgias conceived the idea of marrying to prose the polish, the finish, and the embellishments of poetry. Accordingly he sowed figures and rhetorical devices as with a sack, and achieved a style which was characterized by a plethora of words and a paucity of ideas. . . . Gorgias' great contribution to Greece was this: he was the founder of artistic prose, and with him begins epideictic literature, or the rhetoric of display. (163)

Van Hook's portrait of Gorgias's achievements is interesting. In Van Hook's narrative, Gorgias's new language, this "artistic prose," this "rhetoric of display," begins to resemble an elegant dandy or a beautiful woman, all dressed up with no place to go.[12] Gorgias, we are meant to understand, deals in words, not ideas,[13] in surfaces, not interiors. We will see that Hecuba in *Trojan Women* accuses Helen of concerning herself only with appearances; but Van Hook accuses Gorgias of doing exactly the same thing in his epideictic compositions. Like Helen in Euripides' play, Gorgias's epideixis, "marrying" poetry and prose, offers us displays of beauty, grafted and cosmetic.

If Gorgias's rhetorical innovations are represented as *excessively* rhetorical (and thus effectively emblematic of all rhetoric), then the *Encomium on Helen,* a series of fragments generally attributed to Gorgias, is itself excessively Gorgian. The very subject matter suggests for Van Hook a challenge particularly Gorgian in nature:

A vindication of this glorious but shameless woman, whose misconduct in abandoning her husband Menelaus to elope with Paris to Troy had caused the Trojan war, was a difficult undertaking and was a challenge to the powers of the most accomplished rhetorician. Gorgias of Sicily had attempted the task in his extant *Encomium on Helen,* a brilliant *tour de force,* but he confesses, at the end of his composition, that his composition was, after all, a παίγνιον, or "sportive essay." (1945:54)

What is significant here is the assumption that Gorgias could not be serious in authoring a work in praise of Helen. Van Hook's Helen is definitively guilty, and he considers the idea of defending such a figure absurd. I cite this to show not that Van Hook is wrong, but that he is typical. The modern critic tends to find it necessary to justify Gorgias's craft, particularly in the case of the *Encomium on Helen.* This justification generally consists in re-rhetoricizing an already rhetorical form. By treating the praise of Helen as a rhetorical challenge, or what Rosalie Colie refers to as a rhetorical paradox,[14] and by labeling Gorgias's piece a game, Van Hook emphasizes the rupture, constitutive of all rhetoric in the Aristotelian model, between intention and language, surface and depth, appearance and reality.

In this sense Van Hook's description of the *Encomium* may remind us of the longstanding confusion over the "proper" way to appreciate Euripides' *Helen.* In both cases, the critic's efforts to justify the text seem to reinstate the very problems in the text that seemed to make that justification necessary. For what is the face of Helen of Troy but a living epideictic surface, the archetypal instance of the rhetoric of display? This brings us to Gorgias's *Encomium* itself, because the premise upon which this speech rests is the analogy of rhetorical and erotic surfaces, rhetorical and erotic powers of persuasion. In the *Encomium,* we will see, *logos, eros, kallos* (beauty), and *opsis* (appearance, sight) are all interchangeable substitutes, all instances of coercion, seduction, persuasion. In the end, Gorgias's *Encomium on Helen* is really a encomium of the rhetorical craft itself, and a demonstration of its power over us.[15]

Gorgias's *Encomium* immediately sets out in its proemium to lay out this system of analogous surfaces and forces:[16] "Embellishment to a city is the valour of

its citizen; to a person, comeliness; to a soul, wisdom; to a deed, virtue; to discourse, truth" (1.1–2; trans. Van Hook 1945).[17] The parallelism at work here is
clearer in the original: σώματι δε κάλλος [. . .] λόγωι δε ἀλήθεια, beauty is to
body as truth is to word. These two forces—beauty and truth—will converge as
the *Encomium* proceeds. Gorgias proceeds, after this opening, to a declaration
of purpose: to clear Helen's name (2). This he begins to do by establishing, at
the outset, the superlative quality of her beauty (κάλλος): "That in nature and in
nurture the lady was the fairest flower of men and women is not unknown" (3.1–
2). Her parentage and birth are recounted, and a general portrait sketched with
all of the standard features. Helen's beauty is "godlike" (ἰσόθεον κάλλος), and
is clearly visible, "expressed not suppressed" (λαβοῦσα καὶ οὐ λαθοῦσα, 4.1–
2). Moreover, Helen, "by means of her body" (ἑνὶ δὲ σώματι) has the power to
"assemble" (literally, "lead" or "bring together") many bodies in contention
or competition, πολλὰ σώματα συνήγαγεν ἀνδρῶν ("she brought together
many bodies," 3–4). This image of bodies *led* and *misled,* brought together and
led apart, is of paramount importance in Gorgias's speech.

So far Gorgias has provided us with a kind of biographical premise for the
central question to which the rest of the *Encomium* is devoted: "Why did Helen
go to Troy?"[18] Everything else hinges upon that question. The answer, which
Gorgias immediately offers in preliminary form, constitutes the substance of
the rest of the *Encomium:* "For either by the disposition of fortune and the rati-
fication of the gods and the determination of necessity she did what she did,
or by violence confounded, or by persuasion dumbfounded, or to Love surren-
dered" (6.1–3). The first possible cause—that of divine necessity or preordained
fortune—requires little in the way of justification, but the three that follow are
crucial and more complicated. Translating in more literal terms: either Helen
was "seized or made captive by force," ἢ βίαι ἁρπασθεῖσα, or "persuaded by
words," ἢ λόγοις πεισθεῖσα, or "captivated by love," ἢ ἔρωτι ἁλοῦσα. These
different explanations, separable in theory, are in fact inseparable: Helen has
suffered all these fates, and suffered them simultaneously. Accordingly, each
will soon reveal itself to be a metaphorical substitute for the other two. This
is something powerfully expressed in the Greek at the level of sound itself,
where, for example, "being persuaded," πεισθεῖσα, closely resembles "being
made captive," ἁρπασθεῖσα. Much of the strength of Gorgias's argument rests,
then, upon rhetorical strategies that are almost completely lost in translation.
His description of analogous forms of subjugation sound alike, and that very
resemblance is itself a force that subjugates, in rhetorical terms, the audience at
whom it is directed. We are, in the end, victimized by a system of resemblances,
just as we are when we gaze upon the face of Helen. (Van Hook's translation
is labored, but his efforts to mimic much of the original word-play allow the
reader to see and hear these resemblances in the text.)

Gorgias, then, does not select the right defense from the panoply of possible causes he lays out, since the difficulty of keeping them distinct itself serves to exonerate Helen. Although he sets out to treat each explanation individually, it is generally difficult to extricate one form of coercion from another. For example, concerning physical violence Gorgias asserts the following:

But if by violence she was defeated and unlawfully she was treated and to her injustice was meted, clearly her violator as a terrifier was importunate, while she, translated and violated, was unfortunate. Therefore, the barbarian who verbally, legally, actually attempted the barbarous attempt, should meet with verbal accusation, legal reprobation, and actual condemnation. (7.1–5)

Van Hook's efforts in this passage to preserve Gorgias's word-play are truly heroic: *defeated, treated,* and *meted* stand for the Greek group ἡρπάσθη (seized, carried off), ἐβιάσθη (coerced), ὑβρίσθη (outraged, mistreated). What I want to stress is the way those pseudo-homonyms conjoin distinct facets of what is, in fact, a single violence, a violence expressed here in verbal, legal, and physical terms. Word-play again is the most powerful strategy by which this conjoining is achieved: it was Paris, Gorgias insists, who committed the crime in this affair, not Helen, and he did so "verbally, legally, actually," or, more literally, "in word, in law, in deed" (καὶ λόγωι καὶ νόμωι καὶ ἔργωι).

When Gorgias turns to the second agent of compulsion, that of persuasion, he falls into digression. But one begins to suspect that it is not a digression at all, but the orator's real subject. Gorgias now takes full advantage of the opportunity to glorify the essential instrument of his own art, at the very moment he turns its full force upon us:

But if it was through persuasion's reception and the soul's deception, it is not difficult to defend the situation and forfend the accusation, thus. Persuasion is a powerful potentate, who with frailest, feeblest frame works wonders. . . . All poetry I ordain and proclaim to be composition in metre, the listeners of which are affected by passionate trepidation and compassionate perturbation and likewise tearful lamentation, since through discourse the soul suffers, as its own, the felicity and infelicity of property and person of others. (8.15–25)

Somewhere in the course of this passage, one is no longer certain if Gorgias is still referring to Helen. According to this description, rhetoric seduces us and overcomes us as surely as Helen overcame Menelaus, as surely as Paris overcame Helen. And these correspondences are far from contingent. For it is the nature of poetry (which in Gorgias's case is not meant to be distinguished from rhetoric) to replicate itself authoritatively in the real world in the manner of a contagion. To hear the word of the poet (or the orator) means to act it out, to repeat it, to mimic it. What Gorgias extols here is precisely what Plato feared in the *Republic:* "persuasion's reception," λόγος ὁ πείσας, as the "soul's deception," καὶ τὴν ψυχὴν ἀπατήσας.

Thus poetry for Gorgias is a kind of incantation that leads or misleads the listener. One might think of the excursus on poetic sorcery that follows as a description of Helen the storyteller in *Odyssey* 4, pouring her *pharmakon* into the wine as she pours her words into the ears of her captive listeners: "Inspired incantations are provocative of charm and revocative of harm. For the power of song in association with the belief of the soul captures and enraptures and translates the soul with witchery" (10.1–4). Instead of "are provocative of charm," Kathleen Freeman translates "can induce pleasure," which brings us closer to the Greek: ἐπαγωγοὶ ἡδονῆς, are able to lead us into, draw us, lure us, toward pleasure. Poetry for Gorgias performs a figurative *abduction* upon the listener, it "enraptures and translates the soul," or, in Freeman's version, "persuades and transports," ἔπεισε καὶ μετέστησεν (Freeman 1966:132). The fragment that follows is not included by Van Hook because the text is considered corrupt, but it provides a fitting summary of this argument: "Persuasion by speech is equivalent to abduction by force," τὸ γὰρ τῆς πειθοῦς ἐξῆν ὁ δὲ νοῦς καίτοι εἰ ἀνάγκη ὁ εἰδὼς ἔξει μὲν οὖν, τὴν δὲ δύναμιν τὴν αὐτὴν ἔχει (12.1–2). In Gorgias's *Encomium on Helen,* to fall under the sway of rhetoric is to reenact the dislocation of metaphor, and relive the exile of Helen.

Trojan Women 914–1041: Helen Persuades Menelaus

Rhetoric, we have seen, is distrusted in much the same way that Helen is. Both are said to require careful moral supervision. Recall Aristotle's cautionary advice in the *Rhetoric* (1355a31): "for we must not make people believe what is wrong," οὐ γὰρ δεῖ τὰ φαῦλα πείθειν (trans. W. R. Roberts in McKeon 1941).[19] Aristotle's admonition sounds like Hecuba's warning to Menelaus as he prepares to confront his wayward wife in the *agon* in Euripides' *Trojan Women.* Let us look more carefully at this confrontation between husband and wife, for it is nothing if not a *rhetorical* confrontation. Even before it begins, Hecuba urges Menelaus: "But keep your eyes away from her. Desire will win" Ὁρᾶν δὲ τήνδε, φεῦγε, μή σ'ἕλῃ πόθῳ (Way 1912, trans. Lattimore 1958: 1. 891).[20] More precisely, the phrase is: "lest she seize/capture you with desire." Helen, however, will be captivating Menelaus with words and appearances, both joined in the rhetorical debate that follows.

Who wins the *agon* between Helen and Hecuba in *Trojan Women* 914–1041? Critics seem predisposed to give the prize to Hecuba. It is that predisposition I want to explore here. In general, it is Helen's defense that is condemned, ironically enough, for its evasive rhetoricity, despite the fact that Hecuba's speech is as smoothly crafted and opportunistic as Helen's.[21] The play itself refuses to pronounce so neat a verdict: Menelaus's sentence is hesitant and contradictory; Hecuba appears skeptical of his ability to carry it out; and the shadow of *Odys-*

sey 4—the image of Helen the happy homemaker—hangs over the debate, regardless of its resolution. But for the critics there has been little question either that Hecuba wins or that Euripides steals her victory from her.[22] In short, the *agon* and its dénouement prove difficult for the critic to digest, and leave a bad taste in his or her mouth; for this *agon* teaches that rational argumentation is impotent before the seductive lure of appearances; *logos* loses, *opsis* wins.[23] Critics have less often acknowledged that this is precisely the argument upon which Helen bases her defense. This makes her a far more perceptive critic than her modern-day counterparts; her speech, she knows, consists of words doomed to go unheard, which is, paradoxically, what her speech is about—if we could only be bothered to hear it. Helen knows this, and so does Hecuba. If we remain deaf to Helen's words, it is because, like Menelaus, we are too busy looking at her face. We would like to believe we convict Helen because she is wrong; in fact we do so because she is beautiful. Beauty is what condemns and saves Helen; beauty is both her crime and her defense.

Trojan Women 895–965: Helen's Defense

At first glance the *agon* in *Trojan Women* seems to promise that it will be easy to listen to and understand. The debate is formally announced and conventionally structured, clearly based on juridical models.[24] And yet it soon becomes apparent that this is no ordinary *agon,* if such a thing exists. First, the organization of this *agon* inverts the customary order of speeches, thereby making its outcome undecidable. Generally speaking, in Euripidean *agones* the second speaker always wins, and that second speaker is generally the defendant.[25] In *Trojan Women,* however, Helen is the defendant, and yet she speaks first; is it fair to say she wins then, or loses?[26] Second, this is not so much an *agon* as a mock-*agon,* one whose verdict has already been decided in advance. Menelaus is at first unwilling to play the judge in any contest of words: "I did not come to talk with you" (for *logous*), he says, acknowledging the traditional Greek antithesis of words and deeds (*logoi men . . . ergoi de*),[27] "I came to kill" οὐκ ἐς λόγους ἐλήλυθ᾽ ἀλλά σε κτενῶν (905). He agrees to play his appointed role only on condition that he be permitted to render his verdict *before* the contest begins (905, 911–13). Finally, Helen herself appears to invalidate the *agon* from the start, suggesting that she cannot win and that it matters little, therefore, what she actually says (914–15).[28]

Surely we—like Menelaus—ought to reserve judgment until we hear the substance of Helen's *rhesis?*[29] The critics certainly appear to have been listening, for they have painstakingly dissected Helen's arguments, and just as painstakingly refuted them. Their strategy amounts to "exposing" those arguments as a self-serving and deceptive rhetorical surface. That, too, we shall see, is the gist of Hecuba's response.[30] I have suggested that if this makes Helen's argument wrong, then it also makes it right. For what, in fact, is the substance of her argument? It is that surface always triumphs over substance.

More specifically, Helen's defense has been regarded as a series of evasions, efforts to pin the blame on anyone but herself: on Hecuba (919–20), on Priam (920–22), on Paris and Aphrodite (924–50), on Menelaus (943–44), on Deiphobus (952–60).[31] In fact, all of these evasions amount to the same essentially Gorgian defense: that beauty (*kallos*) is an irresistible force (*bia*), a form of coercion. Hence the emphasis Helen puts upon the Judgment of Paris (924–37)[32] — a myth about beauty triumphant. Less often remembered is that the Judgment is itself an *agon*, much like the one that pits Helen against Hecuba, and that, by the same token, the *agon* in *Trojan Women* is a second Judgment (*neîkos*), in which beauty will, once again, triumph over words.[33] Both *agon* and *neîkos* belong to a larger category of verbal structure: language as graft, word pitted against word, argument sutured to argument, as in the *antilogoi* that constitute the building blocks of dialectic. Dialectic, as Socrates "invents" it in the *Phaedrus,* is another way of joining words together (collection) and keeping them apart (division); that too is a process, it was suggested in chapter 4, ultimately played out on a much larger scale in the *neikos* of the Trojan war itself.

Helen's defense in *Trojan Women* is very close to that spoken for her by Gorgias in the *Encomium on Helen.*[34] Gorgias argues that *logos, eros, kallos,* and *opsis* are interchangeable terms, forces alike of compulsion (*bia*). He makes this argument, in large measure, as much through sound (paranomasia) as sense. Like Helen's defense, Gorgias's *Encomium* seeks to demonstrate the seductive power of appearance and to equate it with the persuasive force of language; like the defense, it has always been criticized itself as an irresponsible and seductive rhetorical display. The *Encomium* has been attacked as a rhetorical showpiece, language for the sake of language, framed in the forensic manner but never designed for the courtroom—an exercise, in other words, in epideixis, disguised as forensics.[35] That, too, is precisely the critics' accusation against Helen: that her speech is not to be taken seriously, that her courtroom defense is really *a rhetoric of display.*

Trojan Women 969–1032: Hecuba's Response

In Euripides' play, this is precisely what Hecuba accuses Helen of: *making a display of herself.* Priam's queen takes her cue here from the chorus: "Break down the beguilement of this woman, since she speaks / well, and has done wickedly" (πειθὼ διαφθείρουσα τῆσδ', ἐπεὶ λέγει / καλῶς κακοῦργος οὖσα [967–68]). This is what Hecuba will try to demonstrate—through persuasiveness of her own, of course. We are once again faced with the ironic spectacle of rhetoric undoing rhetoric, and therefore inevitably undoing itself.[36] Hecuba, in other words, will counter the charm of Helen's speech with a countercharm, just as Socrates defends against poetry by means of more poetry. Helen, Hecuba asserts, is a chronic rhetorician, too skilled at saying exactly what is required by the situation at hand: "when the reports came in that Menelaus' side / was winning, you would praise him" (εἰ μὲν τὰ τοῦδε κρείσσον᾽ ἀγγέλλοιτό σοι, / Μενέλαον ᾔνεις [1004–5]). This line should remind us that the Trojan war itself was but another, larger *agon,* whose outcome was equally problematic.[37] Much of Hecuba's speech, it has been noted, seeks to achieve its ends by exposing the myths in which Helen so deftly "wraps" her motives *as myth*—mere appearances. The Judgment could not have *really* happened as Helen said it did (969–82); Aphrodite did not *really* force Helen to join Paris, as Helen said she did (983–90). Although these arguments have convinced many a critic that Helen is guilty, what is finally most significant about them is that whether right or wrong, they actually support Helen's defense. For if the Judgment is only a myth, Helen is right—for then a myth has toppled Troy. If Aphrodite is nothing but a word for lust, Helen is again right—for then lust, a penchant for appearances, has toppled Troy. Hecuba's "realism" ends up validating Helen's "myths." "My son," she says, "was handsome beyond all other men. / You looked at him, and sense went Cyprian at the sight" (ἦν οὑμὸς υἱὸς κάλλος ἐκπρεπέστατος, / ὁ σὸς δ᾽ ἰδών νιν νοῦς ἐποιήθη Κύπρις [987–88]). Hecuba would replace Helen's myths with reasonable facts, a history that could then be verified or rejected. But history in fact proves Helen right, for the "fact" of Paris's beauty is precisely its irresistible power.[38]

The arguments heard during the *agon* are ultimately betrayed, in both senses of the word, by the references to appearance that frame the debate. Hecuba initiates the proceedings, we have seen, with a warning for Menelaus: "keep your eyes away from her. Desire will win. / She looks enchantment, and where she looks homes are set on fire; / she captures cities as she captures the eyes of men" (ὁρᾶν δὲ τήνδε φεῦγε, μή σ᾽ ἕλῃ πόθῳ. / αἱρεῖ γὰρ ἀνδρῶν ὄμματ᾽, ἐξαιρεῖ πόλεις, / πίμπρησιν οἴκους· ὧδ᾽ ἔχει κηλήματα [891–93]). Similarly, she closes the debate with this final "proof": "And now you dare to come outside, / figure fastidiously arranged" (κἀπὶ τοῖσδε σὸν δέμας / ἐξῆλθες ἀσκήσασα [1022–23]). This charge merely extends and restates those that precede it: Helen's beauty, Hecuba is saying, in several different ways, is a rhetorical device, an artificial surface, carefully crafted. "Throughout Helen's speech it is not clear which might be the more effective, her looks or her words," N. T. Croally writes. The truth is that it is probably both" (1994:145). This is true enough, but the truth is also that the distinction between looks and words is precisely what Helen and, as we now see, Hecuba reject.

It has been noted that Menelaus participates only reluctantly in this debate, and that it is Hecuba who urges Menelaus to let Helen speak. This is not surprising. Hecuba knows that a silent Helen is the most dangerous Helen of all,[39] and the only chance to convict Helen is to let her speak.[40] Such a strategy must inevitably fail. Helen's words are drawn into the circle of *opsis* and soon become indistinguishable from appearances. Indeed Helen's words are judged precisely as appearances, as something hypnotic, beautiful, deceptive, and purely superficial: in other words, rhetoric.

Looking Instead of Listening: The Critic as Menelaus

"Rhetoric": that is how, in effect, the critics have disparaged Helen's speech in *Trojan Women,* and the *agon* in its entirety. It is interesting that critics have been, on the whole, as reluctant as Menelaus to "participate" in the debate, and now we can begin to understand why.[41] Lattimore, for example, sees the *agon* as the weakest part of the play, a distraction, a digression from the matter at hand.[42] The irony is that this *agon* is precisely about language as distraction. All this verbiage, it tells us, is beside the point! All of it is, as Menelaus puts it (without knowing what he means), for "show" (1038–39).

This is, for Menelaus, what the debate has been from the beginning: a *show.* He brings the *agon* abruptly to its conclusion, saying, "Enough, Hecuba. I am not listening to her now" (παῦσαι, γεραιά· τῆσδε δ᾽ οὐκ ἐφρόντισα [1046]). The truth is, he never listened to her at all. The modern critic appears to base his verdict on the substance of Helen's speech—neatly separating the speaker's words from her appearance. The critic appears to be listening to Helen, not looking at her. In truth, like Menelaus, the critic has never stopped looking—and never really listened. His verdict, like Hecuba's, accuses Helen of rhetoricity, reduces her to a conspiracy of deceptive surfaces: her words, her clothes, her beauty. Despite the careful dissection of her *logos, logos* is never judged as anything but *opsis.* And thus Menelaus says at the close of the *agon:* "all this talk of Aphrodite / is for pure show" (χἠ Κύπρις κόμπου χάριν / λόγοις ἐνεῖται [1038–39]). The critic, who appears to speak Hecuba's lines, inevitably performs Menelaus's role. This would explain, for example, why critical readings have been so eager to find Helen guilty. Critical readings of this *agon* are bound to repeat the arguments they purport to elucidate. And this makes sense: the reader, after all, is in the same "position" as Menelaus (who is himself in the same position as Paris before him): that of a judge in a beauty contest.

Thus the critic's condemnation of Helen's rhetorical duplicity is always a displaced acknowledgment of her beauty. This is the case for Gellie, for example, whose scorn—unmistakably suggesting desire, only half-heartedly repressed—is unusual only in its stridency:

What this debate demonstrates is not that Helen is wicked but that she is empty. We are not being asked to hate her but to despise her. . . . When Helen comes out in her finery and plays the rhetorician with her schoolgirl arguments, our enjoyment of the fun must be seasoned with a feeling of disgust; can so contemptible a creature have been the cause of the Trojan War? . . . The Helen scene uses Hecuba to see through the glamour of myth and expose Helen for the shallow wanton that she is. (Gellie 1986:117–18)

Every reader of *Trojan Women* suffers from this kind of repetition-compulsion.[43] Where this play is concerned, literary appraisal soon becomes character assassination.[44]

I offer no way out of this repetition. My point here is not to find fault with critical readings, but rather to suggest that critical reading — or critical listening — is condemned to fail here, that the critic cannot listen to Helen, but is doomed to look at her. The critic is always Menelaus. In a battle of words, when no one is listening, or when listening is really looking, Helen can only lose, then, as she herself well knows, and, by losing, she knows, she wins. I am not suggesting that we need to try harder to "hear" what Helen has to say. When we do listen to the substance of Helen's argument, what we hear, after all, is that it doesn't matter what we hear, that *opsis* must always triumph over *logos,* that *logos* is *opsis.* Some have argued that *Trojan Women* ultimately displays the defeat of language — or reason — in a world dominated by appearances. Others assert, on the contrary, that *logos* here finds its ultimate triumph, for *logos* is all the Trojan women have left. Perhaps it would be more accurate to say that the *agon* in this play aims to jeopardize the very distinction between words and appearances.

There is another sense in which *logos* in *Trojan Women* must always give way to *opsis* — a sense in which our listening must always be a form of looking. We are supposed to be watching a tragedy, after all, in a theater. Tragedy itself, Croally (like others) reminds us, is a "dramatized *agon*" (1994:160), not only in the sense that a tragedy is a debate of ideas, but in the social context of performance itself, where tragedians are competing against each other. Performance in this sense has played little or no role in the critical appraisal of the *agon* in *Trojan Women,* and yet it clearly ought to be a crucial feature in a debate on the power of spectacle over reason.[45]

Conclusion: Rhetoric as Abduction

In a passage from the *Philebus,* Protarchus is questioning Socrates on the art of rhetoric. "How," he asks, "ought we to describe her?" Socrates responds: "Plainly everyone will recognize her whom we now speak of." Protarchus recalls Gorgias's own definition: "he regularly said, Socrates, that the art of persuasion was greatly superior to all others, for it subjugated all things not by violence, but by willing submission" (57e–58a8; trans. Hackforth 1945). Recognizing Helen is just as easy, and just as dangerous. Both rhetoric and Helen specialize in likenesses that mislead. To be seduced by the rhetor's art is thus to reenact the story of Helen's own seduction (her seduction of and her seduction by others). Epideixis, in its conventional characterization as a rhetoric of "display," always entraps us in this contagious system of abductions and possessions:

> To begin with the danger issuing from the dynamic quality of rhetoric, it is clear that the power of oratory works upon an audience, but even more does it work upon a speaker. He can only too easily be led on, "inebriated with the exuberance of his own verbosity," as Disraeli said of Gladstone, to statements beyond what he intended and to an irresponsibility unsuspected at the beginning of his speech. (Kennedy 1963:24)

Much like Aristotle in the *Rhetoric,* George Kennedy feels it necessary to caution the practitioner of this dangerous art with sober moral injunctions: "The good orator, good both in a moral and an artistic sense, must be aware of his power and must never forget his responsibility. No rhetoric can be better than the character of its orator, and sometimes it seduces him." The terms employed here are not, it must be clear by now, fortuitous. They are the language of Gorgias describing the power of persuasion. These are the metaphors we continue to employ in our own moments of submission, to *logos* as to *eros* (I was swept away . . . I got carried away . . . I was transported . . .). Every time we use those metaphors, we reenact the story of Helen and Paris.

Let me cite two very different examples of this reenactment. Gorgias's Helen may well remind one, for example, of Socrates' "stone of Heraclea" in the *Ion,* which transmits the same force of attraction along a chain of contiguous rings. "Just so the Muse," says Socrates (533e–534a):

> She first makes men inspired, and then through these inspired ones others share in the enthusiasm, and a chain is formed. . . . So it is also with the good lyric poets; as the worshiping Corybantes are not in their senses when they dance, so the lyric poets are not in their senses when they make these lovely lyric poems. No, when once they launch into harmony and rhythm, they are seized with the Bacchic transport, and are possessed. (Trans. Cooper 1938)

And a moment later Socrates completes the analogy he has been elaborating since the beginning of the dialogue: "Well, do you see that the spectator is the last of the rings I spoke of, which receive their force from one another by virtue of the loadstone? You, the rhapsodist and actor, are the middle ring, and the first one is the poet himself" (536a). It is in very much these terms that Gorgias celebrates the virtues of his art. What is the precise way, Socrates goes on to ask, to describe the attachment of the poet to his patron Muse? "One poet is suspended from one Muse, another from another; we call it being 'possessed' [κατέχεται], but the fact is much the same, since he is *held* [ἔχεται]" (536b). Socrates' own seductive imagery here suggests that all rhetoric functions as a form of graft. When rhetoric exerts its power upon us, it binds us to its structures.

Compare Socrates' image of contagious possession—an early variation on metaphor as metonymy—in the *Ion,* with Johann Joachim Winckelmann's rapture over the Apollo Belvedere some two thousand years later, cited by Hugh Honour in *Neo-Classicism:*

In the presence of this miracle of art I forget the whole universe and my soul acquires a loftiness appropriate to its dignity. From admiration I pass to ecstasy, I feel my breast dilate and rise as if I were filled with the spirit of prophecy; I am transported to Delos and the sacred groves of Lycia—places Apollo honoured with his presence—and the statue seems to come alive like the beautiful creation of Pygmalion. (Honour 1968:60)

Winckelmann's admiration of this piece of ancient culture is a way, we can see, of reenacting its exile. Note, too, that Winckelmann is not just transported *to* Delos, in spatial terms; he is transported *back,* as well, along a temporal axis, to antiquity. Such a moment points toward the poetic articulations of cultural exile and nostalgia that we will be confronting in part 2.

6

Deixis

Introduction: Helen in the Lyric

"Eros is always a story in which lover, beloved and the difference between them interact," writes Anne Carson (1986:169). This is arguably the essential plot of the lyric, reduced to its basic outlines. This chapter focuses primarily on the role Helen plays in the works of the lyric poets Alcaeus, Alcman, Theocritus, and, above all, Sappho. The lyric Helen, I contend, always acts as a pivot or a point of articulation, as that "difference between" that constitutes the very possibility of the erotic narrative. This difference opposes not just lover and beloved, but also past and present, epic and lyric. Helen is both lyric's superlative individual (most desired, most desirous) and a synecdoche for all Homeric epic ("Helen" is always a reference to the Trojan war), so that putting her into a poem makes it both a "private" confession and a "public" or "intertextual" dialogue. By way of Helen, Sappho is both soldered to and sundered from Homer, so that Helen becomes the very emblem of what makes literary history—as continuity—both possible and impossible.

What makes Helen such an effective point of reference for the lyric? On the most obvious—that is, thematic—level, taking Helen's side allows the lyric poet to renounce the theme of war (Homer's theme par excellence), and to do so by means of the very terms in which that theme has traditionally been articulated. This is lyric as *recusatio*. On the level of language itself, however—and it is this level with which I am most concerned in this chapter—Helen may be said to function in the lyric as one of its most reliable *deictics*. Deictics are signifiers that point (pronouns such as "I" or "you," adverbs such as "here" or "now"), and upon them lyric may be said to pin its success. What is distinctive about deictics is that while belonging to a preexisting system (that is, language, what Saussure calls *langue*), they have no meaning except in reference to a particular speaker, in the context of a particular speech act (again in Saussurian terms, *parole*). Helen is always part of Homeric language, that is, but to cite her is to give voice to subjective desire. Chapter 4, "Speculation," has already demonstrated how lyric can be a form of graft to the extent that it refers back to a prior system of epic motifs, capitalizing, as it were, upon a Homeric commonwealth. This chapter suggests that lyric subjectivity (the lyric "I") is a graft in at least two senses: (1) it is fashioned from an intertextual splicing of an epic past and a lyric present, and (2) it is viable only when attached to a particular site and moment of enunciation—when, that is, it is spoken by a designated speaker.

Implicit here is a view of Sapphic lyric that runs contrary to a number of longstanding critical conventions: (1) to read lyric poetry is to play at hearing the voice of a subject who speaks it; (2) early lyric *monody* (poetry sung by an individual to the accompaniment of a lyre) represents the emergent voice of individualism, the declaration of a now-differentiated subjectivity formerly dissolved into the communal expressions of cult and polis;[1] (3) Sappho's poetry is a personal record—whether of a private crisis or a public ritual—rather than a rhetorical script.[2] *The Oxford Companion to Classical Literature* concludes its entry on her with this appraisal: "Sappho created a form of subjective personal lyric never equaled in the ancient world in its immediacy and intensity" (Howatson 1989:507). These terms—*immediacy* and *intensity*—consistently govern interpretations of Sapphic verse. On the one hand, critics deploy these terms as if they were conventional feminine attributes; on the other, because within this convention the feminine is equated with the natural, these terms are constitutive elements in our definitions of subjectivity itself.[3] The important point here is that the effect of these interpretations is to read Sappho *out* of history by inserting her back into it. Not only can lyric be said to graft the past onto the present, but critical approaches to lyric have always tried to graft the present back onto the past. Critics—including Denys Page (1955b), Anne Burnett (1983), C. M. Bowra (1936), and Martin West (1970)—have tended to explain Sappho's poetry by referring it back to a historical origin, treating the poem either as "a burning page from a diary," as Burnett puts it (1983:229) or as part of a social or ritual occasion. In both cases Sappho is returned to the past by grafting her to a particular context. I call this *forensic* or *referential* criticism.

My reading of lyric as essentially *deictic* relies on the work of two linguistic philosophers: J. L. Austin's conception of the performative utterance and Emile Benveniste's writings on self-referring pronouns. The primary site in which I test these assertions will again be Fr. 16, Sappho's "Defense of Helen." My analysis of this poem also depends on the contributions of classicists: Gregory Nagy's identification of the lyric "I" in classical Greek monody as a species of choral voice (regardless of the actual performative setting, Sappho speaks *like* a choral leader *as if* to a chorus), and Elroy Bundy's and William Race's discussion of lyric as a conventional arrangement of comparative claims or *priamels*, competing predications that depend upon the deployment of mythic-literary (that is, Homeric) themes and structures. These critics help us understand the lyric not as event but as reenactment or performance. For example, if we read Sappho's erotic hyperbole as a rhetorical display of passion, not passion itself, if we agree that Sappho employs myth, and even "improves" upon it ("I think that not even Hermione was such as you . . ." [Fr. 23])[4] as part of a conventional performance, then the lyric looks less like confession and more like self-promotion, the validation of one genre (lyric) over another (epic). A mythic intertext that repeatedly intervenes in Sappho's verse is the Trojan conflict; and the figure of Helen (Frs. 16, 17, 23, 44, 68[a], 166) is paramount. From the forensic perspective Helen is an excuse for personal confession; in the deictic model, she is a pivot, the heroine of both lyric and epic traditions, a figure of superlative and superlatively catastrophic beauty. Nagy's conception of the chorus in, for example, Alcman and Pindar suggests a body at once fractured and fused (divided and collected, to use Plato's dialectical terminology) by gestures of representation and competition. If we think of Fr. 16 as a choral performance, Helen appears to play the part of a choral leader. In fact, here as elsewhere in Archaic and Classical poetry and prose (in Homer, Gorgias, Isocrates, and Theocritus), Helen takes on the attributes not just of a choral leader but of a "panhellenic" choral leader, a figure who in both literary and political terms constitutes (i.e., collects) Hellenic culture as she fractures (i.e., divides) it.

Forensic Criticism

"Sappho's poetry, written for her own need or the pleasure of her friends, is concerned with her emotions — her loves, hates and jealousies — and with the activities of her family and friends." Taken from David Campbell's school edition, *Greek Lyric Poetry* (Campbell 1967:xxiii), this is a typical example of *forensic criticism*. Whether the poem is read as interior monologue or as a script, its *subject* (that is, its source and/or referent) is understood to be Sappho herself. In either case, poetry is evidence: a fingerprint, tear, suicide note, or, less dramatically, minutes of a meeting, lines for a performance. Either way, reference is converted neatly into causality. We can call these two versions of forensic readings the *private* and the *public model*.

In the private model Sappho's language is less a matter of *techne* than of unmediated nature. Willis Barnstone writes: "Simplicity and directness are the manner of all monody, in contrast to choral poetry. In Sappho these qualities are at their highest" (1962:10).[5] This so-called natural language is without artifice or literary precedent. It is, above all, *sincere*. Sincerity is the ethical equivalent of referential immediacy. A. R. Burn admits that homosexuality was rampant in ancient Greece; what *saves* Sappho, he avers, is the intensity of her passion, her utter "absence of shame," and her absolute *sincerity:* "She loved many of her girls with a fire of which few are capable; and she said what she felt" (1960:231). Thus critics have tended to divorce Sappho's poetry from its *literary* context, as they seek to resituate it in a historical or biographical one. (Borrowing Jakobson's linguistic functions, one can say that the standard Sapphic *message* in the eyes of these critics is *emotive, conative,* and *referential*—anything but *poetic.*)[6] If Page concedes that in Fr. 31 (which begins, φαίνεταί μοι, "He seems to me fortunate as the gods," "Homeric symptoms and Homeric phraseology are here adapted to describe the passion of love" (1955b:29), and that it "would not be safe to assume that Sappho writes quite independently of models which must have been well enough known to her," he nevertheless consistently detaches Sapphic verse from literary precedent: "Rarely . . . shall we find language so far independent of literary tradition . . . so close to the speech of everyday. Style is in harmony with dialect, both products of nature, not artifice" (30). Sappho is, moreover, to be clearly distinguished in this respect from male poets such as Alcaeus or Archilocus: "Whereas Archilocus speaks a dialect which readily assimilates the Epic dialect and style, Sappho's vernacular resists those influences" (30). It is hard not to see gendered biases at work in this image of an all-natural Sappho. That image relies on the assumption, Mary Lefkowitz argues, that "because women poets are emotionally disturbed, their poems are psychological outpourings" (1981:59).[7]

In the public model, Sappho's poetry is read as ceremonial libretto. The picture Bowra paints is emblematic of this approach: "She was the leader . . . in an institution which trained young girls. . . . primarily concerned with the cult of Aphrodite" (1936:187); and the members of the cult constituted "a *thiasos*" (187).[8] Burnett compares Sappho's poetic circle to the all-male symposiastic *hetaireia* of Alcaic verse (1983:210). Wilamowitz's theory of Sappho as headmistress of a formal school-organization remains influential; this scholar famously attempted to convert Fr. 31 into an epithalamium, inserting it into an extended ritual context (1913). Within this model, poetry functions less as a confession than as a photograph (and preferably a Polaroid). In this view Sappho's "naturalness" is a guarantor of her poetry's truth-value, and is distinguished from the complex doublings and deceptions of masculine rhetoric. "The original experience had been a real one," West insists of Fr. 31. Bowra's reading of Fr. 2 ("Come hither to me from Crete"), which certainly sounds like a prayer to Aphrodite, is chiefly an attempt to find the situation (some "religious occasion") to which the lines refer (1936:196). The ceremonial proposition is just another species of biographical criticism. Reference still has its assigned causality outside the text.

Readings of Sappho's Fr. 17 (a prayer, at least in form, to Hera) and Fr. 1 (a prayer to Aphrodite) illustrate both of these critical paradigms: the private and the public. Page, as we might expect, works to distance Fr. 17 from its epic source in *Odyssey* 3. Sappho's version of the Achaean sojourn at Lesbos is really a personal matter: "the revelation of Hera to the Atridae is quoted not for its own sake but as a precedent for her appearance to Sappho . . . it is the prayer, not the precedent, which is the primary theme of the poem" (1955b:61).[9] In other words, Fr. 17 is not a prayer; it just looks like one. Similarly, Fr. 1 "is not a cult-song . . . yet it is constructed in accordance with the principles of the cult-song." [10] Bowra agrees: if Fr. 1 is "cast in the form of a prayer and obeys the usual rules for entreating the gods to do something," nevertheless it is "not a public but a private poem, not a hymn for a festival but a personal appeal from Sappho to her goddess" (1936:200).

In the other camp Wilamowitz suggests that Fr. 17 refers to the founding of a cult to Hera (1913). Burnett, likewise, approaches Fr. 17 as a formal prayer (1938:211). Burnett tends to read Sappho literally and to justify that reading by reference to imagined historical contexts. When Burnett cites the line "These things I sing among my friends to bring them joy" (Fr. 60) as proof that "Sappho performed for her girls in order to amuse them" (216), she assumes that the very content of the line she cites is not itself dictated by a forgotten convention; she assumes that it is not rhetorical. It is easy to imagine, however, that the "I" in Fr. 60 may not be Sappho or may refer to a role she plays and that the friends here designated are not necessarily Sappho's or are hers only within the horizons of the particular act performed by the speaker. Of Fr. 94 (τεθνάκην δ' ἀδόλως θέλω, "I candidly want to die"), Burnett asserts: "Nothing about the text proves that its first line was delivered by the poet in her own persona" (293). But can any line of Sappho be proved to belong to Sappho? And even if it does, is the Sappho about whom Sappho is singing the same as the Sappho who sings? Fr. 94 is, according to Burnett, "an anecdote told in dramatic form with the singer-narrator cast as one of its characters" (293). It is difficult to see why all of Sappho's poems could not be classified in the same way, whether or not Sappho is present in name and whether or not we want to imagine Sappho herself doing the singing.

Deictic Criticism

All of the critics cited above agree that, whatever Fr. 17 and Fr. 1 actually are, they certainly look like prayers, and even designate themselves as such. This is very much how J. L. Austin defines *performative utterances*.[11] To utter a performative is to do something by saying it, as in "I bet" or "I promise" —or "I pray." *Constatives,* on the other hand, to which Austin opposes performatives, are descriptions or statements of fact. Performatives do what they say they are doing, by virtue of being said.[12] To say "I do" in the marriage ceremony is not to describe the marriage ceremony, but—as long as the ceremony is valid—to perform it.

Austin's conception of the performative is useful in reading Sappho because it challenges the kind of referentiality upon which forensic criticism is based. Like the traditional philosophers of language from whom Austin distances himself, Sappho's forensic critics make language refer to an intention, to a particular state of mind in a particular historical situation. For these philosophers a performative like "I promise" describes an "inward and spiritual act" (Austin 1962:10). Austin shows that a promise, however, even made dishonestly, is still a promise—it is just one that is not carried out. Constatives assert, and are therefore always either true or false. Performatives are under no such obligation: they are neither true nor false, but felicitous or unfelicitous, and for reasons which have nothing to do with intention. When performatives "misfire," it is because their social context is somehow faulty: the occasion or the speaker or the addressee must be improper. Saying "I now pronounce you husband and wife" will not have the desired effect unless the person saying it is "certified" to do so, and the situation is "proper." Performatives underscore the extent to which all language is a theatrical affair: a question of saying particular things in particular roles to particular audiences in particular settings. (Thus, the priest who performs the marriage ceremony is playing the role of "priest" in a designated situation called a "wedding.") The point is that poems, like performatives, may be better understood as exploiting conventions, not intentions.

Austin himself attempts to forestall this kind of widening of the performative field and to contain the more radical consequences of the performative perspective he has opened up (isn't everything, in a sense, a performative?). Why do Sappho's readers reject her poems as actual prayers? Their reasons are the same ones advanced by Austin in disallowing certain performatives: "Surely the words must be spoken 'seriously' and so as to be taken 'seriously'? . . . I must not be joking, for example, nor writing a poem" (1962:9). Austin's exclusions here depend, we can see, upon the very assertions of intentionality he is elsewhere trying to undermine.

The performative perspective, however, ought to have important consequences for reading lyric poetry. To begin with, it would settle the debate as to whether Fr. 17 and Fr. 1 are "really" prayers or not. Considered as performative utterances, we may agree that these poems are not *successful* or *legitimate* prayers, but we would have to insist that they are prayers all the same. They are *performances* of prayers, both the carrying out of, and the dramatic representation of, prayers.[13] More generally, the performative encourages us to think of lyric as reenactment rather than confession, and moves us toward a conception of subjectivity in the lyric as something *structural:* as a position to be repeatedly occupied and evacuated.

Sappho's poems, in fact, do not designate themselves as "actual" confessions, personalized artifacts tied to a specific time and place, but capitalize instead upon their own repeatability. Lefkowitz remarks with regard to Fr. 31: "The time is indefinite, the illusion happens over and over: 'whenever I look at you' (*os* with subjunctive *ido*)" (1981:66). The forensic view cannot acknowledge that the poetic voice is essentially transposable, that the lyric "I" has no objective reference. This is Benveniste's point in "La nature des pronoms," where he defines the first-person pronoun *je* tautologically as "the person enunciating the present instance of the discourse containing *I*" ("la personne qui énonce la présente instance de discours contenant *je*" [1974, 1:252]). Like Austin, Benveniste leads us toward a structural conception of subjectivity, one that depends not upon a psychological notion of intention, but upon the occupation of a position in a system: "It is by identifying oneself as the sole person pronouncing *I* that each speaker assumes the role, in turn, of subject" ("C'est en s'identifiant comme personne unique prononçant *je* que chacun des locuteurs se pose tour à tour comme 'sujet' " [254]). Other pronouns (*you, me, he, she*) similarly refer to their own enunciation (Fr. 17 begins: πλάσιον δή μ'[ε], "close to *me*"), as do certain adverbs (*here, now, today*) and demonstratives or deictics (*this, that*). Like Austin's performatives, Benveniste's deictics, "which assert nothing . . . are not bound by the condition of truth and escape all denial" ("n'assertant rien . . . ne sont pas soumis à la condition de vérité et échappent à toute dénégation").

What of those poems, however, that explicitly bear the name *Sappho?* This would seem to be the quickest and surest route, in forensic terms, from poem to poet. Readers of lyric see the name of the poet as contractual proof of a confession's authenticity. It is the signature of the real. We can compare it to the traditional interpretation of a celebrated passage of the *Theognidea,* where the speaker asks that a seal (*sphregis*) be placed upon his verse. Andrew Ford underscores how the *sphregis* has generally been understood as an early declaration of individual authorship (1985:82–95). But after noting the anachronism of such a reading (given that the normal mode of poetic transmission in the time of Theognis was oral, not written), Ford argues that the exhortation of the *sphregis* suggests instead the instability of poetic authorship, and thus represents an attempt to control it (or to be seen doing so). Ford compares it to the inscribed *mnema,* or memorials, set up to glorify and immortalize early Classical tyrants. West classifies the erotic poetry of the *Theognidea* with its anonymous addressees as "amorous sympotic," and notes, "Such songs have the best chance of being propagated, for anyone can sing them with his own love in mind" (1970:308). The poetry of Sappho, on the other hand (Fr. 1 is cited as evidence), is inexplicably dismissed as private property: "We cannot take it so far with Sappho. It is not a love song for Everyman, it is labeled as hers." That it is *labeled as* hers is precisely what should make us suspicious. The signature may be, in other words, a trope of lyric mimesis.[14] West reads the signature as a contractual guarantee of subjective presence, and never allows for a rhetorically crafted Sappho, a Sappho persona. What does it mean to say that Sappho refers to herself? It means, at best, that her name is cited. In Fr. 1 that name happens to occupy the position of a wounded lover. Despite West, it *is* a song for every man (or woman). The proof of this is simple: we continue to read Sappho's poem today.

Classicists have long traced the rise of the lyric genre as an offshoot of choral poetry and tied it to the emergence of a new kind of individualism, thereby encouraging a reading that takes "confessional" monody at face value. More recently, critics have offered alternative explanations for lyric's distinctiveness. Nagy argues that monody can just as easily be understood as a "differentiated offshoot" of choral performance. The lyric speaker would represent a choral leader (*khoregos*) as a character now distinct (at least on the level of the poem's own fiction, if not in actuality) from the performer, as in Pindaric epinician (Nagy 1990:339–81). In other words, monody continues to promote the illusion of a *khoregos* singing to a chorus, even if that chorus is no longer singing or dancing, and, in fact, may now be purely theoretical. What we are meant to hear then in the monodic "I" is a choral voice now converted into authorship. Thus Sappho, even as she promotes the fiction of authorial confession, is still speaking, as Nagy puts it, "as a choral personality" (371).

The implications of these deictic perspectives are far-reaching for our understanding of lyric as a part of literary history instead of history "proper," or, in other words, as a system (*langue*) instead of an utterance (*parole*). To call monody a form of choral singing is to reconceptualize it as a competitive sport. Not only is the internal space of the choral entity marked by hierarchical differentiation and rivalry (as in the rivalry of semichoruses, or the superiority of *khoregos* to chorus), but the chorus competes with other choruses in public contests. In both intratextual and intertextual terms, that is to say, monody says what it says by way of graft. In Alcman 1, his *partheneion* or maiden song (Page 1962), a figure named Agido competes with a Hagesichora for preeminence in beauty and skill. Nagy calls this song "a particularly striking example of the choral form as a hierarchical construct" (1990:345).[15] We do not have to side with either Page or Wilamowitz to see that Sappho's verse always predicates some kind of communal space, whatever its "real" nature, and that one of the central gestures of her poetry is to valorize those within that space and to devalorize those outside it.[16] Internal competition, too, is a way of reinforcing the boundaries of a community, real or theoretical, as in Fr. 82 (a): εὐμορφοτέρα Μνασιδίκα τὰς ἀπάλας Γυρίννως, "Mnasidica is more shapely than Gyrinno." Such contests, Nagy argues, are always ritual reenactments of mythic rivalries, and the choral leader is always in some sense a substitute for a mythic or royal predecessor. The idea of choral reenactment helps us regard Agido and Hagesichora as characters rather than "real people" per se. Thus Hagesichora, whose name means literally "she who leads the chorus" (Nagy 1990:345), may be a substitute on the level of ritual for a corresponding mythic cult figure.[17] A similar depersonalization occurs if we think of lyric monody as reenacting choral song, which in turn is reenacting mythic event. Sappho, then, like Mnasidica and Gyrinno, becomes a "character" in a ritual reenactment. This in turn would designate Sappho's amorous evaluations, with their mythic-epic antecedents, as intertextual gestures, maneuverings vis-à-vis the poetic past. The voice of the lover speaks, always of other, prior voices: epic voices above all. The successful completion of the lyric prayer, for example, depends on citing epic precedent. To return to the genre of the prayer: perhaps what Fr. 17 promulgates, in the end, is a lyric occasion equal to or greater than the epic model.

Sappho, Fr. 16: Revisited

I previously discussed Sappho Fr. 16 as an instance of the speculative economy Helen tends to set in motion in classical poetry. In revisiting this poem now, I want to position it in an intertextual economy: in other words, to show how it grafts epic and lyric genres, as it grafts its reader and speaker into its structures.

> Some say a host of horsemen, others of infantry, and others
>   of ships, is the most beautiful thing on the dark earth:
>   but I say, it is what you love
> Full easy it is to make this understood of one and all: for
>   she that far surpassed all mortals in beauty, Helen, her
>   most noble husband
> Deserted, and went sailing to Troy, with never a thought for
>   her daughter and dear parents. The [Cyprian goddess] led
>   her from the path [παράγαγ' αὔταν] . . .
>   . . . [Which] now has put me in mind of Anactoria far away:
> Her lovely way of walking, and the bright radiance of her
>   changing face, would I rather see than your Lydian
>   chariots and infantry full-armed.

Fr. 16 has traditionally been read as amorous confession, another chapter in Sappho's autobiography. According to West: "In songs such as these Sappho entertained her current companions with candid expressions of her feelings towards past or absent ones" (1970:318). Bowra similarly makes his exegesis of the poem into a biographical narrative, a story of Sappho and her "girls" (1936:179). The verb *eramai* in line 4 of Fr. 16 is cited as a way of drawing an equation between poem and passion.[18] Although Page notes that the reference to Helen as exemplum here is "a commonplace device," he nevertheless works hard to divorce Fr. 16 from all literary precedent (1955b:56). Helen's crime is a crime of passion, but so is Sappho's writing of this poem. Page does not exactly approve, for the poem's weakness lies precisely in its departure from Homeric style and ethics. It is revealing to compare Page's analysis of Sappho Fr. 16 with his view of Alcaeus N1,[19] another poem on the theme of Helen at Troy, but one that takes a dimmer view of her amorous adventures. Of Alcaeus N1 Page writes: "The story of Helen and Paris is portrayed as a great misfortune to the world.

. . . It is noticeable here . . . that Epic theme and Epic style go hand in hand"
(1955b:278). Here, Page lays the stress on literary precedent; not a word is said
about what Alcaeus may think or feel. Sappho's poems are submitted to a very
different set of criteria, despite the fact that Alcaeus's poem shares many of the
motifs at work in hers, motifs that are essential features of the literary Helen:
her madness; her subjugation to Aphrodite, by whom she is diverted; her family,
abandoned in Sparta. Page, again, is less interested in Sappho's poetry than in
Sappho herself. Her poems are read, we might say, at *face value*.

To read a poem *at face value* is to reject its figurative or rhetorical status while
simultaneously submitting it to a figurative operation: anthropomorphizing it,
turning it into a portrait of the poet herself. This is the trope of *prosopopoeia:*
the "giving of a face." Prosopopeia is the principal mode of reading Sapphic
and, one might argue, all lyric poetry. De Man examines the operation of that
trope in readings of lyric in "Autobiograpy as De-Facement":

are we so certain that autobiography depends on reference, as a photograph depends
on its subject . . . ? We assume that life produces the autobiography as an act produced
its consequences, but can we not suggest, with equal justice, that the autobiographical
project may itself produce and determine the life and that whatever the writer does is
in fact determined . . . by the resources of his medium? And since . . . mimesis . . . is
one mode of figuration among others, does the referent determine the figure, or is it the
other way round . . . ? (1984:69)

It is easy to make a story out of Anactoria's absence, to hear the yearning of
the poet in lines 15–16, με νῦν Ἀνακτορί[ας ὀ]νέμναι-/ σ' οὐ] παρεοίσας
"[Which] now has put me in mind of Anactoria, far away," in Page's translation.
It is easy because the rhetorical strategies of poetic mimesis are designed to
make it easy. Sappho's poetry, I am suggesting, should be read less as a "portrait
of the artist" and more like "fragments d'un discours amoureux" ("fragments
of an amorous discourse").[20]

Barthes's *Fragments d'un discours amoureux* provides some useful directions
for a deictic reading of Sappho. In that work Barthes decomposes the language
of love, turning it into a warehouse of commonplaces culled from diverse texts
from antiquity to the present. One of these topoi is what Barthes calls "Identification": "The subject painfully identifies himself with some person (or character) who occupies the same position as himself in the amorous structure"
(1978:129). I would suggest that the concept of intertextual competition or reenactment is closely related to this notion of *identification*. Helen's status as a
mythic exemplum allows Fr. 16 to perform the work of identification: *I am to
Anactoria as Helen is to Paris*.[21] Helen, in such a structure, is clearly more than
an illustration of a private concern. To identify with Helen is to play the role of
Helen (and of Homer), to repeat that role and rival it.

Barthes is suggesting in the *Fragments* that eros is an entirely rhetorical domain. He argues, in effect, that it is impossible to say "I love you" without quotation marks (1978:147–54). This is true as well of the lyric poem, which is always a citation of prior poetic statements, but designed to sound spontaneous and original. It sounds that way as long as it is spoken (or thought of as being spoken), and it is designed to be spoken and re-spoken over and over again, and always in the present tense. If lyric competes with epic, by doing so it affirms the atemporal immediacy of the lyric moment—which is the moment of enunciation itself. We have already seen how the *imperative* + *pronoun* pair that opens Fr. 17 meets Benveniste's criteria as a shifter or deictic, and effectively detaches the poem from a historical genesis. Whatever may have preceded the μe νῦν in Fr. 16.15 ("[Which] *now* has put *me* in mind of Anaktoria,"μe νῦν Ἀνακτορί[ας ὀ]νέμναι-/ σ' οὐ), it performs the same function as Benveniste's shifter, establishing a swift scene change from mythic history to lyric presence, and referring the discourse to its own production and reproduction. Carson attributes the frequency with which such deictics recur in erotic Greek poetry to an exaggerated concern with time, due either to an archaic psychology of love or to a transformation from orality to writing (1986:118). But I would suggest that these deictics, like the *nun* (*now*) of Fr. 16 are, more importantly, the operational signals of the performative work of the lyric voice. And the pronoun *me* is a kind of subjective *sphregis,* a seal on the poem. It signs the work—but the way a statesman signs a law into effect by doing it in public, so that all can see—and gives it an explicitly "subjective" status.

Other formal features of the priamel already discussed in chapter 4, such as the ἔγω δὲ of line 3 (ἔγω δὲ κῆν' ὄτ-/ τω τις ἔραται, "but I say, it is what you love")—a personal pronoun plus adversative signaling the climax of the priamel—suggest other varieties of what we might call *lyric deictics.* Not only do the priamels that structure Fr. 16 shift the perspective away from an absolute and stable economy to a relativizing chrematistics,[22] but they set in motion a continual back-and-forth between an epic past and a lyric present. I would thus have to differ somewhat from Leah Rissman's assertion that "in mythic terms, the two sides of the comparison are the troops of the Trojan war and Helen and Paris, while on the contemporary plane, they are the Lydian army and Anactoria, beloved of Sappho" (1983:31). I accept the gap Rissman posits here between the mythic and contemporary planes, but I would move away from the residual biographical perspective (Anactoria, beloved of Sappho) toward one more in line with Benveniste. The contemporary plane, we might say, is the moment of enunciation of the poem: the eternally lyric moment. Nevertheless, Rissman has exposed something significant about the structure of Fr. 16, an essentially hybrid structure, built out of two sides, linked intimately in embrace and divided by grim contention: Helen and Troy, Anactoria and Lydia, Helen and "Sappho," Paris and Anactoria, Troy and Sparta, Lesbos and Lydia, home and exile, present and past, Sappho and Homer, lyric and epic.

Helen as Panhellenic *Khoregos*

Rather than asking, in the manner of the forensic biographer, "Who is Anactoria?" suppose we accept her as a name, a position in a rhetorical and repeatable drama. The name itself, like *Hagesichora* in Alcman's *partheneion,* confirms its own climactic position in the intersecting priamels of the poem. *Anactoria* is related to *anax,* "master" or "protector" (compare *Astyanax,* "lord of the city" in *Iliad* 6.403). She is, quite literally, the "one who leads (the chorus)." In the Homeric Hymns, *anactoria* refers to the "management of horses" (Chantraine 1968). Finally, the *anax* root, Pierre Chantraine stresses, has a long association with the Dioscuri, and this hardly seems fortuitous in a poem about Helen, horsemen, ships, and nautical distances and separations. The name of Sappho's heroine, like Alcman's *Agido* and *Astumeloisa* (Nagy 1990:347), is thus lyrically overdetermined: it is, etymologically speaking, superlative, just as Helen is superlative in epic terms.

We do not have to presume an actual choral or ceremonial origin for this poem to assert that Anactoria and the speaker are characters in a ritual scenario. There are, however, signs that point toward precisely such a ritual history. Striking connections emerge between the mythic background to Alcman 1 (in which the divinity who corresponds to Hagesichora seems to be, on at least one level, Helen, or divinities associated with her) and Sappho Fr. 16. More and more, the latter seems to function like a variant of the former or, in any case, like a reenactment of a lost or forgotten ritual close to that reenacted in Alcman 1. Let us examine for a moment Alcman's *partheneion* as an example of choral performance reenacting ritual event, and see what light may be shed thereby upon the figure of Helen in Sappho Fr. 16.[23] Alcman's poem implies the presence of two semichoruses, one praising the figure Agido, the other Hagesichora, the ultimate leader of the united chorus. The very names of these characters suggest a conventional or ritualistic position: Hagesichora, again, is literally the "leader of the chorus." Hagesichora is thus performing a mimesis, precisely in the way we have seen Helen herself performing mimeses in various literary settings. In just a moment we will turn to more specific scenes of Helen as choral leader and mimetic performer. Hagesichora, in any case, has been identified as "a local Spartan version of Helen" (346). Nagy believes a more important connection exists between Hagesichora and two local Spartan divinites, the Leukippides (meaning "white horses"; the rival choral leaders in Alcman 1 are in fact compared to competing racehorses). The figures of Agido and Hagesichora would then be "acting out, on the level of the ritual presented by the chorus, the roles of the two Leukippides." These local divinities are in turn associated with Helen and the Dioscuri.[24] Walter Burkert notes, finally, that the thematic motifs addressed in the *partheneion,* and specifically the choral references to Artemis, often conspire to project a mythic setting which appears "as a predestined occasion for rape, whether it is the Dioskouroi seizing the Leukippides or Theseus taking Helen" (1985:150).

Evidence for the various cults of Helen practiced in Archaic and Classical Greece, cited earlier, is essential to understanding how the lyric Helen may be said to reenact prior and primordial sacred dramas. Such cults existed, we know, at Therapna in Sparta (where Helen was worshiped along with Menelaus and where, according to Herodotus, a temple housed a cult image of the goddess),[25] Rhodes (where Helen was worshiped as Helen *Dendritis,* or Helen of the Trees), and Attica. Nilsson suggests that the rape of Helen is a desacralized version of the Kore and Ariadne myths,[26] and that Helen was originally a Mycenaean vegetation goddess.[27] Nagy (1990:345), who describes the choral leader as the substitute for or reenactment of a divinity or royal figure involved in cult, lists a number of literary works from the late Classical and Hellenistic periods where Helen as object of cult veneration is figured as a choral leader: *Lysistrata* 1296–321, for example, and Theocritus 18, the *Epithalamium for Helen.*

In Theocritus 18 a chorus of maidens are celebrating Menelaus's victory over his rivals for Helen's hand and at the same time lamenting the departure of the bride from their circle. Their praise of Helen is reminiscent of Sappho's encomia of departing or departed members, and of Alcman's virgin half-choirs lauding their respective leaders. In effect, it is Helen as choral leader they are celebrating:

> Girls though we are, we love to swim and run,
> To strip and smear ourselves with oil. But none
> Who gathers by Eurotas for our sport
> Dares match herself with Helen. Each falls short.
> Lovely after the night the rising dawn.
> Lovely the whitening spring when winter's gone.
> So Helen shines, golden among her peers.
> A trace-bound filly, a cypress tree that rears
> Its dark adornment over field and garden,
> Helen, the rose-flushed, graces Lacedaemon.
> None, seated at the loom, is half so deft
> As she with yarn and shuttle, or cuts a weft
> More finally woven from the crossbar strings.
>
>   (Trans. Wells 1988)

Helen's superlative beauty raises the authority of the choral leader to epic or panhellenic levels.[28] Affirming this authority both maintains the unity of the choral group (in other words, *collects*) and provokes schisms of rivalry (that is, *divides*). That paradoxical gesture of fracturing within a unified collectivity is acted out on a global scale in the Trojan war. Theocritus's maidens sing of Helen's attributes in competitive, comparative terms, just as the assertion of Helen's beauty in Sappho Fr. 16 sets up a hierarchy of competing values. Note, too, that Helen's talents as performer are emphasized, whether at the loom or at the lyre. Like Sappho herself in the words of Maximus of Tyre (Lobel and Page 1955: fr. 188), Helen is a preeminent "weaver of fictions," Σαπφὼ μυθοπλόκον (Carson 1986:170). We may recall the beginning of Sappho, Fr. 1.2, cited earlier, in which Sappho calls upon Aphrodite, παῖ Δίος δολόπλοκε, "daughter of Zeus, weaver of wiles." Aphrodite, like Helen, is a seductive and dangerous weaver, in Sappho as in Theocritus as in Homer. The very act of weaving—collecting and sorting threads, leading them in and out, up and down, fashioning interpenetrating and intersecting patterns—suggests the Platonic conception of mimetic beauty itself, a misleading and captivating flux. Finally, the latter part of Theocritus 18 appears to be an aetiology of a cult to which we have already referred: that of Helen Dendritis. A plane tree is selected and inscribed with the legend: "Worship me. I am Helen's tree." [29]

Early and late in the post-Homeric classical tradition, Helen is represented as a choral leader. As late as Virgil, we find Helen as the malevolent performer of the choral dance, from Deiphobus's perspective at least, in *Aeneid* 6. But Homer's Helen, already, has a tendency to perform her own mimesis. Helen in the *Odyssey* is always weaving, narrating, miming, deceiving, reenacting. In the *Iliad* Helen narrates the portraits of the Achaean heroes, weaves the tale of Troy at her loom, and imitates the voices of Achaean wives. Helen in the *teichoskopia* is playing the role of choral leader. The elders of Troy see her as a *khoregos* acting out the role of a divinity, a simulacrum of a goddess.

Nilsson sees Paris as a late intruder into the Helen myth, which, in this theory, represents an epic trivialization, a misreading, as it were, of a prior cult belief. Without speculating on her origins, I would like to suggest that Helen's role in the Trojan conflict makes into a panhellenic *khoregos,* and a pivotal link between epic and lyric systems. We have seen the competitive and comparative tensions at work in both choral and lyric poetry. Nagy, examining the apparently contradictory semantic fields of the term *stasis* (meaning paradoxically, on the one hand, "establishment" or "setting up," and, on the other, "division" or "strife"), and citing various myths in which the *institution* (*stasis*) of a chorus entails the *division* of a social collectivity into rival groups, asserts that the "very constitution of society, as visualized in the traditions of a polis like Sparta, is choral performance" (1990:367). Now, another crucial example of Helen linking epic and lyric forms is one that we have already treated—the *Palinode* of Stesichorus. But Nagy notes that the very figure of Stesichorus suggests a choral persona: the name means, literally, "he who sets up the chorus" (1990:422). Stesichorus's performance would thus represent an example of local lyric striving for the panhellenic status that is the prerogative of Homeric epic.

Helen, I am arguing, is a crucial figure in the elaboration of a panhellenic collectivity. Nagy's characterization of choral mimesis should be understood,

I would suggest, in connection with Socrates' eroticized dialectic and Helen's dialectical eroticism: both variations upon graft. "In sum," writes Nagy, "the ritual essence of the choral lyric performance is that it is *constitutive* of society in the very process of *dividing* it. For this reason, the concept of *stasis* is simultaneously *constitution* and *division*" (1990:367). What is this constitution and division, after all, but another instance of that paradoxical method of *collection* and *division* with which Socrates is *in love* in the *Phaedrus?* Eros in Sappho, as Carson clearly shows, is a grafting of lover and beloved, a force that both divides and conflates, something γλυκύπικρον (*glukupikron*), "bittersweet" or, more literally, "sweetbitter" (Fr. 130). That predicate is itself a word-graft and captures the tension and instability we have already seen in the erotic relation. Plato's *Phaedrus* has already told us that Socrates and Sappho are engaged in parallel pursuits, that Socrates' dialectical system of collections and divisions *is* an erotic methodology, the pursuit of a continually receding and seductive truth. To lead us toward the truth, Socrates must mislead us: weave tales, spin out metaphors and myths. Helen is the crucial figure and agency of graft, through whom "lover, beloved and the difference between them interact" (Carson 1986: 169). Helen indeed weaves fictions, and in Sappho that weaving is a way of joining past and present—and of keeping them separate.

Helen, as preeminent victim and agent of this method, forces us to make connections between poetic, erotic, and, now, political domains.[30] The Trojan war is Greece's national myth, and the rape of Helen its foundational event, the crisis that gives birth to a panhellenic identity. It is the moment both of primordial division (between, for example, Europe and Asia, as in Herodotus 1.1) and of constitution (of an Acheaean or Greek identity, as in Isocrates' *Encomium on Helen*). Kennedy suggests, in his reading of Isocrates' *Encomium,* that Helen's link to the Trojan conflict is more important than Helen herself (although it is difficult to imagine what or who that is): "the work is to be regarded as a praise of Hellenism rather than Helen throughout" (1958:80).[31] Kennedy, I believe, is right, but in a much more radical way than I think he intends. For it is indeed possible to argue that Helen is Hellenism's emblematic founder. But why? Because it is Helen's special property to destroy as she establishes, to mislead as she leads, to gather together as she divides. This is the story reenacted in all choral poetry. Understood thus as rhetorical reenactment, rather than autobiographical reference, Sappho's mimesis of erotic lyric becomes a gesture of intertextual connection rather than private effusion. Sappho's mimesis of Helen, that is, is also the reenactment, the recognition, and the reappropriation of Homer. Or perhaps it is more than that: perhaps the mimesis of Helen reenacts the very constitution (and division) of Hellenism itself.

Part 2

Helen in France

7

Idolatry

Cum inhaesero tibi ex omni me, nusquam erit mihi dolor et labor, et viva erit vita mea tota plena te.

[When I shall with my whole self cleave to Thee, I shall nowhere have sorrow, or labour; and my life shall wholly live, as wholly full of Thee.] (Trans. Watts)

— Augustine, *Confessions*

Introduction: Remembering Helen

In "Se j'ai esté lonc tens en Romanie," a *chanson courtoise,* or courtly love song, from the thirteenth century, the troubadour Raoul de Soissons (active 1243–55) resurrects the image of his beloved from afar. He is remembering her, in other words, but not only her. In order to confer upon his *dame* the greatest possible value, the troubadour remembers others, like him, who remembered before. They did not, however, remember as well as he, and because they did not remember as well as he, what they remembered is not as valuable:

> Car quant je pens a son tres douz visage,
> De mon penser aim meuz la conpaignie
> C'onques Tristan ne fist d'Iseut s'amie.
>
> . . . .
>
> Si puisse je sentir sa douce alaine
> Et reveoir sa bele contenance
> Com je desir s'amor et s'acointance
> Plus que Paris ne fist oncques Elaine!
>
> (16–18, 28–31)

> [For when I think of her face so pretty, I love the company of my thought more than Tristan did that of Iseut, his beloved. . . . . If I could feel her sweet breath and see her beautiful face again! I want her love and her company more than Paris ever did Helen's!] (Winkler 1914)

And so Helen becomes an exemplum, in a medieval French poem that, like Sappho Fr. 16, measures the value of the present by reference to the worth of the past. But can Helen truly be said to play the same role in both poems? Obviously not. Exactly what role, then, does Helen play in the *chanson courtoise?* More specifically, in a culture now removed or cut off from Greek antiquity, are we right to suspect that the classical exemplum is a sign of medieval anachronism and a mark of historical rupture? Or is it proof, on the contrary, of some kind of historicizing perspective? Can Raoul de Soissons be said to "remember" who Helen is in the way that Sappho does?[1] Does it matter if he doesn't?

I return to this poem, and to these questions, at the close of this chapter. For now, I want to suggest that this is a poem about the eroticism of the asymptotic, and that the classical allusion may be part of that asymptotic mechanism. What the speaker prizes here, it would seem, is the approach, the ever-receding spectacle, of an object or body never to be possessed. In the meantime, what the poet has instead is so many substitutes and simulacra, or what I will be calling, in this chapter, *idols:* images, dreams, memories, exempla. Helen is one of these memories. But is the memory the same as an exemplum? Such a notion would seem to clash with the conventional ways of thinking about the exemplum. In fact, we will see that the literary allusion in the medieval love poem, such as the reference here to Tristan and Iseut, or to Helen and Paris, has more than the simple utility of an analogy, for perhaps these names from the past are themselves only more substitutes and simulacra: memories on a cultural scale.[2]

L'amour de loin: Medieval Culture and Amnesia

In *The Light in Troy: Imitation and Discovery in Renaissance Poetry,* Thomas Greene compares the historical isolation of the European Middle Ages to a state of amnesia. "Just as an amnesiac recovers his identity with his memory," Greene writes, "so it is with words; we learn them as they acquire a past for us" (1982:16). The literary text that lacks what Greene calls "historical self-consciousness" is like the amnesiac who cannot even make the effort to recuperate the past because he is unaware that he has lost it:

If we examine the intertextuality of medieval poems before Dante, if we consider particularly the estrangement from antiquity they reflect, then we do not find any historical construct because the awareness of estrangement was very restricted. . . . the use of elements from Virgil and Ovid found in the *Roman de Thebes* or the *Roman d'Eneas* does not provide an etiological construct to deal with cultural discontinuity, to connect subtext with surface text; they fail to provide this because they fail to register the discontinuity. They lack historical self-consciousness just as the *Iliad* lacks it. (1982:17)[3]

That the medieval poet fails to speak out loud his estrangement from antiquity is undeniable; it is the crucial fact with which this chapter will be grappling. But does that mean that the medieval poem fails to "register" the "discontinuity" of history? Perhaps there are different ways of registering estrangement—including denying that estrangement exists. What would happen if we approached the medieval text not as confessors or psychotherapists before a mute or traumatized victim, trying to make it speak the past, but as archaeologists or geologists before a landscape in ruins, looking for traces of cataclysm and repair? To do this would mean resisting the lure of interpretive ventriloquism, the temptation to make silent stones speak the words we lend them. Reading this way will allow us to see, I hope, that if the medieval text (like the *Iliad*) lacks historical self-consciousness (something I am not contesting), it nevertheless betrays signs, not only of historical exile, but of the effort to restore its connection to the past and, moreover, to disguise that very effort. In all senses of the word, the past for the medieval poet is something that must be *fixed*.

To speak of the "discontinuity" of Western history, as Greene does, is, in fact, to point to its essential continuity, a continuity, however, now concealed or deferred or deformed. The problem with the medieval poet is his failure to acknowledge that deformity. In the traditional model outlined above, Western humanism is defined as the recognition of estrangement, the bold confrontation with rupture. Petrarch, in this paradigm, is the great modernist hero, setting out paradoxically to "retrieve" a past now recognized as irretrievable. This is, for example, the view Giuseppe Mazzotta adopts in a discussion of "Antiquity and the New Arts in Petrarch" (1991). Mazzotta focuses on Petrarch's wanderings in Rome with Giovanni Colonna, an event narrated in *Le familiari* 2.6.2. Petrarch portrays himself as a ventriloquist of stone, a confessor to the ruins around him, discerning "discontinuities at the heart of the tradition that someone like Dante would still view as a uniform reality" (Rossi and Bosso 1933, 42:54). For Mazzotta, Petrarch's poetic project emerges out of this perception of cultural passage and represents the conscious effort to suspend that passage. It is "Thought"; that is, "a suspension [Mazzotta is here playing on the root of *pensier* in the Latin *pendere*, "hang" or "suspend"], the insertion of a break in the flow of history, the effort to arrest the unseizable flight of time" (1991:63). "This in-between time, which historically we call *medium aevum*," Mazzotta concludes, "is the unavoidable, recurring time of audacious thought—which is what poetry is." [4]

I want to focus on this story of rupture and retrieval, amnesia and recollection, as another love story. Thus I begin my exploration of classical intertextuality and imitation in European vernacular literature in what may seem at first an unlikely setting: the love poetry of *troubadour* and *trouvère,* the poetry of *la fin' amor* (courtly love) that emerges at the end of the eleventh century in *l'Occitanie* and then is taken up by the poets of the north. [5] The subject of this poetry, after all, is the erotic crisis of solitude and separation, and the solace afforded by poetic performance. The poet sings of what he cannot have; that is

why he sings.[6] So goes, at least, the conventional fiction of *la fin' amor*. Em-
manuèle Baumgartner describes the erotic crisis that provides the standard narrative in courtly love poetry, and the role played by poetry in resolving that
crisis. "Distance, *the love from afar,* which the code itself creates between the
vassal-lover and the lady-sovereign, makes almost impossible, and always de-
layed . . . the joy of possession—which would spell the death of desire. The
lover can only speak desire, and the song remains his only recourse. The great
invention of these poets is in this way to have linked love and writing, love and
song" ("la distance, *l'amour de loin,* que le code lui-même crée entre l'amant
vassal et la dame souverain rend presque impossible, toujours différée, la . . .
joie de la possession, qui serait peut-être la mort du désir. L'amant ne peut que
dire le désir et le chant reste son seul recours. L'invention de ces poètes est
ainsi d'avoir lié amour et écriture, amour et chant" [Baumgartner and Ferrand
1983:10–11]). My discussion of Greek poetry in part 1 has suggested, however,
that love and poetry were conjoined in this way long before the troubadours.
Carson, exploring what she calls the "triangulation" of desire in Archaic Greek
lyric, points out that standing between the lyric lover and beloved was a necessary third party, an obstacle or rival. Distance itself is always the first rival:
"Mere space has power. *L'amour d' loonh* ('love from a distance') is what the
canny troubadours called courtly love" (1986:18).

   L'amour d' loonh also serves well, I think, as a description of the restorative,
imitative, classicizing impulses that are the larger subject of part 2 of this book.
How to possess the beloved is the question at its center. Asking it (and therefore
keeping it unanswerable) is essential to the identity of the poet and the lover
alike. Possession would spell, of course, the end of the troubadour's career. With
regard to the highly standardized conventions of *la fin' amor,* what the troubadour ultimately seeks, and is condemned forever to pursue, is *joie* (joy): in
Eugene Vance's definition, "the principle of unmediated presence between two
beings" (1975:51). (Incidentally, this is the essential principle driving all acts
of *imitatio.*) For the poet to articulate that principle is already to acknowledge
its futility: "merely to spell out *joie* . . . is already to dispel it . . . joy implies
surpassing the production of all signs in the tranquility of a silent stasis, *facie
ad faciem,* in the presence of the other." The dream of *joie* is the dream of the
perfect graft: to be *facie ad faciem* with the past.

   Because the troubadour longs for what he cannot have—according, at least,
to the prescribed narrative to which the poet adheres—he must make do instead
with substitutes and supplements: memories, images, fantasies, words, myths,
poems. All of these effectively function as relics or *idols.* Courtly love, I am
arguing here, is essentially a form of *idolatry,* a way of replacing the past with
a stock of surrogate pasts.

Courtly Love as Idolatrous Cult

Scholars have long remarked that courtly love, which regularly assumes the form of a prayer for reunion with an unattainable and abstracted beloved, is organized as a kind of cult, an imitation of Christianity. "Thus the song becomes in effect a ritual cult of the lady, a liturgy, parallel to that glorifying God," Baumgartner writes. "In the *service of love,* the lover abdicates his own will and places it in the hands of the lady, just as the mystic abandons himself to God, or as the vassal submits to his earthly lord" ("Le chant se fait ainsi rituel du culte de la dame, liturgie parallèle à celle qui magnifie Dieu. Dans le *service d'amour,* l'amant abdique sa volonté propre entre les mains de la dame, comme le mystique s'abandonne à Dieu, comme le vassal se soumet à son seigneur terrestre" [1983:10]). C. S. Lewis argues in *The Allegory of Love* that courtly love's cult of the god *Amor,* or what he terms *Frauendienst,* is more properly understood not so much as an *emulation* of Christian practice as a *parody* of it (1936:9).[7]

If courtly love resembles a cult, then its basic tenets are spelled out in Andreas Capellanus's *De arte honeste amandi* of ca. 1185, also known as the *De amore* (The art of courtly love).[8] It may be Capellanus's work that is referred to in the famous condemnatory decree issued by Etienne Tempier, bishop of Paris, on March 7, 1277 (Curtius 1953:126; Nelli 1963:247), rejecting, as one of various Thomist and neo-Aristotelian tendencies within the Faculty of Arts at the University of Paris, the doctrine of courtly love. In René Nelli's reading of the *De amore,* Capellanus elaborates a tripartite hierarchical system of love, borrowing from the Christian conception of love, Provençal poetry, Arab mysticism (see also Walsh 1982:20–21 on Arabic sources such as Avicenna), and Aristotle's reflections on friendship in the *Nicomachean Ethics* (Nelli 1953:251–53). Thus at 1.470–71 *amor purus* (pure love, spiritual love, at the top of the chain) is distinguished from both *amor mixtus* (mixed love, physical love, combined with and preceded by spiritual love) and *amor per pecuniam acquisitus* (venal love, love that is purely physical, such as libertinage, or purely prescriptive, such as marriage) (Trojel 1892:182). What the courtly love poet seeks, in general, is the second type of love, *amor mixtus.* Alfred Jeanroy characterizes it, uncertainly, as a "union almost uniquely spiritual" ("union presque uniquement spirituelle" [1934:374]). Nelli calls it, equally confusedly, a "pure, inter-sexual, love" ("amour pur inter-sexuel" [1963:252]). Looked at from this perspective, *fin' amors* would appear to be a systematic pursuit and evasion of graft: a continual substitution of metaphorical for literal unions.

Consider one metaphor that frequently recurs in courtly love poetry: that of the exchange or joining of hearts. Capellanus relies on the image in his definition of *amor purus:* "Pure love is that which joins the hearts of two lovers with universal feelings of affection" ("Et purus quidem amor est, qui omnimoda dilectionis affectione duorum amantium corda coniungit" [Trojel 1892:1.470–

71, trans. Walsh 1982:180]). Nelli suggests that the entire system of cardiac conceits (placing the heart "en gage," sending the heart as messenger, engaging it in dialogue with the eyes and the ears) functions as a kind of working mythology in the poetry of the troubadours (1963:209–10). But perhaps metaphor—the joining of what remains distinct—is the real point here, and not a means to an end. Courtly love, in other words, may be an elaborate mechanism for producing *only* metaphorical unions. "When love is reciprocal," Nelli writes, "it creates a sort of joining of the hearts" ("Quand l'amour est réciproque, il se produit une sorte de liaison des coeurs" [211]). This *liaison* Nelli calls a "sungcrasis sentimentale"; one cannot help but note the proliferation of rhetorical unions here. A citation from the poet Peyrol helps to illustrate: "No matter where my lady is, my heart is under her rule, for Love unites and enchains, even under different skies, two hearts burning for each other" ("N'importe où ma dame se trouve, mon coeur lui est toujours soumis, car *Fin'Amors* unit et enchaîne, même sous des cieux divers, deux coeurs brûlant l'un pour l'autre" [Diez 1845:157]).

Union in courtly love poetry remains metaphorical. There is no joining, except on the level of language: a succession of substitute encounters, mediated marriages, imitation bodies. Love originates, according to Capellanus, in the contemplation of sensible beauty, but its development depends upon the transformation of what has been contemplated into a system of replicated images:

Nam quum aliquis videt aliquam aptam amori et suo formatam arbitrio, statim eam incipit concupiscere corde; postea vero quotiens de ipsa cogitat, totiens eius magis ardescit amore. . . . Postmodum mulieris incipit cogitare facturas, et eius distinguere membra susosque. . . . Postquam vero ad hanc cogitationem plenariam devenerit . . . sed statim procedit ad actum; statim enim iuvamen habere laboret et internuntium invenire. (Walsh 1982:1.1.9–12)

[For when a man sees some woman fit for love . . . he begins at once to lust after her in his heart; then the more he thinks about her the more he burns with love. . . . Presently he begins to think about the fashioning of the woman and to differentiate her limbs. . . . after he has come to this complete mediation . . . he proceeds at once to action; straightaway he strives to get a helper and to find an intermediary.] (Parry 1990:29)

Meditation and mediation from afar: this is an apt description not only of the courtly lover, separated from the beloved, but of the medieval poet, separated from the past. Both are idolaters: image-hunters and -gatherers. Bernart de Ventadorn (1966) gives us a textbook case in line with Capellanus's analysis—for example, in "Tant ai mo cor ple de joya" ("My heart is so full of joy," ll. 25–30): "Let her make me keep my distance from her love—there's still one thing I'm sure of: I have conquered nothing less than her beautiful image. Cut off from her like this I have such bliss" ("De s'amistat me reciza! / Mas be n'ai fiansa, / que sivals eu n'ai conquiza / la bela semblansa. / Et ai ne a ma deviza / tan de benanansa" [Goldin 1983:131]).[9] The courtly lover, cut off from what he loves, depends upon the very rupture he laments. Courtly love in this sense is always grafted, constituted by rupture and elision. And because the real is forever distanced and deferred, the troubadour must settle for a reconstituted real: an idol or image (*semblansa*).

For the Middle Ages, Augustine is the authority on the seductiveness of the image. In *City of God* 4.30, Augustine fulminates against idolatrous worship and the depiction of gods in epic battles and genealogies. Regarding Lucilius Balbus's veneration of images in *De natura deorum,* he asserts: "He makes himself also an accomplice, for although he tries with all his eloquence to extricate himself from their toils, he found it necessary to worship them" ("inplicat et ipsum, qui, quantolibet eloquio se in libertatem nitatur evolvere, necesse habebat ista venerari" [trans. Greene 1963:115]). The possibility of somehow salvaging these images from the pagan past is obviously one of the great problems for the medieval Christian poet. Augustine does not escape that problem.[10] Henri Marrou phrases the question in its Augustinian form: "Can't one borrow from it a certain number of elements, of useful materials?" ("Ne pouvait-on pas lui emprunter un certain nombre d'éléments, de matériaux utiles?" [1958:390]). Allegorical exegesis is Augustine's principal strategy, as it is for most medieval humanists before and after him.[11] Exegesis of this sort involves a linguistic purification and compartmentalization of the pagan past: "Little by little," Marrou suggests, speaking of the medieval authors who had grown accustomed to the allegorical method, "they had learned to analyze the content of ancient culture and dissociate its elements, to break the links which had joined those elements to paganism, to purify them, repossess them, use them." ("Peu à peu on avait appris à analyser le contenu de la culture antique, à en dissocier les éléments, à briser les liens qui les rattachaient au paganisme, à les purifier, à les reprendre, à les utiliser" [393]). By leaching from the pagan myth its theological content, allegorical exegesis, ironically enough, represents a form of linguistic idolatry.

For the problem of idolatry is both solved and reinstated by language itself. Language at once permits us to approach the divine and prevents us from reaching it.[12] In the *Confessions,* Augustine says that material creation itself is another obstacle, a kind of static or screen between the human and the divine, a chorus eternally proclaiming: "We did not make ourselves, but he who abides for ever made us" (trans. Pine-Coffin 1961:198). Creation means authorship. Augustine, his readers have long pointed out, is a semiotician; he reads the universe as a text, a sign system proclaiming its referentiality and pointing to that which alone grounds it and gives it meaning: God as transcendental signifier and signified.[13] What refers here (the visible or material world) both points to and conceals the referent. With the Fall as the fundamental fact, the "remedy was plain," Peter Brown writes (1967:262), and he cites Augustine's *Sermons* 22.7: "For the meantime, let the Scriptures be the countenance of God." The remedy is also the problem. A new idolatry here takes the place of the old.

Language both points to God and shuts him out. As in the epigraph to this chapter, God is that with which man longs to unite. God is the principle of unification and synthesis. Thus when Augustine turns in *Confessions* 10.29 to the issue of continence, or the adherence to God's law, he writes: "By continence we are collected together and brought to the unity from which we disintegrated into multiplicity" ("per continentiam quippe colligimur et redigimur in unum, a quo in multa defluxiumus" [trans. Chadwick 1991:202]). But this notion of collection and unification is also a literary method—scriptural reference, for example, represents the binding principle of the *Confessions* itself—and one which makes Augustinian prose a synthesis of classical and Christian: "Echoes of the Christian Scriptures . . . could be heard, winding in and out of the more accustomed classical phrases of a master-rhetor in the old tradition" (Brown in Sheed 1993:xi–xii).

Referentiality is central to John Freccero's discussion of Augustine in "The Fig Tree and the Laurel: Petrarch's Poetics" (1975). For Augustine, only God provides an "escape from the infinite referentiality of signs" (Freccero 1975: 36). Augustine elaborates this theory of signs, Freccero notes, in *De doctrina Christiana* 1.2. In that text the relation between referentiality and idolatry is made explicit. All signs but God *refer,* according to Augustine; only God is *referred to.* God alone is to be enjoyed, *frui,* while all other things are to be used, *uti* (38). What would it mean then, to deny the referentiality of the sign, to enjoy it in and of itself? It would mean idolatry. Idolatry, for Augustine, is a "fetishization" or "reification" of the sign, a "deceptive attempt to render presence" (37). Freccero contends that Petrarchan poetics depends upon such fetishization, and that more generally "idolatry, however repugnant to an Augustinian moralist, is at the linguistic level the essence of poetic autonomy" (40).

This last claim is essential to my reading of medieval love poetry. I would emend it, however: idolatry is also the essence of erotic autonomy. Poetic *and* erotic autonomy is what the troubadour claims in the *le grand chant courtois.* A number of critics have focused recently on courtly love as a semiotic enterprise carried out by means of an erotic fiction. Their work attempts to reverse the long tradition of reading troubadour lyric as an erotic enterprise carried out by means of a semiotic fiction. Julia Kristeva, in her 1983 discussion of courtly love in *Histoires d'amour,* maintains a difficult balancing act when she asks: "Is love a metaphor for the song, or the song an image of love?" ("Est-ce l'amour une métaphore du chant, ou le chant—une image de l'amour?" [268]).[14] Eugene Vance argues that the frustration of unrequited love is a fiction sustained by a conspiracy of poet and audience seeking the satisfaction of "readerly" —as opposed to corporeal— "desire": "if I were really to enjoy that lady . . . the *je* of the singing poet and his audience would instantly die: semen and ink cannot flow in the same vein, If I may abuse a profoundly medieval analogy" (1985:101). Stephen Nichols speaks of Guillaume IX's "ambition to make the poet's movement from *trobar* [composition, invention] to *chantar* [performance], a celebration of the body's quest for pleasure, concur with the audience's quest for the pleasure of the song" (1989:35).[15]

The new concern with the performative aspect of *le grand chant courtois* bears some striking similarities to recent approaches to Classical Greek love poetry (as discussed in chapter 6, "Deixis"). In both cases poetry is read as rhetoric instead of confession. Both Kristeva and Paul Zumthor offer performative analyses of *troubadour/trouvère* lyric based on a Benveniste-style approach to the personal pronoun. The third-person pronoun standing in for *la dame* may be said to have two different meanings, Kristeva argues (1983:268); on the one hand, it has its "signification littérale" ("literal signification"), its "objet référentiel" ("referential object")—that is, *la dame* herself, and, on the other hand, it may be a "signe" ("sign") of the song itself, "referring only to joy" ("se référant à la seule joie"). For Zumthor in general, *la dame* is a pretext for song. In "The *I* of the Song and the *Me* of the Poet among the First *Trouvères* 1180–1220" ("Le *je* de la chanson et le *moi* du poète chez les premiers trouvères 1180–1220"), Zumthor writes of the first-person pronoun: "It is remarkable that these *I* and *me* do not refer back to any referent included in the text; they designate only . . . the speaker . . . the singer (whom we assume to be changeable) of the song" ("Il est remarquable que ces *je* et *moi* ne renvoient à aucun référent inclus dans le texte: ils désignent purement . . . le locuteur . . . le chanteur (que l'on peut supposer variable) de la chanson" [1974:12]).[16] Like Kristeva, Zumthor emphasizes the pronoun's role in making the chanson an act of music rather than language, a self-referring incantation rather than an object-referring narration; he speaks of the modulation of the personal pronoun, "I-me-I-me, the untiring and repetitive cry of radical desire, the simple affirmation of life in and through song" ("je-moi-je-moi, le cri inlassablement répétitif d'un désir radical, simple affirmation de vie dans et par le chant" [14]). What this means, in effect, is that, like the Greek rhapsode performing Homeric epic, the troubadour is essentially a rhetorical role, a dramatic position to be filled over and over again. Nagy, as we might expect, makes precisely this connection in "The Homeric Nightingale and the Poetics of Variation in the Art of the Troubadour": "The rhapsode is a recomposed performer: he becomes recomposed into Homer every time he performs Homer"; similarly, for the *jongleur* to "perform the song" is "to recompose it, to change it, that is, *move* it" (1996:16). As in the poetry of Sappho, then, we might say that the Provençal *jongleur* always grafts himself into the position of *troubadour*.

Another feature of the performative model of Provençal lyric should retain our interest. A number of critics have begun approaching troubadour poetry as essentially oral-performative poetry, like Archaic Greek epic. The performative theory here acts as a response to a different sort of idolatry at work in modern readings of courtly love lyric. Those readings often seek to identify a definitive or "authentic" text among the variant forms that generally exist for any troubadour poem. Critics who have promoted the oral-performative model, such as Zumthor and Bernard Cerquiglini, stress the futility of such a search and the distinctive roles (as least rhetorical roles) played by the *troubadour/trouvère* or "composer," and the *jongleur* or "singer." [17] In this view there is no *chanson,* only versions, performed by different *jongleurs.* Performative critics instead stress Provençal lyric as *mouvance,* a term that lyric itself uses to refer to its own dynamic variability, its dissemination or movement. Zumthor uses *mouvance* as a term to describe the essential fluidity and instability of the *chanson,* which he characterizes as an oral phenomenon (1972:65–75). Troubadour lyric, in this approach, needs to be thought of as a graft of alternative texts: what Cerquiglini calls "variance." For Cerquiglini, Nagy asserts, "medieval writing does not produce variants: it is variance" (1996:10).

The characterization of the courtly love song as a self-referring and autonomous sign-system is mirrored by Freccero's discussion of Petrarch. Petrarch's *Rime sparse* seeks to be a perfectly original and absolutely self-contained work: a set of signs without reference to any "anterior logos," as Freccero puts it. This makes Petrarch's poetry "idolatrous in the Augustinian sense" (1975:38). The laurel—central and emblematic signifier of the *Rime*—is a circular sign, referring both to the love-object and to the poet who authors it. Freccero's discussion assumes, however, that Petrarch engages in an implicit dialogue with Augustine as his precursor throughout the *Rime sparse,* and indeed, throughout Petrarch's career. Behind Petrarch's laurel stands Augustine's fig tree. We are reminded of the passage in the *Secretum* where Augustine reproaches Petrarch for his egotism, enjoining him to let the fig tree—site of Augustine's conversion in the *Confessions*—replace the laurel. The fig tree is Augustine's way of moving from autobiography to allegory; only incidentally a landmark in Augustine's personal history, it is also a sign offering the pattern of salvation for all Christians. This is a pattern of repetition and reference. Freccero calls Augustine's conversion a "gloss" on previous "textual" moments. Augustine, under the shade of the fig tree, hears children's voices and remembers Ponticianus's story of the sinner who read the Word of God and was converted. Augustine reads. Augustine is converted. Thus the fig tree "stands for a tradition of textual anteriority." Augustine's story makes sense only by reference to Ponticianus, whose story makes sense only by reference to Genesis and The Text which has no anteriority (37). Augustine's conversion, writes Freccero, "demands that there be both a continuity and a discontinuity between the self that is and the self that was" (36).

Petrarch's *Rime sparse,* on the other hand, never moves beyond conversion. Its speaker never leaves the shade of the laurel and refuses to acknowledge (explicitly at least) any anterior narrative (in chapter 11, "Miscegenation," we will see Valéry trying to make a similar refusal).[18] Here conversion seeks to remains idiosyncratic or self-referring, constituted solely by the figures of Petrarch and

Laura. It is, in other words, an idolatrous conversion. And yet the fig tree stands behind the laurel, just as Beatrice stands behind Laura. Despite Petrarch's attempts to exclude referentiality, the shadows of other poets lurk throughout the *Rime:* of Dante, for example, and of the poets of the classical past. Freccero goes on to identify Petrarch's rivalry with Dante as the first example, in Western culture, of Bloom's anxiety of influence (1975:40). It is neither the first nor the last time we will see a critic attempt, somewhat anxiously, to locate the first example of that anxiety. Dante's Beatrice is, above all, a mediator; Petrarch, on the other hand, would have his Laura remain a surface, a "pure signifier." (This motif in both Petrarch and Ronsard is taken up in more detail in chapter 10, "Cosmetics.") In the image of Beatrice unveiled in the last canto of the *Purgatorio,* we see the familiar medieval topos of the veil, standing for the relation of sign to referent. But in Petrarch 52, "Non al suo amante più Diana piacque" ("Not so much did Diana please her lover"), the poet watches Laura take off her veil and wash it (trans. Durling 1976:122). This is a very "real" veil, detached, fetishized, a sign "wrenched free of its semantic content," and one that "must be read as an affirmation of poetic presence" (Freccero 1975:39–40). And yet there is no escaping referentiality. Freccero concludes by conflating the semiotic and erotic fictions he has been separating:

> all of the fictions of courtly love have their semiotic justifications: the love must be idolatrous for its poetic expression to be autonomous; the idolatry cannot be unconflicted, any more than a sign can be completely referential if it is to communicate anything at all. Spiritual struggle stands for the dialectic of literary creation, somewhere between opaque carnality and transparent transcendency. . . . Finally, it might be suggested that the illicit or even adulterous nature of the passion has its counterpart in the "anxiety of influence": communication demands that our signs be appropriated; poetic creation often requires that they be stolen. (40)

I would say that it *always* requires that they be stolen.[19] Freccero confirms our suspicions that Petrarch's conversion is meant to stand for a literary as much as an erotic conversion, an absolute rupture with the past and an escape from all signifying contingency. At the same time, the narration of Petrarch's guilty, self-indulgent, and frustrated fixation upon that conversion throughout the *Rime* betrays its second-hand nature: the debt it owes to other conversions, other authors, other texts.

Textual Anteriority and Images of Graft in Courtly Love Poetry

Long before Petrarch, the *chanson courtoise* performs a similar sleight-of-hand, carefully staging its own poetic autonomy, carefully hiding its own poetic anteriority backstage. Here, in our earliest examples of European vernacular verse, a poetry of illicit love is the same as a love of illicit poetry. We do not have to wait for Petrarch to find a poet seeking refuge from the referentiality and anteriority of history. Long before Petrarch, poets in France are guiltily transplanting poetic themes from the past. Where there is guilt, there is graft, its symptom and cure.

In "The Promise of Performance: Discourse and Desire in Early Troubadour Lyric" (1984), Nichols discusses a poem by the twelfth-century troubadour Marcabru as a thematized contest between competing voices of originality and tradition—a contest that is elaborated in an image of graft. By skillfully moving from highly conventional topoi to less conventional ones, or by combining topoi in ways that do not finally work, Marcabru's "Al departir del brau tempier" succeeds in narrating its own ambiguous relation to the early "founders" of a genre from which it descends. In the beginning the poem adheres self-consciously to the familiar conventions, but then it abruptly veers, promoting itself as something new. The first stanza opens with a highly conventional image of the natural world in springtime, full of promise (as springtime generally is, in the courtly cliché), and complete with "willows and elders" ("sauzes et saucx") —trees that cannot normally be cultivated, and that supply the poem's refrain. It is only at the very end of the first stanza (line 8) that the voice of the speaker intervenes explicitly, disrupting the illusion of mimesis, and declaring his intention to make a *vers,* a poem: "I am minded to make a poem" ("Suy d'un vers far en cossirer"). Mimesis now becomes an intertextual or artificial affair. In the second stanza we move from a wilderness to an orchard, the very figure of nature as artifice or intervention. The image of the graft, above all, suggests the possibility—and yet the impossibility—of realizing the promise and potential of the first stanza:

> Cossiros suy d'un gran vergier
> Ont a de belhs plansos mans lucs;
> Gent sont l'empeut e l frugs bacus,
> Selh qu'esser degran sordegier,
> Fuelhs e flors paron de pomier,
> Son al fruchar sautz' e saucs.
>
> (9–14)

> [I am concerned about a great orchard where there are beautiful saplings all about: the grafts are fine and the fruit fleshy; those (trees) that ought to be worse appear to flower and leaf like an apple tree; but at harvest time they are rather like willows and elders.] (Nichols 1984:99)

The first stanza is essentially metaphorical, according to Nichols; in the second, we have moved into an allegorical realm in which the promises of metaphor fail to bear fruit. The disjunction between these two modes is itself figured, that is, in the image of failed graft. Instead of apples, we have only sterile willows and elders, trees that do not belong in an orchard. The incompatibility between metaphor and allegory thus dramatizes for Nichols the poet's own attempted rupture with the voices of the past, and suggests the notion of failed promise or continuity that is the underlying theme of the poem. Marcabru's allegory "short-circuits because an antithetical figurative language has been grafted on, to use the image of the stanza. Or, rather, the allegory fails because the palimpsest has not been sufficiently forceful" (1984:100). (Nichols's language here displays an ironic repetition typical of critical efforts to expose the metaphorical structure of graft, for in moving from the image of the graft to the palimpsest, Nichols thereby replays the figurative grafting he is attempting to describe.) The graft here is too openly displayed, the seam too visible. One might locate it formally in the chiastic transition from the concluding line of the first stanza to the opening line of the second, from "Suy d'un vers far en cossirer" to "Cossiros suy d'un gran vergier," the *cossirer–Cossiros* pair privileging the role of poetic intention, doomed to failure, *vergier–vers* suggesting the distance and distinction between nature and mimesis. But through the image of the sterile graft, Marcabru's poem succeeds, ironically, in representing its own ambition to be at once perfectly original and perfectly conventional.[20]

Marcabru's orchard provides a rare moment where the graft is openly exposed to view. "Tout autresi con l'ente fet venir," by Thibaut de Champagne (active 1230–60), is another poem that thematizes its own grafts, its own strategies for capitalizing upon the past.[21] At the start of its second *laisse*, the speaker exclaims: "Would to god that, to cure my sorrow, She were Thisbe, for I am Piramus" ("Pleust a Dieu, por ma dolor garir, / Qu'el fust Tisbe car je sui Piramus!" [ll. 11–12, trans. Brahney 1998:96–101]). Here the authenticity of the troubadour's passion is guaranteed by the reference to a classical exemplum and yet appears to fall short of it. This is a rhetorical device to which I return in the next section. Thibaut's chant begins, however, with a vegetative conceit that insists upon the proper *positioning* of the lover:

> Tout autresi con l'ente fet venir
> Li arrousers de l'eve qui chiet jus,
> Fet bone amor nestre et croistre et florir
> Li ramenbrers par coustume et par us.
> D'amors loial n'iert ja nus au desus,
> Ainz li couvient au desouz maintenir.
>
> (1–6)

> [Just as falling water
> Makes the grafted scion grow,
> So does remembrance give birth to true love
> And make it grow and flower through habit and use.
> No one ever overcomes true love,
> Thus one must be content to stay under its spell.]
>
> (Brahney 1998:97)

That position is one of submission: submission to the memory, the image, the idol of desire. The graft will not take, will not bear fruit, if it is not constantly tended and nourished by memory, by the unceasing return to the source. It is the ideal position for the poet building something new out of the remnants of the old. But the artifice and intervention implicit in the graft are, as we might expect, elided; what is stressed here is the effortless fluidity of memory, something as natural as water falling. Thibaut's image of graft provides us with an early European paradigm of imitation as both continuity and discontinuity.

Medieval Poetry and the Currency of Love

More often, however, graft in courtly love is less open to view, and the troubadour relies on a hidden economy, a covert corruption of the sign. Graft as semiotic self-sufficiency and/or debt is the implicit subject of Vance's "Love's Concordance: The Poetics of Desire and the Joy of the Text" (1975). Vance here treats the *troubadour/trouvère* as both a historical product and a self-historicizing subject. He accomplishes this by linking courtly love to two concurrent historical movements: the spread of writing in the vernacular and the rise of monetary finance. Vance's theory finds confirmation in Henri Pirenne's *Economic and Social History of Medieval Europe,* which points to the increasing appropriation in the twelfth century of coinage, or what Pirenne in another work calls the "monetary prerogative" (Pirenne 1937:112), by monarchs who were beginning to replace feudal lords.[22] We know that *courtoisie* emerged within the economic culture of feudalism (Bloch 1961:305–11).[23] Although money played a role in financial transactions in Europe as early as the ninth century, commercial exchanges at this time were extremely limited, for the "economy of the domain is a natural economy," or a closed market.[24] With the severing of the Eastern and Western Empires, gold disappeared as an instrument of exchange (Pirenne 1903:106). Perhaps the most significant event of the Carolingian reform was the usurpation of coinage by the state and the return to (silver) monometallism (107). With the disintegration of the Carolingian Empire, however, Charlemagne's monetary reforms remained in place. By the twelfth century, new coins were being minted by monarchs. Bloch speaks of a veritable economic revolution between 1050 and 1250 and points to a rapid increase in currency and circulation (1966:70). For Pirenne, the clearest sign of economic growth and the revival of trade in twelfth-century France was Louis IX's creation of the *gros tournois* and the *gros parisis* in 1266: "These two coins immediately spread all over Europe, just as Gothic art and the literature of chivalry and courtesy were spreading from France at the same time" (1903:114).[25]

For both Pirenne and Vance, money and poetry are mutually equivalent or homologous semiotic systems. Vance characterizes the *chanson courtoise* as a place where the first vernacular authors confront the authority of textual tradition. At a moment in European history when secular vernacularization was beginning to assert itself against the long textual tradition of Latinity, the issue of authorial presence suddenly acquired a great deal of urgency. For Vance, with the new importance of writing in the twelfth century came a new and diachronic understanding of history: the conception of a *"modernitas* that marked a cleavage from the authorial past" (1975:42). Courtly love poetry would, for Vance, contain the fossilized record of this new, vernacular author, struggling to be born. Vance sees medieval erotic lyric as "the earliest secular text to be marked decisively by the conditions of its own textuality" (42). These assertions can be linked to Cerquiglini's and Zumthor's arguments for an essentially oral-performative basis for early Provençal lyric. By the end of the twelfth century, we are to assume, the oral-performative model has already become obsolete, a now-rhetorical model embedded in a written system that has superseded it.

As secular writing rose in twelfth-century France, commerce revived. Central to that revival was the liberation of money, so to speak, as an autonomous, circulating, self-referring entity detached from its origins in labor. This monetary revolution is not entirely distinct from that transpiring in the domain of letters, and treating these issues as separate may be anachronistic. After all, Vance points out, medieval writers tended to treat money, too, as a sign-system, as a species of language. The important change to take note of is the shift, within this language, from reference to self-reference. Previously, the " 'referentiality' of a piece of money was only the system of currency itself. By the end of the twelfth century, money had not only become the mediator for all other manifestations of need or desire; it had finally substituted itself as a primary object of desire" (1975:44). This was a shift toward which the ecclesiastical authorities were hostile. The Church did not admit the auto-referentiality of money. As a sign, money—stamped with name and value—was supposed to be fixed, stable, like language itself. Hence the condemnation of usury, profit, hoarding, inflation, and graft, so analogous to the traditional complaints made against rhetoric: "rhetoric as an inflation of signs, rhetorical tropes as substitutions of the proper value of signifiers with what is improper, the practice of rhetoric as a lucrative (hence reprehensible) art, and so forth." If this sounds familiar, it is because we have already explored this analogy in chapter 4, "Speculation," in our discussion of Aristotle's writings on money. In the twelfth century, in any case, both money and texts had begun to circulate freely. The vernacular lyric poem, like the coin, was now detached from an absolute Origin. Instead of a gold standard and a transcendental signifier grounding the system, what we encounter is a free-floating system of differences. The name for this free-market system in textual terms is intertextuality. Poetry, like money, became an arbitrary system of differences, its value entirely a function of internal, reciprocal relations, its meaning subject to instability and inflation. Think of the twelfth-century troubadour, then, as a ruthless entrepreneur dealing in the commodity of meaning, and seeking to inflate his profits by all available means.

Profiting from the Past: Grafting the Mythic Exemplum

One of the most effective mechanisms for turning a profit on a poem is an allusion to a mythic referent or exemplum. I rely here on Vance's conception of *la chanson courtoise* as a radically autonomous and self-referring semiotic system. But while I would agree that the troubadour profits all he can from a textual economy that, ideally, is grounded in no extratextual referent, I would argue that he retains a persistent nostalgia for such a referent. In the economy of courtly love, the preferred currency is the coinage of the mythic and erotic past. Citing the name of the mythic hero as *exemplum* of the past can be a quick way, in other words, for the poet/profiteer to make a lot of money.[26]

Curtius defines the *exemplum* or *paradeigma* as an "interpolated anecdote serving as an example" (1953:59). There are at least two things to take note of here: the act of interpolation itself and the function of the interpolation. Curtius suggests that this function is above all edification. I would suggest another function that has not perhaps been sufficiently appreciated. Perhaps the point of the exemplum is interpolation itself. This would mean, in other words, that the exemplum is a double interpolation, or, to put it another way, that the fact of interpolation is far more significant than its content. Exempla are rhetorically useful because they are ruptures in the text, intrusions from the past. What is interesting about J. T. Welter's comprehensive catalogue in *L'exemplum dans la littérature du moyen âge* is that the more specific he tries to be—the more examples he gives, one might say—the less specific the content of the exemplum appears:

Celui-ci comprenait, d'après les compilateurs mêmes des receuils d'exempla, non seulement les historiettes et les légendes *d'origine* sacrée et profane, les anecdotes *extraites de* l'histoire *et de* l'antiquité classique et du Moyen Age ou *empruntées aux* souvenirs de l'auteur . . . mais encore les fables et les contes orientaux et occidentaux, les récits plaisants, les moralités ou les descriptions *tirées des* bestiaires ou des traités d'histoire naturelle, bref tout le fond narratif et descriptif du passé et du présent. (1927:20; my italics)

[[Exempla] included, even according to the compilers of collections of exempla, not only stories and legends of sacred and profane *origin,* anecdotes *taken from* history, both *from* classical and medieval history or *borrowed from* the author's memories . . . but also fables and tales from the West and the East, entertaining narratives, edifying lessons and descriptions *taken from* bestiaries or from treatises in natural history, in short the entire narrative and descriptive background of the past and the present.]

In other words, everything is an exemplum (which itself suggests a variation of Derrida's assertion that all writing is in essence a citation). As the italicized passages emphasize, what is important about the exemplum is not what it is, but where it comes from—that is, the fact that it comes from elsewhere.

Things become even more complicated, however, when the exemplum in question is an "exemplary figure" (the *eikon* or *imago*). Curtius characterizes the exemplary figure as the "incarnation of a quality" (1953:59–60). Quintilian, he notes, recommends that the orator have at hand a ready stock of exempla borrowed from myth. Helen, of course, has been a favorite exemplary figure in post-Homeric literature, but her role as persistent *eikon* or *imago* should give us pause. Helen, we recall, is never stable as a referent; she is always an "incarnation of a quality." Perhaps the exemplary figure always functions in the same way, as quality made incarnate, as *logos* become body. There is an intimate connection, I am suggesting, between exemplarity and idolatry. The exemplum is an idol, material language invested with the ideal. The idol, of course, is by definition a fiction. And as with the idol, the exemplum "works" precisely to the extent that its ideality is purely conventional.

The exemplum in troubadour poetry appears most commonly in what Paolo Cherchi calls "asseverating adynata" of the form *A* (the speaker) is "plus . . . que," "more . . . than" *B* (the exemplary figure) (1994:118). Bernart de Ventadorn (1966) concludes the stanza cited earlier, from "Tant ai mo cor ple de joya," with the claim: "I have more pain of love than had Tristan the lover, who experienced so much pain for Isolde the blonde" ("Plus trac pena d'amor / de Tristan l'amador, / que n sofri manhta dolor / per Izeut la blonda" [ll. 45–58, trans. Cherchi 1994:119]). Helen is a frequent choice for such exemplary comparisons, as in these lines from a song attributed to Arnaut Daniel: "Such is (the lady) I like that I get more joy from it than Paris got from Helen; yes that Paris of Troy" ("tal m'abelis / don eu ai plus de joia / non ac Paris, de Lena, sel de Troia" [trans. Cherchi 1994:164n87]).[27] In this structure the exemplum may simply be a form of rhetorical hyperbole. That Bernart suffers more than Tristan is, Cherchi argues, "an *adynaton,* because it is not possible to suffer more than Tristan did: his sorrows are written in the *historia,* and have attained the exemplarity of myth" (119). One may question whether the literary exemplum is impossible to surpass. The crucial point here, however, is that the exemplum is impossibly distant, coming, as it were, from infinitely far away. And that, perhaps, is the point. For given this distance, Bernart is admitting—without saying it out loud, without perhaps "wanting" to say it or "meaning" to say it—that he is estranged not just from his lady, but from the past. At the same time, Bernart's boast is a way of nullifying that estrangement. *Grand chant courtois* can thus be understood as mimetic substitution in this sense: as a repetition and a reenactment, in the manner of Classical Greek monody or choral poetry, of the amorous and literary exploits of the past. In the *grand chant* of Thibaut de Champagne and Raoul de Soissons, for example, the poet regularly validates his rhetorical claims upon the object of his desire by citing mythic or antique paradigms. The allure of the beloved, like Helen on the walls of Troy, sets in motion a competition or comparison with anterior objects of desire, a proliferation of analogies and metaphors that serves to fix the moment of poetic enunciation in a hyperbolized present (too often read as naïve timelessness). The effect (whether deliberate or unwitting) is to intensify, not erase, the ruptures and distances of history.

Sometimes this intertextual competition is staged explicitly. Thibaut de Champagne is a master at using the exemplum in his performances. The exemplum may be drawn from old French sources or classical Greek and Roman texts; the important thing is that it signifies a past now infinitely distant and distinct from the performative present. In Thibaut's "Ausi conme unicorne sui," for example, the deployment of the love-as-battle analogy and an exemplum borrowed from the *chanson de geste* tradition leads to the kind of lyric–epic contest we saw in Sappho: "Who could bear the grief / And the assaults of these three (Fair Seeming, Beauty, and Danger, Love's doorkeepers)? / Never were Roland or Olivier / Victorious in such hard battles" ("Qui porroit souffrir les tristors / Et les assauz de ces huisiers? / Onques Rollans ne Oliviers / Ne vainquirent si fors estors" [ll. 28–31, trans. Brahney 1998]). In "Pour conforter ma pesance" (Brahney 1998:26–29), an exemplum borrowed from Greek antiquity functions similarly: "In order to ease my pain / I am making a song. / It will be good if it helps me, / For Jason, / He who won the fleece, / Never had such penance" ("Pour conforter ma pesance / faz un son. / Bons ert se il m'en avance, / Car Jason, / cil qui conquist le toison, / n'ot pas si grief penitence" [ll. 1–6]). It may be, as some critics have suggested, that Thibaut's use of exempla is strikingly "original," [28] but originality is not really the point here. Rather, exempla provide a way of tying the poet's performance to a prestigious past and simultaneously of outdoing it.[29]

In the early thirteenth-century *descort* "La douce pensée" (Huet 1912:61–63), *chansonnier* Gautier de Dargies valorizes his beloved through the technique of the *blason* and builds up to an antique-epic term functioning very much as the priamel cap did in Classical Greek lyric: "She's my lady and my joy, and all my wealth. Indeed, without her, why even try to rival Hector?" ("C'est ma dame et ma joie / Et mon riche tresor. / Certes je ne voudroie / Sanz li valoir Hector" [ll. 19–22]). We have seen how Helen as a figure of epic beauty generated in Greek lyric a rhetoric of comparison and competition, a lyric present positioning itself in relation to an epic past. Similarly, referring to the classical past in courtly love poetry makes that poetry a site of remembrance and recovery as much as amnesia. It is not clear that Gautier knows exactly who Hector is. What is clear, and what is important, is that Gautier makes a pretense of knowing. That makes Hector an important ally for Gautier's literary project by turning him into a literary and erotic rival.

Another poem by Thibaut, "Li rossignox chante tant" ("The nightingale sings so fully"), demonstrates the mythic exemplum's centrality to the rhetorical claims of the courtly love poet. Much of this poem is staged as a succession of exempla borrowed from antiquity, both classical and biblical. Thus Thibaut announces: "Never has there been haughtiness as great / As that of Julius toward Pompey, / Yet my lady has even more for me / Who die desiring" ("Onques fierté n'ot si grant / vers Pompee Julius / que ma dame n'en ait plus / vers moi, qui muir desirrant" [ll. 15–18, trans. Brahney 1998]). Thibaut offers the Roman exemplum as unsurpassable, only to suggest that he has surpassed it. A moment later he returns to this comparative mode, moving through a medley of exotic analogues, exempla borrowed from the past, the foreign, or the animal:

> Je ne cuit pas que serpent
> n'autre beste poigne plus
> que fet Amors au desus;
> trop par sont li coup pesant.
> Plus tret souvent que Turs ne Arrabiz,
> n'onques oncor Salemons ne Daviz,
> ne s'i tindrent ne qu'uns fox d'Alemaigne.
>
> (ll. 29–35)

> [I do not think that the serpent
> Or any other animal strikes
> As fiercely as does Love;
> Her blows are exceedingly heavy.
> She strikes more steadily than a Turk or an Arab,
> And not even Solomon or David,
> Or a madman from Germany could withstand the assault.]
>
> (Trans. Brahney 1998)

Let us return to the poem with which this chapter opened. We are perhaps better equipped now to appraise the role that Helen could play in troubadour poetry. In Raoul de Soisson's "Se j'ai este lonc tens en Romanie," Paris and Helen serve, we can see, as foils or priamels allowing the poet to magnify the prestige of a lyric present. Feeling greater passion must mean writing better poetry, or so this poetry would have us believe. The troubadour dwells not so much on the woman he loves as on the pleasure and pain of his own meditation upon her, a meditation that is built into the poem as its subject and, above all, in its emphasis upon re-viewed images (*penser, reveoir*). Those images are only substitutes, imitations that resemble what the poet cannot possess. Poetic technique can also suggest this focus on resemblance, as when Raoul rhymes *Elaine* with *alaine*. The troubadour's verse presents itself, then, as the final simulacrum of an irretrievable original. Citing the erotic exemplum, to return to the economic mode we have been emphasizing, is like inserting a coin in a mythic jukebox. (Helen as coin figures prominently in the discussion of Sappho Fr. 16 in chapter 4.) The songs in such a machine are powerful, familiar, nostalgic shortcuts to cultural memories of the past (even if those memories are no longer one's

own). This insertion of the coin is a form of graft: a quick link to the prestige
of the past.

Grafting Helen: A Medieval Zeuxis

We began this chapter with an image of amnesia. Helen may function effectively in medieval poetry precisely to the extent that the poet has forgotten who
she is. Raoul de Soisson's Helen is a relic, a highly prestigious piece of the past.
As such she fills a space, occupies a position, serves the poet's syntactical and
rhetorical needs, and, at the same time, gives his work the illusion of historical depth. Onomastics in such a system is a powerful mechanism for sustaining
cultural continuity—or at least the image thereof. It is also a system that privileges, even fetishizes, the word. Poetry is no longer a reliable mirror of nature,
or a reliable conduit to the past; it is instead at best a simulacrum, a substitute,
an idol.

This is precisely the point of the story of Zeuxis told by Jean de Meun in
the *Roman de la rose* (finished in 1275). For the medieval poet for whom the
world is God's creation, Zeuxis can no longer serve as a heroic emblem of the
artist perfecting nature, as he did in Cicero's *De inventione:* Art, even the art of
Zeuxis, is inadequate to represent the Rose:

> Zeusis neïs por son bel peindre
> Ne pourroit a tel fourme ataindre,
> Qui, pour fair l'image au temple,
> De cinc puceles fist essemple,
> Les plus beles que l'en pot qurerre
> E trouver en toute la terre,
> Qui devant lui se sont tenues
> Tout en estant trestoutes nues,
> Pour sei prendre garde en chascune
> S'il trouvait nul defaut en l'une,
> Ou fust seur cors ou fust seur membre,
> Si con Tulles le nous remembre,
> Au livre de sa Retorique,
> Qui mout est science autentique.
> Mais ci ne peüst il viens faire,
> Zeusis, tant seüst bien pourtraire,
> Ne coulourer sa pourtraiture,
> Tant est de grant beauté Nature.
>   (Langlois 1914–24: ll. 16185–202)

[Even Zeuxis could not achieve such a form with his beautiful
painting; it was he who, in order to make an image in the temple,

used as models, five of the most beautiful girls that one could
seek and find in the whole land. They remained standing quite
naked before him so that he could use each one as a model if he
found any defect in another, either in body or limb. Tully recalls
the story to us in this way in the book of his *Rhetoric,* a very authentic body of knowledge. But Nature is of such great beauty
that Zeuxis could do nothing in this connection, no matter how
well he could represent or colour his likeness.] (Trans. Dahlberg
1995)

The passage certainly represents an old topos, the inexpressibility of the beauty
of the beloved: "I would willingly describe her to you, but . . ." ("Bien la vous
vousisse descrire, / Mais . . ." [Langlois 1914–24: ll. 16165–66]). But at least two
features make this reworking of the topos distinctive: the image of the naked figures posed, in statuesque fashion ("devant lui se sont tenues"), before the artist,
and the reference to the source of the topos (Cicero's "book of . . . Rhetoric,"
by which the author refers to *De inventione* 2.1–2) as something authentic. In
The Gothic Idol Michael Camille discusses this passage, specifically in a chapter on medieval representations of Pygmalion as artist/idolater (1989:316–37).
For Zeuxis is a second Pygmalion, and Jean de Meun's Pygmalion (Langlois
1914–24: ll. 20817–1227), borrowed from Ovid's *Metamorphoses* 10.242–99, is
the archetypal idolater. The poet makes the connection between the two proto-
idolaters explicit when he measures the beauty of Pygmalion's Galatea by the
familiar gold standard of Helen (and Lavinia): "Neither Helen, nor Lavinia,
however well-formed, were of such perfect complexion or development, nor
did they have a tenth the beauty" ("N'onques Helen ne Lavine / Ne furent de
couleur si fine / Ne de si bone façon nees, / Tout fussent eus bien façonees, /
Ne de beauté n'orent la disme" [Langlois 1914–24: ll. 20832–35]).

   In Jean de Meun's version as in Ovid's, it is only with the intervention of
Venus—the goddess "sent a soul to the image" ("A l'image enveia lors ame"
[21117])—that the idol is transformed into something living: "Then he [Pyg-
malion] saw that she was a living body" ("Lors veit qu'ele est vive e charnue"
[21133]). Art itself, in the *Roman de la rose,* is a poor substitute for nature. Just
before the passage cited above, Art is made to kneel before Nature and "imitates her like a monkey" ("E la contrefait come singe"). At least two familiar
medieval tropes are at work here, according to Camille: Art's "secondariness,"
and Nature's "inexpressibility" (1989:317). Zeuxis, like Pygmalion, can imitate
but he cannot invent; his art is an idol, not a living body.

   At this point Camille cites an illustration from a 1282 manuscript of Cicero's
Rhetoric that represents Zeuxis at work (Chantilly, Musée Condé MS. 590, fol.
45v; reprinted in Camille 1989:318, fig. 170). It is clearly not an illustration of
Helen "herself," but of an idol representing Helen, and still unfinished. As such

it serves us well as an emblem of all the Helens we have encountered, and will encounter, in the course of this book: never Helen "herself," always second-hand, always unfinished. The illustration, comments Camille,

shows the artist about to "colour" the face and hand (key life-signifiers) on his column-statue matched against his model maidens. . . . These not only have been depicted clothed but they are all identical, surely defeating the object of Zeuxis' comparative synthesis. . . . The medieval Zeuxis follows a "general" type of uniform schema, as does the artist of this miniature, rather than select from flawed nature's repertoire to create a unified new whole. (1989:318)

A different reading of the image is possible, I think. First, while the differences between the models are slight, they are nonetheless distinct (note the variations in clothing, and in the gestures adopted by the maidens). Zeuxis's artistry is still, apparently, an act of synthesis and transference, although its power, as we would expect, is severely curtailed.

I want to focus on, and conclude with, the face of Helen, which, Camille tells us, the artist is about to paint. The illustrator has arrested his action at a critical moment: the moment when the generic idol will "come alive," will become an individual. Is this a statement about the inability of Art to bring Nature to life? Perhaps. But what the empty face of Helen also suggests, it seems to me, is the infinite recyclability of Art and the infinite transposability of the classical past. The blank face of this illustration has its verbal equivalent in Jean de Meun's description of Zeuxis, where Helen is never actually mentioned by name. Helen's story is that of an individual who always remains generic. Helen's face must remain an empty space, a space that can be repeatedly filled, emptied, and filled again.

8

Translation

Introduction: Translation as Metaphor and Method

This chapter examines the myth of Trojan origins, and Helen's role in it, in late medieval and early modern France. This myth functions as a genealogical graft in which (pagan) past is sutured seamlessly to (Christian) present through a repetition of migrations: Trojans become Romans, Romans become French, and thus France is Troy translated, linguistically, temporally, and geographically. Translation in its various guises—euhemerism, parallelism, plagiarism, citation, genealogy, and anachronism—is a favorite strategy in the medieval and early modern periods for simultaneously acknowledging and refusing historical precedent. Indeed, Jennifer Goodman has suggested that *translatio* should be regarded as the "governing metaphor of the whole period" (1992:89).

Translation is not just a metaphor, however, but a method. *Metaphor,* after all, is also another word for *translation;* each term is a translation of the other. Both suggest that the mechanism of reading and writing history is a continual transference. In this sense, translation is the principal method behind the medieval romance of antiquity. This chapter focuses on one of the earliest and the most influential—that is to say, the most translated—of these romances: Benoît de Sainte-Maure's *Le roman de Troie*. Translation in *Le roman de Troie* is both a catastrophic rupture, because Helen's transference from Sparta to Troy will destroy both cultures, and the only way to begin repairing that rupture, because Benoit proffers his text as an act of cultural retrieval and redemption. Translation in the medieval period is thus the guarantor of continuity and, by the very fact that it must be undertaken, the proof of discontinuity.

By the fifteenth century, as we will see in the following chapter, metaphors of translation have become political methods. The tropes of *translatio studii* (trans-ference of learning) and *translatio imperii* (transference of empire) provide the nascent European state with genealogies of national origin, apologies for cul-tural conquest, and strategies for achieving political hegemony. Translations, then, are genealogical strategies. Upon this premise is founded Jean Lemaire de Belges's prose epic of cultural origins, *Illustrations de Gaule et singularitez de Troye*. Not only is the *Illustrations* a translation of countless histories, includ-ing Benoît de Sainte-Maure's—stories collected and conflated; it is itself, from start to finish, a history of countless translations—bodies collected and con-flated. It is a history, in other words, of sexual and political liaisons, abductions, copulations, and weddings, legitimate and illegitimate. It begins with Helen of Troy.

Medieval Historiography: Euhemerism, Allegory, Parallelism, Correspondence

Chapter 7 approaches idolatry in courtly love as a fetishization of the textual sign, a way of transforming cultural debt into self-sufficiency. Before turning to *translatio* as the preferred secular story of historical origination for Western medieval culture, I want to explore briefly the implications of textual idolatry for the medieval recovery of a pagan past. For, paradoxically, the medieval con-demnation of classical idolatry goes hand in hand with the period's antiquari-anism and its cultivation of the classical text. Augustine's method for reading amounts, we have seen, to a mining operation for hidden meanings; it is essen-tially allegorical, following the strategy applied since late antiquity to Homer and Virgil (Curtius 1953:74).[1] There is nothing particularly reverential about mining, and we can begin to see already how the proscription of idolatry as a religious practice can become a prescription for idolatry as a poetics. A good example can be found in Patristic readings of ancient mythology, which often resorted to *euhemeristic* methods (named after the third-century Greek reader Euhemerus of Messene). *Euhemerism* is a translation, really, by rationalization. Rather than disposing of the pagan gods altogether, the medieval poet reads them as *god-like* human beings (mistakenly) worshiped in antiquity as divini-ties.[2] The euhemerists saw the error of antiquity as a misguided translation, the substitution of a likeness for the real thing.[3] Turning idolatry into translation allowed the Latin Middle Ages to recuperate what would otherwise be lost, to make the pagan past part of or parallel to contemporary history.[4] Baal, the rival god, was indigestible; in Eusebius's *Chronicles* he has been reborn as the first king of the Assyrians.[5]

To strip the ancient gods of their divinity means to treat them—and the texts in which they figure—as so many relics to be revered, recovered, bought, and sold. It is through this allegorical-textual commerce that medieval culture con-structs its own history. Out of the differences of diachrony, it constructs a synchronous, contiguous narrative.[6] Because that narrative is openly constructed and explicitly synthetic, because its essential feature is rupture and repair, it works as an argument both for and against continuity. Medieval historiography is essentially a form of graft. Baal as king already suggested the transformation of an alien antiquity into a familiar genealogical and cultural extension by grafting pagan and Christian, like and unlike. What was the past? The past was like today, says the euhemerist, only a long time ago. Hence the proliferation, in the Latin Middle Ages, of history, chronicle, encyclopedia, and genealogy, syntheses of pagan and Christian figures organized into a vast continuum.

This structure of parallelism may be rooted, as Curtius suggests, in Jerome's system of correspondences (1953:362); Alcimus Avitus (d. 518), in his Christian epic, is already drawing parallels between the giants of the Bible and those of Greek mythology (Curtius 1953:220). But by the twelfth century, parallelism has become the central organizational principle in historiographic narrative. Appearing at about the same time as *Le roman de Troie* (1160), Petrus Comestor's influential *Historia scholastica,* for example, presents pagan and Christian history in symmetrical terms. Martianus Capella's *De nuptiis Philologiae et Mercurii* is an encyclopedia of knowledge, a "text-book for the Middle Ages" (Lewis 1936:81), an allegorical compendium typical of the medieval period. In the *Historia Romana a Noe usque ad Romulum* (cited by Sanford 1944), Noah sails to Italy and founds a city that Romulus will incorporate into Rome.[7]

E. M. Sanford's "The Study of Ancient History in the Middle Ages" cites these works and others as evidence of historical awareness (1944:21–38). Sanford would "indicate some channels through which the stream of ancient history reached medieval readers," to show that pagan–Christian historical syntheses "gave medieval readers a strong sense of continuity with the past." [8] The very images Sanford employs here collaborate with that sense of continuity. I prefer to emphasize the discontinuity (in which continuity as a failed idea is implied) at the heart of medieval historiography. It is easy to mistake the medieval penchant for synthesizing and encyclopedic compendia for a static or flattened vision of history as continuity and repetition. Such a view of medieval culture is traditional and remains persistent. What it fails to see is that the medieval narration of the past is an act of repair and replacement. In medieval history the past, irreparably sundered from the present, must be bandaged, sutured, and replaced with makeshift substitutes.

This is why I both agree and disagree with Nicholas Birns when he argues in "The Trojan Myth: Postmodern Reverberations" that medieval historiography was not really interested in history as origin, but rather sought to confirm the potential presence of Christian "modernity" in the past. This so-called modernity "was not reverent of sources, nor did it triumphantly graft what had gone before into a unitary, holistic, Hegelian narrative. Rather, medieval Christian modernity asserted a distinction, enacted by the Christ-event, so absolute that history before and after need not partake in a coherent continuum" (Birns

1993:47). I would prefer to say that medieval historiography was a search for distinction from *and* identity with the past; it was *both* reverent *and* irreverent of sources; it *did* seek to graft past and present into a unitary whole and, therefore, made the vision of a continuum both coherent and counterfeit.[9]

Translatio: The Myth of Trojan Origins

That continuum has its assigned point of origin in Troy.[10] The myth of Trojan origins relies on the genealogical trope that describes history as the recurrent exile, dislocation, transmigration, and revival of empire (i.e., Trojans = Romans = fill in the ethnic or national group of your choice). This trope is referred to in the formulae *translatio imperii* (the transfer of power) and later *translatio studii* (transfer of culture), which are central to medieval historical theory.[11] For the task of the medieval historiographer, converting mythic terms into Christian ones, splicing one to the other, is not only a translation of history, but a history of translation.[12] The *translatio studii/imperii* functions as a viable genealogy for Western authors from classical Rome to the Renaissance. We find a classic example near the beginning of Chrétien de Troyes's second *roman breton, Cligés,* composed at roughly the same time as *Le roman de Troie:*

> Par les livres que nous avons
> Les fez des anciiens savons
> Et del siecle qui fu jadis.
> Ce nos ont nostre livre apris,
> Que Grece ot de chevalerie
> Le premier los et de clergie.
> Puis vint chevalerie a Rome
> Et de la clergie la some,
> Qui or est en France venue.
> Deus doint qu'ele i soit retenue
> Et que li leus li abelisse
> Tant que ja mes de France n'isse.
> L'enor qui s'i est arestee,
> Deus l'avoit as autres prestee:
> Car de Grejois ne de Romains
> Ne dit an mes ne plus ne mains;
> D'aus est la parole remese
> Et estainte la vive brese.
>   (Micha 1982: ll. 25–42)[13]

[Through the books which we have, we know the deeds of the ancients and of times long passed. Our books have taught us that Greece had the first fame of chivalry and learning. Then came chivalry to Rome, and the sum of learning, which now is come to France. God grant that it remain there, and that it find the place so pleasant it will never depart from France.

> The honor which has taken up its abode here, God had but
> lent to the others: for of the Greeks and the Romans no one
> any longer says either much or little; their word has ceased,
> their bright flame is put out.] (Trans. Curtius 1953:385)

Occupying the last position in this genealogical chain is, for the poet, a mixed blessing. On the one hand, the past lives on, here and now, in Chrétien's France. On the other hand, France may one day fall as silent as Greece and Rome, and live on only in someone else's books and someone else's voice. Etienne Gilson reads these lines as an expression of "medieval humanism" (1932:184); Curtius disagrees, suggesting that they represent "the reverse of a humanistic creed" (1953:385). I think it is perhaps more accurate to understand humanism as a self-negating embrace of the past.

The trope of *translatio* has its own genealogy, of course. Its most influential adumbration for medieval European culture is to be found in Virgil's *Aeneid*. A work called *De familiis Troianis* matched up Roman families of the late Republic with Trojan ancestors. Cassiodorus gave Theodoric the Ostrogoth a Trojan family tree. As early as the seventh century, the Frankish historiographer Fredegarius refers to a Francus or Francion as the son of Hector and the eponymous founder of the Frankish kingdom.[14] Something like the same story is recounted in variant forms by medieval authors across Europe, before and after Benoît de Sainte-Maure, in Latin and in the vernacular, in historical works and in romance. In the twelfth century we find the *Pergama flere uolo,* a narrative in Latin on the subject of Troy.[15] The romance *Eneas,* roughly contemporary (ca. 1158–60) with the *Roman de Troie,* includes the story of Troy and the Judgment of Paris. Of course, it is not easy to distinguish between "history" and "fiction" in this period; the line between them is considerably blurred. Paul Meyer, in a study of the earliest extant French prose "history," argues that the *Histoire ancienne jusqu'a César* (1223–30), in which the Judgment of Paris figures prominently as a pivotal historical juncture, represents in essence a combination of extant Latin histories such as the *De excidio Troine* or the *Compendium historiae troianae-romanae* and a prose redaction of Benoît's romance (Meyer 1885:63–67; see below).[16] Troy plays an equally significant role in other medieval hybrid narrative-histories, such as Vincent of Beauvais's *Speculum naturale, historiale, doctrinate.* The Trojan war is a historical event; so is the Judgment of Paris: "The cause of the war was, however, as Eusebius writes, that argument of three women for the prize of beauty, one of them promising Helen to the shepherd judge" ("Causa autem belli fuit ut scribit eusebius quod trium mulierum de pulcritudine certantium premium fuit una earum helenam pastorali iudice pollicente" [Mentelin 1473:3.60, trans. Ehrhart 1987:70]). That work also provides some textbook cases of the technique of parallelism discussed above: in chapter 59, for example, we learn that in the same year that Jephte, the judge of Israel, dies, Paris rapes Helen (Ehrhart 1987:69). (Note here as well the way the author ratifies his assertions by means of a prior literary authority.) A discussion follows comparing Augustine's and Orosius's views on exactly how long before the founding of Rome the rape of Helen occurred. Later historical works continue to give Troy an originary position. In the fourteenth century Christine de Pisan begins her *Des fais et bonnes moeurs du sage Roy Charles V* with Troy as historical starting point (Thibaut 1888:162).

Le roman de Troie is but the most influential in this lineage of Trojan narratives, a genealogy that will eventually find its most grandiose and most explicit expression in Jean Lemaire de Belges's *Illustrations de Gaule et singularitez de Troie,* where the subject is really genealogy itself.[17] I deal with this development in chapter 9, "Genealogy." With the breakdown of feudalism and the advent of new, powerful dynasties with an interest in legitimating and perpetuating lineages (Capetians, Plantagenets, etc.), the Trojan myth, at first a simple adaptation of Virgil, will become, as Birns puts it, "a worthy equivalent to the ecclesiastical claims of apostolic succession" (1993:49). In *Etymologies and Genealogies: A Literary Anthropology of the French Middle Ages,* R. Howard Bloch suggests that the popularity of the myth is explained, in part, by a historical shift in which the ideal of the extended family began to give way to that of the dynasty centered on a male lineage.

To speak of the genealogy of a myth is to perform the figurative work of genealogy itself. Francisque Thibaut's history of the myth of *translatio studii* is typical in the way it encourages genealogy-speak: "It had long since become a *sort/species* of official dogma, *transmitted without interruption* from century to century, and consecrated by an *affiliation* of ideas which needs to be traced" ("Depuis longtemps, c'était une *espèce* de dogme officiel, *transmis sans interruption* de siècle en siècle, et consacré par une *filiation* d'idées qu'il est nécessaire d'établir" [1888:159–60; my italics]). Genealogy is, in effect, a powerful species of translation, a figure that links as it suppresses. Genealogy-speak is always, at the same time, graft-speak: this again, is the premise of the next chapter in this study. On the euhemeristic recuperation of the Trojan heroes in the early romances of antiquity, Jean Seznec comments: "Such is one of the effects of euhemerism in the Middle Ages: mythic characters . . . are the patrons of such and such a people, the stock from which it issues and from which it takes its glory" ("Tel est un des effets de l'évhémérisme au Moyen-Age: les personnages mythiques . . . sont les patrons de tel peuple, la souche dont il est issu et dont il tire sa gloire" [1939:23]).

Translation in *Le roman de Troie*

Le roman de Troie begins by exposing its own genealogical mission. The prologue (verses 1–144) argues in botanical terms: "Who has knowledge and does not teach it cannot escape being forgotten; while knowledge truly received germinates, flourishes, and bears fruit" ("Qui siet e n'enseigne ou ne dit, / Ne puet estre ne s'entroblit; / E scïence qu'ist bien oïe, / Germe, flurist e fructifie" [Baumgartner 1987: ll. 21–24]).[18] This image evokes the dream of perfect continuity, history without rupture. And yet the past must be retrieved, counterfeited, or stolen. *Le roman de Troie* begins, in fact, by suggesting the temptations of graft. It does so not in a botanical conceit, but with a literary citation: "Solomon teaches us and tells us, so one can read in his writings, that no one should conceal what they know; rather one should show it, so that he can profit from it, receive honor from it; so the Ancients acted" ("Salemons nos enseigne e dit, / E sil lit hon en son escrit, / Que nus ne deit son sens celer; / Ainz le deit hon si demonstrer / Que l'on i ait preu e honor, / Qu'ensi firent li ancessor" [ll. 1–6]). Solomon warns us against the dangers of intellectual hoarding, and Benoît shows us what a good pupil he is by acknowledging his source. It should not surprise us if this is the exception that proves the rule. From its very opening, in any case, Benoît's romance identifies itself as an exercise in bibliographic genealogy and textual reconstruction: a translation. The term *roman* itself refers to the translation of a Latin text into a vernacular tongue.[19] The *romans d'antiquité* that begin to emerge in the Carolingian renaissance—*Le roman de Troie* is one of the earliest—can be viewed as part of the encyclopedic, text-centered tradition of medieval historiography already discussed.[20] The 30,000 verses of Benoit de Sainte-Maure's *Roman de Troie* (1154–60) are meant to be, one might say, an assemblage of everything known on the subject of Troy. Benoît's goal, as Baumgartner puts it, is to "appropriate all the materials brought together by his predecessors, to grind them up, to mix them together, to pour them into this immense mold of more than thirty thousand lines" ("reprendre tous les matériaux réunis pas ses prédécesseurs, les broyer, les mélanger, les couler dans cet immense moule de plus de trente mille vers" [1987:130]). There is no question that the romance, in Jean-Charles Huchet's words, is a "a humanist gesture" and represents a "desire to reestablish connection with classical culture" (1989:38). But when we look at how that desire is repeatedly satisfied and frustrated, it also becomes clear that the romance is a way of dissolving and—to use a term associated of late with ruthless juntas—*disappearing* that culture.

Benoît portrays himself from the beginning of his romance as a translator, one who will make texts accessible to the *illiterati:* "I want to work to begin a History, which, from the Latin in which I found it, I will translate into Romance . . . so that those who do not understand the letter can take pleasure in the *romans*" ("E por ce me vuell travailler / En une estoire conmencer / Que, de latin ou je la truis, / Se j'ai le sens e se ge puis, / Le voudrai si en romanz metre / Que cil qui n'entendront la letre / Se puissent deduire el romanz" [trans. Birns 1993: ll. 33–39]). We should not be too concerned with the particular text Benoît may or may not be referring to in the opening to the prologue. It is the act of referring itself that is significant. It is the *ancessor,* the Ancients, pagan or

Christian, and their *escrit,* their Writings, that he invokes, and cites, at the start of this epic. Chrétien de Troyes's *Cligés* begins almost exactly the same way, citing as its source "one of the books in the library of Saint Peter's Cathedral in Beauvais" ("un des livres de l'aumaire / Mon seignor saint Pere a Biauvez" [trans. Staines 1990: ll. 20–21]), and, as we have seen, praising the written word inherited from the past.

Benoît, however, does not value all books equally. Homer is a talented poet—

> Mais ne dist pas ses livres veir.
> Car bien savons, sens niul espeir,
> Qu'il ne fu puis de cent anz nez
> Que li granz osz fu asenblez.
> N'est merveille s'il i faillit,
> Qui unc n'i fu ne rien n'en vit.
> Quant il en ot son livre fait
> E a Athenes l'ot retrait,
> Si ot estrange contençon:
> Dampner le voustrent par raison
> Por ce qu'ot fait les damedex
> Cumbatre o les homes charnex.

> [But his books do not tell the truth. For we know well, without any doubt, that he was born more than one hundred years after the great armies gathered. It is not surprising therefore if he was in error, since he was not there, and saw nothing himself. When his book was done and it was heard in Athens, then there was a strange argument: they wanted to condemn him for having made the gods fight against men of flesh.] (Trans. Birns 1993: ll. 51–62)

It does not matter that Benoît could not have read Homer, or that his dates are wrong. What does matter is that Homer is rejected for *historical* reasons, because he is (like Benoît) *belated.* What is needed is an eyewitness, someone who was *there,* and who *saw.* (The model here would seem to be the Gospels, the testimony of those who *saw* Christ.) Homer is rejected as an idolater, a faulty translator of history.

If Homer is apocryphal, Benoît does have his canonical texts: the *De excidio Troiae historia* by a certain Dares Phrygius, which is referred to throughout *Le roman de Troie,* and the *Ephemeris belli Troiani,* by one Dictys Cretensis, cited explicitly as a source only toward the end of the romance (Baumgartner 1987:13). The first is by far the more important: Benoît calls it his *Livre,* or the *Escrit,* and its author is the *Auctor.* These apparently authoritative sources, upon which much of *Le roman de Troie* is indeed based, are in fact Latin texts based upon late Greek texts themselves derived from the post-Homeric poems of the epic cycle, all of which in turn refer back to or supplement the Homeric epics—

Both take great pains, however, to demonstrate their authenticity through elaborate scenarios of translation and archaeological recovery. Thus the *Ephemeris belli Trojani* is supposed to be a translation of a lost Phoenician manuscript, a war journal kept by one of the victors, discovered in a Cretan tomb (Highet 1949:52). The *De excidio Trojae* is another Latin "forgery" modeled upon any number of Greek texts, including Philostratus's *Heroicus* (ca. 215 A.D.), but again presented by its narrator, one Cornelius Nepos, as a translation of an eyewitness account of the Trojan war by one of the losers.[21] Benoît repeats and confirms these scenarios of textual retrieval and translation, recounting Cornelius's "discovery" of the *De excidio:* "One day he was looking for old textbooks in a chest, searching in all directions, until among the other books he found the history which Dares had composed and written in the Greek tongue" ("Un jor esteit en un almaire / Por traire livres de gramaire; / Tant i a quis e reversé / Qu'entre les autres a trové / L'estoire que Dares ot escrite, / En grecque langue faite et dite" [trans. Birns 1993: ll. 87–92]). The bibliographic history of Benoît's romance is thus itself a kind of romance of imitations, translations, and counterfeits. Despite its show of rejecting idolatry, it is itself a new form of idolatry, I would argue, in which textual surfaces are revered as oracular truths. In retelling the story of Dares' recovery as alleged by Cornelius Nepos, Benoît accepts, or at least makes a show of accepting, the explanations of the Latin "translator" at face value. Of Dares he asserts, in effect translating Cornelius Nepos: "He wrote the truth about what happened. For a long time his book was lost, neither found nor seen. But Cornelius found it in Athens, and translated it: from Greek into Latin, with intelligence and skill" ("De l'estoire la verté escrist. / Lonc tens fu sis livres perduz, / Qui ne fu trovez ne veüz, / Mes a Athenes le trova / Cornelïus quil translata: / Du grec le torna en latin / Par sons sens e par son engin" [116–22]). Benoît's romance is thus only the last in a series of *translations.* It is, in fact, the translation of a pseudo-translation (Dares) of an imitation (Greek text) of an imitation (epic cycle) of an imitation (Homer).

Benoît ends the prologue professing that his translation is faithful, but he contradicts himself as he does so: "I will follow the Latin to the letter. I will add nothing else to what I find written there, except I will not refrain from adding some good things. But I will stay close to the matter" ("Le latin sivrai e la letre; / Niul autre rien n'i voudrai metre / S'ensi non cum jel truis escrit. / Ne die mie qu'aucun buen dit / N'i mete, se faire le sai, / Mais la matire en ensirrai" [139–44]). The hesitation here suggests an early example of the dangers of the supplement. How to add without really adding? "Such additions," writes Huchet, "bear witness to something specifically novelistic, that something conceived as a surplus meaning added to the Latin model" (1989:38). Benoît insists that he will add nothing as he informs us that he will add something. In fact, Benoît adds quite a bit. Beneath the ideal of reverent conservation in *Le roman de Troie* lies the subterfuge of graft. Benoît's translation (like those by Cor nelius and Dares) is a synthesis of textual relics, another collection—worthy of Petrus Comestor and Martianus Capella—like the heap of books among which ("entre les autres") Cornelius finds his Dares. This is Birns's conclusion: "Even as Benoît is constructing a literary pedigree expected by his patrons and readers, he is admitting that the entire process is laden with falsehoods and betrayals" (1993:58).[22]

The Judgment of Paris, Translated

Why does Benoît favor Dictys and especially Dares as his sources instead of more prestigious Roman epics like the *Thebaid* or the *Aeneid?* Perhaps it is because their very limitations made them easier to build upon. This is Baumgartner's view (1987:15): "the phrases of the Latin text, in fact, are but anchoring points, nodes to which are grafted and out of which flower the discourse of the medieval writer" ("les phrases du texte latin ne sont en fait que des points d'ancrage, des noeuds à partir desquels se greffe et fructifie le discours de l'écrivain médiéval"). Baumgartner's use of the figure of graft serves to justify the dubious strategies of the medieval poet.[23]

One of the motifs that Benoît "borrows" from Dares is that of the Judgment of Paris, a topos that medieval poets tend to read as a story about dubious transactions: titles improperly conferred, property illegitimately transferred. The Judgment of Paris plays a prominent role in Benoît's narrative, as it does in many medieval renderings of the Trojan story. But Benoît's preference for late Classical readings of the Homeric tale has far-reaching implications for the particular valence the scene of the Judgment—and Helen's part in it—will have in medieval literature.

Following Dares, the Judgment in *Le roman de Troie* (3855–928) is a dream recollected by Paris. Turning the event into a dream serves, of course, to rationalize and demystify it, a critical move typical of late Classical and Hellenistic reworkings of Homeric themes. But Benoît is not wedded, we know, to Dares as a model; he also borrows from the romance of *Eneas* and from a number of possible Celtic folkloric sources (see Ehrhart 1987:41).

Benoît's Judgment would seem to belong to, or point ahead to, the medieval genre of the "dream-vision," long before the *Roman de la rose.* Many of the motifs of that genre are here: the story takes place in the spring; Paris is hunting for a stag, in a place called the "valley of Venus"; the setting for the vision is a garden, where the hunter has fallen asleep beside a fountain.[24] Thus the Judgment in *Le roman de Troie* is converted into romance. But beyond that, the Judgment can now be treated—as it will be, over and over again by Benoît's successors— as either allegory or history, or, to put it in other terms, as either translation or genealogy. I discuss the former treatment in this chapter; the latter is the subject of chapter 9.

Helen in *Le roman de Troie:* Anachronism

Critics who find fault in Benoît often refer to the persistent anachronism of his text. Anachronism is indeed Benoît's major *fault* or *flaw;* by which I mean only that it generates the numerous seams between the grafted elements that constitute his work. Anachronism is not a weakness in *Le roman de Troie,* I would argue, but its essential stylistic feature. Homer, Benoît declares in the prologue, was "an extraordinary scholar/cleric" ("clerz merveilleus" [45]); Menelaus "a very powerful king" ("iert mout riche reis" [4227]). Antenor, who betrays his city to the Greeks, is "that vile Judas" ("li cuiverz Juadas" [26135; see also Raynaud de Lage 1976:154]). Such anachronisms may be evidence of historical amnesia, but they are also empirical marks of historical rupture and suture.

Suppose we think of graft for a moment as a temporal variation on Jakobson's *poetic principle,* which "projects the principle of equivalence from the axis of selection into the axis of combination" (1987:71). Anachronism, the graft of pagan and Christian, antique and modern, foreign and indigenous, projects, Jakobson might say, the principle of equivalence from the axis of diachrony into the axis of synchrony. In narrative terms, the medieval humanist converts the temporal proposition *a then b* into *a and b.* The second proposition, which confirms that the task of the medieval poet is to conjoin distinct and disconnected terms, describes the work of the romance not only on a formal but on a dramatic level as well. Graft, in other words, is a figure not only for the intertextual genesis of *Le roman de Troie,* but for its narrative subject. That subject is the triumph of abduction over marriage. The drama of this romance is a succession of violent possessions (of the Golden Fleece, Esïona, Heleine, Briseïda) and failed unions (Jason and Medea, Paris and Heleine, Achillés and Polixena, Troïlus and Briseïda, etc.), unions which, as Baumgartner puts it, "take up again in the sphere of love the antagonism between Greece and Troy" ("redoublent dans la sphère de l'amour l'antagonisme de la Grèce et de Troie" [1987:21]). One of my aims here is to show that this "antagonism between Greece and Troy" is always re-enacted by the humanist poet in pursuit of his or her own literary Helen. When, in the following passage, the love of Jason and Medea is consummated— "They were together all night, for so the book tells me, both naked, in each other's arms; I hide nothing" ("Tote la nuit se jurent puis, / Ensi cume je el livre truis / Tot nu a nu e braz a braz. / Autre celee ne vos faz" [1643–46])—we may notice how carefully Benoît refers his reportage to his Source (the book, the "livre"). Furthermore, the image of naked embrace, and the defensive "I hide nothing" that follows could refer as much to Benoît's commerce with Dares as to Jason's with Medea.

According to Baumgartner, the writer weaves (*entrelace*) the love story into the narrative of military exploits (1987:21). What I want to stress is how that interlacing repeats, on the textual level, the amorous embraces that are so often the subject of the romance. Anachronism in *Le roman de Troie* suggests a graft of lyric and epic modes such as we saw at work in *la chanson courtoise,* and earlier in the poetry of Sappho. In each case love and war are in competition: lyric rivaling epic, *courtoisie* rivaling *antiquité.* Paris's expedition to Sparta in *Le roman* is a military affair (he has been sent to avenge the rape of Hesione), but his meeting with Helen is more Ovidian than Homeric:

> Mout s'esgarderent anbedui.
> El ot demandé e enquis
> Cui fiz e don't esteit Paris.
> Fiere biautié en lui mirot:
> Mout l'aama e mout li plot.
> Paris fu saives e artos,
> Veiziez, cointes e sc̈ientos:
> Tost sot, tost vit e tost conut
> Son bon senblant e aperçut,
> E que vers lui ot bon corage:
> Ne fu mie vers li salvage,
> Anceis s'est puis mis en itant
> Qu'auques li dist de son talant.
> El veeir e el parlement
> Qui il firent assez briefment,
> Navra Amors e lui e li
> Ainz qu'il se fussent departi.
>   (4342–58)

[The two of them looked at each other for a long time. She has made inquiries as to who Paris was, and whose son he was. Her extraordinary beauty fascinated him: she loved him very much, and he pleased her very much. Paris was wise and talented, sensible, courtly, and knowledgeable; right away he noticed her friendly attitude, he saw that her heart was well disposed toward him. As for him, he was not shy with her at all, but rather set out to speak his mind to her. In the little time they had to see each other, and to speak with each other, before they could separate, Love had wounded both him and her.]

Love in *Le roman de Troie* obstructs heroic action.[25] Achilles withdraws from the fray not with the wounded pride of a warrior, but with the wounded heart of a lover, a Homeric warrior trapped in Ovid's *Amores.* The romance continually plays at *recusatio,* where matters of war give way to matters of the heart. The effect, however, is not to dispose of epic but to bind opposing genres in an uneasy alliance.

Perfect love, within the system of *courtoisie,* is by definition adulterous, and yet marriage is esteemed in *Le roman de Troie* as the only means of maintaining social stability and continuity. It is an ideal that fails. It is the promise of marriage with Polyxène, a legitimate and stable union, that lures Achilles to the temple of Apollo and death at the hands of Paris. Baumgartner notes that both Paris and Achilles attempt, and fail, to replace the cycle of abductions and adultery pitting Troy against Greece with conjugal alliances. Marriage is the dream of love as perfect graft, the graft that will mature and bear fruit. When the Greeks decide to sacrifice Polyxène in order to gain favorable passage home, it is the failed dream of her union with Achilles and the now-extinguished hope of a scion common to Troy and Greece that Benoît regrets: "How much better the world would have been, if from it an heir had been born! Its beauty was lost; how admirable they would have been, how extraordinarily beautiful, those who were its descendants!" ("Ancor en fust le mont meillor / Se de lui fussent heir eissu. / Ço qu'ert de bel i fu perdu: / Sor autres fussent remirables / E de beauté resplendissables / Cil qui de li fussent estrait" [26458–63]). Huchet is among those critics who have suggested that the idealization of marriage in the romance seems to reflect a historical transition from feudalism to centralized power, and the rise of dynastic ruling families placing a new value upon an identifiable patrilineage: "In telling the history of a successful or failed, impossible or annulled, marriage, and in assessing its consequences, the genre shared the preoccupations of the chivalric class in its frantic quest for heiresses who would provide land and assure the continuance of a lineage" (1989:40). The myth of Trojan origins paints these genealogical-matrimonial concerns on the broadest possible scale, as a national search for a "mythic ancestor" (39). Gaston Paris calls the romances, with their emphasis upon marriages, "ethogenic fables" (quoted in Seznec 1939:22). This is not just a national search; it is also a poetic one. Just as the advocacy of adulterous love (*fin' amor*) in *la chanson courtoise* was shown in chapter 7 to be parallel to the pursuit of poetic autonomy; so married love in the *roman d'antiquité* may be said to figure the return to an ancestral referent, a poetic lineage and origin.

Marriage in the Medieval Period

A brief reference to the rhetoric of marriage in the Middle Ages is required in this context. Marriage in the medieval period, Nichols argues, is always "mimetic, a symbolic representation of the political order"—and the cultural order, too, as we have seen. But in a larger sense, we can begin to see that marriage represents one of the essential typologies of graft in medieval thinking. That thinking is dominated, of course, by the narratives of the Old and New Testaments. I want to stress two elements from Genesis 2 among those cited by Nichols: first, that the female sex is conceptualized as the supplement to the male; second, that marriage represents the return of the supplement to that which it supplements, and thus the "merging" of the two sexes: "A man shall leave his father and mother, and shall cleave unto his wife: and they shall be one flesh" (Nichols 1991:71). Thus marriage, Nichols writes, referring to Genesis

2:24, "restores the original unity of male flesh by the marital union of 'two in one flesh' " (75). It also serves to confirm the hierarchical place of the female, legislating her role in patriarchal, heterocentric culture. But marriage, at the same time, poses a problem for the Latin church fathers because it appears to legitimize sexuality and the body (see Augustine, *City of God* 14.15.346–55).[26]

George Duby in *Medieval Marriage* sheds some light on the political and economic ramifications of marriage as both a rhetorical and a literal act of joining, potentially profitable, but also potentially destabilizing. This idea has consequences, not only for the present discussion, but for our examination in chapter 9 of dynastic unions, and literature celebrating those unions, in early modern France and Burgundy. For Duby argues that the essential structure of feudal power in medieval Europe—the relation, for example, between vassal and lord—is based on the image of the conjugal household, the *domus* (1978:3). Marriage is a very real means of maintaining social and familial stability, and the standard rhetoric and social recognition attached to the ritual of marriage convey that reality. Rhetoric and recognition come together in the standard "marriage agreement" or "treaty," the *pactum conjugale* that ratified the event (4). What the *pactum conjugale* ratifies, however, is not a simple act of conjugation, a joining of equals. The ecclesiastical model of graft sketched out by Nichols above remains the norm: it is the groom to whom the bride is joined: "Under such a pact, one of the houses would give up, the other receive or acquire, a woman." That joining is, we know by now, a potentially violent and coercive act. The marriage treaty, the public celebration of marriage, is a way of defusing that violence, of promoting the union as something legitimate. "Marriage thus inserted procreation into the order of things," Duby writes. "And order also implied peace, because the institution of marriage was the very opposite of abduction" (4). This is not exactly right in my view; I would suggest, rather, that marriage is a variation on abduction, which is precisely why the event is socially ratified and rendered official.

That marriage remains uncomfortably close to abduction is suggested a moment later, when Duby turns to the respective consequences of the marriage agreement for the two families concerned. Most of the discussion here bears upon the husband's family: not surprising, since the institution of marriage is in essence patriarchal and meant to ensure the stability of the male lineage. Marriage, even where institutionally ratified, remains a rather precarious affair for the husband's family, which has "introduced a foreign body into its midst, namely, the bride" (1978:5). The parallels with the Trojan fear of the foreign bride are striking. "To some extent," Duby continues, "this woman always remained an intruder, the object of tenacious distrust, of a suspicion that was invariably focused upon her should some unusual misfortune befall her husband" (6). The insertion of the foreign woman into the *domus* already poses a potential threat to the purity and stability of that body. The fear of this threat, Duby suggests, goes a long way toward explaining the strict and standard prohibition of adultery on the part of the wife.

Helen in *Le roman de Troie:* Amplification

Given the affinities between medieval marriage and abduction, we should not be too surprised if, in the marriage game that is central to the romance of antiquity, Helen is the ultimate prize and the ultimate weapon. Helen is doomed to make all marriages fail, to subvert all genealogies, political and poetic. Thus the moment when Paris gazes upon Helen is crucial on more than one level. The requisite scene of *le regard* (the look) is also a moment of narrative stasis, an interlude, an interruption of epic action. It is as if the fascination with the face of the beloved, a lingering upon his or her features, is translated simultaneously into a kind of narrative stupor. Wherever the beauty of a woman is concerned, the narrator is in danger of delay and digression. The narrator of *Le roman de Troie* runs this risk when he describes Polyxène: "Of her beauty I must say no more, for I could not describe her, even If I had half a day without interruption" ("De sa beauté m'estuet taisir / Quar ne la porreie descrire / En demi jor trestot a tire" [26454–56]).

Thus love in *Le roman de Troie* is an obstruction not only to heroic but to poetic action as well. Erotic beauty is a threat not only to the epic hero of the romance, but to its epic author. Sexuality is a dangerous and seductive digression for Paris and Benoît alike. Benoît hesitates before the face of Polyxène, as he does before the face of Helen; he goes on, however, to describe what, it has been claimed, exceeds all description. Beauty is an irresistible temptation for the poet in love with poetic language, and with his own poetic skill. Writing on the capacious description of Camille in *Le roman d'Eneas* (ll. 3959–4098), Rebecca Gottlieb notes that the length of a portrait in the romance will generally be proportional to the importance of the figure. Here, too, the poet's protestations—"what could I tell about her beauty? In the very longest day of summer I would not be able to tell"—amount to a merely rhetorical denial, and indicate "confidence in his poetic and rhetorical skills" (1990:155).

This feigned narrative impotence before the face of a beautiful woman, followed by a display of narrative prowess, shows the rhetorical gesture of *amplificatio* at work. Numerous Latin didactic treatises from the twelfth and thirteenth centuries touch upon the opposition between *dilatatio* or *amplificatio* and *abbrevatio* (brevity).[27] Geoffrey of Vinsauf's category of *amplificatio* in his *Poetria nova* (ca. 1200) includes *descriptiones, circumlocutiones, digressiones, prosopopeia,* and *apostrophationes* (Curtius 1953:490). Curtius suggests that a recurrent "frustration" with "epic breadth" is expressed in these treatises, where authors such as Matthew of Vendôme in his *Ars versificatoria* (ca. 1175) criticize the ancients for their "long-windedness" (Curtius 1953:490). But *am-*

plificatio in the medieval romance is clearly a rhetorical tactic with particular benefits for the humanist *translator.* As rhetorical denial, it seeks to do battle with the specter of poetry past while claiming to acquiesce in that poetry's supremacy. As rhetorical expansion, it seeks to overcome the rival precursor through sheer verbal weight. As such, amplification can be linked to the issue of *copia,* so important in early modern discussions of poetic imitation. Remember, however, that amplification in the romance tends to be a response to an erotic stimulus and demonstrates the intersection of courtly love with epic. What I am trying to suggest here is that *amplificatio* in the medieval romance is a form of textual idolatry, a fetishization of language and a celebration of poetic invention, of language as an autonomous and self-referring plenitude.

If idolatry is antithetical to epic action in *Le roman de Troie,* then the *Chambre des Beautés* that Priam gives to Helen and Paris as a wedding gift is the idolater's sanctuary. Benoît places it, we should note, at the very center of his poem (14631–14958), immediately following a passage in which the Trojans compare the beauty of Helen and Polyxène, who have gathered to tend to the wounded Hector: "Very often they would talk of who was more beautiful, lady Helen, or the young maiden" ("Assez en ont sovent parlé / La quele tienent a plus bele, / O dame Heleine, o la pucele" [14622–24]). This is, in effect, a second Judgment, affording the poet the opportunity to describe at leisure two alternative models of superlative beauty. (The Judgment of Paris is narrated earlier by Paris himself as a vision that comes to him in a dream, a familiar medieval topos: see 3869–923.) [28] Some three hundred lines follow, describing an alabaster chamber filled with jewels, columns, mirrors, statues, and automata (all common exotic motifs in the medieval romance). Everything is beautiful, rare, expensive. One statue dances, another plays instruments gently enough so that all who listen are soothed, but loud enough so that lovers may speak their thoughts without fear of spies. Decorum is strictly monitored here; one statue is designed to state what should or should not be done or said. The *Chambre de Beautés* is, we can see, Benoît's utopia of idolatry and *courtoisie.* It is a good example of *amplificatio,* and of the tendency found in medieval writing toward encyclopedic inventory: the delight, not only in collecting things, but in describing what has been collected.

The Judgment of Paris, Translated Again

The collector's fate is to be collected. Benoît himself will become part of literary history, valuable stock to be grafted and pruned and replanted over and over again. But before turning to that rather ruthless history of genealogical succession, I want to look again at the persistence of a contrasting impulse toward idolatry and stasis in the poetry of Troy. This is an impulse essential to translation, or allegory. How are the figures of Helen and Paris translated by French poets after Benoît? A kind of antihistory emerges here as we look at the way poets resist the momentum of classical narrative and, by holding it still, by fixing it, transform it into an ethical or theological truth. I turn briefly, since we have already discussed this scene, to allegorical treatments of the Judgment of Paris in a handful of late medieval poems.

The sources of the fables that appear in the *Ovide moralisé* (1316–28) are, as we might expect, eclectic, and include Benoît and Dares (Demats 1973:68). The Judgment of Paris itself does not, of course, figure in Ovid's *Metamorphoses,* but the version of the Judgment that appears in the *Ovide moralisé* is the "classical" or Homeric version, not Dares' dream-vision. As for the allegorizations that follow the narratives, the author of the *Ovide moralisé* would appear to have borrowed much from commentaries accompanying earlier editions of the *Metamorphoses,* such as those by Arnulf of Orleans or John of Garland (Engels 1945:42), most often Christian in their orientation, but sometimes euhemeristic or cosmological, to use Joseph Engels's terms (43). As we would expect with medieval allegorizations, the influence of Fulgentius is preponderant. Thus in the *Ovide moralisé,* the wedding of Peleus and Thetis (ll. 1200–2372) is read as an allegory of creation and the promise (in Achilles) of redemption. Discord is Satan; the apple can, of course, remain the apple. Thus the Judgment of Paris is read through the lens of salvation theory and becomes an allegory of the Fall. The Judgment itself (ll. 2425–27), following Fulgentius, is read more tropologically, as a reflection on human cognition and will. The strategy, already conventional, persists as late as Jean Lemaire de Belges, as we will see. Margaret Ehrhart puts it concisely: "Juno signifies the active life, Pallas the contemplative, and Venus the voluptuous" (1987:90).

What I want to stress is the way allegory in the *Ovide moralisé* cooperates with its own narrative strategies. Essentially, these strategies resist narrative ironically, since they stress Helen's iconic beauty and Paris's idolatrous fixation on it. But the poet of the *Ovide moralisé* makes the connection between Helen's beauty and the narrative poem, both illusory surfaces: "these fables . . . seem completely false, but there is nothing there which is not true: to one who would know the sense of it, the truth, which lies covered beneath the fables, would be obvious" (ll. 41–45, trans. Ehrhart 1987:85). The poet of the *Ovide moralisé* turns both the choice of Paris and the reading of the poem into acts of translation: Helen is the bribe that gives Venus her victory, and the delightful surface of the poem is the honey that allows the reader to swallow the medicine of truth.

Guillaume de Machaut's *Dit de la fonteinne amoureuse* (1357–64) provides an even more explicit example of the Judgment of Paris fixed as ethical/aesthetic image. Machuat follows the conventions of the medieval dream-vision: here the Judgment appears as a message in a dream (borrowed from the *Ovide moralisé*), delivered by the figure of Venus to a nobleman asleep in a garden beside a "love fountain" ("fonteinne amoureuse"). The genre of the dream already presupposes translation in terms of the story's production and reception alike. Machuat turns the story of the Judgment into a lesson in the primacy of love, or a lesson, if we prefer, in the folly of believing in the primacy of love. Either way, there is no doubt that both the nobleman and the reader are meant to read the Judgment as an allegory. Again, the poet is there to make the connection for us, reminding us that the language of the dream is a beautiful but deceptive surface, and that the truth must be found beneath the surface (ll. 1625–28). But Machaut goes further, multiplying the allegorical surfaces in this scene. For the fountain that marks the site of Venus's theophany is decorated with scenes from the Trojan saga, including Venus leading Helen to Paris, and Helen in love (ll. 1313–24). *Ecphrasis* becomes another mechanism for translation: here is another surface to read. And this is not any ordinary surface; it is the perfect representation of the truth: carvings commissioned by Jupiter, executed by Pygmalion himself (ll. 1394–98).

Finally, everything conspires in Christine de Pisan's *Epître d'Othéa* (ca. 1400) to translate epic narrative into moral picture. Consider the structure of this work, addressed to Hector as the ideal *chevalier:* one hundred chapters on distinct mythological subjects, each chapter comprising three distinct elements: the *texte,* a text borrowed from classical mythology; the *glose,* a passage offering background and ethical extrapolation; and an *allegorie,* showing the reader (or Hector) the text's spiritual import. Chapters 60 to 73 take us from the wedding of Peleus and Thetis to the Judgment of Paris, which is offered in its "Homeric" version. Nonetheless, the allegorical dream-genre, with its insistence on the dangers of seductive surfaces, continues to exert its dominance here. The *glose* in chapter 68 exhorts: "Do not base a great undertaking, whether for good or evil, on a vision or false illusion—remember Paris" ("Ne fonde sur auision / Ne dessus folle illusion / Grant emprinse soit droit ou tort / Et de Paris ayes recort" [150–53, trans. Ehrhart 1987:263n150]).

Benoît de Sainte-Maure: From Idol to Ancestor

Idolâtrie is the term that Benoît de Sainte-Maure's renowned commentator, Aristide Joly, uses to characterize the medieval poet's substitution of Latin texts for their Greek originals (Joly 1870:15). The passage from medieval idolatry to modern classicism (Joly's own true religion) is made by way of masks, supplements, names:

Les hommes de moyen-âge n'étaient pas capables encore de contempler la divinité face à face et dans sa gloire. . . . Ils apprenaient à aimer les noms antiques et les choses antiques, et lorsque la vraie antiquité se révèlerait à eux dans sa beauté sévère, ce ne serait plus une chose nouvelle . . . . ils devaient se précipiter avec joie de l'autel des fausses divinités à celui du vrai Dieu, le jour où il se manifesterait à eux. (Joly 1870:15)

[The men of the Middle Ages were not yet capable of contemplating divinity face to face and in all its glory. . . . They learned to love ancient names and ancient things, and when true antiquity showed itself to them in all its severe beauty, it was no longer something unexpected . . . they would rush with joy from the altar of the false divinities to that of the true God, on that day when it would be revealed to them.]

Joly's story recalls that of Pomona, overcome by the true face of the god Vertumnus. It is a story of genealogy as idolatry. But meanwhile, in the four centuries before the faithful would finally "overturn the idol" ("renversaient l'idole"), the history of Benoît's text itself, which "had spread throughout Europe" (Joly 1870:397), was like the propagation of a false religion. Very soon after Benoît, four prose versions of *Le roman de Troie* appeared, indicating the immense popularity of his work. One of these prose narratives, the so-called Southern version (pre-1270) will be the basis for Guido delle Colonne's Latin adaptation of Benoît (1270–87), the *Historia destructionis Troiae,* and the direct model for almost all succeeding versions of the Troy narrative.[29]

The "religion" of Troy is propagated by means of repeated conquests and suppressions: plagiarism, imitation, wholesale appropriation. The case of Benoît offers, Joly asserts, "one of the most remarkable examples of literary despoilment" ("un des plus curieux exemples de spoliation littéraire" [399]). Thus Joly accuses Benoît's "plagiarizers" ("plagiaires") of the very sins that Benoît practiced in his own work. He presents them "impudently bedecking themselves in the remains of our old trouvère" ("se parant impudemment des dépouilles de notre vieux trouvère" [422]). In the thirteenth century, Joly informs us, a Jean Malkaraume "had seized the poem of our *trouvère* and had shamelessly inserted it into a kind of religious tale, following the narration of the death of Moses" ("s'était emparé du poème de notre trouvère et l'avait intervalé sans façon dans une espèce d'histoire sainte, après le récit de la mort de Moïse" [406]). This appropriation is simple and brutal: the poem is copied and inserted, and the author's name replaced with that of Jean Malkaraume (a practice hardly restricted, it should be noted, to the medieval era; much the same process is at work in Jacques Peletier du Mans's translation of Horace's *Ars poetica* in the sixteenth century). Malkaraume, however, supplements the text, just as Benoît did. He adds, for example, a translation of two fragments from Ovid's *Heroides* on Paris's first love for the nymph Oenone (Joly 1870:409). Sometimes Joly refers explicitly to the process of intercalation and stitching as graft. Two fourteenth-century works found in the same manuscript of the *Bibliothèque impériale* narrate, respectively, the childhood of Hector and the exploits of his son Landomata: "Two works," writes Joly, "which came to be *grafted* on to that of Benoît" ("deux œuvres qui sont venue *se greffer* sur celle de Benoît" [410n1; my italics]).[30] Benoît's text is ultimately completely overshadowed by its popular imitation in Latin prose, Guido delle Colonne's *Historia destructionis Troiae.* Colonne's Latin is, ironically, often mistaken for the original, and Benoît's version for a translation.[31] And yet Joly finds something to commend in Guido's "forgery": "If he caused Benoît's name to be forgotten, at least he saved his work" ("S'il a fait oublier son nom, il a sauvé son œuvre" [473]). Guido's *Historia* will, however, be turned back into French at the court of Burgundy by Raoul le Fèvre in his *Recueil des histories de Troye* (1464).[32] This is the tangled ancestry of Jean Lemaire de Belges's *Illustrations de Gaul et singularitez de Troye* (1509–13).

The transformations of Benoît de Sainte-Maure's *Le roman de Troie* present a perilous genealogy. *Troie* lives on, as it were, only as it is copied, recopied, mutilated, pillaged, plagiarized, camouflaged, suppressed. But it does live on; and that survival tends to be celebrated by modern readers in familiar images of flow and growth, unspoiled by breaks or seams or gaps. The line of the graft disappears. Joly writes, reviving the conceit of the Heraclitean-Pythagorean river: "Benoît was the river where all the classical vernacular poetry of the Middle Ages came to draw water" ("Benoît a été le fleuve où toute la poésie classique du moyen-âge en langue vulgaire est venue puiser" [1870:6]). Faral, on the other hand, employs the familiar arboreal mode: "The romances of Thebes, of Piramus and Thisbe, of Aeneas, and of Troy, were the mother roots of an abundant genre which produced numerous and varied branches, all nourished by the same sap" ("Les romans de Thèbes, de Piramus et Tisbé, d'Eneas et de Troie, ont été les racines maîtresses d'un genre abondant qui s'est développé en rameaux multiples et variés, mais tous nourris de la même sève" [1913:419]). A similar image is found in Jacques Millet's *Lystoire de la destruction de Troye la grant,* composed circa 1452 and popular well into the sixteenth century. This history of France converted into dramatic form is, Joly insists, another work stolen from Benoît by way of Guido or some other prose version.[33] In the prologue Millet reports a vision of a tree bearing the arms of France. A shepherd informs him: "If you want to know who planted it, you have to find the root" ("Si tu veux savoir qui l'à semé, il te faut chercher la racine" [trans. Joly 1870:435]). Upon digging, Millet discovers: "The coat of arms of the Trojans / From whom the French are descended / Some five thousand years ago. / Then I decided / To undertake a history of Troy / And to write it / To the best of my abilities" ("Les armes des Troyans, / Dont les François sont descendus, / Passé a près de cinq mille ans. / Lors je me prins à pourpenser / De faire l'histoire de Troye, / Et à mon pouvoir composer, / Tout au mieulx que je pourroye" [cited in Joly 1870:435]). Here Millet discovers the roots of an uninterrupted genealogy of France and justifies his own narration of that ancestry. But the fact that he has to dig to find them suggests a different view of history, one in which the past is dead and buried.

9

Genealogy

Introduction: Medieval Romance as Genealogical and Intertextual Fable

Marriage in the twelfth-century romance promises the possibility of a stable intertextual genealogy, a seamless transference of the past to the present, and the present to a future still to come. Helen, classic exemplum of adultery, figures in this setting above all as a threat to cultural succession and therefore legitimacy. At the same time, ironically, her example proves that the poet is the successor of the past and certifies his own legitimacy.

Consider the reference to Helen in Chrétien de Troyes's romance *Cligés,* a tale, as we have already seen, about cultural succession. Chrétien begins by inserting himself into a cultural genealogy, the latest heir to the *translatio studii* that moves from Greece to Rome to France. The story Chrétien proceeds to tell, itself inherited from his cultural fathers, is about dynastic genealogy gone wrong. Alexandre, heir to the throne of Constantinople, marries Soredamor, attendant to Queen Guenièvre; their son is Cligés (Cligés is thus a hybrid figure, half-Byzantine and half-Celtic). When Cligés's uncle Alis usurps Alexandre's throne and weds Fenice (that is, the Phoenix), the daughter of the empress of Germany, the lineage that leads to Cligés is threatened. Cligés and Fenice, meanwhile, have fallen in love. Here institutional marriage has been rendered fraudulent; the "real" marriage, still unrealized, is that between Cligés and Fenice. To preserve the legitimacy of this marriage, Fenice ensures that her union with Alis remains unconsummated and her love for Cligés secret. She is trying to avoid the example, set by earlier poets, of Iseut and Tristan. Thus Fenice refuses Cligés's offers to "kidnap" her: "I shall never go away with you in this fashion, for then the entire world would talk of us the way people do of the Blond Iseult and Tristan" ("Ja avoec cos ensi n'irai, / Cars lors seroit par tot le monde / Ausi come d'Ysolt la Blonde / Et de Tristant de nos parlé" [Micha 1957: ll. 5250–53, trans. Staines 1990]).[1]

But Fenice's refusal, it must be said, serves Chrétien's purposes well. For the poet, too, is interested in legitimacy and wants to avoid the examples set by others. At the same time, and for the very same reasons, he relies on those examples. And, indeed, *Cligés* is everywhere haunted by the ghosts of Tristan and Iseut.[2] But other ghosts loom as well: most notably, that of Helen of Troy. It is Cligés who mentions Helen as he tries to persuade Fenice to flee with him to Arthur's court: "For never would there be so much joy as when Helen came to Troy brought by Paris" ("C'onques ne fu a si grant joie / Eleinne reçüe a Troie, / Quant Paris li ot amenee" [ll. 5239–41]). Fenice chooses not to play either role—Iseut's or Helen's. Or not intentionally. For Fenice manages to remain both married and faithful to Cligés only through an elaborate series of ruses, "pharmacological tricks and rhetorical figures" (McCracken 1998:42) that deceive Alis and create illusory Fenices: "He believed that he held her and he held her not. But he took much pleasure in nothing, for he received nothing, kissed nothing, held nothing" ("Tenir la cuide, n'an tient mie, / Mes de neant est a grant eise / Car neant tient, et neant beise" [ll. 3316–18]). One cannot help but note the irony here: in the very moment when Fenice strives hardest to avoid the example of one Helen, she plays the part of another, assuming the role of the *eidolon*. The irony is intertextual as well, for the more Chrétien strives to distance his work from prior poetic traditions, the more firmly he ties himself to them. Peggy McCracken puts it this way: "The accumulation of Fenice's literary predecessors in the narrative suggests that adultery . . . cannot remain hidden" (1998:45). Neither, I would add, can Chrétien's adultery, his commerce with the poetic past. Perhaps what Chrétien is haunted by, in the end, are the ghosts of all those books that came before him: so many phantoms of empires now dead and buried.

Genealogy and Translation in Early Modern Europe

By the fifteenth century, marriage, with all of its genealogical implications, is a state affair. For the nascent Western European nation-state, patrilineage is now more than a figure of speech; it is foreign policy, a justification for plagiarism *and* political conquest, a strategy for embezzling what belongs to others and what belongs to the past. If patrilineage presumes marriage—the promise of lasting union and the propagation of the (male) name, or the legitimization of graft—then fifteenth-century France and Burgundy, family members related as suzerain and vassal, each engaged in efforts at expansion and self-definition that require the *annexation of* or *secession from* the other (read *marriage* or *divorce*), provide textbook lessons in the politics of paternity and wedlock. Jean Lemaire de Belges's *Illustrations de Gaule et singularitez de Troye* is just such a textbook. It is a defense of French or Habsbourg (and, by extension, Burgundian) hegemony, a theogonic history, the drama of a lineage in which father and sons play the principal roles. What they play, however, are recurrent scenes of seduction, abduction, and, sometimes, marriage. A genealogy, it is easy to forget (we are supposed to forget) is not just a succession of filial inheritors of paternal power; it is also a lineage of sexual liaisons. Within Lemaire's myth of Trojan origins, no figure more gravely threatens that lineage, and yet is more responsible for its direction, than Helen of Troy.

Copulation, coercion, and parturition make up the underground commerce that finances the corporate public mergers and expansions of patriarchal genealogy. Thomas Greene's model of literary history in the early modern period, sketched out in the introduction to *The Light in Troy,* is an effort to rescue genealogy from graft:

The text adopts its legitimate progenitor . . . not without certain risks. As individuals, we have to recreate our origins in our memories. . . . If we are to stay sane, we have to pattern images of our origins that simplify and distort them. But certain kinds of distortion . . . turn out to be destructive. There has to be a healthy circular interplay between our patterning of our beginnings and our free action as we try to move out from them. The interplay is never free from the risk of an intertextual pathology. (1982:19)

Greene's understanding of literary history begins with the premise that *imitatio* is a cure for the trauma of history (recall the image of the belated poet as an amnesiac). It is a homeopathic cure: trauma administered in measured doses. The desire to isolate a healthy intertextual vaccine is powerful, but it is difficult to see how the imitative therapy recommended here can be anything but a sustained form of schizophrenia. Greene, who remains committed to critical study as a science of the intentional (and thus the ethical), suggests that "legitimate" intertextual references must be self-aware and explicit. For Greene there is a healthy way of recuperating the past and there is an *intertextual pathology.* Behind Greene's prescription, however, is the fear that there may be no truly "legitimate" progenitors, and that *all* intertextuality may be pathological. And much as we would like to see ourselves as the rightful "heirs" to classical culture, as purebred scions of good Homeric stock, we may have to admit that we are a bastard culture.

Jean Lemaire's *Illustrations de Gaule et singularitez de Troye* makes adopting legitimate progenitors its main business. This is, we will see, a highly profitable business—but also an illicit one.[3]

A Family Romance: France and Burgundy

To say that *patriotism,* the discourse of nationhood, is inescapably genealogical is to state the obvious. But in early modern Europe, still emerging out of
medieval feudalism, families and nations are not yet fully distinct. As Emile
Telle puts it, "All the princes of Christendom . . . found themselves 'allied' by
some sort of relation. . . . They formed a European family" ("Tous les princes
de la chrétienté . . . se trouvaient 'alliés' par quelque sorte de parenté. . . . Ils
formaient une famille européenne" [1950:7]). Because the history of the Burgundian "state" is so precarious (always almost coming into being without ever
achieving full existence), it dramatically acts out and promotes the familial rhetoric of union, divorce, affiliation, legitimacy. This is one reason why the cult
of antiquity in general, and the myth of Troy in particular, proves more popular
here than perhaps anywhere else in Europe.

Even a cursory account of the rise and fall of the Burgundian state reads like
a family romance, the story of a prodigal son or a wayward wife straying too
far from home. The feudal origins of Capetian Burgundy and France mean, in
a very real sense, that the history of the father *is* the history of the state. As
Joseph Calmette puts it: "From 1031 to 1361 in Burgundy . . . there had always
been . . . an heir . . . who succeeded. From father to son, from grandfather to
grandson . . . or from brother to brother, the ducal crown has thus been transmitted without any hitches" ("De 1031 à 1361 en Bourgogne . . . il y avait toujous
eu . . . un héritier . . . pour succéder. De père en fils, de grand-père à petit-fils
. . . ou de frère à frère, la couronne ducale s'était donc transmise sans a-coups"
[1949:41]). When the last Capetian duke of Burgundy, Philippe de Rouvres, ex-
pires intestate in 1361, Jean le Bon, king of France, is recognized as legitimate
heir. But when Jean moves for annexation pure and simple, the General Estates
resist: marriage proves, for now, premature. Instead, Jean gives Burgundy in
apanage to his son, Philippe le Hardi (41).

In time, the son will come to threaten the preeminence of the father. Burgundy proves to be a potent adversary of Charles VI and VII. The history of the
duchy through the fourteenth century looks more and more like that of an independent state: political centralization, monetary unification, proclamation of
the *coutume* or private law, development of schools of painting and sculpture—
all testify to this process of maturation. Philippe le Bon and Charles le Téméraire
both seek out royal crowns to confirm their power and marriages to extend it.
Marriage means alliance or, in time, annexation; Philippe's successive designs
upon Joanna, widow of the king of Naples, Elizabeth, niece of the king of Hun-
gary, and Marguerite, daughter of the count of Flanders, are so many means to
Burgundian expansion. Only the last will come to fruition.[4] Despite Marguerite,
the Burgundian state remains theoretical. As Jean Favier remarks, "What makes
the Burgundian state is the strong cohesion of its territories through their par-

ticipation in a common foreign policy" ("Ce qui fait l'état bourguignon, c'est la forte cohésion de ses territoires dans leur participation à une politique extérieure commune" [1984:386]). Burgundy, in other words, remains a tenuous marriage of distinctive and independent entities. Pirenne writes of Jans sans Peur in his *Histoire de Belgique,* "In him, the Valois cedes completely to the Burgundian" ("Chez lui, le Valois a fait place complètement au Bourguignon" [1903, 2:209]). A *Bourguignon,* then, is something real. But Favier's remarks on the power of rhetoric to engender identity apply as much to Pirenne as to the court historiographers of *les grands ducs:* "One also finds state chroniclers composing historiographic portraits where the Burgundian state appears to be an obvious reality. The more one speaks about it, the more it is" ("On entend aussi les chroniqueurs gagés composer la fresque historiographique où l'état bourguignon apparaît comme une évidente réalité. Plus on en parle, plus il l'est" [1984:387]).

In the end, the father destroys the son; the bride and groom are wed; the duchy of Burgundy ceases to exist—or takes the name of her husband. Charles le Téméraire is killed at the battle of Nancy in 1477; Louis XI takes possession of Burgundy proper; Marie de Bourgogne, Charles's heiress, retains Holland as dowry but, to Louis's chagrin, marries the Habsbourg Maximilian instead of the dauphin. Their daughter is Marguerite d'Autriche: patron of Jean Lemaire de Belges, historiographer of the House of Austria and Burgundy.

The Cult of Troy: Humanism as Property Rights

The cult of antiquity is a crucial strategy in the elaboration of an autonomous Burgundy. It is an attempt to find a worthy foster parent. Nostalgia for the kingdom of Lotharingia, propagated at this time, is one example;[5] the creation of the *Ordre de la Toison d'Or* in 1430 by Philippe le Bon, with Jason as "patron saint," is another. Guido delle Colonne's popular version of the Trojan romance begins, like Benoît de Sainte-Maure's, with the tale of Jason and the Golden Fleece—a tale that includes the first destruction of Troy by Jason and Hercules on their way back from Colchis (an act of revenge against King Laomedon, who had refused them hospitality on their way *to* Colchis). The institution of the Order of the Golden Fleece is thus but one manifestation of the Burgundian Troy cult. A cult practiced to some extent in every European state at this time, it has a particularly official status in the duchy of Burgundy, as is suggested by Chastellain's treatment of the phenomenon in the *Concile de Basle.*[6] The 1467 inventory of the ducal library of Philippe le Bon indicated seventeen manuscripts on the subject of Troy—out of only nine hundred volumes.[7]

Alphonse Bayot's brief study of "La légende de Troie à la cour de Bourgogne" (1908) provides us with some observations on the survival and cultivation of the Troy myth in Burgundy at the textual level. Bayot is solely concerned with trac-

ing the bibliographic origins of specific manuscripts, but his data are relevant
to our discussion of genealogy and graft. Bayot focuses primarily upon certain
editions of Raoul le Fèvre's *Recueil des histories de Troye.* Raoul le Fèvre is one
of Benoît de Sainte-Maure's most illustrious (or notorious) imitators, by way of
Guido delle Colonne and Boccaccio.[8] The frontispiece of one manuscript of the
Recueil (Bruxelles, Bibl. roy., 9261), located in the dukes' library in Brussels,
represents Philippe le Bon "commanding the author to execute the work" ("faisant à l'auteur la commande de l'ouvrage" [Bayot 1908:6]). Now, the prologue to
this work refers to translations of the matter of Troy already in circulation: translations of Colonne's *Historia destructionis Troiae* (1287), which Bayot calls "an
audacious forgery of the French romance of Benoît de Sainte-Maure" ("contre-
façon audacieuse du roman français de Benoît de Sainte-Maure" [18]). Bayot
proceeds to examine three French versions of Colonne's text and concludes that
one of them has been taken, almost in its entirety, to form the third book of the
Recueil des histories de Troye. Almost in its entirety: certain lines have been
replaced by others, forming a "*raccord*" or "bridge" between the second and
third books. "Except for this small amputation," writes Bayot, "the translation
took its place, in its entirety and without any changes, just after the original
Receuil" ("Hormis cette légère amputation, la traduction a pris place, intégrale-
ment et sans subir nulle retouche, à la suite du *Recueil* primitif" [23]). Note
the structure of the joint here presented, and the use of *amputation* to describe
what must be left out to make the joint fit. Bayot furthermore establishes that
the origin of this suture lies not in an authorial decision, but rather in a *tradition*
"which little by little imposed itself upon the copyists of the *Recueil.* Apparently, the origin of this practice is to be found in a simple juxtaposition of the
two texts. The new section came to attach itself to the earlier one by steps which
can be traced in the editions of the work in three Books" ("qui s'est imposée peu
à peu aux copistes du *Recueil.* Apparemment, le point de départ réside dans une
simple juxtaposition des deux textes. La section nouvelle ne s'est agglutinée à la
partie ancienne que par degrés dont les exemplaires en trois Livres ont conservé
la trace" [23]). Bayot now turns the microscope up to full power and focuses on
the end of Book 2 and the opening of Book 3 in four manuscripts. From one case
to the next, the line of the joint grows harder to detect. The first manuscript (B.N.
Fr. 253) openly states the source of the last Book.[9] In the third manuscript (B.N.
Fr. 252), Book 2 ends thus: "And now afterwards, this Book, in its completion,
treats of the general destruction of Troy, which followed the rape of lady Helen,
wife of the noble king Menelaus of Greece, as here afterwards is recounted"
("Et ycy après, pour la perfection de ce livre, traicte de la generalle detruc-
tion de Troyes, qui vint à l'occasion du ravissement de dame Helayne, feme du
noble roy Menelaus de Grèce, comme cy après s'ensieut" [Bayot 1908:24–25]).
Book 3 of the same manuscript begins: "And even though the story which I am
here narrating is better known than those which preceded, and though many

have already told it in many ways, nonetheless I will treat it in detail, based on what I've been able to find in diverse Books, and in the best way which I am able" ("Et non obstant ce que l'istoire de laquelle je traicte soit plus connue que les precedentes, et que plusieurs l'ayent en plusieurs manières, toutesvoyes si le traicteray-je et metteray au long, ainsi [comme] je ay peut trouver en divers voullumes, au moins mal que possible me sera"). And so Colonne disappears, or is camouflaged. Bayot's bibliographic microscope reveals a different story of cultural transmission than the one to which we are accustomed. It is a history, not just of recurrent imitations, copyings, compilations, revisions, translations, and paraphrasings, but of plagiarism, theft, concealment, suppression, mutilation, truncations, amputations, splicings, and solderings. It is a vision of an intertextual pathology, and an illegitimate genealogy, at work.

The literary historian tends to view bibliographic "crimes" of this sort as a feature of medieval ignorance. Bayot speaks of "the clumsiness of writers, with their disregard for anything that has to do with the art of composition" ("la maladresse des écrivains, avec leur insouciance pour ce qui touche à l'art de la composition" [1908:27]). He goes on to rectify the errors of the past and point out, with modern exactitude, what belongs to whom. With regard to Book 3, he declares that "Lefèvre . . . has absolutely no rights over the translation of . . . Colonne from which this last section was borrowed; he has wrongly been considered to be its author" ("Lefèvre n'a . . . aucun droit sur la traduction de Gui de Colonne à laquelle a été empruntée cette dernière section; c'est à tort qu'on l'en a considéré comme l'auteur" [30–31]). Bayot begins with bibliographic research and finishes by legislating property rights.

Property rights may be, in a sense, what the myth of Trojan origins is about. Hence the frequency with which the *grands rhétoriqueurs* exhort the monarchs of Europe to crusade, not only for the liberation of the Holy Land, but also for, as Pierre Jodogne puts it, "the recovery of territories formerly possessed by the Trojans, founders of the European dynasties" ("la récupération des territoires possédés jadis par les Troyens, fondateurs des dynasties européennes" [1970:161]). Francisque Thibaut compares fifteenth-century Europe's attachment to the myth of Trojan origins to nineteenth-century Europe's interest in the Ottoman empire: the states were "as determined then to be descended from the comrades of Hector, as they are now to divide up the spoils of Turkey" ("aussi jalouses en ce temps-là de descendre des compagnons d'Hector, qu'elles le sont actuellement de se partager les dépouilles de la Turquie" [1888:168]). Interestingly enough, Seznec employs the same word, *dépouilles* or spoils, to describe the names of the Trojan heroes assigned by Lemaire to the separate European states as founding ancestors: "Lemaire divided among them, like spoils of war, the names of the different Trojan heroes" ("Le Maire leur partageait, ainsi que des dépouilles, les noms des différent héros troyens" [1939:27]). Jean Lemaire's humanist treatise *La concorde des deux langages* moves from an image of French and Tuscan conjugal harmony and shared origins to a crusade call against the Turks. The *Illustrations* begins with the same exhortation. There is always this call to arms in what we refer to, innocently enough, as *classical humanism.*

Intertextuality in *Illustrations de Gaule et singularitez de Troye*

In 1508, when Jean Lemaire de Belges begins Book 1 of the *Illustrations de Gaule et singularitez de Troye,* he is a servant of the empire, *indiciaire* for Marguerite d'Autriche; by 1510, when he is composing Book 2, he has shifted his allegiance to France and Anne de Bretagne. The change does little to alter the essential purpose of the project: to establish the unity and prestige of the European states by documenting a common origin in Troy. In doing this, Lemaire seeks both to promote Burgundy as a legitimate subject—with its own Trojan hero as *souche*—and to justify its inclusion in a greater political whole. The general plan of the *Illustrations,* with its three volumes, should remind us of le Fèvre's *Recueil,* of the *Histoire ancienne jusqu'à César,* and of other late medieval and early Renaissance hybrid works (see chapter 8, "Translation," where these hybrid genres are discussed). Book 1 narrates the history of the world from the Flood to the kings of Troy and the childhood of Paris; Book 2 presents the abduction of Helen and the Trojan conflict; Book 3 traces the diaspora of the Trojan nobility, demonstrating the shared ancestral origins of France, Burgundy, and Austria. Thibaut calls the first Book "a pleasant romance" ("un roman agréable"); the second "a bit of epic poetry" ("un . . . morceau d'épopée"); and the third "a history" ("une histoire") (1888:165). The goal of the entire project is characterized, at the start, as a celebration of the Gallic nation and language: "to illustrate in the French language, which the Italians with their customary scorn call Barbarous (but which is not), the very venerable antiquity of the blood of the Princes of Gaul both Belgian and Celtic" ("esclarcir en ce langage François, que les Italiens par leur mesprisance acoustumee appellent Barbare [mais non est] la tres-venerable antiquite du sang de nosdits Princes de Gaule tant Belgique, comme Celtique" [Stecher 1885, 1:11]). This work, the author asserts, should serve the state in two vital respects: by reaffirming the respect and service of its subjects toward its masters and by unifying it against a common enemy and pretender to the Trojan throne: the Turk.

The *Illustrations* is typical of its time in being at once a work of humanism, historiography, genealogy, and patriotism. The *grands rhétoriqueurs* were, almost without exception, "court functionaries" (Zumthor 1978:9). As Jodogne puts it, writing prose or verse for the *rhétoriqueur* was a "public duty" ("devoir public" [1970:160]). This explains, to some extent, why I have been moving between politics and literature in this chapter—there being little difference between the two in this period—and why the *Illustrations* must be understood not only as a humanist enterprise but as a political program. Zumthor suggests that the *rhétoriqueur*'s principal obligation toward his prince is to produce a "discourse of Glory" ("discours de la Gloire" [1978:10]). This is, I think, a more interesting way of explaining the mythological framework within which the *rhétoriqueur* tends to work, and his propensity for obsessive word-play, than the customary assertions of excessive erudition and deficient sensibility.[10] The *rhétoriqueur*'s job is not to *represent* the world of the court, but to *reproduce* it as Law (10). Moreover, Zumthor underscores the connection between the law of the land and the law of the letter: "The *rhetoriqueur* makes it possible to hear/understand and read the Law. What writes the Law, through his hand, is a kind of violence" ("Ce que le rhétoriqueur donne à 'entendre' et à lire, c'est la Loi. Ce qui, par sa main, l'écrit, est une violence" [11]). It is that violence I am trying to expose.[11]

In the *Illustrations* that law may be summarized as "finders keepers" or "crime pays." Jodogne defends the frequently maligned *rhétoriqueurs* as a group of proto-humanist poets, many committed to translation and the cultivation of the vernacular (1970:166). Many critics treat the *Illustrations* as an early achievement of this humanism. Jodogne praises Lemaire for his responsible erudition, pointing out that each Book of the *Illustrations* lists the "authors referred to" ("acteurs alleguéz" [167]). Lemaire himself describes his work as a bibliographic-humanist enterprise, as in his summary of Book 2: "My principal intention is . . . to gather together in a single work . . . all that the ancient authors laid down, in many texts, concerning the exploits of Paris, Helen, Oenone, in order to create a comprehensive history. Which is a thing that, as far as I know, no one else has attempted, either in French or in Latin" ("Mon intention principale est . . . de rassembler tout en un corps . . . ce que les anciens acteurs autentiques ont couché de gestes de Paris, Heleine, et Oenone, en escrits divers . . . pour en forger une histoire totale. Laquelle chose nha esté ancores attentée de nul autre, qui ie sache, ny en Français ny en Latin" [Stecher 1885, 2:59–60]). Authorship is characterized both as an originating act and as a process of retrieval and collection, hunting and gathering. But upon closer examination it becomes clear that Lemaire is doing less hunting and gathering than he would have us believe, and more stealing. Generally Lemaire quotes as if directly sources that have, in fact, been prepackaged by previous authors. Jean Frappier, in "L'humanisme de Jean de Belges," defines Renaissance humanism as "an improved knowledge, direct, critical, of Greek and Latin authors" ("une connaissance amélioré, directe, critique, des auters grecs et latin" [1963:289]). On this score Lemaire must be said to fail; Frappier, sounding like Greene, decides that Lemaire "does not seem to have felt any rupture between what we call the Middle Ages . . . and the Renaissance" ("ne semble pas avoir senti de rupture entre ce que nous appelons le Moyen-Age et . . . la Renaissance" [290]). Frappier then proceeds to run through a list of some of Lemaire's sources; Lemaire gets his *Iliad*, for example, from Lorenzo Valla's prose translation in Latin—as Lemaire acknowledges (Stecher 1885, 2:152, 319). Lemaire's humanism is, on the whole, a mediated pseudo-humanism. Georges Doutrepont disagrees with Thibaut's assessment of Lemaire as a humanist, noting that Thibaut fails to mention where Lemaire gets his information (1934:153). In the section of his *Jean Lemaire de Belges et le Renaissance* devoted to "Borrowings from Annius de Viterbe" ("Emprunts à Annius de Viterbe," pp. 17–19), Doutrepont examines a passage from the *Illustrations* that explains the origins of the word *Gallus* and cites Xenophon as the source (Stecher 1885, 1:16–17). But Doutrepont shows that the entire passage, including the reference to Xenophon, has been taken from Annius. In fact a vast list of authors cited by Lemaire as sources actually comprises references made by Boccaccio (Doutrepont 1934:26).

Like Benoît de Sainte-Maure's *Le roman* and Raoul le Fèvre's *Recueil*, Lemaire's *Illustrations* presents us with the spectacle of cultural genealogy as citation. Doutrepont castigates Lemaire for this technique, which he sees as a subterfuge, a pure show of erudition. But that *show* is precisely what I am interested in: the effort to fashion, by whatever means are available, a *surface* of intertextual complexity. Doutrepont regards Lemaire's plagiarism exactly as Bayot did the editorial interventions of le Fèvre's copyists: as a moral and artistic shortcoming. "He combines," he writes of Lemaire, "he extends, but he doesn't invent" ("Il combine, il allonge, mais il n'invente pas" [1934:75]). When Doutrepont finds something positive to say, his praise is dubious: "Here he adds, there he cuts, elsewhere he modifies the argument. Thus, these translations deserve, in certain respects, to be called 'unfaithful beauties' " ("Ici il ajoute, là il retranche, ailleurs il change des arguments. Ainsi, ces traductions méritent-elles, pour certains points, la qualification de 'belles infidèles' " [239–40]). Lemaire's textual borrowings are all Helen of Troys, *belles infidèles.* The romance inside the text imitates the one outside. What is told imitates the way it is told—so much so that it becomes impossible to decide, and meaningless to ask, which is a metaphor for the other.

Illustrations 1: On Men and Their Names

The romance of the *Illustrations* is a patrilineage. Lemaire's patriarchs are Hercules de Libye, ancestor of the Trojans; Francus, son of Hector, who "gave the French their name" ("donna le nom aux François") (Stecher 1885, 1:13); Bauo, king of Phrygia and cousin of Priam, founder of Belgium; and the Duc Austrasius, "who first gave their names to [qui premierement donna le nom au] Royaume d'Austrasie and Austriche la basse" (3:364).The proof of continuity is the name; every name is the legacy of a prince who once ruled, the sign of the father who endures: "But no matter how much place and fortune may change, in no way does it change the direct genealogy of the illustrious blood of Her-

cules. . . . In both its feminine and masculine lines, this Genealogy is passed
on from father to son: from Francus, legitimate son of Hector of Troy, to Pépin le Bref" ("Mais combien que se fasse transmutation de liue et de fortune,
si ne change en riens la droite genealogie du tresnoble sang d'Hercules. . . .
Laquelle Genealogie tant en lignne feminine comme masculine est deduit de
pere ne filz: depuis Francus, filz legitime d'Hector de Troye, iusques à Pépin le
Bref" [Stecher 1885, 1:102, 3:259]). With *Charles le grand*— "who was monarch of Europe, and of all the Western nations" ("qui fut monarque d'Europe,
et de toutes lesdites nations Occidentales")—the *Illustrations* comes to a close
(3:259).

This genealogy is another instance of the medieval historiographic catalogue,
linking the disparate and the distant, asserting similarity in difference, synchrony in diachrony. Genealogy translates historical change into metaphor, asserting relationship by way of likeness. What stays alike is the Name. Here is
Thibaut on Lemaire's eponymous genealogy: "He only needed to cite a figure
whose name bears some resemblance to those by which the cities are called"
("Il lui suffisait de citer un personnage, dont le nom présentât quelque ressem-
blance avec celui qu'elles portaient elles-mêmes" [1888:173]). Regarding this
folk etymology Frappier comments: "Let us not heap too much abuse on Jean
Lemaire, if he is in love with puerile or comic etymologies based on the resemblance of letters and sounds (resonances and not reasonings)" ("N'accablons
pas trop non plus Jean Lemaire, s'il est féru d'étymologies puériles ou cocasses
suscitées par des ressemblances de lettres et de sons [des résonnements et non
des raisonnements]" [1963:296]). Frappier goes on to suggest what he calls a
"letter symbolism" ("symbolisme de lettres") at the origin both of Lemaire's
particular brand of etymology and of the all-pervasive emphasis upon word-play
in *rhétoriqueur* poetry. Rather than the mystical symbolism of "resonance,"
something closer to Cratylean idolatry is at work here, a faith in the perceptible
shape of the name as image or substitute. The Pyrenees owe their name to a fire
that melted the mountains between France and Spain, as Lemaire explains: "For
pyr in Greek means *fire* in French" ("Car pyr en Grec signifie feu en François"
[Stecher 1885, 1:59]). The example suggests that names in the *Illustrations* are
representational; it also shows that names, too, have their preferred genealogies
and ancestors. Etymology by resemblance is, in fact, another form of *prosopopoeia,* where names are effectively turned into faces. The name is beautiful,
seductive, is coveted, fetishized, idolized. To cite the name of the ancestor is to
point to the tomb of the eponymous hero, like the relic of a saint.

In Lemaire's patrilineage, names are prized like women, but the names that
count belong to men. Charlemagne is the ultimate target: Lemaire's *Illustrations*
moves toward him, a succession of fathers and sons converges upon him. If Lemaire admits that Charlemagne may be related, through Queen Berthe, to the
Eastern Roman Empire, he quickly reduces the importance of that relationship:

"there is no need to confirm his nobility and generosity in this way" ("de ren-
forcer sa noblesse et générosité par ce moyen, nest ia besoing" [Stecher 1885,
3:464]).[12] A woman's name belongs only to the individual; it cannot be per-
petuated: "the great Hercules of Libya had with his wife Galatea, the beautiful
giant, a son named Galatas: who gave his name to the Gallic nation" ("le grand
Hercules de Libye eut de sa femme Galatee la belle geande un filz nommé Galatas: qui donna son nom à la nation Gallicane" [1:12]). The female name can,
however, perpetuate itself. Women are valued in the *Illustrations* to the extent
that they marry and propagate, and they are condemned to the extent that they
depart from that role. The feminine, in other words, is valued to the extent that
it mediates the masculine. Of course that makes the masculine contingent upon
the feminine. The overarching structure of the *Illustrations* suggests that if the
protagonists are male, the space in which they move is feminine. In the prologue to Book 1, Lemaire declares: "I will dedicate each of the three individual
Books . . . to the dominions and lofty natures of three great Goddesses . . . Pallas,
Venus, and Juno. These will also represent . . . the three ages of Paris Alexander" ("Les trois liures particuliers, seront par moy dediez . . . aux seigneuries
et hautesses de trois grands Deesses . . . Pallas, Venus, et Iuno. Et representeront
. . . les trois aages de Paris Alexandre" [Stecher 1885, 1:5]). The first Book of
the *Illustrations* is devoted to the exploits of the young Paris: his education and
marriage to the nymph Oenone. But Paris has yet to learn the power of beauty.
His turning point, which is civilization's, is where Book 2 begins: the Judgment
of Paris.

Illustrations 2: On Women and Their Faces

Thibaut laments what he sees as Lemaire's lack of focus in Book 2: out of 44
chapters in the first part, 15 deal with the Judgment of Paris; out of 100 chapters
in the second part, 60 are devoted to Helen (1888:165). It is clear, however, that
these two, Helen and Paris, are the central protagonists in the central Book of the
Illustrations. If Lemaire's genealogy is an alternative to the biblical narrative,
then the Judgment of Paris is the Fall.[13] Lemaire is not alone, we have seen, in
giving this kind of prominence to the Judgment: precursors here include Benoît
de Sainte-Maure's *Le roman de Troie,* Christine de Pisan's *L'epîstre d'Othéa à
Hector de Troye,* and the *Ovide moralisé* (see chapter 8). But in Lemaire's ren-
dition the Judgment determines not only the direction of human history, but
the structure of the *Illustrations* itself. As Lemaire declares in the prologue to
Book 1, speaking with the voice of Mercury and putting the seal of authenticity
upon the forthcoming narrative: "of all the celestial spirits it fell to me to ensure
the restoration of this history, given that I ministered in person at the judgment
of the three Goddesses, in which event is to be found the key to this entire Trojan
history" ("à moy . . . des esprits celestes appartenoit de procurer la restauration

dicelle histoire, attendu, que ie fuz . . . ministre presential ai iugement des trois Deesses, auquel gist lesclarcissement de toute lhistoire Troyenne" [1:4]). Lemaire reenacts the Judgment in the very organization of the *Illustrations,* which comprises, we have seen, three Books, each brought under the auspices of one of the three goddesses who competed for Paris's favor. Book 1 belongs to (Pallas) Athena; Book 2 to Venus; and Book 3 to Juno. The Judgment also provides one of the moments where the political aspirations of the *Illustrations* are most openly voiced. Lemaire explicitly translates the parable of the apple of discord (parallel to Eve's apple) into contemporary terms. Marguerite will be the new Pallas Athena, and her nephew, the future Charles-Quint, the new "Paris Alexandre": "I will present him with the golden apple, which is to say, his own free will: And I will make him judge of the beauty of the three goddesses: this is, Prudence, Pleasure, and Power" ("je luy presenteray la pomme dor, cesatdire, son propre franc arbitre: Et le feray iuge de la beauté des trois Deesses: cestasauoir Prudence, Plaisance, et Puissance" [1:6]). Paris's education will serve as a model for the education of the future emperor.

What happens at the Judgment, and why is it so important? The beauty of a woman leads Paris (as it led Adam) and, ultimately, all of civilization, astray. Paris, Lemaire laments, "by bad judgment, preferred Venus, that is, corporal beauty and sensual pleasure, over the two other Goddesses, Juno and Pallas, who stand for spiritual knowledge and the riches of temporal dominion" ("par iugement abusif, prefera Venus, cestadire beauté corporelle et volupté sensuelle, aux deux autres Deesses, Iuno et Pallas, qui signifient science spirituelle . . . et richesses de domination temporelle" [2:2]). The presence of Helen, of course, is always implied in any version of the Judgement. Lemaire's prologue to Book 2 makes this connection perfectly clear. Paris in the Judgment "fixed his whole gaze upon the body of Venus, that is, on that of Helen, whom he ravished and detained unjustly, breaking and corrupting his marriage, and others" ("arresta du tout son regard sur la corpulence de Venus, cestadire, de la belle Heleine, laquelle il rauit et detint iniustement, en brisant et corrompant le sien marriage, et dautry" [2:2]). The Judgment here merges into the rape of Helen almost without a seam; Venus is but a substitute for Helen. In fact, Lemaire's picture of Paris's fall from grace offers at least two aspects that explain its prominence in the *Illustrations:* the Judgment is a crisis for the institution of marriage, and it is a dramatic allegory about the fatality of beauty and the dangers of idolatry.

Paris's error, I would note, is the very one committed by Lemaire in his idolatry of his precursors' texts and his ancestors' names: a belief in or a love of surfaces.[14] The Judgment of Paris is a moment of exposure in which truth is unveiled only to reveal another veil: the illusory veil of beauty. Here is Frappier on Lemaire's schooling in the humanities: "In short, Greek literature reached him only as if reflected in a mirror. But these reflections, especially the Homeric ones, retained enough power and brilliance to enchant and dazzle him" ("En somme, la littérature grecque n'est venue jusqu'à lui que par reflets. Mais ces reflets, surtout les homériques, ont gardé assez de force et d'éclat pour l'enchanter ou l'éblouir" [1963:301n3]). Isn't Lemaire, as much as Paris, enchanted and seduced by a vision of beauty, a vision that is but a likeness, a substitute for the real? Frappier says that Lemaire, true to his time, did not "believe" in the myths he narrates (301n3). This may be true, but that skepticism, as we have seen, paradoxically encourages a different form of worship: a cult of myth as pretty picture or seductive image.[15] Thus Lemaire ends up practicing the very idolatry he condemns, as when, in euhemeristic fashion, he attacks the ancient cults of Helen: "after her death, antiquity, blind and misguided, a time prodigious in its idolatrous creation of new Gods and Goddesses, placed Helen among the list of the immortal Goddesses" ("après la mort d'icelle, l'aage aveuglee et erronee du temps . . . qui estoit prodigue de forger nouveaux Dieux et Deesses par idolatrie, meit et rengea ladite Heleine au nombre et catalogue des Deesses immortelles" [2:301]).

That rejection does not prevent Lemaire from amplifying Helen's beauty or from recounting her power as a goddess of beauty or from citing the miracles she works at her shrine at Therapna. Lemaire vents his spleen at Helen and yet lingers all too long—following the tradition of *amplificatio*—over the temptations she offers to the eyes of Paris and others. "Heleine," we are informed, "was famous as the most beautiful being who had ever been seen on earth" ("fut renommee pour la plus belle creature que iamais on eust veüe sur terre" [2:23]). At this point Lemaire retells the tale of Theseus and Peirithous, complete with scenes of Helen wrestling naked at a festival: "And then they found entertainment at the palestra, where the maiden Helen wrestled naked, covered in nothing more than olive oil" ("Ainsi sesbastoit à la palestre ou luitte la pucelle Heleine toute nue, oincte sans plus dhuile dolive" [2:25]). No wonder, Lemaire seems to say, Theseus could not resist. Lemaire does not fail to include the scene of seduction par excellence: his own version of the *teichoskopia*. Helen stands, once again, upon the walls of Troy, at the "Skaian gates" ("porte scee"), and this time Lemaire is with the elders, gazing upon her: "Certainly it is not at all strange that the Trojans and the Greeks endure so much suffering, and for so long, for such a face, which seems to be not at all that of a human woman, but rather that of an immortal Goddess" ("Certes ce nest point chose estrange, si les Troyens et les Grecz soustiennent tant de maux, et par si longue espace, pour un tell visage, qui ne semble point estre de femme humaine, ainçois plustost dune Deesse immortelle" [2:158]).

As Lemaire looks upon Helen, the reader might well ask what he or she is reading. Could it be Homer? This is apparently what Lemaire has acknowledged only moments before: "I will translate Homer in this passage almost word for word" ("je translateray presques mot à mot ledit Homer sur de passage" [2:152]). And yet two sentences later Lemaire segues into the scene at Troy with: "Now this is what the noble prince of Greek poets says as put into Latin by Laurens Valla" ("Or dit iceluy noble prince des poëtes Grecz mis en Latin par Laurens Valla"). As with the face of Helen, it is not clear exactly what we are looking at. Is this the real thing, or just a likeness?

Lemaire's Helen owes less to Homer than to Ovid, Virgil, and Benoît; she is the villain, not the victim, of the story. The original sin of Lemaire's cosmology is ultimately not rape but *seduction* and, following that, *infidelity*. Helen is too seductive and too disruptive to win much sympathy in a treatise on political stability and union. Like Benoît, Lemaire discounts the Homeric epic—more favorable to Helen—as Greek propaganda (not that Lemaire would have had access to the Greek original). Regarding his decision to include Homer at all in his recounting of the Trojan war, Lemaire insists: "nonetheless I will not diverge too far from the historical truth of our author Dictys" ("nonobstantant ie ne relenquiray point de trop loing la vérité historiale de nostre acteur Dictys de Crete" [2:152]). Homer may be a "prince of poets" ("prince des poëtes"— the phrase is Valla's: "Homerus poetarum princeps"),[16] but he is no historian. Helen's rape is really a question of simple adultery. Lemaire, like Ovid in the *Heroides* (from which Lemaire, at least in part, takes his romance of Paris and Helen),[17] asserts that Helen wanted to be abducted (2:70–72). If Paris is Lemaire's Adam, then Helen is his Eve. Lemaire's scorn for this "feminine monster" ("monstre feminin" [2:76]) is boundless. But in the following apostrophe, we can see how easily Lemaire's moral proscription cooperates with voyeuristic indulgence: "O felonious heart . . . stranger to reason, distant from feminine pity . . . o angelic face of Venus, with the tail of a serpent or a dragon" ("O coeur felon. . . aliéné de raison, loingtain de pitié feminine . . . ô visage angélique et venerien, ayant queüe draconique et serpentine" [2:77]). Helen is a heroine out of the courtly love tradition; she cannot be loved and married at the same time. Helen's foil, symbol of purity and goodness, is Paris's legitimate and abandoned spouse, the faithful Oenone. This is clear as Lemaire fulminates against Helen: "O detestable bitch, mad dog, viper most dangerous! What a difference there is between you and the noble nymph Oenone" ("O chienne tresdestable, lisse enragee et vipere tresdangereuse! Combien y ha il de difference de toy à la noble Nymphe Œnone" [Stecher 1885, 2:219]).

When Lemaire comes to narrate the ascent of France's own founding father, Clovis, the ghost of Helen returns in the figure of Clotilde de Bourgogne. Clotilde, the dispossessed daughter of Chilperic, brother of Gundebaud, king of Burgundy, comes upon the scene at a critical juncture in Lemaire's history: her marriage to Clovis, first Christian Frankish ruler, confirms the legitimate unity of Burgundy and France. But that legitimacy is subtly threatened by Lemaire's own admission that coercion—or the outward appearance of coercion— may have been at work: that "Clotilde de Bourgogne agreed in secret to be ravished by [consentit secretement destre rauie par] Clouis, king of France." Like

Helen, Clotilde is "tall and perfectly beautiful" ("grande et belle en perfection"[3:399]). As with Helen, Clotilde's beauty is first reported by an ambassa-
dor to the man who will abduct her. Clotilde's abduction, like Helen's, occurs
while the man of the house is away on business, and Clotilde as much as Helen is
taken "willingly, with her consent" ("de son bon gré et consentement"[3:403]).
Like Helen, finally, Clotilde is an especially destructive figure, a "woman too
vindictive" ("femme trop vindicative"); her vengeance for Gundebaud's murder of her father is maniacal, "beyond all measure" ("oultremesure"[3:410]).

Illustrations 3: On Husbands and Wives

Unlike Helen and Paris, Clotilde and Clovis are legitimately united. We have
seen cultural and political union figured—and realized—as wedlock in
fifteenth-century Europe. We have seen how the history of Burgundy—its sub-
ordination to France, its recurrent flirtations with a foreign seducer (England)—
is like a long saga of marital infidelity, wavering between divorce and reconciliation. We know that behind the history of European alliances there is another
story of political maneuvers for conquest and annexation. The figures of Clotilde
and Clovis in the *Illustrations* represent marriage as the primordial step toward
European union (read conquest) and anticipate the overarching objectives of
Book 3:

> Par la deduction de ce deuxieme Traicté ha este veu, comment le tresnoble sang des pre-
> miers Roys de Bourgongne fut coniont avec celuy de France, es personnes de Clouis et
> de Clotilde. Si reste de monstrer au Traicté ensuivant, comment le sang Romain et la
> genealogie d'Austriche la basse furent meslez avec celles de France et de Bourgongne.
> (3:421)

> [By the arguments of this second Book we have shown how the noble blood of the first
> Kings of Burgundy was conjoined with that of France, in the persons of Clovis and Clo-
> tilde. It remains to be shown, in the following Book, how Roman blood and the genealogy
> of lower Austria were mixed with that of France and Burgundy.]

These objectives are realized in the figure of Charlemagne, who reunites the
disparate lineages that Helen had dispersed.

The entire third Book of the *Illustrations* is dedicated to Anne de Bretagne
as a new Juno, queen of the Olympians, goddess of marriage: "lady of . . .
earthly wealth, who rules over Kingdoms and principalities, mistress and pa-
troness of the holy alliances of faithful marriages" ("dame des . . . richesses
mondaines, dominateresse des Royaumes et seigneuries, maistresse et patrone
des saintes alliances des loyaux mariages" [3:249]). Marriage as a figure of
viable power allows the triumph of a feminine, matriarchal rhetoric. Lemaire's
very dedication of the *Illustrations* to either Marguerite d'Autriche or Anne de
Bretagne suggests a scenario of conjugal submission and betrayal. We know that

Lemaire—like many of his fellow *rhétoriqueurs*—is a kept poet, a servant to a woman of vast power. A kept poet, but one who is unfaithful to his betrothed. The first prologue, written in 1508, begins with a dedication to Marguerite, "another Pallas, and wise Minerva, that is, immortal" ("une autre Pallas, et tressage Minerve, cestadire, immortelle" [1:7]). By 1510, when he is writing Book 2, as we have already seen, the poet is working for Anne de Bretagne, singing *her* praises, comparing *her,* not Marguerite, to Juno. The opening of the first Book proper of the *Illustrations* is more than the hyperbole of dedication to a patron; it is on several levels a valorization of the feminine as the power to reconcile, unify, or marry. Burgundian and Austrian, French and Habsbourg, Marguerite is celebrated as integrating "the two noblest houses of all the world" ("deux maisons les plus nobles de tout le monde" [1:10]). As arbitrator of the Ligue de Cambrai of 1509, a pact allying Emperor Maximilian and King Louis XII against the Venetians, Marguerite is extolled as both peacemaker and matchmaker. Finally, it is declared that "all Princesses, ladies and maidens" ("toutes Princesses, dames et damoiselles"), now joined in peace, may turn to Lemaire's history as a source of entertainment and edification; it is for them Lemaire has written. In consequence, the Sovereign Princess and her female subjects may be brought together, may communicate, "like those with whom she has engaged in conversation" ("comme celles avec lesquelles elle ha eu conversation [1:11]). It is only after this lengthy invocation that Lemaire formally announces the principal question to be addressed by the work at hand and presupposed in its title: "by what means one can make the two terms and words GAUL and TROY signify and agree with each other, given that these are the names of regions very distant from one another, and which have no proximity whatsoever" ("par quel moyen on peult faire symboliser et convenir ensemble ces deux termes et vocables GAULE et TROYE, attendu que ce sont noms de regions si tresdistantes lune de lautre, et qui nont proximite ne voisinage aucun" [1:11–12]). The question Lemaire asks here is, in effect, the one I am posing throughout this Book; and the very terms in which it is posed suggest the answer. For *symboliser* here retains its original meaning, *to throw together* (*sumbolon*) the halves of a coin or bone that two people broke between them. *Convenir,* originally *to come with,* is thus a restatement of *symboliser.* In both verbs we can detect the outlines of an ideal marriage. How to link that which is irrevocably cloven, both geographically and temporally? By a recurrent *zeugma,* yoking like and unlike. By means, in other words, of graft.

   The central premise of the *Illustrations* is that marriage functions as a graft. We have learned "how the noble blood of the first Kings of Burgundy was conjoined with that of France" ("comment le tresnoble sang des premiers Roys de Bourgongne fut coniont avec celuy de France" [3:421]). Clovis and Clothilde are the new Baucis and Philemon of Lemaire's mythology. Thus the call for political cooperation among the nations of Europe, justified by an image of shared arboreal origins: "that the two Peoples who came from the same trunk/ stock share a common perpetual alliance" ("que les deux Peuples et nations sorties dun mesme tronc, on fasse une commune perpetuelle alliance" [3:250]). Thus the prophecy spoken by King Bauo, founder of a "large city in Belgium" ("grande cité de Belges"), that "the noble line of the Trojans would be extirpated in Asia, in order to be planted in Europe" ("la noble lignee ses Troyens seroit extirpee d'Asie, pour estre plantee en Europe" [3:284]. Thus the etymological digression upon *Alexia,* the name of a city founded by Hercules, king of Gaul, in that land "which is now called the Duchy of Burgundy" ("quon dit maintenant la Duché de Bourgongne" [1:61]); *Alexia* "signifies conjunctive or copulative: because the noble blood of two different nations was there conjoined" ("signifie coniunctive ou copulative: pource que le tresnoble sang de deux diverses nations y fut conioint" [1:61]). And thus the myth of Hermaphroditus, fulfilled in the perfect amalgamation of Gaul and Troy: for "the Gauls and the Trojans are not only tightly bound together, now as in the past, but are so intertwined that one cannot clearly distinguish or separate the one from the other" ("les Gaulois et les Troyens ont non seulement grande adherence ensemble tant vieille comme nouuelle, mais sont si meslez quon ne les peult bonnement discerner ne separer lun de lautre" [1:13]).

Marriage as graft also provides, we should remember, the central organizing principle of the *Illustrations.* As Lemaire's genealogy is designed to join the Houses of Burgundy, France, and Austria into one happy family, so his work is designed, as we have already seen, to synthesize the texts of the past, to "gather together in a single work . . . all that the ancient authors laid down" ("rassembler tout en un corps . . . ce que les anciens acteurs autentiques ont couché"). In Lemaire's grand question of the first prologue, GAULE and TROYE are specifically labeled *termes* and *vocables*—they are units of language, elements of a title. The question is not just how to make Gaul and Troy *one,* but how to make *one Book* out of them. We can watch Lemaire building his title out of larger and larger blocks: "And to better authorize the Illustrations of Gaule with the singularities of Troye . . . we will mix the Gallic Kings among the Trojans" ("Et pour mieux autoriser les Illustrations de Gaule avec les singularitez de Troye . . . nous meslerons les Roys Galliques entremy les Troyens" [1:16]). At such a moment it is no longer clear if the book is there to justify the genealogy or the other way around. The two coincide in an image from the prologue of Book 3, where that book is compared with Books 1 and 2; they "are but the buds and the flowers: but here is the fruit come to its maturity. There is the peel and here is the pit: over there is the painting, and over here is real life: those are merely the two premises of the syllogism, but here is the conclusion" ("ne sont que les bourgeons et les fleurs: mais voicy le fruit parvenu en maturité. Là est le scaille, et icy le noyau: droit là est la peinture, et cy dedens le vif: illecques sont sans plus les deux premices du syllogisme, mais voicy la conclusion" [3:250]).

Obviously the images here employed refer as much to Lemaire's *Illustrations* as to the genealogical history narrated therein. The passage, in its shift from metaphor to metaphor, is itself a marriage of disparate discursive modes. Each mode points toward the conclusion of the *Illustrations* as successful, organic graft, in contradistinction to an artificial and failed synthesis: (1) fertility, not sterility; (2) substantive interiority, not superficial exteriority; (3) living origin, not imitative likeness; and (4) knowledge in the sense of the embracing of difference (saying *this is like that*), rather than the preservation of distinctions (saying *this* and then saying *that*). Lemaire's is a vision of genealogical wholeness and intertextual health: achieved without violence, rupture, deception, pathology, or appropriation. It seems to be the fulfillment of Greene's search for a healthy, natural, legitimate cultural genealogy.

The distinction between inner truth and outer veil is an essential motif in the *Illustrations*—a title that itself refers at once to pictorial production and to revelation and elucidation. That distinction is a way of justifying, at the outset of the work, the narrative project, "which . . . is rich in great mysteries and poetic and philosophical wisdom, containing the fruitful substance beneath the skin of artificial fables" ("laquelle . . . est toute riche de grans mystères et intelligences poëtiques et philosophales, contenant fructueuse substance souz l'escorce des fables artificielles" [1:4]). And yet the crucial moment of the *Illustrations,* when the veils are removed and the "truth" exposed, is the catastrophe of the Judgment: a moment of deception, seduction, and violence. Venus's beauty is itself a mere veil, an illusory truth. In the cases of both Venus and Helen, beauty is only skin deep.

10

Cosmetics

Introduction (Cleanser): Cosmetologies

What if new poetry is just old poetry, stolen, stitched together, and given a makeover? Early modern lyric continues to be judged almost solely by the criteria of originality and authenticity. Even when it appears to be nothing more than a collection of conventions and clichés, a good poem must refer, we persist in believing, to something "real," "true," "sincere." But what if reference is itself a convention? If we were to read lyric as a graft of prior passages, only thinly disguised, originality might then become a question of cosmetic changes. Perhaps Ronsard's last sonnet cycle, the *Sonets pour Helene,* can best be appreciated as a *recycling* of earlier poetic models. As one might expect in a work that adheres closely to the Petrarchan code, the addressee of the *Sonets pour Helene* is nowhere to be found. But perhaps the speaker does not wish to find her. Poetry, here, is not a way of recovering Helen, but a way of replacing her. The business of the *Sonets pour Helene,* I will argue, is not passion or praise but production: it functions in the manner of an industry dedicated to the replication and dissemination of phantom or supplementary Helens (Helen, for example, as portrait, name, dream, gaze, letter, public figure, poem, myth), pieced together out of premanufactured parts.

Ronsard's love sonnets are often miniature cosmologies. The following is from his earliest sonnet cycle, the *Amours* (1552): "When the Woman whom I adore / First came to adorn the realm of the heavens, / The son of Rhea called all the Gods, / To make her another Pandora" ("Quand au premier la Dame que j'adore / Vint embellir le sejour de nos cieulx, / Le filz de Rhée appella tous les Dieux, / Pour faire encore d'elle une aultre Pandore" [ll. 1–4]).[1] As in any typical *blason, Amours* 32 goes on to praise this celestial body by enumerating its parts: "Then Apollo dressed her opulently . . . Mars gave her his fierce cruelty, / Venus her laughter, Dione her beauty, Peitho his voice" ("Lors Apollin richement la decore / . . . . Mars luy donna sa fiere cruaulté, / Venus son ris, Dione sa beaulté, / Peithon sa voix" [5–11]). Critics have disparaged this poem, and for reasons that point toward a more general dissatisfaction with Ronsard's poetry: first, it is not very original; second, it doesn't seem to care. Donald Stone, for example, calls *Amours* 32 "derivative" and without "depth," an "artificial list" of Petrarchan clichés. He argues that the entire *Amours* "is laden with Petrarch, but in bits and tatters; its piecemeal execution fails" (1966:220). My goal here is not to dispute Stone's terms, but to show that they are part of a larger set of cultural presuppositions that continue to inform the way we read lyric poetry.

Stone prefers Ronsard's last sonnet cycle (1578),[2] the *Sonets pour Helene* (hereafter referred to as *SpH*), a "deeper" and more "original" work. At first glance, a cosmogony such as *SpH* 1.4,[3] with its all-real, all-natural heroine, looks like a plea for that kind of depth and originality: "All that is holy, honorable, and virtuous, / All the good which Nature can do for mortals, / All that artifice here can fabricate, / My mistress had in her spirit at birth" ("Tout ce qui est de sainct, d'honneur & de vertu, / Tout le bien qu'aux mortels la Nature peut faire, / Tout ce que l'artifice icy peut contrefaire. / Ma mistresse, en naissant, dans l'esprit l'avoit eu" [1–4]). We can only imitate ("contrefaire") perfection, through the labor of art ("artifice"), but Helen is primordial, her birth without labor. At least that's what the first quatrain seems to say. But there are at least two ways to read lines 3 and 4 of this poem: (1) Helen is blessed at birth with all the virtues, which art can only imitate; or (2) Helen is blessed with only imitation virtues, those, in other words, which art can imitate. What of the second quatrain, then, which appears to assert Helen's authenticity and essential goodness? "Of that which is just and honest vied for enviously / In the schools of the Greeks: of that which can lead / To the love of the true good, to flee the opposite, / As with a dress her body was clothed" ("Du juste & de l'honneste à l'envy debatu / Aux escoles des Grecs: de ce qui peut attraire / A l'amour du vray bien, à fuyr le contraire, / Ainsi que d'un habit son corps fut revestu" [5–8]). How to read line 8? Does it mean that Helen wears her virtues as naturally as a dress, or that Helen *only* wears her virtues as naturally as a dress? The speaker concludes: "Seeing her so perfect, I must cry out, / Happy he who adores her, and who lives in her time!" ("La voyant si parfaite, il faut que je m'escrie, / Bien-heureux qui l'adore, & qui vit de son temps!" [13–14]). Is line 13 a final salute (1) to Helen's perfection or (2) to Helen's apparent perfection? (What is important is "la *voyant* si parfaite": "*seeing* her so perfect.") Perhaps what *SpH* 1.4 argues for is not *poetics* but cosmetics. The lesson here may be that we ought not to take originality and depth too seriously.[4]

This would appear to be the lesson of *SpH* 2.18, another *blason* that returns to the model of Pandora even as it rejects that model. Creation comes first: "Nature and the Heavens / Poured upon you their gifts each vying with the other, / Then in order never to make another broke the mold" ("La Nature & les Cieux / Ont versé dessus toy leurs dons à qui mieux mieux: / Puis pour n'en faire plus ont rompu le modelle" [6–8]). This is followed by enumeration: "Here Chastity is joined to your beauty, / Here is the respect for God, here Piety" ("Icy à ta beauté se joint la Chasteté, / Icy l'honneur de Dieu, icy la Pieté" [9–10]). And the poem concludes with a baptism: "Thus instead of my heart, or Helen, or my life, / I will henceforth call you my Penelope" ("Pource en lieu de mon cœur, d'Helene, & de ma vie, / Je te veux desormais ma Pandore appeler" [13–14]). Mechanistic theogony, *SpH* 2.18 reads like a promotional exhortation: build your own Pandora! The poem itself is built in this way, assembled from the tropes of poets past. Since the original has been lost (so goes the cliché of the second quatrain), Ronsard can declare his Helen unique.[5] A rather tired campaign, perhaps, but Ronsard's Helen, like his *Sonets pour Helene,* is never anything but a cheerfully generic product. A product must have the right name if it is to sell; hence the second tercet's testing and rejecting of competing brand *names* (*mon coeur [my heart], Helene, ma vie [my life]*), a process that should discourage us from treating any of these images too seriously.[6]

Stone's reading of Ronsard rests on the cherished assumption that lyric is always an act of origination (the making of something entirely new) and confession (the revelation of something entirely true). Poetics as such has always been opposed to cosmetics. Reading poetry in the tradition of poetics has always conformed to a very specific topological and tropological model: it has always meant excavation, unveiling, exfoliation. According to this model a good poem is *deep,* the *meaning* of a poem *invisible, hidden* within its *interior.* Poetics as such is also an *erotics:* the poem playing coy mistress to a critic/seducer who will settle for nothing less than the *naked* truth. This is why poetics (when performed "properly") resembles a striptease. Poems like *Amours* 32 refuse to play the game: such poems start out already naked, as it were, and are considered unworthy of serious critical attention. That critics prefer the *Sonets pour Helene* is the inevitable consequence of these assumptions. The best readers will concede that the dichotomy between imitation and invention is a false one in the sixteenth century, but the "originality fallacy" condemns even the best readers to resurrect that dichotomy at some "deeper" level of Ronsard's poetry, even when that poetry appears to be entirely "derivative." The "confessional fallacy," meanwhile, will just as inevitably lead the critic to recast it as a personal artifact, an articulation of the poet's experience. The "confessional fallacy" has its corollary, the "developmental fallacy," which argues that more experience makes for better (deeper) articulations. Thus Ronsard's last sonnet cycle must be his best (deepest, most heartfelt, most original).

But what if all poetry, to use Stone's terms, were a way of creating the new piecemeal, out of bits and tatters? Suppose we read *Amours* 32 as a confession without a crime, or a surface without depth, or a representation that has no referent (or that refuses to take its referents seriously): as not a cosmology, but a *cosmetology?* We may start by agreeing that *Amours* 32 is a shamelessly derivative poem, and then decide that there is nothing to be ashamed about. Cassandra, addressee of the first *Amours,* is herself a copy, "another Pandora" ("une aultre Pandore"); she is not so much born as fabricated: synthesized and sutured. In just the same way, the sonnet itself is grafted from spare parts (Italian, French, Greek, Latin): stories, all, about grafting from spare parts, like Hesiod's story of the birth of Pandora (Evelyn-White 1914: ll. 70–80). His theogony is as cosmetological as Ronsard's: "the . . . Lame God molded clay in the likeness of a modest maid . . . . Athene girded and clothed her, and the divine Graces and queenly Persuasion put necklaces of gold upon her . . . . And Pallas Athene bedecked her with all manners of finery. Also the Guide, the Slayer of Argos, contrived within her lies and crafty words and a deceitful nature." Pandora is manufactured; her beauty, skin-deep, a mask hiding only other masks. The example of Hesiod suggests that Ronsard can hardly be considered the first "cosmetic" poet (an "original cosmetics" is a contradiction, in any case). Rather, Ronsard represents a particular moment in a classical-humanist tradition that has always been "pro-cosmetic."

I will argue that all of the *Sonets pour Helene,* like *Amours* 23, simultaneously promote and critique the poetics of originality and depth. This makes Ronsard's work a powerful piece of postmodern criticism, and long before postmodernity. That suggests, in turn, both the elasticity of a term like *postmodernism* and the contemporaneity of the sixteenth-century sonnet cycle. Terry Eagleton defines the postmodern as a cosmetic mode of reading: "playful, self-ironizing . . . embracing the language of . . . the commodity. Its stance towards cultural tradition is one of irreverent pastiche, and its contrived depthlessness undermines all metaphysical solemnities." [7] The same can be said about the *Sonets pour Helene.*

Exfoliants and Astringents: Poetics in an Age of Cosmetics

There are good reasons why early modern poems look so much like postmodern products. In many respects the sixteenth century is a cosmetic era, an era dominated by representation and textual dissemination. This is what contemporary critics acknowledge when they set about reading Ronsard, without putting it in those terms. Acknowledging that, however, means losing Ronsard as a creative subject, and that is what the critic, in the next moment, will struggle to salvage.

Both critical moments operate in the following exhortation by Terence Cave:

Preoccupations of Romantic origin with "originality" or with the sense of a direct com-
munication of lived experience ("sincerity") have to be drastically modified if one is
to appreciate a sixteenth-century poem; the influence of the . . . discipline of rhetoric . . . predisposes the poet to present individual experiences within the framework of
established modes of expression, to the point at which a declaration of love in a mid-
sixteenth-century poem may be almost indistinguishable from its equivalent in Petrarch
or a classical Latin poet. Once such factors have been taken into account, a new kind of
enjoyment may be *released* for the reader, not only in the full perception of Ronsard's
brilliance in modulating a well-worn theme, but also in the search at *a deeper level* for
those recurrent *preoccupations and anxieties,* absent from lesser poets, which give his
work a fundamentally *human centre.* (1973:1; my italics)

The first sentence is a perfect example of the attempt to situate Ronsard historically. With the second, however, Cave performs a strategic *volte-face.* But this
pivoting is not a mistake; on the contrary, it is determined by the same cultural
presuppositions Cave attempts to dismiss as Romantic concerns. I would argue that these presuppositions go farther back than Romanticism: when we read
poetry as the external representation of a "truth" both "hidden" and "human,"
we speak not just as Romantics, but as Platonists and Neoplatonists. It is also
typical that the closer Cave approaches the specificity of the poem (that which
makes it original), the less he is able to articulate that specificity. What is a
"human centre"? Exactly what "deeper level" is Cave talking about? These
terms are rhetorically effective precisely to the extent that they remain imprecise.[8] Criticism of early modern poetry remains almost exclusively an anticosmetic tropology.[9]

In his *Pléiade Poetics,* the more Grahame Castor succeeds in dissolving the
poet in the solvent of sixteenth-century convention, the more anxious he is to
save his hero from utterly disappearing. Much of Castor's study rests on the
distinction between *imitation* and *invention,* an opposition he works hard to reject and retain. Like Cave, Castor locates this distinction historically after the
Renaissance: "Originality did not become the antonym of imitation until the
seventeenth century at the earliest, and creativity was not regularly attributed
to poets or poetry until the eighteenth century" (1964:5). A few pages later,
however, he hastens to reinsert invention into the equation: "Invention was the
name used to designate the element of originality, as we would nowadays call
it, in a work of art; in this sense it was the opposite of imitation" (11). Castor
goes on to say that invention "was also used to refer to the relationship of the
poet with his subject-matter, which he was said to 'invent' or find . . . in reality.
Invention was thus the first step in the Aristotelian process of imitation. Once
the objects of imitation had been found, then they could be represented in the
form of an artifact" (11). The gesture toward Aristotle does not expel Plato or
his Neoplatonic descendants from the picture: poetry remains, as it always does
in the anticosmetic model, representational, referential, or revelatory.[10]

It also remains, of necessity, confessional. In the anticosmetic reading the "subject-matter" which the poem "represents" is the subject, plain and simple: the poet. All of the critics cited here perform the ritual "death of the author" only to resurrect him in the next instant, by turning Ronsard's poems into chapters in a biographical narrative. Here is the "developmental fallacy" at work. I am focusing on Ronsard's last sonnet cycle because the critical tradition has approached it as the culminating moment in a literary history-as-*Bildungsroman* that moves from the "cosmetic" to the "poetic." In Stone's narrative of Ronsard's career, only the work of the "mature" artist is marked by what he calls poetic "vision," another Neoplatonic figure the precise meaning of which remains obscure (1966:17). If Ronsard imitates Petrarch 192 in *SpH* 2.3, it is now an example of "mature borrowing" instead of "piecemeal insertion"; Ronsard "looks beyond the level of vocabulary to the more central issues of structure, tone, and even vision" (207). A. H. T. Levi ties every phase of Ronsard's poetic output to specific historical events and their impact upon the poet; the more he lives, the more he has to say, and the better he can say it. Thus the *Sonets pour Helene* is Ronsard's greatest accomplishment; in it he "shows real emotional power." Levi allows that this was court poetry, but poetry "into which Ronsard distilled his most deeply personal concerns" (1973:135).

We have seen that Ronsard's readers, even when they labor to preserve the integrity of the poetic subject as an originating force, have always been ready to concede that originality is under severe constraints in the sixteenth century. But constrained by what? If originality is an eighteenth- or a nineteenth-century invention (as critics tend to argue), then what kind of world is the sixteenth century? It is a world, it would appear, very much like ours, revolutionized by technologies for replicating, disseminating, and marketing images and words—the technologies, for example, that Walter Benjamin (1968) groups under the term "mechanical reproduction," and among which printing is certainly the most important. Michael Camille (1989) sums up the transition from the Middle Ages to the early modern period as a proliferation of new kinds of buildings (for example, cathedrals) and new kinds of books, including psalters, picture books, and illuminated manuscripts.

The implications of these technologies are enormous. Castor (1964) links them to all the developments in early modern culture that are generally grouped under the rubric of *humanism:* the diffusion and imitation of Greek and Latin texts (classicism), the popularization and emulation of Italian literary traditions (Petrarchism, Ficinian Neoplatonism), the promotion of a national literature in the vernacular. In "The Work of Art in the Age of Mechanical Reproduction," Benjamin writes that "the technique of reproduction detaches the reproduced object from the domain of tradition" (1968:221). For the first time, the image becomes a commodity.[11] Without tradition, there is no possibility of distance or ritual, what Benjamin calls "aura." The "cult value of the work," which appreciates the object as an idol, is replaced by the "secular cult of beauty," in which the object becomes *art* in the modern sense of the term (224). Henri Weber's *La création poétique au XVIe siècle en France* makes it clear that the "secular cult of beauty" is simply another term for humanism. The return to Greco-Roman sources, Weber reminds us, did not begin with early modern culture; what was new was a return to those sources as texts: material, formal structures. Humanism for Weber "attaches as much importance to the beauty and the charm of expression as to the rigor of the reasoning" ("attache autant d'importance à la beauté et au charme de l'expression qu'à la rigueur du raisonnement" [1956:11]).[12] What is distinct in early modern humanism is "the consciousness of the necessary union of ancient thought and ancient style" ("la conscience de l'union nécessaire de la pensée antique avec le décor antique" [25]).[13] Humanism, in other words, is a way of thinking cosmetically.

For Michel Foucault textuality is the defining feature of the early modern period. In *Les mots et les choses* (The order of things), Foucault speaks of the "absolute primacy of writing" ("privilège absolu de l'écriture") in the Renaissance (1966:53). By this he means the newfound importance of writing not only as a distinct technology (printing), but as a way of thinking about the world in semiotic terms. To the early modern mind, the universe, Foucault argues, is a text, plain and simple: a collection of signs. There is no way "out" of this text: signs do not "signify" in the sense of pointing back to some extralinguistic referent, but *correspond* with or *resemble* each other (48–49). Indeed, *resemblance* is the defining feature of all knowledge up to the end of the sixteenth century (32). The implications for reading early modern poetry may be far-reaching. For if reading itself is a question of finding resemblances — "Finding meaning is about bringing to light resemblances" ("Chercher le sens, c'est mettre au jour ce qui se ressemble" [44]) — then criticism (the meta-textual) may not be entirely distinct from poetry (the textual). Knowledge in the sixteenth century "consists, then, in moving from language to language" ("consiste donc à rapporter du langage à du langage"); the interpretation of one text (for example, a poem) is the production of a second, such as a commentary, or criticism (55). The crucial point is that the second text does not elucidate the first; it resembles it: "Commentary resembles indefinitely that upon which it comments and which it can never state" ("Le commentaire ressemble indéfiniment à ce qu'il commente et qu'il ne peut jamais énoncer" [56–57]). We are very close here to the idea of criticism as cosmetics (searching for resemblances), as opposed to poetics (searching for extratextual significations). The distinction between these two hermeneutics is the subject of the next section.

Foucault's pan-textual sixteenth century looks a lot like Frederic Jameson's postmodern twentieth, a space without depth, a place where the present is consumed by a nostalgia for the past, and the past is a product to be bought and sold (which brings us back to humanism as a marketing of the past). Both would appear to be "cosmetic" eras. There are, however, some crucial differences between the early modern and the "postmodern." The sixteenth century is happily cosmetic; the twentieth, unhappily. The truth is that all eras are cosmetic in nature; some eras deny it, however, while others accept it. Our culture is intensely ambivalent about the reign of the image, an idea so central to postmodern visions of contemporaneity. But postmodernism as a theory is no less ambivalent. Is it a critique or a celebration? A new brand of iconoclasm or idolatry? It is both. Foucault argues that we remain denizens of the "âge classique," the great era of Signification that began when the age of Resemblance came to a close at the end of the sixteenth century (1966:58). I would agree. We are, today, intensely cosmetic and intensely nostalgic for a precosmetic world.

Foundation: Cosmetics

... tiny jojoba beads gentled with oats, nettles, and aloe vera lift the shroud of dulling flakes off skin to reveal the radiance.
—From *Swept Away: Gentle Slougher for All Skins*

What is a cosmetic? Something you add in order to subtract. In an unhappily cosmetic world, the cosmetic industry can be understood only as a Platonic enterprise: an effort to *render* (restore, represent, redeem) beauty. The entire cosmetic armamentarium—foundation, exfoliant, rouge, mascara, lipstick, eyeliner, moisturizer, scruffing lotion, astringent—is designed to restore nature through artifice. The cosmetic is always, in other words, a *supplement,* in the Derridean sense: an addition to and/or a substitute for natural beauty. But, as Derrida has shown, the very possibility of the supplement threatens the coherence of that which was prior or plenary: the supplement can always be said to constitute that which it was thought to complete. The cosmetic artifice can function only if nature is no longer deemed sufficient. This is the accusation Naomi Wolf levels against the cosmetic industry in *The Beauty Myth:* "Second-rate . . . the female body is always in need of completion, of man-made ways to perfect it" (1994:94).

Americans are born cosmeticians. The archetypal figure of the self-made man is a cosmetic hero, safeguarding an identity that he continually constructs and reconstructs. Only in an unhappily cosmetic world could Madonna, the ultimate self-made woman, made-up and made-over (and over and over), be celebrated as subversive. She is, in fact, an eminently conservative figure. Cosmetic surgery, Wolf argues, is "the American dream come true: one can re-create oneself 'better' in a brave new world" (1994:252). Cosmetics today are Platonic to the extent that they are mimetic (estranged from the real), and Neoplatonic to the extent that they promise redemption (a real more real than the real). Wolf calls skin cream the "holy oil" of a "new religion," an industry that "offers to sell back to women in tubes and bottles the light of grace, to redeem women's bodies" (1994:104).

The dominant discourse of another American phenomenon, the television talk show, would appear to be that of *truth,* or of what Foucault, referring to our culture's preferred strategy for "producing the truth of sex," calls *confession* (1990:57–58). But because the talk show is a place where we market ourselves, confession has become a genre, structured, like poetry, to look unstructured. Shows typically focus on crises of appearance—mothers who think their daughters dress like prostitutes, etc.—and conclude, triumphantly, with a favorite American ritual of rebirth: the makeover. Prostitute becomes Princess: not just a "new" woman, but the "real" woman, the one who was there (inside) all the time! The subject of the *Sally Jessy Raphael Show* on November 7, 1996, was "My Teen Needs a Makeover." One of the featured mothers laments of her daughter: "There's a very nice person hiding down there underneath." [14]

Consider the artist Orlan, once featured in the television magazine program *Eye to Eye with Connie Chung.* Orlan's aim is to "make a spectacle of herself" through repeated cosmetic surgery: "To create her new face Orlan pieced together parts of some of the most famous women in art history. She took the forehead from the 'Mona Lisa,' and borrowed other body parts from mythology: the chin of Venus . . . Psyche's nose; Diana's eyes . . . the mouth of Europa" (CBS 1993). Orlan is a living *blason.* This may or may not be an example of postmodern performance art, but it is, in any case, an eminently classical recipe for beauty: recall Hesiod's Pandora or Cicero's Zeuxis, whose portrait of Helen of Troy combined features of the five most beautiful women of Croton. Both myths are themselves favorite prescriptions for poetic method in the Renaissance. Orlan simply *realizes* those prescriptions: her poetics really is cosmetics, her body surrogate and spectacular. Ronsard's last sonnet cycle is just such a spectacle of surrogate bodies: a triumph of cosmetics. That Orlan's body of work is a work of the body means only that it *embodies* what was *disembodied* in the sonnet *cycle,* a genre that has always been a ritual for *recycling* bodies (lovers, beloveds, other poems). Orlan's return to the body is less a radical subversion of the humanist tradition than an affirmation of its most conservative tendencies: an attempt, in other words, to vindicate Plato and close the gap between the real and the ideal, the representation and the model.[15] Ronsard's sonnets always promise to close that gap, but always teasingly, disingenuously.

Ronsard's method appears close to Orlan's and is often the explicit subject of his poetry. Perhaps the most celebrated example of his verse as *ars poetica*— or *ars cosmetica*—is the beginning of "L'Hylas," where the poet compares his labor to that of the bee: "Passerat, I am like the bee / Which goes about picking, now the vermilion flower, / Now the yellow, wandering from prairie to prairie" ("Mon Passerat, je resemble à l'Abeille / qui va cueillant tantost la fleur vermeille, / Tantost la jaune, errant de pré en pré").[16] The metaphor is then made explicit: "In the same way, reading and leafing through my books, / I collect, select, and choose that which is most beautiful, / Which I turn into a painting with a hundred colors" ("Ainsy courant et feuilletant mes livres, / J'amasse, trie & choisis le plus beau, / Qu'en cent couleurs je peints en un tableau"). True to the part, here Ronsard borrows, now from Cicero, now from Seneca, grafting a wide range of classical models.[17] But what kind of labor is this? Labor that looks like leisure. Many a critic, reading this passage, has taken its lack of seriousness all too seriously. Ullrich Langer suggests that Ronsard's image as a "light" poet has contributed to his depreciation: "critical neglect is partially explained by an apparent lack of depth" (1986: vii), he writes; Ronsard's "optimism and sensuality do not endear him to the modern critical world."[18] His "lack of depth," for Langer, is only apparent. I want to show that Ronsard's poetry is, in fact, neither serious nor original nor deep. That's what makes it good poetry.

This would seem to be the lesson of a *blason* like *Amours* 23: "This beautiful coral, this marble which sighs, / . . . Are in my heart held in such esteem, / That no matter what object I behold, / The beauty I adore is their beauty" ("Ce beau coral, ce marbre qui souspire, / . . . Me sont au cuoeur en si profond esmoy, / Qu'un autre object ne se présente à moy, / Si non le beau de leur beau que j'adore" [5–10]). Everything here is familiar: nature translated into artifice, the female body converted into mineral mosaic, the beloved broken down and put back together again. But it is precisely the *familiar* that is embraced as supreme aesthetic law: what is beautiful is what resembles the beloved, the beloved in turn being nothing but a congregation of resemblances. The pleasure this poem affords us is the pleasure of the poet in the last stanza: "And the pleasure, which cannot be refused, / Of dreaming, thinking, and thinking about them again, / And once again dreaming, thinking, and thinking about them again" ("Et le plaisir qui ne se peult passer / De les songer, penser, & repenser, / Songer, penser, & repenser encore"). What kind of pleasure is this? The endlessly productive and reproductive pleasure of repetition (the sonnet's closing couplet is a practical demonstration of that principle). What *Amours* 23 suggests is that the work of poetry is not to make but to make-over, and over. The *Sonets pour Helene* is just such a *makeover* (as opposed to a "deeper," more "mature," more "original" version) of the *Amours.* Helene delights not because she is distinct from Cassandre, Marie, Sinope, Astrée, but because she reminds us of them (and of Petrarch's Laura, Propertius's Cynthia, Homer's Helen, etc.).

Amours 23 appears to be an unambiguous statement of the cosmetic method. But what is one to make of a passage from the *Hymn de l'automne* in which Ronsard defends the use of pagan mythology to "dissimulate and hide stories in the right way / And disguise well the truth of things / with a fabulous coat in which they are enclosed" ("feindre et cacher les fables proprement, / Et à bien deguiser la vérité des choses / D'un fabuleux manteau dont elles sont encloses" [Laumonier 1914–75, 12:49])? Isn't this an argument for poetics? Doesn't the poet here hold out the promise of a truth deferred, truth as something immanent, naked, invisible? Or is this, rather, just another example of poetry playing hard-to-get? The cosmetic text is always capable of posing as a poetic one. Just as there are only cosmetic eras (some more happy than others), so there are only cosmetic texts: those which deny it (poetic texts), and those which affirm it (cosmetic texts, properly speaking).

We should hardly be surprised, then, to hear Ronsard sounding sometimes like his most "poetic" readers. Levi (1973) argues that Ronsard's attachment to Neoplatonism is scarcely more than skin deep, as it were. Ronsard does not "believe" in it, any more than he believes in the pagan myths that constellate his poetry. Both are convenient vehicles for conveying poetic truths or personal messages. Ronsard himself, in a number of passages cited by Levi, would appear to make a similar point, in similar terms. In the *Hymn de l'automne,* Ronsard explains why he relies on pagan myths in his poems: "In order that the vulgar desire to seek out / the hidden beauty which they dare not approach" ("A fin que le vulgaire ait desir de chercher / La couverte beauté dont il n'ose approcher" [72]). But while we are measuring Ronsard's poetry by the barometer of belief (standard practice in the poetic model), how do we know Ronsard "believes" what he says here, any more than when he praises Jupiter? Isn't the promise of revelation just another cliché, just as much a part of the poetic "décor" as Neoplatonic "furies" and Olympian gods?

This tension between the "poetic" and the "cosmetic" has always existed. Ronsard's method, which would appear to leave little room for "originality" in the modern sense of the term, is hardly original; his theory of cosmetics is itself a remake of numerous classical and medieval formulations. Quintilian's *Institutio oratoria* is the quintessential statement of poetics (in the sense in which I have been using the term) from the classical world. At 8 *praef.* 18–21, Quintilian fulminates against "the people who neglect content, the sinews of a case." He continues:

They do it for the sake of "beauty" . . . a most attractive feature in oratory — but only when it comes naturally. . . . Healthy bodies . . . get their beauty from the same source as their strength — for they are of good complexion, spare, muscles showing. But suppose these bodies were to be plucked and rouged and effeminately prinked; they would become hideous just because of the trouble taken to make them beautiful . . . . splendid dress gives a man authority (as a Greek verse testifies); but when it is womanish and luxurious it does not beautify the body — it lays bare the mind. In the same way, the diaphanous and multi-coloured way of expression that some affect takes the manhood from the matter which they clothe in such verbal costume.[19]

In the poetic model good writing is always naked, natural, and masculine. Not that there is anything particularly naked or natural or masculine about Quintilian's elaborate figures, each of which says the same thing and in ways that have been said long before (by Horace and Plato, among others).[20] Like all poetics, Quintilian's is ultimately a cosmetics, but one that takes its figures seriously.

Ronsard, however, is a cosmetician, not a poetician. If Ronsard has a model, it is not the *Institutio oratoria* but the *Ars amatoria,* which celebrates beauty as something second-hand and superficial. "You know," Ovid's speaker declares (3:199), ostensibly addressing his female readers, "how to gain a bright hue by applying powder; art gives complexion if real blood gives it not (trans. Mozley 1929)." I say ostensibly, for Ovid's conspiratorial confession is but a mask for an exercise in voyeurism, intended for men. This is poetry as striptease or ex-foliant, playing at revelation. Truth is promised, and deferred: "I have a book . . . wherein I have told of the paints that will make you beautiful (3:205–6)." This "book" is the *Medicamina faciei [Face cosmetics]:* "Learn, O women, what pains can enhance your looks. . . . What is cultivated gives pleasure. Lofty halls are plated with gold . . . earth lies hid under marble buildings. . . . You wish your bodies to be covered with gold-embroidered gowns . . . to have hands that shine with gems" (Mozley 1929: ll. 1–24).[21] These are the cosmetic arts, dedicated to the care and camouflage of surfaces. Among these arts Ovid in-cludes that of graft: "and the grafted tree is granted adopted fruit" ("Fissaque adoptivas accipit arbor opes" [6; my translation]). We may add poetry to the list, the trade that Ovid is plying at the moment he pretends to engage in exposé. If the *Medicamina faciei* looks like a confession, its real aim, as in the *Ars ama-toria,* is seduction. Our job, as readers, is to play along, to pretend we are privy to a peepshow of truth, which makes us poetry's victims at the very moment we are its voyeurs. As with all cosmetics, poetry's power lies in the way it calls attention to itself at the moment it effaces itself. Cosmetics always make the disingenuous demand: *I'm not here, don't look at me.* And the poet/cosmetician always performs, ostentatiously, his own undoing: "Why must I know the cause of the whiteness of your cheek? Shut your chamber door: why show the un-finished work? Here is much that it befits men not to know" (*Ars amatoria* 3:226–29). Close the door, says Ovid, but it is he who has opened it. So Ron-sard's *Sonets pour Helene* affirms, as it exposes, the poetic; it, too, is an *ars cosmetica.*

Makeover: Homeric Features

The *Sonets pour Helene,* I have suggested, is just like Ronsard's earlier sonnet cycles. It is different, too. The differences, we might say, are cosmetic. To begin with, Helen is always a synecdoche for Homer. In *La deffence et illustration de la langue françoyse (Defense and illustration of the French language),* Joachim du Bellay reserves supremacy for the poet who would contend with Homer and Virgil and give France an epic in its own tongue. The *Franciade* (1565–72) is Ronsard's abortive effort in this line (only the first four books of a projected twenty-four were ever written). Few critics have words of praise for this work, which is generally felt to imitate ancient epic too closely.[22] Ronsard's epic ambitions are more effectively realized, perhaps, in the *Sonets pour Helene*.[23] Realizing them means doing something new and doing something very old, a point made by *SpH* 2.10: "Farewell beautiful Cassandra, and you, beautiful Marie . . . . In my first April, with amorous desire / I adored your beauties" ("Adieu belle Cassandre, & vous belle Marie, / . . . . Sur mon premier Avril, d'une amoureuse envie / J'adoray voz beautez" [1–6]). Now an old man, Ronsard is in love again: "I live as in Spring, still amorous, / So that despite my age I am at the mercy of my suffering" ("Je vy comme au Printemps de nature amoureux, / A fin que tout mon âge aille au gré de la peine" [10–11]). The poet is resigned to his elected role: "And now that I ought to be exempt from the harness, / My Colonel sends me with my quiver / To lay siege once again to Ilium and conquer Helen" ("Et ores que je deusse estre exempt du harnois, / Mon Colonel m'envoye à grands coups de carquois / R'assieger Ilion pour conquerir Heleine" [12–14]). *Conquerir Heleine?* Or *Homère?* Both, of course. To sing of Helen is always to compete with Homer. *SpH* 2.10 is not only the lover's way of justifying one more infatuation; it is the poet's way of justifying one more sonnet cycle. Ronsard presents his latest passion both as a new "chapter" in his life (this is the drama taken at face value in "developmental" readings of Ronsard's poetry) and as just another literary installment. The poet's latest sonnet cycle is introduced as a biographical and bibliographical addition: after the early experiments with Cassandra (*Amours* I, 1552) and Marie (*Amours* II, 1560) comes Helen (*Sonets,* 1578).[24]

In Helen, however, Ronsard chooses not only the preeminent Homeric subject, but the preeminent classical emblem of perfect beauty. Helen is the quintessential cosmetic heroine. Hers is a myth about beauty, and not transcendent beauty, but visible, present, on the surface (to speak in poetic terms). To gaze upon her is always to be compelled to ask: what is *re*-presented? What lies *behind* the surface? At the same time, Helen's beauty is never particularized or individualized; it remains ideal, superlative, emblematic. This makes Helen like and unlike other erotic heroines. What makes Helen absolutely distinct, in other words, is her absolute lack of distinction: she is utterly generic. Thus the Helen myth, in whatever form we encounter it, is never a story about Helen herself (a contradiction in terms), but always a fable about Beauty.

In her entrée upon the battlements of Troy in *Iliad* 3.154–60, Helen's beauty, we know, is a spectacle that simultaneously seduces and terrorizes her admirers:

> And these, as they saw Helen along the tower approaching,
> murmuring softly to each other uttered their winged words:
> "Surely there is no blame on Trojans and strong-greaved Achaians
> if for long time they suffer hardship for a woman like this one.
> Terrible is the likeness of her face to immortal goddesses.
> Still, though she be such, let her go away in the ships, lest
> she be left behind, a grief to us and our children."

Helen's beauty is always accompanied by the unsettling ethical and epistemological undecidability of this scene. Who is Helen? Real or phantom? Goddess
or mortal? Trojan or Achaean? Helen's intrusion upon the scene never fails to
provoke such ambiguities. They are those Plato fears in the imitation, which
always "pretends" to be that which it is not. The most dramatic example of this
Platonic undecidability in Homer is Menelaus's narrative (*Odyssey* 4.265–89)
of Helen's preternatural mimicry of the wives of the Achaean heroes waiting
inside the belly of the Trojan horse (a scene that Ronsard mimics in *SpH* 2.9).
Helen is not only a symptom of cosmetic undecidability, but its agent. Hence
the proliferation of Helen myths and Helen texts, all posing as the real story of
the real Helen, all masks and surfaces purporting to represent the original, the
real, the true. Thus, the "alternative" tradition of the *eidolon* or phantom Helen
fashioned by the gods to provoke the Trojan war (the "real" Helen having been
spirited away to Egypt),[25] is not alternative at all, we have seen, but the most
literal or explicit rendering of the "standard" myth.[26] Ronsard's Helen, too, is
only the latest model, the newest phantom Helen.[27]

SpH 2.45 adheres closely, in the first eight lines, to *Iliad* 3.154–60. But in the
tercets, Ronsard addresses the elders who speak in the quatrains, blending his
Homer with a little Propertius: "Fathers (who tremble at the thought of force),
you shouldn't / Hold back the young ones with bad advice: / But old and young
alike together you should / Risk body and possessions for her" ("Peres, il ne
falloit [à qui la force tremble] / Par un mauvais conseil les jeunes retarder: /
Mais & jeunes & vieux vous deviez tous ensemble / Et le corps & les biens pour
elle hazarder"). The final couplet of this poem is taken directly from the Latin
elegist (2.3): "Menelaus was wise, and Paris, too, it seems to me, / The one to
demand her back, the other to keep her" ("Menelas fut bien sage, & Pâris, ce me
semble, / L'un de la demander, l'autre de la garder") (trans. Goold 1990). The
sonnet is Homeric and un-Homeric at the same time, a citation plus commentary, neither Homer nor Propertius nor Ronsard, but a Zeuxian quilt, stitched
out of multiple and disparate voices. The tension here between *les jeunes* and
les vieillars parallels that between Ronsard and his precursors, and the prize
so hotly contested here is as much Homer's prestige as Helen's beauty. Read
thus, *SpH* 2.45 is another battle of the ancients and the moderns. Ronsard takes
both sides: the ephebe, doing battle with Homer on the field of poetic immortality, and the old soldier, wearily reentering the arena (see *SpH* 2.10 above). But
the postclassical poet is always, in a sense, one who has arrived too late. The
Trojan fathers speak desires (heroic and erotic) that can no longer be assuaged.
This, too, is Ronsard's position. The elders' impotent idolatry is analogous to the
poet's impotent imitation. Both poet and poet/lover are continually frustrated
(and continually satisfied) by a phantom Helen.

Too weak to cast javelins, Homer's elders in the *Iliad* cast words instead:
"Now through old age these fought no longer, yet were they excellent / speakers

still" (3.150–51). In other words, they are critics. Like critics, Ronsard's *bons vieillars* dream of holding the naked form of that which they love. They sound like Propertius addressing Cynthia in the *Elegies* (one of Ronsard's models for the *Sonets pour Helene*): "What avails it to drench your locks with Syrian perfume and to vaunt yourself in foreign finery, to destroy your natural charm with purchased ornament . . . . Believe me, there is no improving your appearance: Love is naked, and loves not beauty gained by artifice" (1.2.3–24). But if the poet/lover speaks like a critic in search of the truth, his readers are expected to know that that is only a cover story, that the poem is in fact a rhetorical showpiece. Critics, we have seen, tend to practice hermeneutics as a form of seduction, speaking like lovers. Their eroticism, finally, is deadly serious, and thus they fail to see how their writings, comically enough, reenact the erotic dramas of the texts they claim to be elucidating. Propertius's speech, which seems to be a diatribe against cosmetics, is a polished and pretty little poem, artfully blended from a potpourri of Greek and Latin texts. His elegy, which elegantly lists the seductive subterfuges it purports to contemn, is, finally, less a criticism of cosmetics than its display. We are in the Ovidian mode: Propertius's poem is a cosmetics posing as a poetics. Ronsard's critics remain, in contrast, stubbornly Quintilianic in their search for the real Ronsard (the naked Ronsard, Ronsard laid bare). They have as little chance of finding him as Ronsard does of finding the real Helen. The difference, again, is that Ronsard's pursuit is a performance.

Makeover: Petrarchan Features

Ronsard's readers have long been resigned to his Petrarchism (recall Stone on the *Amours*), which they tend to see as a fashion he was forced to wear.[28] Strip the poetry bare, they assert, and you find the real Ronsard. This is an argument Ronsard himself, we have seen, does not hesitate to take advantage of in his poetry. This kind of anti-Petrarchism, however, is already a pose in the sixteenth century, as in du Bellay's "Contre les Petrarquistes" ("Against the Petrarchists"): "I have forgotten the art of Petrarchizing / I want to speak about love frankly / Without flattery, and without disguise" ("J'ay oublié l'art de Petrarquizer, / Je veulx d'Amour franchement deviser, / Sans vous flatter, et sans me déguizer"). And it has always been a part of standard Petrarchism—a few lines later du Bellay puts the mask back on, or takes it off again: "But if Petrarch is more pleasing to you / I will take up that melodious tune again" ("Si toutefois Petrarque vous plaist mieux, / Je reprendray mon chant melodieux").

Is Ronsard really Petrarch in disguise? Ronsard's Helen certainly looks a good deal like Petrarch's Laura. The question is, is that resemblance understood as a liability or a benefit? What is the difference between Petrarch and Ronsard? Compare *SpH* 1.41 and *Rime sparse* 35. Both depend on the familiar paradox of solipsism made public: "Alone and filled with care, I go measuring the most deserted fields / with steps delaying and slow, and I keep my eyes alert so as to flee / from where any human footprint marks the sand" ("Solo et pensoso i più deserti campi / vo mesurando a passi tardi et lenti, / et gli occhi porto per fuggire intenti / ove vestigio uman la rena stampi" [ll. 1–4]).[29] Petrarch's poem is a Platonic nightmare, where signifiers betray their signifieds (of course, the poem itself is just such a public signifier, perfect mirror, we are encouraged to believe, of the poet's soul): "No other shield do I find to protect me from people's open / knowing, for in my bearing, in which all happiness is extinguished, anyone / can read from without how I am aflame within" ("Altro schermo non trovo che mi scampi / dal manifesto accorger de la genti, / perché negli atti d'allegrezza spenti / di fuor si legge com' io dentro avampi" [5–8]). Ronsard's poem begins like Petrarch's, with a soliloquy about solitude: "With solitary step there is no place I walk / Where Love, good artisan, does not imprint upon me the image / In the deepest part of my thoughts, of her lovely face, / And the gracious words of her last Farewell" ("D'un solitaire pas je ne marche en nul lieu, / Qu'Amour bon artisan ne m'imprime l'image / Au profond du penser de ton gentil visage, / Et des mots gracieux de ton dernier Adieu" [1–4]). Solitude, we know, guarantees sincerity. Ronsard's speaker, like Petrarch's, shares his passion with a depopulated landscape, a confessional scenario that is itself only ostensibly, or cosmetically, anticosmetic: "Harder than a rock, engraved in the center / Of my heart I carry them; and thus there is no shore, / Flower, cave or cliff, forest or wood, / To whom I do not recite them, No Nymph, no God" ("Plus fermes du'un rocher, engravez au milieu / De mon coeur je les porte: & s'il n'y a rivage, / Fleur, antre ny rocher, ny forests ny bocage, / A qui je ne le conte, à Nymphe, ny à Dieu" [1–8]).

What is the difference here? Thomas Greene deploys the two works to suggest contrasting positions on cultural nostalgia.[30] Ronsard would be the familiar *naïf,* cheerfully heedless of the debt owed his poetic precursors, while Petrarch broods on all that separates him from the past. Both of their poems are about reading signs as a private affair. But if both speakers seek solitude, it would appear to be for different reasons, Petrarch to escape, Ronsard to embrace, the act of reading (and of being read). In both cases confession is an obvious fiction, Ronsard's sonnet proclaiming its privacy just as loudly and publicly as Petrarch's. Petrarch's soliloquy, however, with its paranoid and fugitive speaker, takes much greater pains at least to appear authentic. Ronsard's, on the other hand, shamelessly enjoys its paranoia, openly celebrating the production and reproduction of textual signs. The poem is one such sign; within it, the speaker's confession is another, itself a reading of a third, the one engraved or imprinted by Love itself. That inscription, finally, is a reproduction of still other, prior texts: the beloved's own face and speech (which are, in turn, only more signs). Suppose these poems are, as Greene would have it, fables about intertextuality. Ronsard's paranoia, like Petrarch's, would then be that of a thief. As Nicolas

Franco put it in 1532: "Do you want to know what a Petrarchist is? It's someone who cannot write a sonnet without stealing lines" ("Voulez-vous savoir ce que c'est qu'un pétrarquiste? C'est quelqu'un qui ne sait pas faire un sonnet sans voler des vers"[trans. Vianey 1909:171]). The difference: Ronsard is a happy thief, a thief who has lost all sense of shame.

Something does change then, between Petrarch's *Rime sparse* and Ronsard's *Sonets:* the former declares allegiance to the dictates of courtly love and is ostensibly marked by the guilt of idolatry; the latter, openly exploiting courtly love as a set of conventions, no longer even bothers to profess guilt. Petrarch's cosmogonies (e.g., *Rime sparse* 159) are both seductive *and* terrifying (just as Helen in *Iliad* 3 both seduces and terrifies); in Ronsard's (cf. *SpH* 2.18), all terror has been dispelled.[31] I would compare Laura to another idol, a matinee idol: Garbo as seen by Barthes in "Le visage de Garbo" ("Garbo's face"). The *divine* Garbo remains for Barthes a Platonic idol, her beauty masked, transcendent, and terrifying. In *Queen Christina* Garbo's "make-up has the snowy thickness of a mask" ("fard a l'épaisseur neigeuse d'un masque"); Garbo's is "a plaster face, forbidden" ("un visage plâtré, défendu"), a mask, the very "archetype of the human face" ("archétype du visage humain"), offering "a kind of Platonic idea of a being" ("une sorte d'idée platonicienne de la créature"). But Petrarch's "confessions" are not Augustine's. Laura is a fallen idol, an excuse for good poetry. So, too, is Garbo: her face "represents a fragile moment, when the cinema will extract existential beauty from essential beauty, when the archetype will incline towards a fascination with perishable forms. . . . As a moment of transition, Garbo's face reconciles two iconographic ages, it guarantees the passage from terror to charm" ("représente un moment fragile, où le cinéma va extraire une beauté existentielle d'une beauté essentielle, où l'archétype va s'infléchir vers la fascination de figures périssables. . . . Comme moment de transition, le visage de Garbo concilie deux âges iconographiques, il assure le passage de la terreur au charme" [1957:71]). It is a transition that leads straight to Ronsard's Helene. If Laura is Garbo, Helene is Hepburn: "Garbo's face is the Idea, Hepburn's is the Event" ("Le visage de Garbo est Idée, celui de Hepburn est Evénement" [70–71]).

Cosmetics: Helen™

Helen of Troy Corporation . . . developer, designer and marketer of personal care products, today reported results for the second quarter and six months. . . . Helen of Troy's products include . . . hairsetters, lighted mirrors and combs and brushes . . .

—1990 PR Newswire Association

Petrarch's Laura was the object of a cult; Ronsard's Helen is a business.[32] In Benjaminian terms, Helen is more "modern," a cult object without a cult.[33] Helen is Laura without the aura. And the *Sonets pour Helene* is a Petrarchan theme park, an industry dedicated to the production and promotion of an idol. One might compare it to Jean Baudrillard's Disneyland, the capital of the hyperreal, a place where the real is always the "real," simulated, reproduced (Baudrillard 1983:23–26). "What society seeks through production, and overproduction," Baudrillard writes, "is the restoration of the real which escapes it. That is why contemporary 'material' production is . . . hyperreal" (1983:44). Ronsard's task in the *Sonets pour Helene* is not so much Helen's praise as her production and overproduction. (In fact Baudrillard is more conservative than Ronsard, continuing to lament the loss of a real that Ronsard never takes seriously.) To a certain extent this is true of every sonnet cycle, which is designed to be redundant, saying the same thing over and over again in slightly different ways. The difference between shopping *chez Ronsard,* instead of *chez Petrarch,* is captured in Meaghan Morris's discussion of commodity in "Things to Do with Shopping Centres" (1993). Morris disagrees with Eagleton's view that "the commodity disports itself with all comers without its halo slipping," that in "[s]erializing its consumers, it nevertheless makes intimate *ad hominem* address to each" (Eagleton quoted in Morris 1993:317). "What is the sound of an intimate *ad hominem* address from a raincoat at Big W?" Morris asks. "The commodities in a discount house have no halo, no aura. On the contrary, they promote a lived aesthetic of the serial, the machinic, the mass-produced" (318). Such is the aesthetic of Ronsard's *Sonets pour Helene.*

It is an aesthetic that refuses to refer. Mallarmé's "Mimique," Derrida argues in "La double scéance," performs "the displacement without the reversal of Platonism and its heritage" ("le déplacement sans renversement du platonisme et de son héritage" [1972a:240]), what Derrida calls "traditional mimetology" ("la mimétologie traditionelle"). But long before Mallarmé, Ronsard effects the same displacement. For Derrida, Mallarmé's mime acts out the drama of writing itself (the blank page is figured in "the white cream of the pale Pierrot who simulates writing on the greasepaint of his makeup, on the page that he is" ("la crème blanche du pâle Pierrot qui, par simulacre, écrit sur la pâte de son fard, sur la page qu'il est" [222]), which always posits while deferring reference. Pierrot is "a mimic who imitates nothing . . . a double who redoubles nothing, who is anticipated by nothing, nothing, in any case, which is not itself already a double" ("une mimique qui n'imite rien . . . un double qui ne redouble aucun simple, qui rien ne prévient, rien qui ne soit en tous cas déjà un double" [234]). In Mallarmé as in Ronsard, *mimetology* is *cosmetology.* Seeing intimations of Mallarmé in Ronsard appears to be a veritable motif of Ronsardian criticism. What Ronsard's poetry and Mallarmé's appear to share is the specter of the referent rendered obsolete.[34] In "Mimique," Derrida insists, Mallarmé "supports, and is supported in, the structure of the phantasm, as Plato defines it: the simulacrum copy of a copy" ("maintient même [se maintient dans] la structure du *phantasme,* telle que le définit Platon: simulacre comme copie de copie" [234]). This is the structure, too, of Ronsard's *Sonets pour Helene,* a cosmetic industry dedicated to the production of phantom Helens, or hyperreal Helens, or Helen supplements.

As in *SpH* 1.41, where Amour is the *bon artisan,* printing and engraving Helen's face and speech, or 2.18, where Helen's cosmic manufacturers monopolize the market by destroying the model, these Helens are all explicitly *technological* artifacts.[35] They are, in other words, products. Thus Ronsard's Helen corresponds neatly with Benjamin's conception of the work of art in the modern era. Mechanical reproduction, Benjamin asserts, "emancipates the work of art from its parasitical dependence on ritual" (1968:224). The work of art, in other words, is no longer a unique object, tied down to a specific time and place and prescribed mode of viewing, but is a portable and reproducible commodity. This is exactly the case for Helen in the *Sonets pour Helene.*

These simulated and supplementary Helens are all copies, not of an absent original, but of each other. Helen "herself" (always, in any case, an elusive entity) is not missed (a fact that does not prevent Ronsard in many a sonnet from lamenting her absence). That makes it difficult to distinguish clearly the products of this industry (recall *SpH* 1.41, for example, with its surfeit of mutually equivalent Helen texts). Still, one can imagine a provisional taxonomy at this point, breaking down the corporate "Helen," as it were, into a number of product lines.

HELEN, THE PORTRAIT

One of Ronsard's favorite Helen substitutes is her portrait, an object obsessively requested, and rarely obtained, in the *Sonets pour Helene:*[36] "If I had a portrait of your beautiful face / . . . I would be happy. / And wouldn't want to change places with the gods. / But I have nothing of you that I can take with me" ("Si j'avois le portrait de vostre belle face / . . . je serois bien heureux, / Et ne voudrois changer aux celestes de place. / Mais je n'ay rien de vous que je puisse emporter" [*SpH* 1.21.5–9]). Consolation prize in lieu of the *real thing,*[37] the portrait is also valued for its *portability* (see *SpH* 2.48). The *Sonets pour Helene* is essentially a tourist economy, the poet/lover acting like a traveler to a distant country (classical Greece and Rome, most often) looking for souvenirs: an antique vase, perhaps, or at least a plastic replica. Benjamin explains the rise of mechanical reproduction by "the desire of contemporary masses to bring things 'closer' spatially" (1968:223). "But I have nothing of you that I can take with me" ("Mais je n'ay rien de vous que je puisse emporter") is the lament of the belated poet frustrated by a distant, immovable past. Unlike the epic poet, the lyric poet travels light and seeks a portable antiquity. But unlike Petrarch's ecphrastic poems on Simone Martini's portrait of Laura, or Bembo's sonnets addressed to Bellini's portrait of his beloved, Ronsard's *Sonets pour Helene* are about a missing portrait. Not only is Helen absent; so is her representation.

HELEN, THE NAME

Helene is an indexical sign, but one that continually misfires. To what does *Helene* refer? It is the question asked over and over again by the *Sonets pour Helene,* which are a continual assault upon, and exploitation of, the seductive power of *reference.* It is often said that Ronsard is a poet in love with names, not women.[38] But names in Ronsard's sonnet cycles—particularly the *Sonets pour Helene*—function irresponsibly, multiplying or deferring their referents.[39] This is the case in *SpH* 1.3, which begins by invoking Helen's name: "My sweet Helen, no, but rather my sweet breath" ("Ma douce Helene, non, mais bien ma douce haleine"), and then goes on to declare: "Happy he who suffers the pain of love / For such a fatal name: happy the pain, / Most happy the torment, which comes from the value / Of her eyes, no, not the eyes, but the flames of Helen" ("Heureux celuy qui souffre une amoureuse peine / Pour un nom si fatal: heureuse la douleur, / Bien-heureux le torment, qui vient pour la valeur / Des yeux, non pas des yeux, mais des flames d'Helene" [5–8]). Here, at first, the name does what it is supposed to do, pointing unproblematically to its referent. All that is quickly undone, the name (*nom*) undone by the *non* that both rejects and repeats it, as *Helene* is undone by *haleine* (breath), as *yeux* (eyes) are undone by *flames* (flames). What follows is a second, and even more problematic, invocation: "Name, misfortune for the Trojans, subject of my concern / . . . Name, which has lifted me from the earth to the sky, / Who would have thought that I would have found / Even in Helen another Penelope?" ("Nom, malheur des Troyens, sujet de mon souci / . . . Nom, qui m'a jusqu'au ciel de la terre enlevé, / Qui eust jamais pensé que j'eusse retrouvé / En une mesme Helene une autre Penelope?" [9–14]). Now invocation becomes meta-invocation; what is now named is the word itself, "Nom" (Name). As object of address in its own right, the name itself can no longer refer simply and naturally, a fact borne out by the confusion of identity (Helen or Penelope?) in the rest of the poem. Ronsard's subject is, indeed, the name, not the named.[40]

HELEN, THE DREAM

The dream Helen, compliant partner (sometimes) in the lover's recurrent fantasies of erotic union, represents another popular and effective line of cosmetic Helens. In *SpH* 1.57 Ronsard threatens to haunt Helene unless she agrees to haunt him: "I will return tomorrow. But if the night, which gnaws at / My heart, gave her to me, in a dream, in my arms, / Embracing as if true the idol of a lie, / Intoxicated with a false pleasure, I would not return" ("Je reviendray demain. Mais si la nuict, qui ronge / Mon cœur, me la donnait par songe entre mes bras, / Embrassant pour le vray l'idole du mensonge, / Soulé d'un faux plaisir je ne reviendrois pas" [9–12]). Critics have written extensively on the theme of the *songe amoureux* in Ronsard, and almost exclusively as a negative motif, dramatic image of a frustrated lover. But *SpH* 1.54 promotes a poetic strategy, not just an erotic fable; Ronsard as a sonneteer is always, inevitably, "embracing as if true the idol of a lie." [41]

HELEN, THE GAZE

The speaker is never happier in the *Sonets pour Helene* than when he is looking at Helen, or being looked at by her. To see or be seen is Ronsard's humble victory, offering a substitute for the union between lover and beloved: "Like a brilliant mirror, your face drives me mad / Piercing me with its beams, and I feel so good / Watching you converse, that I no longer belong to myself, / And my fugitive soul flies to yours" ("Comme un mirouer ardent, ton visage m'affole / Me percant de ses raiz, & tant je sens de bien, / En t'oyant deviser, que je ne suis plus mien, / Et mon ame fuitive à la tienne s'en-vole" [*SpH* 1.18:5–8]). But the gaze is always also an admission of distance and defeat, proof that there can never be a meeting, only mediation.[42] But distance has its value, allowing the safe release of even the most violent fantasies and desires. Again and again (*SpH* 1.10, 2.20, 2.43, among others), the speaker is penetrated, violated, overpowered by the gaze of the beloved whom he would penetrate, violate, and overpower.[43]

HELEN, THE LETTER

SpH 2.28 apostrophizes a letter Helen has written the speaker; *SpH* 2.29 addresses the speaker's response: "Letter, faithful interpreter of my ardor, / Who speaks without speaking the passions of the heart, / Messenger of lovers, go and tell my suffering / To my lady" ("Lettre, de mon ardeur veritable interprete, / Qui parles sans parler les passions du coeur, / Poste des amoureux, va conter ma langueur / A ma dame" [1–4]). These letters are textual substitutes for speaking, and silent ones at that. They are like the sonnets we are reading. But it is the nature of writing always to speak silently, so that 2.29 indicts all writing as an illusory reference. To apostrophize a letter is to animate it, to give it, in turn, the voice that it lacks and yet supplies for its sender. But Ronsard's apostrophe, again like his sonnets, is a fiction, a trope, voiceless, representing voice. Thus the first stanza of this sonnet becomes an entire rehearsal of the cosmetic tropes that continually seduce us into believing the comfortable fictions of representation. Not only does the letter speak for Ronsard, it also sees and feels for him. In the next stanza the letter is Ronsard's substitute under Helen's eyes and in her hands: "Like a messenger, gracious and discreet, / Observe, when you see her, her face and her color" ("Comme une messagere & accorte & secrete / Contemple, en la voyant, sa face & sa couleur" [5–6]). The letter allows the speaker (and the reader) to enjoy the beloved metonymically, voyeuristically. Thus, again, the epistolary exchange in 2.28 and 2.29 stands as an emblem of the entire sonnet cycle, a series of letters, in effect, addressed to an absent beloved.

HELEN, THE PUBLIC FIGURE

When Helen is confronted in society, what you see is decidedly not what you get. Helene dissimulates (1.26, 1.33, 1.37, 1.45, 2.25, 2.33, 2.48); she is a creature of the court, her Neoplatonism its latest fad (1.42 and 1.43), her friendships guided by its dictates (1.53), her actions designed only to win its favor (2.48). There is only masquerade (from the Italian *mascara,* or *mask*): "While you dance at your pleasure, / And mask your face as well as your heart, / Passionately in love, I cry out . . . . The Carnival pleases you" ("Tandis que vous dansez & ballez à vostre aise, / Et masquez vostre face ainsi que vostre coeur, / Passionné d'amour, je me plains . . . . Le Carnaval vous plaist" [*SpH* 2.4:1–5]). The beloved's duplicity (the mask that conceals) is contrasted here with the lover's authenticity (the face that reveals): "Mistress, believe me . . . I want to die, and nothing consoles me. / If my brow, if my eyes do not convince you, / Let my complaint be the proof" ["Maistresse, croyez moy . . . Je desire la mort, & rien ne me console. / Si mon front, si mes yeux ne vous en sont tesmoins, / Ma plainte vous en serve"] (9–13). We know to what extent such authenticity is itself a pose, another carnival dance, every step of which is choreographed by the conventions of the genre. "Mistress, believe me," the speaker pleads. Helene does not believe him (1.26, 1.60); neither should we.

HELEN, THE POEM

The disavowal of convention is the last convention. Poetry is the mask that figures its own unmasking. As in the second tercet of *SpH* 2.4, the *Sonets pour Helene pose* as mirrors of a real world, urging us to read them simultaneously as *confession* and *confection.*[44] In *SpH* 1.26 Helen herself refuses to read the verse that bears her name as anything but fiction. What she enjoys, she tells Ronsard, is poetry that makes her cry. Ronsard responds: "Your words are lies. If you cared about / Those who had a heart weeping and frozen, / You would pity me out of sympathy" ("Vos propos sont trompeurs. Si vous aviez soucy / De ceux qui ont un coeur larmoyant & transy, / Je vous ferois pitié par une sympathie" [9–11]). Sympathy is precisely what Helen refuses Ronsard, because she does not take his poetry seriously. That is, she reads it *as poetry.*[45] Critics who read the *Sonets pour Helene* as autobiography would do well to follow Helen.[46] Ronsard's poetry everywhere encourages us to read it in just this fashion. *SpH* 1.45 is a lesson in deception and belief that plays on our own desire to "believe" what we are reading as the "truth": "I swore to you my faith, you did the same . . . O oath made up to look like something Good! / O perjurable altar! your God is nothing" ("Je vous juray ma foy, vous feistes le semblable . . . O jurement fardé sous l'espece d'un Bien! / O perjurable autel! ta Deité n'est rien" [5–10]). Ronsard's oath is true; Helen's, its "semblable," only appears to be. Her truth is cosmetic, an "oath *made up* to look like something

Good" ("jurement *fardé* sous l'espece d'un Bien"). The Webers treat 1.45 as autobiography, citing evidence that such an oath was indeed pronounced at such a table at such a time, and so on. But pointing to an elegy (3.20) by Propertius that bears a striking resemblance to Ronsard's sonnet, they conclude: "It is therefore not certain that this scene really happened" ("Il n'est donc pas certain que la scène se soit réellement passée"). Such a reading unwittingly treats the poem itself as another *serment,* sworn truly or falsely. The discovery that the sonnet's *mise-en-scène* may in fact refer, not to contemporary life, but to classical poetry, makes 1.45 itself another *jurement fardé.* Which is, in a sense, what all poetry is.

HELEN, THE MYTH

We have seen the importance of myth in the *Sonets pour Helene.*[47] But it is myth of the Ovidian type that Ronsard tends to favor: narratives, in other words, that return to the motifs of erotic pursuit and metamorphosis. These serve the poet well, I would argue, not just as erotic fantasies, but as literary fantasies of *imitatio* (although I have been trying to demonstrate that the distinction between the erotic and the literary in this sense is meaningless). Ronsard poses as Ixion in *SpH* 1.42 not just because he dreams of embracing Helen, but because he wants to overpower and appropriate the past, a specter equally elusive and equally resistant. Myths of abduction and metamorphosis are thus more than Ronsard's favorite subjects: they are his essential poetic techniques.

Those same myths, one must hasten to add, also serve to disguise those techniques, and therein lies their strategic value. The myth is a decoy, a lure that conceals and reveals, an evasion designed to make the point evaded. What the myth masks, or sanitizes, is the *literal* violence of the poet/lover. This is a general feature of Ronsardian poetics. In the 1552 *Amours* 20, the speaker recites his desire for Cassandre as a succession of mythic possessions:

> Je vouldroy bien richement jaunissant
> En pluye d'or goute à goute descendre
> Dans le beau sein de ma belle Cassandre
> Lors qu'en ses yeulx le somme va glissant.
> Je vouldroy bien en toreau blandissant
> Me transformer pour finement la prendre
> Quand elle va par l'herbe la plus tendre
> Seule à l'escart mille fleurs ravissant.
> Je vouldroy bien afin d'aiser ma peine
> Estre un Narcisse, & elle une fontaine
> Pour m'y plonger une nuict à sejour.
>
> (1–11)

[I would like, turning yellow, to fall, in a golden rain, drop by drop, upon the beautiful bosom of my beautiful Cassandre, when sleep slips into her eyes. I would like to transform myself into a seductive bull in order to take her, gently, when she passes, along the softest grass, alone and apart, picking/ravishing a thousand flowers. I would like, in order to ease my pain, to be Narcissus, and her a fountain, so that I could plunge myself into it one night and stay there.]

Each of the mythic scenarios in this poem reenacts the possession of and integration with a mute and unwilling object of desire. Perfect integration here can mean self-extinction, as in the myth of Danaë, or it can mean the extinction of the other, as in the story of Narcissus. In any case, the recurrent motif of appropriation and integration aptly describes the genesis of the sonnet itself, which "borrows from" or "builds itself out of" many myths and innumerable texts, partaking of a literary past that is, like Jupiter's victims, silent and without defense. The sonnet even puts on display its own methodology in allegorical form: Europa, about to be "ravished" by the gods, is busy "picking/ravishing a thousand flowers" ("mille fleurs ravissant"). Nothing could be more banal than this topos of literary *contaminatio,* but here Ronsard capitalizes on its more darkly erotic overtones. The figures of Europa and Persephone, gently plucking flowers, about to be themselves less gently plucked, returns us to the figure of the poet/bee in "L'Hylas." My earlier discussion of the dissimulative poetics sketched out in that work did not mention the larger narrative of abduction in which it is set, and which gives the poem its title. This narrative turns *contaminatio* into a political imperative, for Ronsard inserts the story of Hylas's abduction (borrowed from Theocritus 13 by way of Apollonius Rhodius) into a genealogy confirming Hercules as the forebear of the French.

Collecting flowers, it would appear, is not always an innocent affair. Nor is the anthologizing of the poet. Ronsard's first collection of *Odes* consistently relies on an abductive methodology whose violence, we might say, is almost always suppressed. In "A Michel de l'hospital," Ronsard returns to the apian image of creativity we saw in "L'Hylas": "Wandering in the fields of Grace / Who paints my verse with her colors / On the Dircean shores I collect / the best of the most beautiful flowers / So that in pillaging, I fashion / With a busy hand / This crown, round and full / twisted three times in a Theban pleat" ("Errant par les champs de la Grace / Qui peint mes vers de ses couleurs, / Sur les bords Dirceans j'amasse / L'eslite des plus belle fleurs, / A fin qu'en pillant, je façonne / D'une laboureuse main / La rondeur de ceste couronne / Trois fois torse d'un ply Thebain" [Laumonier 1914–75, 3:118–19, ll. 1–8]). What is visible here is the same tension between haphazard leisure and methodical industry we saw in "L'Hylas," the same contrast between pastoral unions and acquisitive thefts. This passage is interesting in that it thematizes the architectural matter of the poem itself: the triadic structure of the Pindaric ode, emulated by Ronsard, here figured as an interweaving. The attention to literal structure here begins to blur the distinction between what is literal and what is figural. Is pillaging just a figure of speech, or a literal methodology, too?

This indeterminacy is essential to the erotic and the literary claims advanced by Ronsard's poetry. Critical readings of those claims, as we might expect, tend to reproduce and even intensify that indeterminacy. Here is how Castor describes Ronsard's allusion to Horace's *Odes* 2.12.21–28 in *Amours* 150: "We may take it for granted . . . that Ronsard intended the voluptuous associations of this passage to be drawn into his own poem. It is an illusory embrace which the poet has experienced" (Castor 1973:94). Castor uses the word "embrace" to describe Ronsard's possession of Cassandre, but could we not use the same term to speak of Ronsard's possession of Horace?

Not only is metamorphosis a violence done unto objects and identities: it is a violence done unto language itself, a violence, I have been suggesting throughout this book, constitutive of metaphor itself.[48] We have seen this, to some extent, in the images of mythic abduction cited above. In *Amours* 1.72 Ronsard speaks of his intimacy with Cassandre as an ideal embrace: "I am in you, and you are in me / You live in me, and I live in you" ("En toy je suis, & et tu es dedans moy, / En moy tu vis, & je vis dedans toy" [Laumonier 1914–75, 2:74]). This image, taken literally, seems more than a circumlocution for sexual intercourse; it is a figure for figurality itself, or graft. In the elegy "Le temps se passe & se passant, Madame," love is a gardener who has planted a rose bush in Genèvre's heart, and a juniper in Ronsard's, "so well," concludes the poet, "that you, Madame, / And I are but one body and one soul" ("si bien, que vous, Madame, / Et moy n'estions qu'un seul corps & qu'un ame") (Laumonier 1914–75, vol. 15(2):335, ll. 237–38).[49]

I. D. McFarlane has noted the frequency with which motifs of absorption and osmosis recur in Ronsard's poetry, and how often borders between beings are broken down in images of melting and metamorphosis (1973). Greene refers to these same tendencies as "liquefaction," a fluidity of forms in which identities are transformed and fused with almost surrealistic rapidity and ease.[50] For Greene this metamorphic tendency represents a "willed escape" from the poetry, more static, less dynamic, of Petrarch. In fact, not only is metamorphosis also central to Petrarch's poetry, but Ronsard's metamorphoses often are modeled upon Petrarch's or involve fragments of Petrarchan verse, themselves metamorphosed. More important, the term *liquefaction* fails to register the violent and literal nature of the intertextual changes narrated and performed by Ronsard's poetry. *Liquefaction,* a term that evades the literal and discontinuous violence of *graft,* is another way of stressing continuity, influence, flow. It is reminiscent of the Heraclitean-Pythagorean conclusion to Ovid's *Metamorphoses.* For the *Sonets pour Helene* is Ronsard's own *Metamorphoses* and, like Ovid's, less a paean to pantheistic flux than a catalogue of possessions and perversions.[51]

Conclusion: Helen, the Body; or, Imitation as Necrophilia

The ultimate metamorphosis—in Ovid as in Ronsard—is death. The death of the beloved both liberates and frustrates the lover, just as the mute rigor mortis of the past makes it, for the poet, at once accessible and inaccessible. Imitation, in this sense, may be but one form of necrophilia. The image of the lover and the beloved grafted—sexually, surgically, botanically—is pervasive in the *Sonets pour Helene,* and in the poetry of the Pléiade in general. But often that image of grafting is translated into a longing for death and the refuge of the tomb.[52] "The Grave's a fine and private place," Andrew Marvell tells us, "But none I think do there embrace" (Lord 1984:24). But Marvell is wrong. Death for Ronsard is the perfect embrace, for to be united with the beloved in the tomb is to be perpetually and perfectly conjoined (bones commingling with bones). In intertextual terms, to join the beloved in death is, for the poet, to have joined his precursors and, with them, to have entered the domain of the monument or the ruin. Others then—lovers and poets—will come (perhaps reverentially, perhaps contemptuously) to worship at his tomb, as he once came to worship at the tombs of those who came before him. The poet, dead, can now be mourned.

SpH 1.5 is a horticultural fantasy on the immortality of the tomb:

> Helene sceut charmer avecque son Nepenthe
> Les pleurs de Telemaque. Helene, je voudroy
> Que tu peusses charmer les maux que je reçoy
> Depuis deux ans passez, sans que je m'en repente.
> Naisse de noz amours une nouvelle plante,
> Qui retienne noz noms pour eternelle foy,
> Qu'obligé je me suis de servitude à toy,
> Et qu'à nostre contact la terre soit presente.
> O terre, de noz oz en ton sein chaleureux
> Naisse une herbe au Printemps propice aux amoureux,
> Qui sur noz tombeaux croisse en un lieu solitaire.
>
> (1–11)

> [Helen knew how to charm away the tears of Telemachus with her Nepenthe. Helen, if only you would charm away the pains I suffer now for two years—not that I regret them. May a new plant be born from our love, one which takes both our names as an act of eternal faith, so that I remain your faithful servant, so that the earth is witness to our contact. O earth, from our bones in your warm bosom, may a plant be born in the Spring, auspicious for lovers, that will grow on our tombs in a solitary place.]

The tomb becomes the literal fulfillment of the lover's chiastic longing for embrace with the beloved, a monument declaring: X *marks the spot.* X: the graft that "takes," that yields the fertile hybrid. Such a hybrid, like the tombs from which it springs and which it joins as one, would be a way of *living on* for Helen and for Ronsard: for *living on* is what the poet and the lover both want.[53] It is another delusion, of course, like that given to Telemachus by way of Helen's magic herb, the *nepenthe,* a drug with the power to erase the pain of memory (see my pp. 40–42). This, in a sense, is the boon sought by Ronsard, another son in search of a father. For both Telemachus and Ronsard, *not* finding the father may be better.[54] The encumbrance of memory is a frequent subject in Ronsard's poetry. In *Ode* 3.9 ("A Denys Lambin, lecteur du roy"), for example, Ronsard professes to know Homer so well that it is as if he remembers hearing him. But to remember Homer is to become Homer, something potentially threatening to one's own poetic identity: "In truth since I began to study Greek, / I had become Homer, / For it seemed I could remember / Having heard his beautiful verses" ("veritablement depuis / Que studieux du Grec je suis, / Homere devenu je fusse, / Si souvenir ici me peusse / D'avoir ses beaux vers entendu" [Laumonier 1914–75, 2:15–16]). To remember the beloved, or the precursor — or the beloved precursor — is, thus, another kind of shackle. As Ronsard writes at the end of the "Stances" from "Sur la mort de Marie": "Goodbye a hundred times, goodbye Marie: / Ronsard will never forget you, / Never will Death undo the bond by which your beauty ties me" ("Adieu cent fois, adieu Marie: / Jamais Ronsard ne t'oublira, / Jamais la Mort ne deslira / Le nœud dont ta beauté me lie" [Weber 334]). The belated poet is such a lover, bound to an antiquity which is long since dead, but whose beauty continues to hold him captive.

The worship of the dead is a duty and an obsession — as is well attested by the recollected image of Laura in Petrarch's *Rime sparse,* whose claims upon the poet's psyche are far more tyrannical after her death than they were before (see Durling 1976:21). There is a parallel to be drawn here with Gregory Nagy's theory of hero worship in Greek antiquity: that which is represented as antagonism between god and hero in epic poetry (between Patroklos and Ares, for example) is transformed into alliance or even identity in cultic practice (Nagy 1979, chaps. 9 and 10). But, as James Redfield writes in the foreword to Nagy's *The Best of the Achaeans,* the "poet himself is a kind of hero, since he has an ambiguous relation to his proper god . . . and can at death become the object of cult. . . . He has, however, a privileged position among heroes . . . he can both partake and observe" (in Nagy 1979:xi–xii). Nagy's thesis proves surprisingly apt as a more general model for the production of poetry. For the poet and the lover, we have seen, are antagonists of that which they revere. The writing of poetry is a way of both narrating that antagonism and transforming it into alliance and identification. Competition is part of commemoration. The poem is a tombstone that buries the past at the same time that it celebrates and perpetuates it. The *Iliad,* Redfield goes on to say, is Achilles' "*monumentum* (literally, tomb)" (in Nagy 1979:xiii). Ronsard's *Ode* 4.5, "De l'élection de son sépulcre," provides a grandiose example of poetry as self-perpetuating cult. *SpH* 1.49, "Chanson," records the establishment of a hero cult to Helen and Ronsard. The poem opens with a series of parallel images of grafting: "More tightly than the vine which is wed to the elm, / With arms both supple and strong, / With the bond of your hands, Mistress, I beg you, / Enlace my body. /. . . Then resting your breast upon mine, swooning, / To ease my suffering / Hold me even tighter round my neck and give me back my soul / By the spirit of a kiss" ("Plus estroit que la Vigne à l'Ormeau se marie / De bras souplement-forts, / Du lien de tes mains, Maistresse, je te prie, / Enlasse moy le corps. /. . . Puis appuyant ton sein sur le mien qui se pâme, / Pour mon mal appaiser, / Serre plus fort mon col, & me redonne l'ame / Par l'esprit d'un baiser" [1–4, 9–12]). In death, the happy couple will journey as one to Ronsard's version of the Isle of the Blessed, where "The Heroes and the Heroines speak only of love" ("Les Heros . . . avec les Heroïnes / Ne parler que d'amours" [23–24]). There they will occupy the place of honor among the mythic lovers of antiquity, but their enthronement is represented, at the same time, as a usurpation: "Straight away the holy group, lovers long ago, honoring us above all others, will come to greet us, counting themselves fortunate indeed to make our acquaintance. And sitting us in a meadow in bloom, in the middle of them all, no one, not even Procris, will refuse to give up their place, neither those who keep to themselves, together, Artemis and Dido, nor that beautiful Greek, she whom you are like in beauty as in name" ("D'embas la troupe saincte, autrefois amoureuse, / Nous honorant sur tous, / Viendra nous saluer, s'estimant bien-heureuse / De s'accointer de nous. // Et nous faisant asseoir dessus l'herbe fleurie / De toutes au milieu, / Nulle, & fust-ce Procris, ne sera point marrie / De nous quitter son lieu. // Non celles qui s'en vont toutes seules ensemble, / Artemise et Didon: / Non ceste belle Grecque, à qui ta beauté semble / Comme tu fais de nom" [37–49]). The old Helen makes way for the new. To join the past is to supersede it.

Death for the poet is a way of defeating the past. *SpH* 1.7 is another "Chanson" *d'outre-tombe* that rests upon the ruins of other songs and other tombs. It begins as a recasting of Sappho Fr. 31, with its classic diagnosis of passion. The prognosis, here too, is death: "Upon my tombstone write my pain / In big letters: / The Vendomois who rests here, / Died loving well, / Like Paris. . . . Not for the love of a Greek Helen, / but a Helen from Saintonge" ("Dessus ma tombe escrivez mon soucy / En lettres grossement: / Le Vendomois, lequel repose icy, / Mourut en bien aimant. / Comme Pâris. . . . Non pour l'amour d'une Helene Gregeoise, / Mais d'une Saintongeoise" [43–49]). Ronsard's memorial rejects or supersedes the earlier, Homeric act of commemoration. But there is a third tombstone (at least) concealed here: that of the poet Propertius. In the Latin elegy (2.13) as in the French song, the dying poet transmits his instructions for his funeral, and dictates a few lines for his tombstone. Propertius goes on to prophesy that his resting place will be as famed as Achilles', a shrine to which his Cynthia will make a futile pilgrimage, futile because her entreaties, now made too late, will go unanswered: "in vain, Cynthia, will you call back my silent shade; for what answer shall my crumbled bones be able to make?" (ll. 57–58; trans. Goold 1990). The tombstone speaks, we might say, because it remains defiantly mute, exhorting and ignoring us all at once.

Note that the usurpation of the Homeric tomb is represented as a victory for an indigenous mythology ("Not for the love of a Greek Helen, / but a Helen from Saintonge"), a common motif in Ronsard's work.[55] This is a poem, like Sappho Fr. 16, that seeks not so much to reject the epic as to incorporate it into itself. It promotes its status as a French entity at the same time that it lays claim to panhellenic greatness. In fact, the whole double labor of the Pléiade is to make the French and the Hellenic distinct and, at the same time, to make them coincide.

This kind of cultic promotion is not possible, in *SpH* 1.7, without the mechanism of writing—on both stone and paper. Poetry for Ronsard is always a tombstone, or an extended epitaph. *SpH* 2.8 records the founding of a cult as agrarian ceremony and as inscription: "In your honor I plant this tree of Cybele, / this Pine, where your renown will be read forever: / I have engraved on its trunk our names and our love, / Which will grow, along with the new bark" ("Je plante en ta faveur cest arbre de Cybelle, / Ce Pin, où tes honneurs se liront tous les jours: / J'ay gravé sur le tronc noz noms & noz amours, / Qui croistront à l'envy de l'escorce nouvelle" [1–4]). The proper care for this pastoral shrine is urged, then, upon the fauns and shepherds who frequent the forest. Instructions follow: "Every year hang on this tree a sign / Bearing witness to passers-by of my love and my pain: / Then, while sprinkling it with the milk and blood of a lamb, / Say, This Pine is sacred, it is Helen's plant" ("Attache tous les ans à ceste arbre un Tableau, / Qui tesmoigne aux passans mes amours & ma peine: / Puis l'arrosant de laict & du sang d'un agneau, / Dy, Ce Pin est sacré, c'est la plante d'Heleine" [11–14]). Ronsard's new cult bears the trace of many others: there are echoes of Virgil, Ovid, Bembo, and, of course, Theocritus (Weber 751n1–6). Theocritus 18, in which a chorus of handmaidens serenades Helen and Menelaus on their wedding night, may in fact represent the aetiology of a cult, archaic or Ptolemaic.[56] In the *Sonets pour Helene,* Ronsard is, we can see, attempting his own aetiology—one that, like that of Theocritus, is at once an act of competition and commemoration, encomium and elegy, and, like that of Theocritus, privileges images of inscription and embrace.[57]

Given the ritual and literary history behind a poem like *SpH* 2.8, Ronsard's fantasies of signatures, of leaving his name behind on tombstones, trees, and pages of poetry, reads all the more like megalomaniacal graffiti, a way of saying: "I WAS HERE." What that means, of course, is that others were there, too, and that others will follow. Poetry is always an act of simultaneous restoration and vandalism, a testament to and a desecration of the writing on the walls of the past.[58] Are the various figures for this restoration/vandalism that we have

examined — abduction, metamorphosis, entombment, inscription, and graffiti —
figures for the literal and literary work of writing poetry? Or is it possible that
the literal work of the poet is really a rehearsal for the "real thing": erotic possession? What the poet above all hopes to achieve is *literally* to unite with what
he loves (and hates). Thus the poet writes poetry, which is to say: he dies and
thereby enters the realm of the *literal/literary.*

SpH 2.42 is a poem that articulates this *poetics of the literal:*

> Passant dessus la tombe, où ta moitié repose,
> Tu versas dessus elle une moisson de fleurs:
> L'eschaufant de souspirs, & l'arrosant de pleurs,
> Tu monstras qu'une mort tenoit ta vie enclose.
> Si tu aimes le corps dont la terre dispose,
> Imagine ta force, & conçoy tes rigueurs:
> Tu me verras, cruelle, entre mille langueurs
> Mourir, puis que la mort te plaist sur toute chose.
> C'est acte de pitié d'honorer un cercueil:
> Mespriser les vivans est un signe d'orgueil.
> Puis que ton naturel les fantaumes embrasse,
> Et qui rien n'est de toy, s'il n'est mort, estimé,
> Sans languir tant de fois, esconduit de ta grace,
> Je veux du tout mourir, pour estre mieux aimé.

> [Passing by the tomb, where your other half rests,
> You threw upon her a harvest of flowers:
> Warming it with sighs, and watering it with tears,
> You showed that a corpse held your life within.
> If you love the body that belongs to the earth,
> Imagine the power you have, and think of what it means:
> You will see me, O cruel one, die from a thousand agonies,
> Since death pleases you more than anything.
> It is an act of pity to honor a coffin:
> To despise the living is a sign of arrogance.
> Since it is your inclination to embrace phantoms,
> And since you esteem nothing, unless it is dead,
> Without suffering so many times, exiled from your grace,
> I want to die, in order to be better loved.]

Here it is Helen who has come, a participant in the cult of the dead, to the tomb
of one who is called her *moitié*. Henri and Catherine Weber note that in the 1584
version of the poem, the name of the deceased, Lucrèce, is stated (note 1 on *SpH*
2.42). But here, in the original version of 1578, no name, no specific identity,
is attached. Instead, *moitié,* while remaining a simple term of affection, is left,
all the same, as a figure that resonates with the Neoplatonic images of rupture
and embrace that abound in the *Sonets pour Helene.* Ronsard would like to be

Helen's *moitié,* but it is the dead, not the living, that Helen loves. What Helen loves, in *SpH* 2.42, is death in its most unadorned and literal sense: "the body that belongs to the earth" ("le corps dont la terre dispose"). But what does this mean, to covet a body, to embrace a corpse? It means, paradoxically, embracing a simulacrum without substance, a mere figure of the real: "it is your inclination to embrace phantoms" ("ton naturel les fantaumes embrasse"). That very phrase is, of course, a figure of speech. Indeed, it could be argued that Helen's entire act of mourning is a conventional performance, the fulfillment of a formal ritual.

Ronsard's sonnet is itself, and by the same token, another ritual performance. The poet warns his beloved that he will die for her, but she knows that he will not *really* die, and he knows that she knows this. What Ronsard says he covets is the very thing, he asserts, that Helen loves excessively: (her) body. But does he *really* want this, or is he merely following the conventions of poetry, just as Helen is following the conventions of mourning? On the other hand, it *is* literally the dead that Ronsard worships: the silent ruins and corpses of texts of antiquity. And yet to say that Ronsard has a "love affair" with the past is to fall into just another figure of speech.

On one hand, the poet literally wants to die. On the other, the poet wants to die literally, that is, figuratively: in literary terms. Ronsard explains why: "to be better loved" ("pour estre mieux aimé").

11

Miscegenation

Introduction: Nerval Watches *Faust* at the Opera in Frankfurt

In *Lorely: Souvenirs d'Allemagne,* Gérard de Nerval recalls attending a performance of Goethe's *Faust* in 1850 with a group of compatriots (1961:729–82). "Many times we had talked about the possibility of creating a *Faust* in the French style, without imitating the inimitable Goethe" ("Nous avions si souvent discuté ensemble sur la possibilité de faire un *Faust* dans le goût français, sans imiter Goethe l'inimitable" [776]). Nerval's problem, it would appear, is much like Ronsard's. When Nerval wonders what a French Faust would look like, he is asking, in effect, as Ronsard so often asks, how to make the foreign French. How does one imitate "without imitating"? Nerval is speaking here, it should be noted, as someone who has already (in 1827) translated the first part of *Faust* into French. (The second part of Goethe's *Faust,* in which Helen plays a significant role, was published in its entirety in 1832, after Goethe's death, and published in French only in 1840.) It has been argued that Nerval's importation of Goethe's poem had, at first, a limited impact upon French romanticism, because the post-Napoleonic France of the 1820s was a highly xenophobic place, still gripped by an intense nostalgia for the Empire.[1] And yet romanticism has long been defined, and has long defined itself, as an embrace of the foreign. It is this simultaneous resistance and attraction to the foreign that I want to explore in this chapter. For the past is also the foreign.

This is not a chapter, then, about Goethe's *Faust.* But there are a number of reasons why it begins with *Faust:* (1) Helen's role in the *Faust* tradition has had a significant impact in France; (2) the reception of *Faust* in France is a powerful model for the construction of an indigenous French romanticism (an impossibility, ultimately, since all romanticism is culturally hybrid); (3) *Faust* itself is a paradoxical project committed to the synthesis of a homogeneous national or cultural tradition out of the heterogeneous pieces of the past. The swerve toward the foreign at the start of this chapter thus has a certain logic to it. To want to imitate *Faust* suggests, in a larger sense, what nineteenth-century France wants: to be both itself (purely French) and another, to be French and German, or French and Greek, or French and Latin, and so on. In each case, ideally speaking, the second term is meant to be dissolved in the first. The imitative strategies to accomplish this delicate graft are the subject of this chapter. It is not clear what the modern poet fears most: that the graft will not take and will be exposed as such, or, rather, that it will take too well and go unrecognized. In both cases, graft is now represented as a form of *miscegenation.*

"To create a *Faust* in the French style" ("Faire un *Faust* dans le goût français": the figure Nerval uses is openly superficial, something a tailor or a carpenter might say with the whims of fashion and the demands of the marketplace in mind. In fact, a fashion called the "goût grec" ("Greek style") was wildly, if briefly, popular in France in the late eighteenth century. "Within a few years," according to Hugh Honour, "the 'Grecian taste' became a mania: everything in Paris was *à la grecque* wrote Grimm in 1763—exteriors and interiors of buildings, furniture, fabrics, jewelry" (1968:27–29). But Honour cautions us not to attach too much significance to the style, as far as the development of neoclassicism is concerned: "The *goût grec,* like the *style étrusque* which succeeded it, is but an offshoot, a branch of prettily variegated leaves, stemming from the main trunk of the Neo-classical movement" (29). Honour relegates to the margins of the Neoclassical tendency a phenomenon that one might imagine belongs at its center, if only because it seems to represent that tendency in its most extreme form. The image of the *goût grec* as an arboreal detour, in fact, is ironic, since the style is one that self-consciously rejects the parentage of the classical root, designating itself as artifice, or grafted scion. It is an image, then, that can serve as a model for the way French writings in the neoclassical vein position themselves in relation to the classical. French writings on Helen in the nineteenth and twentieth centuries, one might say, function in the manner of a *goût grec.*[2]

Nerval's interest in making *Faust* French is not only fashion-driven but linked to the question of cultural ancestry and the role of writing in the transmission of that ancestry. In the same work cited above, Nerval reflects on the Faust legend recorded in medieval chapbooks all over Europe.[3] The legend begins, according to Nerval, with a figure named Johannes Fust, who, according to tradition, was one of the inventors of the printing press. The familiar story that Faust sold his soul to the devil is a product of the malicious gossip of jealous monks, convinced that Faust's invention would quickly eliminate their work as scribes, "manuscript copyists" ("copistes des manuscrits" [Nerval 1961:779]). Nerval's story is to a large extent a fable about technology. For him, technology permits the reproduction and dissemination of language. That is not all, however: the printing press also takes the power to preserve culture out of the hands of an elitist oligarchy, liberating and commercializing it. This is clear in Nerval's account. Faust travels to a monastery to receive payment for work completed on a new Bible. Upon arrival he is shocked to discover that the monks are busy scratching lines off a manuscript in order to reuse the pages. The manuscript is the *Iliad,* and the monks are literally erasing it: expunging the past. Faust requests a complete manuscript of the *Iliad* as payment for his services. Books removed from the monastery are customarily stamped with its identifying seal, and it is at the moment when the abbot stamps the parchment that the idea of the printing press is born in Faust's mind. "Faust carried away," Nerval writes, "as an eagle carries away its prey, the manuscript and the idea" ("Faust emporta, comme la proie de l'aigle, le manuscrit et l'idée" [780]). The idea is the possibility of limitless and almost effortless reproduction, and it saves Homer from extinction. It is a powerful idea and, for many, a frightening one. Faust is almost executed "for having sold Bibles that were exactly alike, each one just like the other,—and which could only have been executed by diabolical artifice" ("pour avoir vendu des Bibles entièrement semblables, l'une à l'autre,— et qui n'avaient pu être exécutées que par artifice diabolique"). Faust's power to reproduce is viewed as divine or demonic.[4] This explains the rumors of sorcery attached to his name, the folktales of phantoms conjured up from the past. Helen's role in the poem is a canonical part of that demonic tradition. Nerval suggests that her importance in that tradition can be explained only by Homer's role in the invention of the press:

On se demande pourquoi celle-ci [la tradition] suppose unanimement que Faust avait commandé au diable de ressusciter pour lui la belle Hélène de Sparte, dont il eut un fils, et avec laquelle il vécut vingt-quatre ans, aux termes de son pacte? Peut-être est-ce le souvenir de l'anecdote relative au manuscrit de l'*Iliade* qui conduisit à cette idée. *L'admirateur d'Homère devait être en esprit l'amant d'Hélène.* (Nerval 1961:781; my italics)

[One wonders why [the tradition] always represents Faust ordering the devil to resurrect for him the beautiful Helen of Sparta, with whom he has a son, and with whom he lives for twenty-four years, all according to the terms of their pact? Perhaps it is the memory of the story about the manuscript of the *Iliad* which led to this idea. *The admirer of Homer must have been, in spirit, the lover of Helen.*]

Nerval is right to join these two parts of the tradition. For this is precisely what this book has set out to document, from beginning to end: that the admirer of Homer has always been, in spirit, the lover of Helen.

Goethe's *Faust* II: "I have slept with Greece and found it sweet"

The "Dedication" (1808) to Part I of Goethe's *Faust* (1797) characterizes the poem that follows as a grandiose exercise in *Wahn:* illusion or theater. *Faust* in its entirety is, of course, a dramatic poem subtitled *Eine Tragödie* (the "Dedication" cited above is followed by a "Vorspiel auf dem Theater"). Part II of *Faust,* composed some twenty years after Part I, is another theatrical performance, but the actors now are different and the genre has changed. The great heroine of Part I is the folkloric Margareta, and Faust's romance with her has long been read in the context of Goethe's search for a definitively German romanticism. If the Goethe of Part I is a nationalist-romantic, then the Goethe of Part II is a nationalist-classicist.[5] The medieval and folkloric elements of Part I are marginalized in Part II, where the tone changes from high tragedy to comedy and parody. And the North European *romantic* Walpurgis Night of Part I is succeeded by the *classical* Walpurgis Night of Part II.

Let us briefly review Helen's role in the second part of Goethe's *Faust.*[6] In Act 1 a hall in the imperial palace has been converted into a makeshift theater, and an emperor "has been seated so he faces / The pictured curtains where he may behold / In comfort battles from great times of old" ("setz man grade vor die Wand / Auf den Tapeten mag er da die Schlachten / Der grossen Zeit bequemlichstens betrachten" [6382–84]). The princes and princesses of the court are not disappointed when the phantoms of Paris and Helen appear upon the stage. The phantoms of antiquity play out their assigned literary roles, and we see that the vignette presented today is "The Rape of Helen." Faced with this spectacle, Faust is mad with passion. Even Gretchen's loveliness, "compared with beauty such as this, turns pale!" (6497). But the comparison is typical of the dialogue Goethe sets up between the two parts of his poem: here, we can see, the Hellenic wins out over the Germanic. The drama at the court is Goethe's *teichoskopia,* complete with German scholars as Trojan elders: "I see her plainly, but I'll make so bold / As doubt that this is Helen we behold. / A presence misleads to exaggerations, / I stick to written texts and annotations, / And there I read: She gave exceeding joy / To all the ancient greybeard men of Troy. / And how that tallies here I well can see: / I am no longer young, and she charms me" ("Ich seh sie deutlich, doch gesteh ich frei: / Zu zweiflen ist, ob sie die rechte sei. / Die Gegenwart verführt ins Übertriebne, / Ich halte mich vor allem ans Geschriebne. / Da les ich denn, sie habe wirklich allen / Graubärten Trojas sonderlich gefallen; / Und wie mich dünkt, vollkommen passt das hier: / Ich bin nicht jung, und doch gefällt sie mir" [6533–40]). Goethe's *teichoskopia* is, in fact, a *meta-teichoskopia:* it proves its authenticity by citing Homer's. Another way of putting this is that Goethe's scholar verifies one illusion by reference to another. The phantom scene that unfolds before his eyes, after all, is but a reenactment of the written scene, something he has read over and over again. Faust (both scholar and lover) is not content merely to watch: he wants to possess (both Homer and Helen). The performance turns to disaster, then, when Faust, attempting to prevent one rape, proceeds to engineer another. But Faust fails, and the scene ends with Faust's prayer to recover Helen, and the recognition, "Who knew her once, without her cannot rest" ("Wer sie erkannt, der darf sie nicht entbehren" [6559]), which is a succinct way of paraphrasing the amorous lament of all modern culture for the classical past.

That the past in *Faust* II is always elusive and illusory becomes even more evident in Act 2. At the beginning of this act, Faust, still mad with love for Helen, is dreaming of the rape of Leda. The reader is privy to these fantasies by way of the divining powers of the newly created Homunculus, first test-tube baby of the literary world and Goethe's emblem of all artistic synthesis. It is Homunculus who leads Faust back to the ancient past in search of Helen on the eve of the "Klassische Walpurgisnacht." Says Mephistopheles: "I've never heard of anything like that" ("Dergleichen hab ich nie vernommen"). Homunculus responds: "How could you hear of anything like that? / Romantic ghosts are all that you would know; / Real ghosts are Classical, and must be so" ("Wie wollt es auch zu euren Ohren kommen? / Romantishe Gespenster kennt ihr nur allein; / Ein echt Gespenst, auch klassisch hat's zu sein" [6944–47]). Despite the position the classical tradition here assumes over and against the Germanic tradition, it is difficult to take either very seriously. Homunculus's last remark points toward the illusory nature of all tradition, and the contradiction that fatally marks all imitations. Classical ghosts may be real, but they are still ghosts. And ghosts there are to spare in the "Classical Walpurgis" that follows in the next scene, which takes place, as Homunculus puts it, "in the land of fable" ("im Fabelreich" [7055]). For the next two thousand lines (7005–9126), we find ourselves in a vast generic Greece, a synthetic antiquity called into existence by Faust's prayer. Most of Goethe's mythological fantasy would appear to have its source, we should not be surprised to learn, in a single book, Hederich's 1770 *Gründliches mythologisches Lexikon* (this according to Passage: see Goethe 1965:251n7). For the Walpurgis is a prepackaged mythological encyclopedia, a collage of classical clichés. What gives the scene its comic flavor is the fact that these talking figures of antiquity are never anything but explicitly *literary* figures. Faust, meanwhile, is like a tourist who suddenly awakens to find himself inside the guide book he has been reading all his life.[7] Set down upon the soil of Hellas, Faust, until then in a state of suspended animation, comes instantly to life and asks abruptly, "Where is she?" ("Wo ist sie?" [7056]).[8] The pursuit of Helen continues. Act 3 takes us before the palace of Menelaus in Sparta, in a scene reminiscent of Euripides' *Helen.* Helen is again carried off, this time successfully, to the castle of Faust (now a medieval lord such as might have ruled over one of the Frankish principalities in Greece in the thirteenth and fourteenth centuries). There she will wed Faust, and their marriage is nothing less than a figure for the union of German and Hellenic culture.

It is nothing more than that, however. That this marriage is merely a figure of speech is suggested by the next scene, which takes place in Arcadia (that is, nowhere, in a past that never was). Faust and Helen enter with their son, Euphorion. Euphorion is an incarnation of freedom, a liberating force too power-ful to be limited or controlled. Shortly before his Icarus-like death, he attempts his first abduction, carrying off one of Helen's handmaidens. Who is this Euphorion? He is expressly identified by Goethe as the Spirit of Romantic Poetry and, more specifically, Lord Byron, recently (1824) dead of a fever in Greece (see Heffner in Goethe 1950:94). And the new Holy Family of Faust–Helen–Euphorion is not destined to last for long. As their son sets out to test his wings, Helen and Faust call out to him in unison, "Is nothing due / To us from you? / Is our union all a dream?" ("Sind denn wir / Gar nichts dir? / Ist der holde Bund ein Traum?" [9881]). Euphorion falls, and with his death Helen dissolves, leaving only her veil in Faust's hands. The marriage is over: the graft does not take.

The dream of that marriage is an intensely ambivalent affair when it is a ques-tion of German culture on French soil. Thus the reception of *Faust* in France can stand as a model for the question of foreign influence in general: when it comes from afar, or when it comes from the past. The reception of the foreign can be a matter of emulation or collaboration, as in Robert Brasillach's famous defense, "I have slept with Germany and found it sweet." But as that defense itself sug-gests, reception is almost always figured in gendered and genetic terms. That figurative tendency is central to Jean Giraudoux's first play, *Siegfried* (1928). This is the story of an amnesiac torn between a German present and a French past. Seigfried von Kleist finds himself in Germany at the end of the Great War—and becomes one of its great statesmen—only to discover that he was formerly Jacques Forestier, a Frenchman. Despite Siegfried/Jacques's promise at the end of the play to unite in himself the German and the Frenchman, the possibility of any coherent identity or nationality by now appears elusive. In Giraudoux's later *La guerre de Troie n'aura pas lieu,* Trojans and Greeks have replaced Germans and French, but the story is in many ways the same.

Euphorion in France: André Chénier, "Le Français Byzantin"

As a real-life Euphorion, it would be hard to find a better precursor than the French poet André Chénier (1762–94). It may be worthwhile to note that, in his final days as a prisoner in 1945, Brasillach was finishing a critical study of Chénier's poetry (see Kaplan 1989:968). Here, in one of his *Elégies,* is how Ché-nier himself describes his origins: "Hail, Thrace, my mother, and the mother of Orpheus, / Galatea, whom my eyes have desired since long ago. / For it is there where a Greek woman, in the spring of her youth, / Beautiful, in the bed of a husband the nursling of France, / Gave birth to me, French, in the bosom of Byzantium" ("Salut, Thrace, ma mère, et la mère d'Orphée, / Galata, que mes yeux désiraient dès longtemps. / Car c'est là qu'une Grecque, en son jeune prin-temps, / Belle, au lit d'un époux nourrison de la France, / Me fit naître français dans le sein de Byzance" [*Elégies* 19.72, in Chénier 1950]). Chénier's portrait of his parentage stresses genealogy as cultural and ethnic graft. It is not at all clear if Chénier's mother was really Greek, and the poet was in fact only a child when he left for France.

All the better, for our purposes, if this ancestry is fictive. What is significant is that both Chénier and his readers rely upon it in order to give him a strategic place in the history of French letters. Gérard Walter, for example, in the introduction to the Pléiade edition of Chénier's complete works, refers to *Elégies* 19 in order to endorse its narrative of miscegenation.[9] Chénier's career as a young libertine is understood to be ethnically predestined: his "life of luxury" ("vie de luxe"), writes Walter, "was perfectly in agreement with his character which tended towards the sensual, and which his levantine upbringing had gratified to a fairly large extent" ("s'accordait parfaitement avec son caractère fait de nonchalante volupté dont l'avait gratifié dans une assez forte proportion son ascendance levantine" [Chénier 1950:xi]). What is known about Chénier's early years suggests that this kind of interpretation was encouraged by his own family. While Chénier *père* languishes as a civil servant in Morocco, Mme de Chénier acquires a reputation as a "belle Grecque," sets up a salon frequented by philhellenes, and offers dinners "in the Olympian style" ("a la mode olympienne") at which she sings Greek folksongs for her guests (x).[10] Chénier's future œuvre, we will see, collaborates with this classicizing project, most of it returning to classical forms (*Bucoliques, Elégies, Epigrammes, Epîtres, Odes, Iambes*) and furnished with classical décor.

If André Chénier had not existed, it is clear, Charles Augustin Sainte-Beuve would have had to invent him. Chénier, in Sainte-Beuve's eyes, is one of France's great cultural patriarchs, at once Homeric avatar and romantic messiah, the sacrificial lamb of a revolution that quite literally cut him off from the present (Chénier was guillotined in the last days of the Terror). Chénier's birth and death make him the very embodiment of the romantic–classical graft. And Sainte-Beuve is everywhere eager to sustain Chénier's genealogical self-promotion, as in this passage from his essay "André Chénier": "Born of an ingenious scientist and an exquisite Greek, André left Byzantium, his homeland, when he was very young; but he dreamed of it often in the delightful valleys of Languedoc, where he was raised; and later, when, now enrolled in the College of Navarre, he learned the most beautiful of languages, he seemed . . . to remember the games of his infancy and the songs of his mother" ("Né d'un savant ingénieux et d'une Grecque brillante, André quitta très jeune Byzance, sa patrie; mais il y rêva souvent dans les délicieuses vallées du Languedoc, où il fut élevé; et lorsque plus tard, entré au collège de Navarre, il apprit la plus belle des langues, il semblait . . . se souvenir des jeux de son enfance et des chants de sa mère" [Sainte-Beuve 1930:90]). For Sainte-Beuve, Chénier's poetry, emerging from the neoclassicism of the Enlightenment, looks both backward to antiquity and forward to the present: "André Chénier, who emerges, born from two classical centuries, already holds his arms out to ours, and seems to be the older brother to the new poets of today" ("André Chénier, jeté à l'issue de ses deux . . . siècles classiques, tend déjà les bras au notre, et semble le frère aîné des poètes nouveaux" [89]). Chénier is thus a perfect specimen of the graft that is needed to heal the wounded continuity of European culture. Every poet, ideally, would be like Chénier, who, when he reads Greek, remembers the songs his mother sang to him.[11]

Genealogical heroes, who may or may not be Chénier himself, are frequent characters in Chénier's poetry, particularly where it returns, as it often does, to the motif of exile from a pastoral world of Hellenic perfection. In "L'aveugle," perhaps Chénier's most widely read poem, a wandering Homer is received as a god by three simple shepherds (1950:48). Chénier's Homer is the emblematic figure of poetry from the first source: original, primitive, and natural.[12] "L'invention," on the other hand (Chénier 1950:123–32), is addressed to the contemporary poet who no longer has access to that source. In such an impasse, how to write new poetry? By imitating old poetry, of course: "O so that among us creative spirits / May reach the heights of Virgil and Homer, / Make sure to keep them in your memory as in a temple, / And without following in their footsteps imitate their example" ("O qu'ainsi parmi nous des esprits inventeurs / De Virgile et d'Homère atteignent les hauteurs, / Sachent dans la mémoire avoir comme eux un temple, / Et sans suivre leurs pas imiter leur exemple" [130]).

Chénier's poetics here is self-consciously Horatian in its central principles. Imitating or reinventing classical poetry, in other words, is not the same thing as collecting or preserving it, haphazardly, in the manner of an antiquarian. Chénier goes on to caution the poet in a paraphrase of the opening lines of the *Ars poetica:* "But inventing is not the same thing . . . as piling into a heap, without design, without force, human limbs that belong apart as an enormous colossus. . . . It is not attaching the bloody mane of a lion upon the forehead of a beautiful Nymph. Insane ravings! Monstrous phantoms!" ("Mais inventer n'est pas . . . / . . . entasser, sans dessein et sans force, / Des membres ennemis en un colosse énorme . . . / Ce n'est pas sur le front d'une Nymphe brillante / Hérisser d'un lion la crinière sanglante: / Délires insensés! fantômes monstrueux!" [1950:123]). Bad poetry is an act of miscegenation, and its product is sterile and monstrous. Good poetry looks a lot like bad poetry. But in good poetry incoherence and incompatibility are only apparent. The great exemplum here for Chénier is Zeuxis, naturally, and his portrait of Helen. The poet who succeeds at invention—

> . . . par des nœuds certains, imprévus et nouveaux,
> Unisssant des objets qui paraissent rivaux,
> Montre et fait adopter à la nature mère

> Ce qu'elle n'a point fait, mais ce qu'elle a pu faire;
> C'est le fécond pinceau qui, sûr dans ses regards,
> Retrouve un seul visage en vingt belles épars,
> Les fait renaître ensemble, et, par un art suprême,
> Des traits de vingt beautés forme la beauté même.
>
> (124)

> [by certain bonds, unexpected and new, unifying objects which appear at odds, shows and gives to mother nature things which she did herself not create, but which she could have created. It is the fertile brush which, by its vision, retrieves a single face in twenty separate faces, causes them to be born again, together and, by a supreme art, from the traces of twenty beauties, forms beauty itself.]

Chénier is everywhere concerned in his poetry with what should and should not be combined. Hence his insistence on the distinction between synthesis and miscegenation. For one must be vigilant in maintaining that distinction. Zeuxis's "vingt beautés" leads directly, in the next line, to the "twenty opposed genres divided up by the Greeks" ("vingt genres opposés . . . chez les Grecs divisés"). And Chénier sounds very Horatian again when he pronounces: "No genre, escaping from its prescribed limits, / Would dare invade the borders of another" ("Nul genre, s'échappant de ses bornes prescrites, / N'aurait osé d'un autre envahir les limites"[124]).

Miscegenation for Chénier is not just a poetic problem, however, but a constant threat to language and culture. The deformation and fracture of Latin into the modern European vernaculars, for example, is presented as a disastrous example of miscegenation:

> Quand le Nord, s'épuisant de barbares essaims,
> Vint, par une conquête en malheurs plus féconde,
> Venger sur les Romains l'esclavage du monde,
> De leurs affreux accents la farouche âpreté
> Du latin en tous lieux souilla la pureté:
> On vit de ce mélange étranger et sauvage
> Naître des langues sœurs, que le temps et l'usage,
> Par des sentiers divers guidant diversement,
> D'une lime insensible ont poli lentement,
> Sans pouvoir en entier, malgré tous leurs prodiges,
> De la rouille barbare effacer les vestiges.
>
> (131–32)

> [When the North, weakened by the barbarian hordes, came, in a conquest even richer in evils, to avenge itself upon the Romans through the enslavement of the world, the wild harshness of their hideous accents everywhere polluted the purity of Latin: Out of this savage and foreign mixture were born the sister tongues, which time and usage,

by different paths moving in different directions, with an invisible file,
polished slowly, without, despite all their miraculous effects, being
able to entirely efface, the vestiges of the barbarian rust.]

Miscegenation, too, is a category with contemporary geopolitical force. It explains Chénier's Europe, still under the "awful yoke" ("joug affreux") of the
Turk (1950:644). It explains Chénier himself. What Chénier wants, above all,
is to be *pure,* and the nostalgia for a lost purity drives much of his poetry and
prose. In *Essai sur les causes et les effets de la perfection et de la décadence de
lettres et des arts* (*Essay on the causes and the effects of the perfection and the
decadence of letters and arts*), for example, Chénier imagines antiquity as a state
of Edenic nudity: "The ancients were naked . . . their soul was naked. . . . For us,
it's entirely the opposite. . . . From infancy on, we wrap up our spirit; we restrain
our imagination with cords; cuffs and garters obstruct our articulations and the
movements of our ideas" ("Les anciens étaient nus . . . leur âme était nue. . . .
Pour nous, c'est tout le contraire. . . . Dès l'enfance, nous emmaillotons notre
esprit; nous retenons notre imagination par des lièvres; des manchettes et des
jarretières gênent les articulations et les mouvements de nos idées" [645]). Our
culture, like our clothing and our language, is an addition that binds, constrains,
and corrupts.

If we insist on a biographical reading, we may agree that Chénier had good
cause to look back with nostalgia upon an Edenic–Hellenic past. Much of his
greatest poetry (in particular, "La jeune captive" and the *Iambes*) was written in the prison of Saint-Lazare in the weeks that preceded his execution.[13] It
would seem that in these final poems the poetics of graft—as in the ode "A
Marie-Anne-Charlotte-Corday," where Corday becomes a new Harmodius—
becomes for Chénier a vehicle for personal and political redemption. Victim of
one revolution, Chénier's neoclassicism becomes another. His devotion to the
restoration of the classical can be read, in this sense, as a form of revolution and
resistance. Chénier is guillotined on July 25, 1794, a few days before Robes-
pierre. His poetry, however, will not be published until 1820. A quarter of a
century, in other words, will pass before Chénier's own restoration.

Poetry and Commemoration: Remembering
Paul Valéry Remembering

Chénier's neoclassicism reminds us that revolutions can be deeply conservative. Looking forward, that is, may be just another way of looking back. This
is the problem faced, over and over again, by French poets seeking to expel or
expunge the legacy of romanticism. Let me fast-forward in the second half of
this chapter to the figure of Valéry, who brings this problem to the center of
his poetry as no other poet does. I begin by remembering a conference I at-

tended November 2–4, 1995, at the University of San Francisco. The title of that gathering— "Valéry, Today [Valéry, Aujourd'hui]: International Colloquium in Honor of Paul Valéry on the 50th Anniversary of His Death" — suggested a question that those of us who attended were not really supposed to ask: *is* Valéry today the same as Valéry yesterday? "Banal question" ("Question banale"), suggests Jacques Derrida in an address delivered November 6, 1971, at a conference commemorating not the fiftieth anniversary of Valéry's death, but the hundredth anniversary of his birth. (Birth and death are interchangeable in the commemorative act, for the poet's death allows him to be continually reborn.) "I had not re-read Valéry in a long time" ("Je n'avais pas relu Valéry depuis longtemps"), Derrida confesses; and to re-read, Derrida suggests, is to be trapped, inevitably, in a "ring . . . in the form of that return to the sources which always afflicts the rhetoric of anniversaries of births: Valéry a hundred years after, Valéry now, Valéry today" ("anneau . . . dans la forme de ce retour aux sources dont s'afflige toujours la rhétorique des anniversaires de naissance: Valéry cent ans après, Valéry pour nous, Valéry présent, Valéry aujourd'hui" [1977:331]). Some twenty-five years later, in San Francisco, we found ourselves repeating this act of repeating.[14] This repetition, ironically, is what Valéry spends his career trying to escape. These are illegitimate and heretical gatherings, one and all, by the very terms of Valéry's poetics, which fear above all the persistence of the past in the present.[15] To remember Valéry, in other words, is to betray him.[16]

What seduces in a phrase like *Valéry, Aujourd'hui* is the rhetoric of the here-and-now promising a new and timeless Valéry, a pure Valéry, sundered from origins. But the search for a contemporary Valéry is inevitably, at the same time, an archaeological dig, a way of excavating an original Valéry, an *arche-Valéry*. Our efforts to isolate a pure Valéry produce instead a contagion of different, sometimes incompatible, Valérys: Valérys of yesterday facing Valérys of today. Implicit here as well is the story of a Valéry who changes because *we* change.[17] Never questioned here is the existence, at any given moment in the story, of *a* Valéry with *a* coherent identity. The question we should be asking is not: is Valéry today the same as Valéry yesterday, but rather: is Valéry, today or yesterday, ever the same as himself?

I am not speaking of Valéry proper, but of his poetry. (It is, in fact, the notion of the proper [*le propre*] itself that I am contesting here.) The very substitution of author for text suggests the way we tend to transform theories of intertextuality into psychological narratives. This explains why Harold Bloom's *Anxiety of Influence* has been misread as a form of "psychological naturalism," as de Man puts it (1983:271). It is helpful here to remember what Bloom's theory is really about. "If we admit that the term "influence" is . . . a metaphor that dramatizes a linguistic structure into a diachronic narrative," argues de Man, then "it follows that Bloom's categories of misreading not only operate between authors, but also between the various texts of a single author or, within a given text, between the different parts" (276). I am concerned with the anxiety of influence in the work of Valéry only to the extent that that anxiety is not a psychological but a textual feature.

Jean Pommier's "Leçon d'ouverture prononcée au Collège de France" on March 7, 1946, betrays this anxiety at the very moment that it attempts to master it. Pommier is faced, more explicitly than most, with the shadow of the precursor: he is about to occupy the chair formerly held by Valéry. It is traditional at the Academy for the newly elected member to laud the former occupant of the post he is about to assume. In Pommier's case, the already formidable task at hand is complicated considerably by the particular nature of his vocation. His specialty, and the title of his post, is History of Literary Works in France (Histoire des créations littéraires en France). This is, we might suggest, the chair that Valéry fought all his life to keep empty, or to keep to himself. It is up to Pommier, nevertheless, to lay claim to it. "There remains a link," he insists, "between the chair of Poetics [the title of the post under Valéry's tenure], and the chair that is now entrusted to me" ("il subsiste un lien entre la chaire de *Poétique* et celle qui m'est confiée" [1946:7]). Pommier spends a good part of his address reinforcing this link, demonstrating that Valéry, too, was, in his own way, a literary historian. But what is the task of the literary historian? Not simply affirming or rejecting Influence, but, rather, identifying and rejecting specific influences. History for Pommier is a succession of encounters between nameable figures. Pommier's work, like Bloom's, is a theory of reading disguised as genealogical drama: "the true effect of a work," Pommier proclaims, "is to be the cause of another work" ("le véritable effet d'une oeuvre, c'est d'être la cause d'une autre"). Imagine the magnitude of this effect, Pommier continues, "when the second edition of *Fleurs du mal* falls into Mallarmé's hands, when fragments of Mallarmé fall into the hands of . . . Valéry himself?" ("quand la seconde édition des *Fleurs du mal* tombe entre les mains de Mallarmé, quand des fragments de Mallarmé tombent entre les mains de . . . Valéry lui-même?" [23–24]). Pommier's narrative turns reading into literal and physical contagion: influence as *influenza* (an in-flowing) or *inspiration* (an in-breathing) transmitted with fatal precision from carrier A to carrier B.[18] Pommier even cites Valéry to prove his point: "I left to go to the sea . . . holding those copies [of Mallarmé's poetry], so precious . . . and neither the azure, nor the incense of burning plants, meant anything to me, so much did these unimaginable verses excite me and possess me" ("Je suis parti vers la mer . . . tenant les copies si précieuses . . . et ni l'azur, ni l'encens des plantes brûlantes ne m'étaient rien, tant ces vers inouïs m'exerçaient et me possédaient" [24]). Valéry appears every bit as *scientific* as Pommier here, signaling the impact of Mallarmé's verse and rejecting, at the same time, the impact of the extratextual world. And yet it is that very rejection of the extratextual that reveals the irruption, unnamed and undetected, of the intertextual: in the stubborn (Mallarméan?) presence of the word *azur* upon the page as it is banished from sea and sky. If *azur* is the mark of Mallarmé, then it shows his influence at work in spite of Valéry's attempts to acknowledge it. But that *azur* is the mark of Mallarmé is precisely what we cannot say, *azur* being, as we will see, the ultimate poetic cliché: that which always comes from somewhere else. Pommier's (like Valéry's) attempt to justify literary history only exposes its futility. *L'azur* is that which makes literary history impossible.

Hygienic Poetics

How and why it does this is the implicit problem raised by all of Valéry's work, which I construe as one long effort to evade literary history. Valéry dreams of a perfectly autonomous and self-generating text, a poem *proper,* we might say, *propre:* at once self-sufficient, pure, and without a past. This explains the rhetoric of hygiene consistently adopted by Valéry and his readers. Typical is the following by Claude Hofmann: "What Valéry holds against the past is that it leaves something other than what you have stolen from it, that it doesn't erase the marks of origin. In brief, the past hurts Valéry because it does not pass; the blood, vermilion and warm, which Lady Macbeth sees and smells on her hands" ("Le grief de Valéry contre le passé est . . . de laisser subsister autre chose que les acquêts dérobés, de n'en pas faire disparaître les attaches d'origine. Bref, ce qui blesse Valéry dans le passé, c'est ce qui ne passe pas: ce sang toujours vermeil et chaud que Macbeth voit et sent sur sa main" [1968:137]). Every trace of the past, for Valéry, is the fingerprint of a crime ("literary theft" — "vol littéraire," Hofmann suggests [140]). This makes the critic a detective, hunting down the elusive source (Hofmann again, looking for evidence of Michelet in Valéry: "And so I found that I was, in literature, a detective despite myself" ("Ainsi me découvrais-je, en littérature, détective malgré moi" [46]).

Valéry dreams of a poetry without fingerprints. His is a poetics of purity, of what he likes to call the "pure me" ("moi pur"), "by which I mean the absolute of consciousness, which is the mechanism . . . of separating automatically from everything. . . . I would compare this PURE ME to that precious Zero in mathematical language" ("par quoi j'entends l'absolu de la conscience, qui est l'opération . . . de se dégager automatiquement de tout. . . . Je compare volontiers ce MOI PUR à ce précieux Zéro de l'écriture mathématique" [1952:245–46]). Monsieur Teste is, of course, Valéry's most explicit incarnation of this zero degree of the self. If "literary practice," to cite Vincent Kaufmann, "presupposes the affirmation of an identity or singularity," then Valéry as an author strives to be his own M. Teste: "the main character of an anti-novel that disappears as soon as one tries to write it, because he is a character about whom there is nothing to say" (Kaufmann 1989:877). To act is to leave a trace, is unclean (*impropre*).[19] M. Teste, a man who refuses to act, is Valéry's most hygienic hero.[20]

But every poem is the scene of a crime, and there is always a tell-tale fingerprint. Johnson has defined *intertextuality* as "the ways a text has of not being self-contained, of being traversed by otherness." [21] I want to look, for a moment, at the problem of intertextuality in the poetry of Valéry, at what separates, not so much Valéry from Mallarmé, as Valéry from himself. Valéry's poetry is itself an extended and recurrent reflection on or of that problem. More specifically, I will read Valéry's "Hélène" (1891), from the *Album de vers anciens,* as itself a reflection on its own intertextuality, as the rehearsal (*répétition*) of its own impurity: its own failure to purge itself of origin.[22]

For Suzanne Nash that origin has been erased, or at least camouflaged. In *Paul Valéry's Album de vers anciens* (1983), Nash considers Valéry's "Hélène" a response to Leconte de Lisle's 1852 poem of the same title, an effort to distill the prior work into its Parnassian essence.[23] The result: a poem demonstrating its own autonomy. Helen is the very emblem of this autonomy: she stands for poetry as parthenogenesis. De Lisle's Helen was the protagonist of a drama in verse; Valéry's Helen, freed from the constraints of dramatic narrative, neutralizes history. The "entire epic of the Trojan War," Nash suggests, "is present in Helen's consciousness, simultaneously" (146). This Helen will not be history's victim; she "relies not on any otherworldly power, but on her own natural senses . . . to recover the rhythmic and sonorous presence of the past" (148). Her autonomy, of course, is the poem's: "Through the use of specular imagery," Nash writes, "Valéry locks the poem on itself as an intransitive and self-reflecting structure" (146).

The *poem locked on itself:* this is modernity's favorite image of the lyric genre, and it continues to dominate poetic criticism today. The highest compliment we can pay a poem remains: it says what it does. (What prevents de Lisle's "Hélène" from being a great poem, then, is the disparity it betrays between highly traditional form and relatively revolutionary content.) Indeed, the coincidence of form and content is the central premise of the *explication de texte.* That exercise more specifically, according to the *Princeton Encyclopedia of Poetry and Poetics,* looks for three essential features in a poem: (1) "self-sufficiency," (2) "unity" (or "comprehensive organicism"), and (3) "complexity" (or "*discordia concors*").[24] In all these respects, "Hélène" seems a very good poem indeed. We may convincingly summarize it as an attempt to forge structure out of inchoate raw material. Thus images of nature as discord giving way to concord—in lines such as "Je viens des grottes de la mort / Entendre l'onde se rompre aux degrés sonores"; or "J'*entends les conques profondes et les clairons / Militaires rythmer le vol des avirons; / Le chant clair des rameurs enchaîne le tumulte"—are credible as descriptions of the poem itself (in the explication, the poem is always, in the end, about itself) as a *discordia concors.* The story these lines tell us—Helen listens to a dissonant world and hears consonance—also suggests what these lines do, which is to fashion, from the crude complexity of letters and sounds, an aural pattern, a vocal consonance (above all by privileging, here, the nasal series *en/on/an*). In this passage, verse, as it were, tries to hear itself: the very paradigm of poetic autonomy.[25]

As a thematic statement, "Hélène" tells a story about perception both healing and wounding the self in its quest to be self-sufficient. That which Helen hears, sees, and touches—that is to say, remembers—both dwells within her (past as present, revived) and assails her from without (past as past, irretrievable). As a pattern of images, "Hélène" is a series of antitheses: meetings between things light and dark, natural and artificial, young and old, male and female, and, above all, past and present. On a dramatic level, too, the poem is organized around a series of symmetrical gestures: Helen cries; the kings sing back; Helen's fingers stroke the kings' beards; the gods stretch out their arms to Helen. Does Helen triumphantly unify these gestures, reconcile these antitheses? Nash says yes.[26] But we could argue equally that Helen is the site where past and present are forever at odds.

Valéry Cleans Up Parnassus

Nash's reading forces us to confront the corruption of anteriority in a number of ways. If "Hélène" is truly autonomous, it is strange, first of all, that it must be approached as a rewriting of an earlier work. What Valéry rejects in the poetry of de Lisle is the authority of history, and yet that very rejection turns Valéry's poem into a historical artifact, a dialogue with de Lisle. The return of the impure begins to emerge here as a pattern.

Parnassus had already described itself as a poetics of purity, privileging impersonality and autonomy as formal ideals. Indeed, in de Lisle's "Hélène," Paris's seduction of Helen is condemned as the intrusion of desire and action into a pure and static realm of art. Thus de Lisle's "Hélène" is revisionist poetics, everywhere seeking to banish what was central to epic: action, movement, and the claims of the body. The Parnassian Helen is closer to the Venus de Milo, subject and title of one of de Lisle's most famous poems: a work of art on display in a museum. Paris is less an abductor, here, than an art collector. De Lisle's 1852 preface to the *Poèmes antiques,* perhaps the closest thing to a Parnassian manifesto, exhorts the would-be poet to take refuge "in the contemplative and scholarly life, as in a sanctuary of rest and purification" ("dans la vie contemplative et savante, comme en un sanctuaire de repos et de purification").[27]

Valéry returns to Parnassus, Nash argues, because he believed that the Parnassian sanctuary had never purified itself of an alterity within: the specter, namely, of romanticism (1983:143–44). It is interesting to note that de Lisle's "Hélène" also appears to refer back to George Sand's hyperromantic rewriting of Goethe's *Faust, Les sept cordes de la lyre* (1838).[28] This is another example of hygienic poetics: Sand's Helen, daughter of an instrument-maker named Albertus, inheritor of his magical lyre, is the pure spirit of that instrument, the very disembodied embodiment of poetry itself. "Look at me," Helen commands the lyre, "and see if I am not as pure as the purest crystal" ("Regarde-moi, et vois si je ne suis point aussi pur que le plus pur cristal" [1869:76]). A choir of "Spirits of Harmony" ("Esprits de l'Harmonie") promise to liberate this "Spirit of the Lyre" ("Esprit de la Lyre"), for "what was ravished / abducted from the sky must return there" ("ce qui a été ravi au ciel doit y retourner" [66]). The motif of abduction has now become a purely "spiritual" event, leached of any reference to the carnal. And the end delivers on this promised apotheosis: Helen "flies up to the heavens with the Spirit of the Lyre and the celestial spirits" ("s'envole vers les cieux avec l'Esprit de la Lyre et les esprits célèstes" [162]).[29]

Valéry, in any case, is no better than de Lisle at silencing these voices from the past. But to rewrite the past is to relive it, and Valéry's "Hélène" is everywhere haunted by the voices it attempts to rewrite. Valéry, in Nash's words, would *lock the poem on itself,* but such an act is necessary only if one is terrified of what lies outside. It is also futile, for the outsider is always already inside, the poem haunted by its own self-difference. Valéry's own reflections on the *Album* in *Lettres à quelques-uns* return to this fear of the other within: "I sense that the Parnassian who at first was me is dissolving and evaporating" ("Je sens que le parnassien qui a d'abord été moi se dissout et s'évapore" [cited in Nash 1983:141]).

Perhaps "Hélène" is the story of this persistent haunting. All Troy may be contained within Helen, as Nash suggests, but the poem describes that containment not as a transcendence out of history, but as some form of unresolved traumatic neurosis. The poem's verbal tenses, shifting from the present indicative to the imperfect and back to the present, delineate not so much a sanctuary free from history as something like a temporal border crossing, a place fraught with tension between the comings and goings of past and present. "Azure! It is me. . . . I come from the caves of death" ("Azur! c'est moi. . . . Je viens des grottes de la mort"): these are, indeed, in the first line of the poem, answers to the questions we would expect at a checkpoint: name and place of birth. But that line, in fact, refuses, or is unable, to answer those questions: Helen is an amnesiac obstinately haunted by memories.

J. R. Lawler reminds us, in his reading of another poem from the *Album de vers anciens,* "Orphée," that the "definitive" versions of Valéry's early poems are all rewritings of originals long ago abandoned, that they are, indeed, haunted, not just by the voices of others, but by their former selves (1956:54).[30] The changes made to "Hélène" are minor, but the point is that there is more than one "Hélène" and more than one "Orphée." That there is something we continue to call a "definitive text" suggests how reluctant we are to read poetry as a historical artifact.[31] Lawler's strategy is typical: the later version of the poem is, of course, more original, more liberated from and less influenced by the past. In the 1942 "Orphée," Lawler argues, the "dog-eared Symbolist vocabulary (*azur incandescent, porphyres*)" of the 1926 version has "almost wholly disappeared" (1956:57). This despite the fact that the later text contains phrases such as "pure circuses" ("cirques purs") and "hallucinates toward the azure" ("vers l'azur délire"). Azur will not come out, not so easily: the past is a difficult thing to purge.

Lethean Poetics

What "Hélène," and by extension all of Valéry's poetry, aspires to is the condition of truth as a purity close to oblivion. The threat of anteriority contained in and by "Hélène" is central to other poems in the *Album,* which offer variations, in different mythic registers, on the theme of poetic origination as an immaculate conception. "Hélène," "Orphée," "Naissance de Vénus," and "La Fileuse" are all descriptions of poetry as a willed self-origination, an act whose autonomy is authenticated by a discourse of purity: Helen's "pure fingers" ("doigts purs"), whose touch leaves no stain; the "pure circuses" ("cirques purs") from which Orpheus's poetic fire descends; the "pure gems" ("pure pierrerie") of the sea upon the arms of Venus. This *Lethean* poetics is announced in the epigraph to "Hélène" that appeared in the first edition of the poem in 1891: "To drink of the lilies the fragile water where pure oblivion sleeps" ("Boire des lis l'eau frêle où dort le pur oubli" [*Oeuvres,* 1957, 1:1539]). Here the poet drinks from a *source* (a fountain, an origin) that is both Lethe and Castalia. Valéry returns to the Lethean image in his *Louanges de l'eau,* cited by Derrida in his own interrogation of the rhetoric of origination in Valéry:

> On sait bien que la soif véritable n'est apaisée que par l'eau pure. Il y a je ne sais quoi d'authentique dans l'accord du désir vrai de l'organisme et du liquide originel. Etre altéré, c'est devenir autre: se corrompre. Il faut donc se désaltérer, redevenir, avoir recours à ce qu'exige tout ce qui vit . . . Nous disons que nous avons SOIF DE VERITE. (*Oeuvres* 1, 204, in Derrida 1972b:329–30)

> [It is well known that real thirst is only quenched by pure water. There is I don't know what kind of authenticity in the agreement between the true desire of the organism and the original liquid. To be thirsty is to become another: to be corrupted (to corrupt oneself). One must therefore quench one's thirst, become again, turn to that which everything living requires. . . . We say that we are THIRSTY FOR THE TRUTH.]

To drink from a spring, that is, from an origin that lies outside the self, is, paradoxically, to become pure and whole once again, to return to oneself once more. We drink in order to forget we are thirsty, our bodies incomplete and insufficient.

The body, in Valéry, is indeed the very proof of the impossibility of self-sufficiency. "Hélène" is a poem, we have already seen, about the body and its sense-perceptions. Those senses ("hearing, seeing, touching"), which Nash identifies as guarantors of Helen's autonomy (1983:148), are rejected in Valéry's writings as modes of the self's coming to know itself as origin. For if the origin is the self, the "pure me, source of all presence" ("moi pure, source de toute présence" [Derrida 1972b:335]), then that self is, at the same time, inevitably constructed, contingent, divided. What of hearing? Valéry wonders if the voice is an origin. He imagines the poet waiting for the word as the paradigm of pure origination. But to "hear" the word is to speak it to oneself. Derrida cites Valéry in the *Cahiers* on the "interior word/the word spoken to oneself" ("parole intérieure"): "Who is speaking, who is listening? It's not exactly the same. . . . The existence of this word from the self, spoken to oneself, is the sign of a cut/break" ("Qui parle, qui écoute? Ce n'est pas tout à fait le même. . . . L'existence de cette parole de soi à soi est signe d'une coupure" [cited in Derrida 1972b:344]).[32] What, instead, of vision? For the self-as-origin to see itself as such, it must divide, in the manner of a Narcissus. Narcissus is, of course, Valéry's most explicit figure for the paradox of *la source*. The spring into which Narcissus gazes is not only a mirror; it is that for which he thirsts; and that in which, quenching his thirst, he will drown.[33] (Conversely, the poet must always fear that *la source* upon which he relies will one day dry up.)[34]

Much is at stake, then, in locating *la source*. Johnson distinguishes intertextual readings from source studies: "the latter," she argues, "speak in terms of a transfer of property ('borrowing') while the former tend to speak in terms of misreading . . . infiltration . . . violations of property" (1987:116). Perhaps the question we ought to ask about "Hélène" is not, in the manner of a source study, what is it trying to remember, but rather, in intertextual fashion, what is it trying to forget? More precisely: what is it trying to forget it remembers?

Mallarmé's "L'azur" and Valéry's "Hélène"

Perhaps Valéry's "Hélène" is an attempt to forget (among many things) Mallarmé's "L'azur." That Valéry needed to forget Mallarmé is reflected in an image of decapitation in *Leonardo, Poe, Mallarmé:* "I worshipped that extraordinary man," Valéry writes, "at the very time when I saw in him the one-invaluable-head to cut off in order to decapitate all Rome" (cited in Kaufmann 1989:878).[35] Valéry admires Mallarmé's work, according to Nash, because, although powerfully informed by Baudelaire, it seems untainted by influence. Influence is most powerful for Valéry, Nash argues, where it is most invisible. And yet Mallarmé is hardly the invisible man in Valéry's poetry; on the contrary, the trace of Mallarmé would seem to be everywhere. Nash writes that Valéry's "recognition of . . . Mallarmé's impact on his own work, combined with his craving for autonomy, produce a . . . theory of influence which ends up rescuing only himself and Mallarmé from . . . history" (1983:50). But how does Valéry rescue himself from Mallarmé? Not, I would suggest, by *cannibalizing* him covertly but, rather, by *ventriloquizing* him in broad daylight.

Remember the image of the poem locked on itself. But where, we might ask, is the lock? It must lie both inside and outside the poem; it is that which both seals the poem shut and allows it to open. Valéry has provided "Hélène," I would suggest, with an almost comically literal lock, placed precisely where we would expect it: undisguised, at the poem's periphery, in the first word of the first line: "Azur!" That is, of course, the last word—or, rather, the last four words as well as the title—of Mallarmé's poem ("I am haunted [Je suis hanté]. L'Azur! L'Azur! L'Azur! L'Azur!"). Perhaps Valéry has neutralized "L'azur" by locking it to "Hélène." (The exclamation point makes the echo clearer; the lack of article strengthens the suture tying Valéry's poem to Mallarmé's.) Here decapitation is the necessary prelude to recapitulation; Mallarmé has been *dismembered* in order to be *remembered*—as Valéry.

That *azur* is one of the most frequently employed words of nineteenth-century French poetry does not make this point less interesting—quite the contrary. Mallarmé's poem, Johnson has pointed out, "dramatizes the predicament of the poet who seeks forgetfulness as a cure for impotence (thus implying that what the impotent poet is suffering from is too much memory)" (1987:119). *L'azur,* in this reading, would be the inescapable—and unforgettable—burden of poetic history that always already inhabits the (original) work of the poet.[36] *L'azur* is that which prevents the poet from ever saying anything completely new. And, indeed, Valéry's dilemma is the (already clichéd) subject of Mallarmé's "L'azur"; there, already, we find the same ghosts ("Je suis hanté") and the same Lethean longings: "And you, come out of the Lethean ponds and gather / On your way, mud and pale reeds, / Dear Ennui" ("Et toi, sors des étangs léthéens et ramasse / En t'en venant la vase et les pâles roseaux, / Cher Ennui").

Valéry here would seem to find himself in a double bind; by remembering Mallarmé's poem, he acknowledges its anteriority and concedes the corruption of the origin; by forgetting it, he demonstrates precisely the same thing. Hence the strategy adopted in "Hélène": neither to refer to "L'azur" as something discrete and external nor to refuse to refer to it, by assimilating, transforming, and camouflaging it,[37] but to suture it, undigested, as it were, to itself, shamelessly, the suture there for all to see. (The effect is equivalent to putting the source "under erasure" ["sous rature"]. That Derridean practice functions to problematize a term that the critic no longer wants to refer to, but must, by crossing it out and leaving both the term and its cancellation visible.) Valéry does not write in "Hélène," as Mallarmé did in "L'azur," about a poet condemned to repeat the past; he writes, instead, as repetition itself. Hélène does not speak about *l'azur;* Hélène *is l'azur* ("Azur! c'est moi. . ."). (This suggests another explanation for the omission of the article: it turns what was an abstraction into a name.) How does this poem forget the past? Not by erasing it, nor by pointing to it, as to a distant landmark, but by trying to *be* it.

All of which raises questions about the real influence of the many sources teased out so skillfully by Nash, Hoffmann, Lawler, and other critics. Is Mallarmé's "L'azur" really a source for Valéry's "Hélène"? Typically, the critic reads *azur* as Mallarmé's signature. Pierre-Olivier Walzer, for example: "As for the influence of Mallarmé, it is much more precise here [in "Narcisse parle"] than in his early poetry. . . . It can be divined, besides, throughout the work, by the frequent use of words cherished by the Master: *azure, helmet, mirror*" ("Quant à l'influence de Mallarmé, elle se fait ici bien plus précise que dans les vers de jeunesse. . . . Elle se devine, en outre, dans tout le recueil, par l'emploi nombreux de mots trop chers au Maître: *azur, casque, miroir*" [1953:107]). But are these words Mallarmé's? Mallarmé's poem is itself, we have suggested, about the impossibility of assigning specific origins; for if influence could be named, determined, externalized, referred to, it could, by the same token, be targeted, warded off, destroyed.[38] Is "L'azur" a source for "Hélène"? The very question depends upon a model of poetic influence that Valéry's poem (and, before it, Mallarmé's) rejects: influence, that is, in its "proper" sense—as an irruption, an insinuation, a seamless flowing from one source to another (viewed more ominously, however, influence, we have seen, becomes *influenza,* an infection, a contagion, a communicable disease).

The presence of the word *azur* in Valéry's text can hardly be a guarantee of influence. Its presence is both too specific and too general a fact to tell us anything about influence. That indeterminacy, I have suggested, is the very specificity of *azur*. Nineteenth-century French poetry's emblem par excellence of artistic purity, of that which escapes anteriority, it is, by the same token, that poetry's favorite self-referential cliché, the very signal that one is writing poetry.[39] There is no sense, then, in which one can use *azur* properly, for it is always an *improper* noun. Thus to employ it is to introduce anteriority and impurity into one's text at the very moment one is claiming originality and purity.

Memoir or Treatise? Valéry's Faust

Sometimes all that is required to make that claim is a simple possessive pronoun. I want to conclude this chapter by returning to the figure of Faust and glancing briefly at one last work by Valéry: *Mon Faust* (1940). Comprising two fragmentary dramas, "Lust, la demoiselle de cristal, comédie," and "Le Solitaire, ou les malédictions d'univers, féerie dramatique," *Mon Faust* is a series of sketches organized around the figures of Faust and Mephistopheles. In the preface, Valéry acknowledges, like Nerval, the inimitability of Goethe's work, and the hubris implicit in the attempt to rewrite or renew it. Valéry's response is a self-justifying poetics of *imitatio* that could serve equally well as a defense for Adam, Eve, Lucifer, or Helen: "But nothing proves more surely the power of a creator than the infidelity or insubordination of his creation. The more alive he has made him, the more free. Even his rebellion against him exalts his author: God knows this all too well" (*"Mais rien ne démontre plus sûrement la puissance d'un créateur que l'infidelité ou l'insoumission de sa créature. Plus il l'a faite vivante, plus il l'a faite libre. Même sa rébellion exalte son auteur: Dieu le sait"* [Valéry 1946:7]). And so we return to the cruel paradox that so vexed Valéry in his own efforts to escape poetic anteriority: the fact that to write great poetry is to lose control of its roots and its ramifications. The poem—to borrow a phrase from Wimsatt and Beardsley's essay on "The Intentional Fallacy"— "belongs to the public" (1981:1016). This is a truth that now serves Valéry well: "The creator of those two, Faust and the Other, created them in such a way that after him they became instruments of the universal spirit: they overflow with what they were in his work" (*"Le créateur de ces deux-ci, Faust et l'Autre, les a engendrés tels qu'ils devinssent après lui des instruments de l'esprit universel: ils débordent de ce qu'ils furent dans son oeuvre"* [1946:7]). Valéry would appear to be speaking here of Faust and Mephistopheles, but I would like to think that behind them looms another implicit couple: Faust and Helen.

Goethe himself, one might suggest, is still another Other, haunting Valéry, or speaking through him.[40] For Valéry continues his defense, resorting now to a convention of poetic invention we have seen before in his work: that of the voice speaking within the self, who, passive, taken unprepared, remains absolved of responsibility. And thus more images of doubling or dividing mark Valéry's story of how he came to write another *Faust:* "Now, on a particular day in 1940, I was surprised to find myself speaking in two voices and let myself write whatever came. And so I sketched, very quickly and, I admit it, without any plan . . . the acts, which you have here, of two very different plays" (*"Or, un certain jour de 1940, je me suis surpris me parlant à deux voix et me suis laissé aller à écrire ce qui venait. J'ai donc ébauché très vivement, et—je l'avoue— sans plan . . . les actes qui voici de deux pièces très différentes"*). Valéry is ostensibly explaining how he came to write two *Fausts,* not one. But Goethe also wrote two *Fausts,* and the two voices Valéry refers to may also be his own and Goethe's.[41] The relationship between Valéry's work and Goethe's *Faust* may be characterized, essentially, as supplementary, for there is some question as to whether Valéry conceives of his Faust as replacing Goethe's or merely extending it. He refers to his conception of the piece, after all, as a *"Faust* Part III" (1946:8).

Kurt Weinberg calls Valéry's Faust a Monsieur Teste with a body, a proto-Cartesian intellect now susceptible to the "seductions of the senses" (1976:5). Valéry's Teste was a solitary figure; his Faust shares the stage with other human beings: "incarnations," Weinberg suggests, of carnal temptations. Which makes this *Faust* something like an allegory, much as Goethe's was: Faust standing for reason or intellect, Mephistopheles for the voice of passion or instinct. Valéry's Faust is engaged in the same search as all of Valéry's heroes: the search for intellectual autonomy. That autonomy is constantly threatened, here, by Lust and by Mephistopheles and his demonic proxies, Astaroth, Bélial, and Goungoune. The conflict is contained in the very name of the first part of Valéry's drama, and the name of its protagonist's assistant, "Lust, la demoiselle de cristal." On one hand, there is the ideal of the body become ideal, crystal, transparent, invisible, cognitive; on the other, there is the body as substance, desire, memory. The very word *lust,* as a foreign, indeed German, importation, introduces a kind of lexical opacity into the title, just as the body introduces opacity into the intellect.[42] The bulk of Valéry's *Faust* is a series of encounters between these antithetical forces. In Act 1, Scene 1, for example, Lust is laughing, an act whose physicality apparently suggests the lofty flights of intellect brought down to earth. Faust is dictating an unnamed work to Lust: "Your Memoirs," she asks ("Les Mémoires"), "or your Treatise?" ("ou le Traité?")—genres themselves representative of the respective claims of the body or the intellect, the past or the present. And Faust responds to Lust: "I explained to you yesterday, again, that I was turning these into the same, single work" ("Je vous ai expliqué, hier encore, que j'en faisais un seul et même ouvrage" [1946:17]).

There is something else in Faust's dictation to Lust that might interest us. Perhaps this scenario of transcription is also Valéry's way of figuring the ideal of the autonomous, oral, immediate source. Faust's dictation to Lust is as close as the poet can get to the self-writing text, to the image of the poet *qui s'entendre* (who hears/understands himself). But in Valéry's *Faust* this scenario of transmission is illusory or is supplemented by subterfuge. Reading back her dictation to Faust (the poet hearing himself), Lust comes to the phrase: "Eros energoumenos" (1946:21). But the phrase is not Faust's— "That isn't mine" ("Ceci n'est pas de moi"); it has been inserted, we later discover, by Mephistopheles into Faust's notes. And yet Faust does not hesitate to appropriate the words precisely as his own: "This must be mine. . . . I like it. I'm taking it!" ("Ceci doit être de moi. . . . il me plaît; je le prends!" [21]). And so influence gives way to graft. But it already has, Weinberg notes, in Goethe's *Faust.* In a letter to F. von Müller dated December 17, 1824, Goethe defends himself for having imitated Job 1:6–12 in the "Prologue in Heaven": "Why should he [the poet] shy away from picking flowers where he finds them? Only through the assimilation of alien treasures do great things come into being" ("Warum soll er [der Dichter] sich scheuen, Blumen zu nehmen, wo er sie findet? Nur durch Aneignung fremder Schätze entsteht ein Grosses" [trans. Weinberg 1976:15]). In Goethe as much as in Valéry, it would appear, "mental activity is brutally reduced to the assimilation of mental theft" (Weinberg 1976:16).

Let us return to the Mephistophelean phrase "Eros energoumenos," which Faust a moment later translates as "Eros as source of extreme energy" ("Eros en tant que source d'extrême énergie"). Eros is indeed the Mephistophelean force par excellence, representing the claims of the body—its memories and desires—upon the detachment of the mind. A moment later Faust feels compelled to caress Lust's body—but in particular her ear, organ of hearing (Valéry 1946:28–29). At the same time he protests that his interests have always remained absolutely detached from the body: "I have dictated nothing to you so far that wasn't perfectly pure" ("je ne vous ai encore rien dicté qui ne soit parfaitement pur" [29]), and he calls for Lust to be absolutely transparent, "a crystal woman" ("une demoiselle de cristal" [30])—in other words, all ear, all hearing. Eros will return with renewed energy in Act 2, Scene 5, where a new Adam and Eve, Faust and Lust, share a peach from Mephistopheles' garden (112). The dénouement to this story of temptation and desire is to be found in a series of sketches Valéry left for an Act 4, where Faust articulates the dream of a perfect communion with Lust, a kind of mental copulation:

Nous serions comme des Dieux, des harmoniques, intelligents, dans une correspondance immédiate de nos vies sensitives, sans parole,—et que nos esprits feraient l'amour l'un avec l'autre comme des corps peuvent le faire. Cet accord harmonique serait plus qu'un accord de pensée; n'est-ce pas là du reste l'accomplissment de la promesse, en quoi consiste la poésie qui n'est après tout que tentative de communion? (1960:1414)

[We would be like Gods, harmonic, intelligent, in the immediate correspondence of our sensory lives, without a word,—and so that our spirits would make love, one with the other, just as bodies can. This harmonic accord would be more than an accord of thought; is it not also the accomplishment of the promise, of which poetry consists, poetry which is nothing, after all, but the attempt at communion?]

This is Valéry's rewriting of Faust's illusory conjoining with Helen in *Faust* II, abstracted now from the specifics of any literary history, and spoken of only in the conditional. And yet Goethe's Helen will not be banished from the text, even in absentia. Moreover, between Valéry's Helen and Goethe's stand other Helens: Sand's chaste and spiritualized Helen, for example, a Helen who is "the purest crystal" ("le plus pur cristal" [Sand 1869:76]).

In the second part of Valéry's *Mon Faust,* "Le Solitaire," the Cartesian allegory of the search for the *cogito* is played out in even more abstracted form: as a drama that takes place entirely in Faust's own mind. Weinberg 1976 calls this allegorical form a *charade*—a term that Valéry himself uses in his notebooks as the essential theatrical form: "Every play is a *charade*" ("Toute pièce de théâtre est une charade" [1957–61, 6:230; my italics). We will see, in the following chapter, that this is the theatrical and narrative mode where Helen seems most at home: in games of mimicry.

To be *solitaire,* completely self-invented and detached, is, we have seen, Valéry's "temptation" throughout his poetic career. In a larger sense, it is the temptation that drives Western culture forward as it looks back, over its shoulder as it were, at the past. It is an impossible and hubristic desire: Solitaire is but another incarnation of Mephistopheles. Citing Mark 5:9, Solitaire declares:

"I am LEGION" ("Je suis LEGION" [1957–61, 6:217]). "Because many devils were entered into him," Luke 8:30 continues (cited in Weinberg 1976:71). Those devils take on many forms, as we would expect them to. In the finale to "Solitaire," called "Intermède: Les fées," they assume the shape of a troupe of seductive fairies. Seduction, here, appears to be a matter, above all, of memory. This has always been Valéry's weakness: the lure of return, or resurrection. Here is the Second Fairy offering Faust the gift of the past:

> Je sais rendre au plomb vil la lueur de l'or pur,
> Je reconnais l'enfant dans le visage dur,
> Et la limpidité des premières années
> Parmi la profondeur des amères pensées.
> Je défais, fil à fil, la trame des vieux jours;
> De tes pas inquiets je remonte le cours . . .
> Je songe avec tendresse à ton adolescence.
> Tes yeux, qu'ont assombris tant d'âpres actions,
> Tes traits qu'ont tourmentés toutes les passions
> Ne m'abolissent point la grâce du jeune être.
> J'y distingue celui que tu pourrais renaître,
> Faust, si tu veux me croire et te fier à moi.
> Veux-tu redevenir et reparaître en roi?
>
> (245–46)

> [I know how to restore the glitter of pure gold to vile lead / I can recognize the child in the hardened face, / And the limpidness of the first years / Within the depth of bitter thoughts. / I undo, thread by thread, the web of the old days; / I reclimb the path of your anxious steps. . . / I dream of your adolescence with tenderness. / Your eyes, darkened by so many harsh acts, / Your features, tormented by all of the passions / Do not abolish, for me, the charm of the young being. / I can detect there the one you could be reborn as, / Faust, if you want to believe me and can trust me. / Do you want to become again and reappear as a king?"]

The Second Fairy's promises to turn back the clock are like a litany of the great figures of poetic *imitatio,* now inverted: weaving becomes unweaving; recognizing the father in the son becomes recognizing the son in the father; following in the footsteps of others becomes retracing one's steps. They are promises, in the end, that Faust refuses to believe: for to give in to memory is to submit to just another illusion, to cede one's self-sufficiency.

I conclude by returning to the notion of the double manuscript that Faust is dictating to Lust in the first play of *Mon Faust.* For in "Solitaire," too, Faust is everywhere trying to compose a Treatise, only to find himself writing his Memoirs. Faust, Goethe's great figure of intellectual self-sufficiency, and Valéry's too, is everywhere assailed by the temptations of the past. His is the most detached of minds, and the most distracted as well. In another passage in "Solitaire," those distractions are embodied as a troupe, not of fairies now, but of "swine," Solitaire's "pourceaux" (1946:387), descendants of Circe's enchanted herd. They are figures, simply, for thought. Solitaire watches over them, but they are free to consort with whomever they please, even his favorite sow. Regarding the latter Faust asks: "You allow him to love?" ("Vous lui laissez l'amour?"). Solitaire answers as follows:

Sans doute. Puisque c'est un esprit. . . . La prostitution est donc son affaire, étant le principe même de l'esprit. A qui, à quoi ne se livre-t-il pas, l'esprit? La moindre mouche le débauche. Il s'accouple à tout ce qui vient, et l'abondance de ses produits ne témoigne que de son infâme facilité. . . . Et le langage donc, son principal agent! Qu'est-ce donc que ce langage qui introduit en nous n'importe qui, et qui nous introduit en qui que ce soit? Un proxénète. (Valéry 1946:222–23)

[Of course. Since it is a spirit. . . . Prostitution is thus her business, being the very principle of spirit. To whom, to what, does the spirit not give itself? The tiniest fly corrupts it. It couples with everything that comes, and its rich productivity only demonstrates its unspeakable facility. . . . And what about language, then, its principle agent? What is this language, then, which allows anyone to enter into us, and us to enter anyone? A pimp."]

Autonomy, in Solitaire's response, is impossible, because thought is always corrupt, always infected by something else, something borrowed from someone else. To think is to be violated by language itself. And so Valéry rewrites Descartes: I think, therefore I prostitute myself (and therefore I am). In the next chapter we turn to the implications of this proposition. We have seen Helen the foreigner, agent of miscegenation: now we turn to Helen the prostitute.

12

Prostitution

Introduction: Textual Promiscuity

Chénier, de Lisle, and Valéry share the same fear of impurity, and the same fascination with corruption. Helen is an emblem of that corruption: poetry's sacred prostitute. Why is nineteenth-century France fascinated by the figure of the prostitute? Because the prostitute is a woman with a past and stands for any space that others have traversed. At *Iliad* 3.180 Helen, now Paris's wife, remembers that she used to be Menelaus's and calls herself a whore.[1] (See chapter 1, "Mimesis," for a detailed reading of this scene.) But before Menelaus there is Theseus, and after Paris there is Deiphobus, then Menelaus again, and perhaps later even Achilles.[2] With Helen, sexual promiscuity goes hand-in-hand with textual promiscuity.

This is the equation explored in this chapter by way of several nineteenth- and early twentieth-century novels and dramatic works. A number of nineteenth-century novels such as France's *Thaïs* and Flaubert's *La tentation de Saint Antoine* figure Helen as *femme fatale:* fatal because unforgettable. The protagonist of *La tentation de Saint Antoine* is condemned to remember her. Flaubert's novel is the story of a man in love with literature. For Saint Antoine to purge himself of desire, he must forget what he has read. But he *is* what he has read: he is a graft of books. History in *La tentation* is thus an endless cycle of graft: textual graft (repetition, imitation, citation) and sexual graft (copulation, abduction, adultery).

From Helen's grand entrance on the Trojan battlements on, I have suggested that representations of her tend toward the theatrical—in the sense that her

actions are always performances, and in the sense that they are always spec-
tacles, made to be witnessed and watched. Thus the relationship between Helen
as a novelistic character and Helen as a dramatic persona is a close one. In
nineteenth- and twentieth-century French theatrical works like Meilhac and
Halévy's *La Belle Hélène* and Claudel's *Protée,* Helen, along with the classical
past, is debunked as a fraud. This equation of classical beauty with graft under-
lies Giraudoux's *La guerre de Troie n'aura pas lieu,* perhaps the most extended
modern theatrical meditation on beauty as a Hellenic topos. In that play Giraudoux is asking, in effect: what does it mean to fight for Helen? Giraudoux's
Helen becomes a figure for the dangerous promiscuity of all figuration, for she
can be prostituted to any ideal.

Helen in the Novel: When Reading Around
Is Like Sleeping Around

Helen, I have suggested, has always been at home on the stage. The last chapter
began with an opera house in Frankfurt, where Nerval was entranced by the
spectacle of *Faust,* and with the imperial court in *Faust* II, entranced by the
spectacle of Helen. But wherever Helen is, we have seen, there is an audience,
a performance, a representation, a costume, an illusion. The *teichoskopia* was
itself a theatrical entrance. A number of nineteenth-century novels that take up
the figure of Helen explicitly or implicitly are essentially extended *teichoskopias.* All are stories about actresses or courtesans: Emile Zola's *Nana,* Anatole
France's *Thaïs,* and Gustave Flaubert's *La tentation de Saint Antoine.*

Helen of Troy is never explicitly mentioned in *Nana* (1885), but it would be
difficult to read the first chapter of this novel without thinking of her. A number
of traces are left in place. We are in a *théâtre de boulevard,* awaiting the début of
a new vedette named Nana in a musical called *La Blonde Vénus* (in Offenbach's
La Belle Hélène, Helen enters with the chorus singing "Hear us, fair Venus /
We need love, even if no love is left in the world!" ["Ecoute-nous, Vénus la
blonde, / Il nous faut de l'amour, n'en fût-il plus au monde!" (Halévy and Meilhac n.d.:6)]). The first character we are introduced to, eagerly awaiting the evening's entertainment, is Hector de la Faloise (the first instance of direct speech
in the novel is "What was I telling you, Hector?" ["Que te disais-je, Hector?"
Zola 1885:2]). While the first act of the play takes place "on Olympus" ("dans
l'Olympe"), the second takes us to a "dance hall, the Boule-Noir, in the middle
of Mardi-Gras" ("bastringue de barrière, à la Boule-Noire, en plein mardi-gras"
[23]), something very much like what we will see in *La Belle Hélène.* There, as
here, we are witness to a "carnival of the gods, Olympus dragged in the mud,
an entire religion, an entire poetry held up to ridicule" ("carnaval des dieux,
l'Olympe traîné dans la boue, toute une religion, toute une poésie bafouées"

[24–25]). Nana appears, "her hands on her hips, putting Venus in the gutter, at the edge of the sidewalk" ("le poing à la taille, asseyant Vénus dans le ruisseau, au bord du trottoir" [25]).

There is a another side to this kind of parody, however. In the third act of *La Blonde Vénus,* Nana/Venus performs her long-awaited theophany: "She was naked, with a tranquil audacity, sure of the absolute power of her flesh.... It was Venus, born from the waves.... No one was laughing now.... A wind seemed to have passed, very gentle, carrying a mysterious menace with it" ("Elle était nue avec une tranquille audace, certaine de la toute-puissance de sa chair.... C'était Vénus naissant des flots.... Personne ne riait plus.... Un vent semblait avoir passé, très doux, chargée d'une sourde menace" [31–34]). This passage is, in effect, Zola's own *teichoskopia.* All the expected motifs are here: the actress upon a stage, the gaze of a captive audience, the mixture of admiration and terror in that gaze, the comparison with a goddess (and specifically Venus, Helen's divine doppelganger).

Helen's apotheosis, in *Nana,* is short-lived. In the second chapter Nana discusses payment with two of her clients from the comfort of her bed. It is scenes like these that lead Charles Bernheimer to view Zola's Nana as the crowning example of the figure of the prostitute who played such an important role in French literature in the nineteenth century (1989a). The list of novels that chronicle the rise and inevitable fall of the prostitute-heroine is a long one, including Sue's *Les mystères de Paris* (1842–43), *La dame aux camélias* by Dumas fils (1848), Balzac's *Splendeurs et misères des courtisanes* (1845–47). Why was the prostitute such a popular literary theme at this moment? The discourse of science and above all medicine, increasingly central and increasingly imbricated in political and social policy, may be a factor. Thus for Bernheimer, the prostitute embodied for the readers of that period the temptations and dangers of female sexuality, dangers realized both literally and figuratively in the transmission of venereal disease: "The syphilitic prostitute," Bernheimer asserts, "is the prototype of the numerous versions of the femme fatale that proliferate in the art of the fin de siècle: the vampire, the Sphinx, Salome, Judith" (1989b:784). He could easily have added Helen to the list. There is a danger, I think, in taking this kind of historical explanation too far, as when Bernheimer continues, "The biological panic reflected in these images dissipates after the discovery in 1909 of an arsenic-based treatment for syphilis and the great cataclysm of the First World War." But surely there is a great deal more here than biological panic. It was not the threat of syphilis, after all, that made Helen's beauty terrifying. That beauty, we will see, remains just as terrifying in Giraudoux's *La guerre de Troie n'aura pas lieu,* written in 1935.

Bernheimer has another, more convincing historical explanation of the phobic representation of the prostitute in the nineteenth-century French novel: a new cultural anxiety over impurity. In fact, this second hypothesis is simply a more general variation on the first. Without then trying to correlate too closely to specific historical developments the emergence of the prostitute as a figure for impurity, it would appear that France, from the period of the July Monarchy (1830–48) to the beginning of the First World War, was at the nexus of a number of significant economic and political trends: a rise in urban population, and with it urban poverty, crime, and disease; the development of various institutionalized discourses and technologies for categorizing and quantifying urban life, what Robert Bezucha calls a "fledgling social science" (1989:689); and the evolution of a realist mode of literature that modeled itself upon or borrowed from the discourse of science. In works such as H.-A. Frégier's *Des classes dangereuses de la population dans les grandes villes* (On dangerous classes of the population in large cities) (1840), and Alexandre Parent-Duchâtelet's *De la prostitution dans la ville de Paris* (1836), prostitution is described, categorized, and represented statistically.[3] The latter work, which Bernheimer considers "the first modern study of prostitution" (1989b:780), treats the question of prostitution, for example, simply as an extension of the subject of sewers: "both channels for the disposal of waste were necessary for the well-being of the city and should be properly supervised and regularly sanitized" (780). Meanwhile, in *Le roman expérimental* (published in 1880, the same year as *Nana*), Zola lays the theoretical groundwork for what is essentially a biological novel: a novel in which the social and biological discourses would collaborate, both ruled by the observational principles of experimental science, both acknowledging the unbending principle of causality.[4]

Bernheimer cites Zola's infamous description of *Nana* as a "poem of the cunt." That "poem," according to Zola, has a "moral": "the moral will lie in the cunt turning everything sour" (Bernheimer 1989b:782). The paradigm here, in keeping with the goals of the experimental or biological novel, is medical: a moral society is a healthy one; an immoral society, one that is infected or diseased. But why is disease, within this model, so virulently gendered? Why the identification between promiscuity and impurity in nineteenth-century France? How does the prostitute become, like Typhoid Mary, public enemy number one? What is feared in the prostitute, I suggest, are the dangers, and attractions, of a space where one is not alone. Zola's "cunt" is this "intersexual" space, a site that one must share with others, with those who were there before. Medically, this fear is translated into venereal disease; economically, into speculation and graft; ethically, into impurity; poetically, into anteriority and intertextuality. The prostitute, as the expression has it, is a "woman with a past." That makes her very dangerous.

Thaïs is the story of a monk who cannot forget the past. Alone in the desolation of the Syrian desert, the ascetic Paphnuce is haunted by a vision of Egypt's most celebrated actress and courtesan. He had seen her once upon the stage in his youth: "she was performing one of these shameful stories that the pagans told of Venus, or Leda, or Pasiphae" ("elle simulait quelqu'une de ces actions honteuses que les fables des païens prêtent à Vénus, à Léda ou à Pasiphaé" [France 1984:725]). Frequent references to Leda help to reinforce associations with Helen.[5] Paphnuce believes that the vision of Thaïs is a sign to undertake a great and holy act: to convert her to a life of Christian goodness. But beauty will win out over virtue; by the end of the novel, Thaïs's beauty will have seduced and destroyed the monk.

In the next chapter Paphnuce leaves his monastery and travels to Alexandria in search of Thäis. He finds her, as we might expect, in a theater. Thaïs is upon the stage, playing the role of the virgin Polyxena: "Motionless, like a beautiful statue . . . she made everyone shudder with her tragic beauty" ("Immobile, semblable à une belle statue . . . elle donnait à tous le frisson tragique de la beauté" [754]). Like Zola, France is fond of abrupt scene changes. As in *Nana,* the next chapter shifts from the public space of the theater to the private domain of the boudoir.[6] Thaïs invites Paphnuce to a gathering of Alexandrian intellectuals, and here at last the association with Helen is made explicit. When the conversation turns to Neoplatonic redemption and mystic theories of transmigration, Zénothémis, a gnostic, speaks of the Thought of God, sometimes called Eunoia, the primordial, and feminine, force of cosmic creation—a force that, long ago, embodied itself upon the earth through a sacrificial act of love. Eunoia "descended to the earth and became incarnate in the breast of a daughter of Tyndarus. She was born frail and small, and she was given the name Helen" ("descendit sur la terre et s'incarna dans le sein d'une Tyndaride. Elle naquit petite et débile et reçut le nom d'Hélène" [France 1984:801]). The sacrifice of which Zénothémis speaks is the rape of Helen, an act of violence that redeems all the rapes of the world. After Helen's death, he explains, Eunoia passed into the bodies of other women: "Thus, passing from body to body, and traveling amongst us through evil times, she takes upon herself the sins of the world" ("Ainsi, passant des corps en corps, et traversant parmi nous les âges mauvais, elle prend sur elle les péchés du monde" [802]). A mystic named Hermodore adds that one of her avatars was the companion of the infamous Simon Magus. And the scene concludes when a philosopher, Callicrate, asks: who is Helen today? Zénothémis answers: "As charming as in the days of Priam and of Asia when it flourished, today Eunoia is named Thäis" ("Charmante comme aux jours de Priam et de l'Asie en fleurs, Eunoia se nomme aujourd'hui Thaïs" [803]).

Helen is again paired with Simon Magus in her brief but significant role in Flaubert's *La tentation de Sainte Antoine,* a novel cast in the form of a dramatic script. Flaubert's model would seem to be the Walpurgis scenes from *Faust.* Nerval's translation of *Faust,* we have seen, was extremely influential in France. Edouard Maynial, in the introduction to his edition of *La tentation,* calls Saint Antoine a "naïve Faust seduced by every possible form of universal illusion" ("Faust ingénu que séduisent toutes les formes possibles de l'illusion universelle" [in Flaubert 1968:ix]). And from beginning to end, in fact, Saint Antoine's faith is tested by a long parade of seductive phantoms. The enemy with whom Saint Antoine must do battle here is not very different from the specter of mimesis against which Plato long ago cautioned us:

HILARION: Qui donc te rend triste?
ANTOINE: . . . Je pense à toutes les âmes perdues par ces faux Dieux!
HILARION: Ne trouves-tu pas qu'ils ont . . . quelquefois . . . comme des ressemblances avec le vrai?

(199)

[HILARION: What is making you sad?
ANTOINE: . . . I'm thinking of all the souls ruined by these false gods!
HILARION: Don't you think that . . . sometimes . . . they resemble the true one?]

But exactly who or what are these phantoms against which Antoine must defend himself? They are, in fact, the ghosts of literature past and present, figures from the pages Antoine himself has read.[7] And Antoine's defense against this army of demonic books is another book: the good book, the Bible.

Among the intertextual phantoms that assail Antoine during his vigil are the figures of Helen and Simon Magus. Helen is a somnolent figure, "covered in a purple robe in shreds" ("couverte d'une robe de pourpre en lambeaux"). She is a figure marked, like the page of a book, with the signs of history: "On her face she has the marks of bites, along her arms the traces of blows; her scattered locks cling to the rips in her rags" ("Elle a sur le visage des marques de morsures, le long des bras des traces de coups; ses cheveux épars s'accrochent dans les déchirures de ses haillons" [Flaubert 1968:122]). When this Helen speaks, her first words are turned toward a distant time and place: "I have a memory," she says, "of a place far away, the color of emerald" ("J'ai souvenir d'une région lointaine, couleur d'émeraude" [123]). Flaubert's Helen even seems to resurrect, dimly, the figures of the Trojan war, and the desire of the crowd: "They oiled me with unguents, and they sold me to the people to amuse them" ("Ils m'ont graissée avec les onguents, et ils m'ont vendue au peuple pour que je l'amuse" [125]). Helen does not say much, however; it is Simon Magus who speaks of and for her:

La voici, Antoine, celle qu'on nomme Sigeh, Ennoia, Barbelo, Prounikos! Les Esprits gouverneurs du monde furent jaloux d'elle, et ils l'attachèrent dans un corps de femme. Elle a été l'Hélène des Troyens, dont le poète Stesichore a maudit la mémoire. Elle a été Lucrèce, la patricienne violée par les rois. Elle a été Dalila, qui coupait les cheveux de Samson. Elle a été cette fille d'Israël qui s'abandonnait aux boucs. Elle a aimé l'adultère, l'idolâtrie, le mensonge et la sottise. Elle s'est prostituée à tous les peuples. Elle a chanté dans tous les carrefours. Elle a baisé tous les visages. (127)

[Here she is, Antoine, the one they call Sigeh, Ennoia, Barbelo, Prounikos! The governing Spirits of the world were jealous of her, and they tied her to the body of a woman. She was the Helen of the Trojans, and her memory was cursed by Stesichorus. She was Lucretia, the patrician's wife, violated by a king. She was Dalilah, the one who cut Samson's hair. She was that daughter of Israël, the one who gave herself to the goats. She loved adultery, idolatry, lies and stupidity. She prostituted herself for every people. She sang at every crossroads. She kissed every face.]

Flaubert's Hélène is another version of France's Thaïs. Who is she? All of these: Universal Feminine, Cosmic Mediator, Sacred Prostitute, Intertextual Constant, Historical Link. She is thus never what she seems to be, and is always different from herself. This Helen, Simon's Helen, is a perpetual illusion, an *eidolon* pursued and never possessed. Or, to put this in terms of cultural or literary history, Helen is a Page from the Book of History, torn, pasted, copied, recopied, excised, shredded, cited, stolen. The history of the world for Flaubert in *La tentation* is thus at once the saga of *intertextuality* (which is to say, repetition, plagiarism, citation, imitation) and *intersexuality* (or adultery, abduction, seduction, prostitution).[8]

What does this make Simon Magus? Maynial offers a brief note: "Simon the Magician, Jew who wanted to buy from the apostles the power to perform miracles. He passed himself off as the Messiah, came to Rome, where an statue of him was erected. He had with him a woman named Helen." ("Simon le Magicien, Juif qui voulut acheter des apôtres le pouvoir de faire des miracles. Il se donna pour le Messie, vint à Rome, où on lui éleva une statue. Il avait avec lui une femme nommée Hélène" [Flaubert 1968:127n122]). In short, Simon is one more manifestation of illusion, a priest of the counterfeit. In fact Simon is a false Christ, and even performs a false baptism. And that with which he baptizes is Helen:

Viennent à moi ceux qui sont couverts de vin, ceux qui sont couverts de boue, ceux qui sont couverts de sang; et j'effacerai les souillures avec le Saint-Esprit, appelé Minerve par les Grecs. Elle est Minerve! Elle est le Saint-Esprit! Je suis Jupiter, Apollon, le Christ, le Paraclet, la grande puissance de Dieu, incarnée en la personne de Simon! (127–28)

[Come to me those who are covered with wine, those who are covered with mud, those who are covered with blood; and I will wipe out the stains with the Holy Spirit, called Minerva by the Greeks. She is Minerva! She is the Holy Spirit! I am Jupiter, Apollo, Christ, the Paraclete, the great power of God, incarnate in the person of Simon!]

If we ask, now, who is Flaubert's Helen, we can answer thus: she is Simon Magus's universal solvent, cleansing all impurity, expunging all guilt. If all things are erased and forgiven through Helen, then the Fall is forgotten, and the past is no longer a threat. History as violence, rupture, rape, and exile: all of that, if we believe Simon, is an illusion. The past, Simon tells us, is here and now. Of course, from the perspective of Saint Antoine, that is a lie. Flaubert's Simon is meant to be a counterfeit prophet and Helen a false penance. In the end, Antoine banishes them with a cry for true absolution: "Ah! if only I had holy water!" ("Ah! si j'avais de l'eau bénite!" [Flaubert 1968:130]).

Helen in the Theater: Plato, Parody, and *Poires "Belle Helene"*

Everything is counterfeit in Henri Meilhac and Ludovic Halévy's 1864 *opéra bouffe, La Belle Hélène* (set to music by Jacques Offenbach). In Act 1, Scene 11, the heroes of the Trojan war have gathered to compete in a game of charades. After several feeble efforts by Achilles, the young Paris solves the riddle:

PARIS: . . . *Loch, homme, hotte, ive.*
ACHILLE, *vivement:* Locomotive! . . . j'ai trouvé!
PARIS: Oui, locomotive. . . . Et c'est très fort d'avoir trouvé ça quatre mille ans avant l'invention des chemins de fer.
ACHILLE, *triumphant:* C'est moi qui l'ai dit!
AGAMEMNON, *se levant:* Achille, vous devenez insupportable! . . . Taisez-vous!. . . Le berger a gagné.
HELENE, *à part:* Vainqueur! Il est vainqueur!

(Halévy and Meilhac n.d.:27)

[PARIS: *Loch, homme, hotte, ive.*
ACHILLES, *enthusiastically:* Locomotive! I got it!
PARIS: Yes, Locomotive. . . . And that's pretty impressive, to have gotten it four thousand years before the invention of the railroad.
ACHILLES, *triumphant:* It was me that got it!
AGAMEMNON, *standing up:* Achilles, you're becoming unbearable. Be quiet! The shepherd has won.
HELEN, *aside:* Victorious! He is victorious!]

We return, then, explicitly, to the genre Valéry will call the essential theatrical form: a form perfectly in accord with Helen's performative aspect. Let this scene stand as an emblem of the role played by classical culture in the literature of the nineteenth and twentieth centuries. For the role is almost always that of the *charade,* in both senses: that of a theatrical reenactment and that of a factitious substitution. Antiquity in modern France tends to be, then, both a mock antiquity and an antiquity mocked. Little attempt is made, generally speaking, to disguise the artifice. In fact, artifice itself is often the point.

In a broader sense the charade may suggest what we have suspected all through this book: that all poetic imitation depends on the kind of irreverent anachronism displayed so transparently in *La Belle Hélène.* Perhaps humanism, in the end, is always a matter of dressing up Second Empire Parisians in Homeric armor. This kind of anachronism is also, it should be noted, a form of merchandizing, a way of selling (out) the past to the present. Helen, in this sense, has always been a bestseller. So successful was Offenbach's *opéra bouffe,* Pauline Carton tells us, that *poires Belle Hélène* were sold in stores (in her preface to Halévy and Meilhac n.d.:xiii). We may feel that there is something cheap and impure about this refurbishing or reforming of the past. We look down upon the bestseller while enjoying it. The same could be said for our adoration of Helen. *La Belle Hélène,* Carton writes, is "a vast and truculent parody of the *Iliad*" ("une vaste et truculent parodie de l'*Iliade*" [xvii]).

Both of these aptly describe the treatment of antiquity in *La Belle Hélène.* The central motif in Meilhac and Halévy's operetta is that of disguise and revelation. In the first scene Paris is disguised as a shepherd; in the last he is dressed as Venus's high priest, come to take Helen, in the requisite "abduction" scene, to the island of Cythera. In both scenes disguise gives way to disclosure, and Paris ends up revealing his identity. From start to finish, in fact, at almost every moment, *La Belle Hélène* demonstrates the lure, and limitation, of appearances. In Act 1 the high priest Calchas anxiously awaits the delivery of a sheet of metal, a prop with which he imitates the sound of thunder, thereby conveying to the credulous populace the assent or dissent of Jupiter. Later Calchas is caught using loaded dice in a card game with Ajax, Achilles, and Agamemnon. Antiquity, in *La Belle Hélène,* is a fake: not only is it a trivial world of greed and cowardice (graft in the economic sense), but one we are not meant to take seriously, something fabricated, fictive, synthetic (graft in the medical or botanical sense). Calchas is a con man, Achilles a dunce, Agamemnon a lout, Menelaus a fool. (At the same time, all of these characterizations represent a faithful rendering of Homeric epic.) Helen, shrewder, habitually washes her infidelities clean with her all-purpose refrain: *La fatalité!*

Helen's beauty makes her the play's most treacherous fraud. When Léaena, a courtesan accompanying the young rake Orestes, attempts to gain access to the festival of Adonis, she argues that if Helen can attend, she should be allowed to as well: "that young philosopher, who taught me wisdom and made me understand that the beautiful and the good are the same thing . . . that was also fatality!" ("ce jeune philosophe, qui ma enseigné la sagesse et qui m'a fait comprendre que le beau et le bon, c'était la même chose . . . fatalité aussi!" [Halévy and Meilhac n.d.:12]). For all its frivolity, and perhaps because of its frivolity, *La Belle Hélène* effectively resurrects the Platonic question: is *le beau* the same as *le bon?* In the end the answer is yes, but only because the second term is dissolved in the first, and not the other way around. Like a painting by Boucher, *La Belle Hélène* is a tableau in which beauty is only skin deep, but in which nothing is deeper *than* skin. This goes a long way toward explaining the climactic dream sequence in the second act of the operetta. Helen in her boudoir has veiled herself with an abundance of fabrics, makeup, and jewelry, arming herself against an assault she both fears and desires: the arrival of Paris. She informs Calchas that she longs to see Paris, but only as a dream, a *"songe."* That night the real Paris hides in Helen's bedroom. The authors have attached the following note on his entrance, just in case the drama's anachronistic parodying has not been sufficiently appreciated: "Paris enters casually, just as a young man of today might enter a salon" ("Pâris entre négligemment, comme ferait de nos jours un jeune homme entrant dans un salon" [38]). Helen awakens to see her wish fulfilled. But is this the real Paris or a dream Paris? It is to the advantage of all concerned, of course, to believe that the real is illusory and the illusory real (that is, a bona fide illusion). This, then, is just another game of charades. "Am I as beautiful as Venus?" ("Suis-je aussi belle que Vénus?"), Helen asks Paris (52). Paris responds that he saw rather more of Venus than he is now seeing of Helen. The scene proceeds to turn into a striptease that is aborted when Menelaus unexpectedly returns. The debunking of antiquity can only go so far.

Only so far, that is, until Jules Lemaître's comedy *La Bonne Hélène* (1896).[9] That this play is a response to *La Belle Hélène* and its pseudo-Platonic concerns is made clear by its title. The play opens with a traditional *teichoskopia,* faithfully recalled by Priam.[10] So enthusiastic is Priam in his agreement with the Trojan elders that he proceeds to arrange a rendezvous with Helen for that very evening. Helen is only too happy to oblige. By the end of the first act, Helen's schedule is rather full, since she also has meetings planned with Hector and even with Hector's eldest son, Cléophile. Cléophile being rather young, Helen hesitates at first to comply. When the boy begins to weep, Helen accedes to his request: "I'm a good person, you see?" ("Mais oui, mais oui. Je suis bonne personne, tu vois?" [Lemaître 1896, 1:17]). Helen, we know, is as "bad" as they come. And it is precisely her ethical ambiguity that makes her irresistible. Lemaître's Helen is like Homer's, but without the guilt. Her beauty now is offered freely, repeatedly, shared like the loaves of bread and fishes multiplied by Jesus at Cana. Lemaître's Helen is thus infinitely recyclable, another sacred prostitute.

The second act of *La Bonne Hélène* shows Helen anointed in this role. A priest announces that a lamb must be sacrificed by a male free of sin. But the Trojans soon discover that such a man is hard to find; all the men in Troy, it would appear, have already "sinned" with Helen. The crisis is resolved only when Venus makes her appearance in *deus ex machina* fashion and proclaims the virtues of free love. Interestingly enough, Venus both celebrates Helen's promiscuity and holds out the possibility of her chastity: possessing Helen may well have been, for all the men of Troy, but a dream. Venus thus confirms Helen in her familiar double status: pure and prostituted. The goddess concludes with the proclamation: "And as for you, beautiful Helen, blush no longer at having been the good Helen" ("Et quant à toi, belle Hélène, ne rougis plus / D'avoir été la bonne Hélène" [Lemaître 1896, 2:41]). Plato, in Lemaître, makes peace with Homer—even if Plato has nothing to say in the matter. At the end of the play the sacrificial knife is given hurriedly to Astyanax, as the child begins to stretch out his arms toward Helen.

Lemaître's revisionary classicism thus continues the work of Halévy and Meilhac in dismantling the wall separating ethics from aesthetics. The effect is to cancel the Platonic edict that would banish poetry—and Helen—from the republic. Proust provides some theoretical justifications for reinstating it—and her —in a review of *La Bonne Hélène* in *Contre Sainte-Beuve*. Proust's comments suggest an attempt to reconcile Offenbach with Lemaître, Plato with Helen, the Beautiful with the Good. But this reconciliation takes place at the expense of Helen as figure of corporeal desire. Proust's Helen is abstracted and becomes an emblem of aesthetic perfection: "And the more we are shown that she was only the good Helen," he argues, "the more we understand the extent to which she had to be the beautiful Helen" ("Et plus on nous montre qu'elle ne fut que la bonne Hélène, plus nous comprenons à quel point elle dut être la belle Hélène" [1971:389]).

Proust is now in a position to cite the Homeric *teichoskopia,* without the drooling and the leering, as a demonstration of the power of beauty over man. His Trojan elders become Parisian aestheticians and connoisseurs.[11] He identifies Lemaître as a poet who, like Stesichorus, understood that human beings are, in essence, aesthetic creatures: "And one may well come to the conclusion that Stesichorus, who also wrote his own *Bonne Hélène,* was . . . something like the Jules Lemaître of antiquity" ("Et l'on peut penser que Stésichore, qui fit aussi sa *Bonne Hélène,* fut . . . quelque chose comme le Jules Lemaître de l'Antiquité" [1971:389–90]). It is not clear to what extent Proust is being ironic in this comparison (on the surface, it may recall the familiar T-shirt declaring X University to be the Harvard of the South or the Midwest). But pairing these two "revisionists" certainly serves Proust's efforts to turn the *teichoskopia* into a triumph of aesthetics. For if Lemaître's Helen is promiscuous while Stesichorus's is chaste, both agree that Helen is ultimately a symbol of Ideal and Eternal Beauty. Even when we read Lemaître's *teichoskopia,* Proust declares,

nous sommes aussi émus que nous l'aurions été par la vue d'Hélène. Il y a telle beauté que nous n'avons jamais vue, dont nous nous sentons les sujets, pour savoir l'empire universel de son charme. Nous la connaissons, si l'aimer c'est déjà la connaître. Et jamais, œuvre d'art ou femme, nous ne la verrons pour la première fois. Ainsi le pouvoir que, vivante, Hélène tira de sa beauté, survécut à sa vie et à sa beauté. (1971:389)

[we are just as moved as we would have been by the sight of Helen. There is a certain beauty we have never seen, a beauty we sense we are the subjects of, since we understand the universal empire of its/her charm. We know it/her, if to love it/her is to know it/her. And never, whether as a work of art or a woman, do we see it/her for the first time. Thus the power that, while she was alive, Helen took from her beauty survived both her life and her beauty.]

Lemaître's version of events may be only second-hand, may represent just another palinode. But Beauty, Proust tells us, is always second-hand. There is no new Helen: Helen, again, is always already known.[12] Proust makes this claim by recourse to a familiar rhetorical trick, playing on the interchangeability of the personal and impersonal referent of the feminine accusative pronoun. How convenient, for all of us, that *la beauté* is feminine. This is the fatal figure of speech which ensures that Helen retains a central place in the French theater.

Figures Can Be Fatal:
Giraudoux's *La guerre de Troie n'aura pas lieu*

Figures can be fatal. This, in essence, is the lesson of Jean Giraudoux's *La guerre de Troie n'aura pas lieu* (The Trojan war will not take place), written four years before the start of the Second World War. Giraudoux's play extends the comic theatrical tradition that began with *Faust* II and *La Belle Hélène*. It is, however, a dark and bitter comedy. *La guerre de Troie n'aura pas lieu* is a satire on war's inevitable *desirability,* on the simple fact that war, when it happens, does so because we *want* it to, and because there are always things *for which* we want to fight. When a thing has become something to fight for, it is no longer just that thing: it has become what it is, and something else as well. It has become a *figure.*

In Giraudoux's version of the Homeric saga, Troy is divided between the peace party, led by Hector and Andromaque, and the war party, whose chief proponent, significantly enough, is the town poet, Demokos. For Giraudoux, in this play and elsewhere (*Siegfried,* for example), art and war can be collaborators. The plot centers on a simple question: should Helen be given back to the Greeks? It is the question that has always been at stake in the *teichoskopia.* Giraudoux's version is a vicious parody of the Homeric scene, and perfectly faithful to it in its own way. The very setting for Act 1 sets the cynically ludicrous tone for Helen's epiphany, which is here a daily event: "Terrace of a rampart overlooked by a terrace and overlooking other ramparts" ("Terrasse d'un rempart dominé par une terrasse et dominant d'autre remparts" [1982:483]). When Cassandra describes Helen's morning constitutional for Hector, who refuses to watch, Giraudoux manages to incorporate most of the familiar Homeric motifs, including the cicadas to which the old tribe of Priam's advisers are compared:

CASSANDRE: Regarde. C'est l'heure de sa promenade . . . Vois aux créneaux toutes ces têtes à barbe blanche . . . On dirait les cigognes caquetant sur les remparts.
HECTOR: Beau spectacle. Les barbes sont blanches et les visages rouges.
CASSANDRE: Oui. C'est la congestion. Ils devraient être à la porte du Scamandre, par où entre nos troupes et la victoire. Non, ils sont aux portes Scées, par où sort Hélène . . . Elle est sur la seconde terrasse. Elle rajuste sa sandale, debout, prenant bien soin de croiser la jambe.

HECTOR: Incroyable. Tous les vieillards de Troie sont là à la regarder d'en haut.
CASSANDRE: Non. Les plus malins regardent d'en bas.

(493)

[CASSANDRA: Look. It's the time for her promenade . . . Look, you see by the cren-
ellations all these heads with white beards . . . They're like cicadas cackling on the
ramparts.
HECTOR: What a pretty spectacle. The beards are white and the faces red.
CASSANDRA: Yes. That's congestion. They ought to be at the Skamandrian gates,
where our troops enter, and victory. But no, they're at the Skaian gates, where Helen
goes out . . . She is on the second terrace. She's fixing her sandal, standing, making
sure to cross her legs.
HECTOR: It's unbelievable. All the old men of Troy are there looking at her from above.
CASSANDRA: No. The cleverest ones are looking at her from below.]

Giraudoux's Hector is a realist: a man who understands what war really is. When
Priam commands him to look straight at Helen and report what he sees, Hector
answers only: "I see a woman fixing her sandal" ("Je vois une femme qui rajuste
sa sandale" [495]). Hector refuses, in other words, to idealize. He trades in flesh
and blood, not in abstractions. His wife agrees. There is a moment when Andromaque says: "I don't understand abstractions" ("Je ne comprends pas les
abstractions" [484]). Priam, Demokos, and the elders of Troy, however, see
more than Helen when they look at her. They see her and . . . *something else:*
not simply a *subject,* but a *surjet* (a more-than-subject, a stitch, a seam). Priam
asks Hector: "Did it ever happen to you, at the sight of a woman, to feel that
she wasn't only herself, but that an entire flow of ideas and feelings had been
poured into her flesh and took on its luster?" ("Il t'est bien arrivé dans la vie,
à l'aspect d'une femme, de ressentir qu'elle n'était pas seulement elle-même,
mais que tout un flux d'idées et de sentiments avait coulé en sa chair et en pre-
nait l'éclat?" [496]). What else is Helen, Hector wonders, besides herself? This
time it is the poet Demokos who responds: she is beauty. Similarly, the town
surveyor, as true to his profession as Demokos is to his own, declares that, before Helen, land could not be mapped: "space and volume now have only one
common measurement, which is Helen" ("il n'y a plus à l'espace et au volume
qu'une commune mesure qui est Hélène" [497]). Helen has become the universal standard, that by which all is measured, that to which all must be compared.
Priam's answer to Hector's question, meanwhile, could have been spoken by
Flaubert's Simon Magus:

regarde seulement cette foule, et tu comprendras ce qu'est Hélène. Elle est une espèce
d'absolution. Elle prouve à tous ces vieillards que tu vois là . . . qu'ils avaient au fond
d'eux-mêmes une revendication secrète, qui était la beauté. . . . Hélène est leur pardon,
et leur revanche, et leur avenir. (497–98)

[just look at this crowd, and you will understand what Helen is. She is a form of absolution. She is the proof for all these old men that you see . . . that they had inside themselves a secret demand, which was beauty. . . . Helen is their pardon, their revenge, and their future.]

In short, concludes Hector, "in claiming to fight for beauty, you want us to fight for a woman" ("en prétendant nous faire battre pour la beauté, vous voulez nous faire battre pour une femme"[498]).

Indeed, Giraudoux's concerns are as Platonic as Flaubert's, or Ronsard's. The dialogue between Hector and Helen that follows the *teichoskopia,* for example, centers upon the difficulty of distinguishing between the illusory and the real. What, Hector asks, is real for you? Paris? Menelaus? Probability and possibility are translated into images of color or transparency: the cosmetic discourse of Platonism. Helen explains: "Among objects and beings, some have colors for me. The ones that I can see. I believe in them" ("Entre les objets et les êtres, certains sont colorés pour moi. Ceux-là je les vois. Je crois en eux" [506]). Neither Paris nor Menelaus is, apparently, very *real* in this respect. And what of yourself, asks Hector? When you embrace Paris, what is it that you *really* feel? Love? Pleasure? "My role," she answers, "is finished. I let the universe think in my place. It does that better than I do" ("Mon rôle est fini. Je laisse l'univers penser à ma place. Cela, il le fait mieux que moi" [506]). Helen herself is no better guarantor of her own status than those who exploit her for their own purposes. Cassandra—whose very profession is the identification of the probable and the possible—conjures up two images of Peace, first "pale" ("pâle") and then "extravagantly made up" ("outrageusement fardée"), like Helen herself (511). The game of Ronsardian cosmetics continues when Helen cites one more "watercolor" ("chromos en couleurs"), that she casually dismisses: an image of "an old Helen, toothless" ("une Hélène vieillie . . . édenté" [532]). Dialogue in *La guerre de Troie n'aura pas lieu* insistently returns to the subject of illusion. In Act 2, Scene 8, Andromaque and Helen are speaking of love. Helen, Andromaque argues, does not even love Paris; would it not be terrible for the course of history to turn upon a lie? "And the life of my son, and the life of Hector," she continues, "will rest upon hypocrisy and lies, it's horrible" ("Et la vie de mon fils, et la vie d'Hector vont se jouer sur l'hypocrisie et le simulacre, c'est épouvantable"[530]). But the truth, once again, is that war happens because someone wants it. Helen is, as she herself recognizes, merely an excuse. As Ulysses puts it, "She is one of those rare creatures which destiny puts into circulation on the earth for its own personal use" ("Elle est un des rares créatures que le destin met en circulation sur la terre pour son usage personnel"[547]). His image suggests a form of currency whose value is indeterminate. Helen, Priam has shown us, is but a pretense for something else, anything else—whatever we *want*. To embrace Helen herself, here, again, is a contradiction. In Act 1, Paris identifies lovemaking with Helen as a kind of telegraphic intimacy: "Even in my arms, Helen is far from me" ("Même au milieu de mes bras, Hélène est loin de moi"[491]). It is a phrase that should remind us of Ronsard's fantasy sonnets, and of all the poets who seek to resurrect the ghosts of antiquity.

The idealization or self-effacing metaphoricity Helen sets in motion is something we have observed since the beginning of this book. We know that the consequences can be catastrophic:

P: A quoi ressemble-t-elle, la guerre, maman?
H: A ta tante Hélène.
P: Elle est bien jolie.

                                                                                      (517)

[POLYXENE: What does war look like, mother?
HECUBE: Like your aunt Helen.
POLYXENE: She is very pretty.]

These ominous words invert the traditional role Helen plays in the metaphoric syllogism, the enthymeme, for here Helen is not its premise but its conclusion. The subject is no longer Helen, but War *her*self. Perhaps it would be more accurate to say that the subject of the syllogism in Giraudoux is *resemblance* itself, the always polished poetry of the conceit. Poetry and politics are collaborators in the inexorable march toward war in Troy. Hector's grimace at Demokos's mediocre epigram in praise of Helen's beauty leads the poet to ask: "Why are you looking at me that way? You seem to hate poetry as much as war" ("Qu'as-tu à me regarder ainsi? Tu as l'air de détester autant la poésie que la guerre"). To which Hector responds: "Please! They are sisters!" ("Va! Ce sont les deux sœurs!" [504]). And, indeed, the poet Demokos, slain by Hector as he attempts to rouse the Trojan rabble in the last scene of the play, is the specific cause of the war. For when Demokos falsely names a Greek named Oiax as his assassin, Oiax is promptly lynched by the mob, and general hostilities commence. At that moment the last line of the play engineers an interesting reversal of the conventional imitative scenario. Giraudoux leaves us with the impression that it is now up to Homer to continue the tale. The last words are Cassandra's: "The Trojan poet is dead. . . . It is the Greek poet's turn" ("Le poète troyen est mort. . . . La parole est au poète grec" [551]). Every poet, of course, seeks to make the precursor follow.

Fighting for Camus's Helen: A Figural or Literal War?

That Helen represents Beauty may have once seemed like an innocent abstraction, but for it Troy will fall. Would it be possible, in the name of that same abstraction, to rebuild Troy? This is the question Albert Camus asks in "L'exil d'Hélène" (1954:108–19), an essay written in 1948, at the end of another war. Camus treats modern Europe as another Siegfried, Giraudoux's shell-shocked amnesiac, exiled from his origins and his own sense of self. The essay is a diagnosis of modern civilization's malaise and a prescription for its recovery. For Camus today's Europe is a world in crisis without values. Wars are now battles for acquisition. Tragedies smell of bureaucracy. The modern city has cut us off from nature, and we have cut ourselves off from our past. Camus even doubts the very premise of historical continuity that Western culture has always taken for granted: "This is why it is indecent to proclaim today that we are the sons of Greece" ("Voilà pourquoi il est indécent de proclamer aujourd'hui que nous sommes les fils de la Grèce" [111–12]).

What is it that Europe has forgotten? Beauty. Camus puts much of the blame for the degeneration of Western culture on Christianity's substitution of the internal tragedy of the soul for the contemplation of external, visible beauty. Today we deal in abstractions and theories, until we forget what it means to look at the world with our eyes. There is an irony here. Camus's essay offers us, as an emblem of the beauty that has been cast out from our world, a faceless, idealized, and allegorical Helen, a Helen who can in no way be looked upon. Camus plays, just as Proust did, on the personification of the personal pronoun *elle* (the basis, too, for the standard Giraudoux metaphor linking the feminine and the abstract), which can as easily be attached to abstract as to sentient objects: "We have exiled beauty, the Greeks took up arms for it/her" ("Nous avons exilé la beauté, les Grecs ont pris les armes pour elle" [1954:108]). What does Camus propose? In essence, the re-Hellenization of Europe. In other words, if the aesthetics are there, ethics will follow. To fight for beauty is Camus's way of becoming Greek again: "Ignorance unmasked, the rejection of fanaticism, the limits of man, the face that is loved, beauty, finally, here is the field of battle where we will rejoin the Greeks" ("L'ignorance reconnue, le refus du fanatisme, les bornes de l'homme, le visage aimé, la beauté enfin, voici le camp où nous rejoindrons les Grecs" [118]). Camus thus writes against the horrors of literal war, and proposes a figurative one instead. Rejecting the seductive abstractions of religion, Camus offers the seduction of sensuous beauty instead, and he does so by way of the most conventional of all abstractions: the metaphor of a beautiful woman who is abducted. In other words, Camus's war against metaphor (Beauty, Truth, Nationalism) is itself the oldest of metaphors.

But metaphors are notoriously difficult to control. Helen is the metaphorical prize of Camus's new metaphorical war, but who is to say what Helen really means? Who is to say that Camus's reading is definitive? Who is to say that Camus's metaphor is not worth—quite literally—dying for? "O midday thought, the Trojan war will be fought far from the fields of battle. This time, again, the terrible walls of the modern city will fall to deliver, 'the soul, serene like the calm of the sea,' the beauty of Helen" ("O pensée de midi, la guerre de Troie se livre loin des champs de bataille! Cette fois encore, les murs terribles de la cité moderne tomberont pour livrer, 'ame sereine comme la calme des mers,' la beauté d'Hélène" [1954:119]). To turn the Trojan war into a figure of speech— as I myself have done throughout this book—is a dangerous act, one that sug- gests that all wars could be converted into convenient metaphors, and that all metaphors could be translated into convenient wars. But real wars or metaphori- cal ones? We must always fear that, one day, Camus's essay will be read not as an aesthetic manifesto, but as a declaration of war.

Conclusion: The Example of Helen in
A la recherche du temps perdu

A reading of the Homeric *teichoskopia* from almost the same year as Camus's "L'exil d'Hélène" suggests just how easy it is to enlist Helen in the service of desire, and make her do the required figurative work: "Meanwhile Helen stands helplessly watching the men who are going to do battle for her. She is there still, since nations that brave each other for markets, for raw materials, rich lands, and their treasures, are fighting, first and foremost, for Helen" (Bespaloff 1947:69). There is nothing remarkable about this kind of figurative reading: it is the most familiar move in criticism. And it is, in fact, a move we cannot help but make. There is no escape from the figural. But perhaps we would do well to remember that if Helen is the figure who can be prostituted to any cause, then, to return to Solitaire's figure in Valéry's *Mon Faust,* it is we (and the language we use) who are her pimps. This is essentially what Giraudoux is arguing in *La guerre de Troie n'aura pas lieu.*

   That figuration may be just another form of graft is the possibility raised in an unfinished passage from the manuscript to *A la recherche du temps perdu* where Proust revisits Helen's appearance upon the walls of Troy. This is a very different *teichoskopia,* however, from the one we saw in *Contre Sainte-Beuve.* There Helen was a faceless universal, the familiar gold standard of beauty. Here Helen is an individual, corporeal, specific, with a real face and a real body. Ab- stractions do not age, but this Helen can. The passage in question was meant to replace a sentence (Proust 1954, 2:716) in which Marcel recalls a rumor that Charlus once failed to pay his last respects to a queen on her deathbed in order to keep an appointment with a hairstylist, an engagement preparatory to a ren- dezvous with a conductor on a city bus. In the unfinished interpolation, Marcel returns to the familiar role of eavesdropper, now overhearing a conversation between Charlus and the recent proletarian object of his affections. Marcel, sur- prised to hear the conductor addressing the baron as an equal, embarks on this reflection:

Continuateur des grands maîtres, il traitait le personnage de M. de Charlus comme un Véronèse, ou un Racine ceux du mari de Cana ou d'Oreste, dont l'un montre le mari de Cana et l'autre, Achille comme si ce juif et ce Grec légendaires avaient fait partie, l'un du fastueux patriciat de Venise, l'autre de la cour de Louis XIV. (1954, 2:1188)

[Carrying on the tradition of the great masters, he was treating M. de Charlus the way a Veronese or a Racine treated the husband of Cana or Orestes, the first showing the husband of Cana, and the second, Achilles, as if this legendary Jew and Greek were from the opulent state of Venice and the court of Louis XIV respectively.]

Sometime later Marcel happens upon the conductor himself and is astonished to find that the object of Charlus's obsession is a strikingly hideous figure. Marcel imagines the incredulity of the Princess de Guermantes—in this textual variation she has become the queen in the scandalous rumor—upon seeing the insignificant object for whom she was abandoned: "Well, imagine, upon seeing him, pimply, ugly, vulgar, with red eyes and shortsighted, imagine the shock!" ("Alors, en voyant celui-ci, bourgeonné, laid, vulgaire, aux yeux rouges et myopes, quel choc!" [Proust 1954, 2:1190]). Now, it must be true, Marcel admits, that "the cause of our sufferings, incarnate in a body loved by another, sometimes is comprehensible even to us" ("la cause de nos chagrins, incarnée en un corps aimé d'un autre être, nous est quelquefois compréhensible"). Helen is the example cited to illustrate the point: "the Trojan elders, seeing Helen pass by, said: 'Our suffering is not worth as much as a single one of her glances'" ("les vieillards troyens, voyant passer Hélène, se disaient: 'Notre mal ne vaut pas un seul de ses regards'"). But the narrator finds it too easy to see the other side of the question: "But the contrary is perhaps more frequent, since . . . there are those who, ugly in the eyes of almost everyone, ignite inexplicable loves" ("Mais le contraire est plus fréquent peut-être, parce que . . . il est commun que des êtres, laids aux yeux de presque tout le monde, excitent des amours inexplicables"). The very example cited earlier would appear to undo itself, since it seems to lend support to both sides of the debate, and even render it moot:

D'ailleurs on ne peut même pas dire que le cas des vieillards troyens soit plus ou moins fréquent que l'autre cas (la stupéfaction devant l'être qui a causé nos peines): car, si on laisse seulement passer un peu de temps, le cas des vieillards se confond presque toujours dans l'autre, il n'y a plus qu'un cas. Si, n'ayant jamais vu Hélène et pour peu qu'elle eût le destin de vieillir longtemps et mal, si on avait dit un jour aux Troyens: "Vous allez voir cette fameuse Hélène," il est probable que devant une petite vieille rougeaude, épaissie, informe, ils n'eussent pas été moins stupéfaits que n'eût été la princesse de Guermantes devant le contôleur d'autobus. (1190)

[Besides one cannot even say that the case of the Trojan elders is more or less frequent than the other case (astonishment at the sight of the being who is the cause of our pain);

for, if you simply let a little time pass, the case of the elders almost always merges with the other, so that there is only one case. If, having never seen Helen, and if her destiny had been to grow old, and badly, if one had said to the Trojans: "You will now see that famous Helen," it is more than likely that, before a little red-faced old woman, fat and formless, they would have been no less astonished than the Princess de Guermantes would have been before the bus conductor.]

There is something obviously appropriate about concluding a study of cultural nostalgia with Proust's extended meditation on the retrieval of the past. But the passage serves as a fitting end to this chapter for a number of reasons. It emphasizes the idea of beauty as, at least in rhetorical terms, an essentially specular term, something to be looked at or gazed upon. That in turn helps to efface the distinction between novels and theatrical works—both of which I discuss in this chapter and the previous one—when it comes to the role Helen is generally called upon to play in literature. We may believe that role is fixed—that Helen is destined to play it, that she is a "natural" for the part, that the lines are always the same—but we delude ourselves in doing so. It is we, rather, who write the lines, and we who make the actor fit the part. The possibility that beauty may be only in the eye of the beholder has never sounded like a more radical proposition, not, at least, since Sappho's floating currency of beauty in Fr. 16. The difference between Proust's two *teichoskopias* is thus the same one that separates the first set of terms in the opening priamel in Sappho's poem ("Some say a host of horsemen, others of infantry, and others of ships, is the most beautiful thing on the dark earth," in Page's translation) from the last ("but I say, it is what you love").[13] In Marcel's return to the walls of Troy, then, beauty is not only specular, but subjective and contingent. It is we who fashion it to fit our own particular desires and serve our own particular causes. But the "thing" we call upon to play the part we need has nothing to do with that part, and nothing to do with us. Beauty, in this passage, is neither abstract nor unchanging. On the contrary, it is something material, and thus transient. It is living; it is real; it resists figuration. And thus Proust joins Ronsard when the poet imagines, in *SpH* 2.24, the famous "Quand vous serez bien vieille," Helen as a "vieille accroupie" (Weber and Weber 1963:431).

And yet there is no escaping the figural. For it would be premature to leave this passage without seeing that it depends entirely on the very mechanisms it manages to expose: anachronism, figuration, and graft. That these mechanisms are at some level inescapable may attenuate the irony of this apparent contradiction. But the contradiction is there, all the same, and the irony, too. Proust's reference to Helen, after all, is designed to be a fable, a kind of allegory. Helen is the example cited to make a point. It is because Proust's rehabilitated Helen is stripped of her figural reading that she can stand as a figure for a new way of reading. Eros is anachronism, Proust is arguing in this passage: we fall in love with interpolations, phantoms we pillage from the past and dress up in the latest fashions; and it is precisely by grafting a passage from an Archaic Greek epic upon a fin-de-siècle Parisian epic that Proust can make this assertion.

The example is what it is, and it is something else. To make something an example of something else is always an act of doubling. But to turn Helen into an example, as Proust does in *A la recherche du temps perdu,* is an especially precarious gesture. For it is never entirely clear what she may be an example *of.* Trying to isolate Helen inevitably means watching her divide. Proust's own example proves highly unstable and undoes itself almost the moment it is cited, turning into its own counterexample. And yet both example and counterexample remain: just as the grafted stock and the scion remain two, and one. There is only one Helen in the passage above, and yet there are two. What both separates and joins these two Helens is what separates and joins Marcel, the narrator who remembers, and Marcel, the hero remembered. the passage of time.

Prosthesis
Helen in (Modern) Greece

Modern Greek Nationhood: *Altneuland*

In "The Virgin of Sparta," a sonnet by the modern Greek poet Angelos Sikelianos (1884–1951), Mary, or Helen, is implicitly invoked as the patron saint of
graft: "Not of Pentelic marble nor of brass / shall I erect Thy deathless idol [τὸ
ἀθάνατο εἴδωλό Σου], but / from a tall column made of cypress wood / that
my work may be fragrant throughout the ages. / And on that hill which wears
like a tall crown / an old Venetian castle, I shall build / a massive church, and in
it shall lock Thee fast [καὶ μέσα θὰ Σέ κλείσω] / with mighty adamantine gates
of iron!" (ll. 1–8; Sikelianos 1951:82, trans. Friar 1982). In fact, Sikelianos's addressee would seem to be both Mary *and* Helen.[1] The title alone is more than
enough to suggest a synthesis of the Christian and the Pagan. Other elements
in the poem, however, point to the theme of synthesis, or graft. The Venetian
castle, for example, reminds us that Greece has long been a culture occupied by
the foreign. The "massive church" is also a temple, and a prison. The idol inside
is at once a work of art and a work of nature, tree and column, made of neither
marble nor brass, but of the wood of the indigenous cypress, emblem of per-
petuity. *Grafting Helen* is the story of countless such idols (εἴδωλα), imitation
Helens or Helen substitutes, all fashioned out of the latest vernacular.

Poetically, but also politically, culturally, and linguistically, the modern
Greek nation-state is built upon the rhetoric of graft.[2] During its struggle against
the Ottoman Empire in the beginning of the nineteenth century (culminating
in the War of Independence of 1821), the question of Greece's political and
ethnic status generated a considerable amount of debate in Western Europe.[3]
As Michael Herzfeld argues in *Ours Once More: Folklore, Ideology, and the*

239

Making of Modern Greece: "To be a European was, in ideological terms, to be a Hellene" (1982:15). Many Europeans of the time, however, believed the contemporary Greeks to be an adulterated version of the classical Greeks — "Byzantinized Slavs" (Bernal 1987:292), a people debased by foreign grafts.[4] Others took for granted the existence of an unbroken connection between the Greeks of antiquity and today. That premise was central to the folk movement developing in Europe at this time. Claude Fauriel in his *Folk Songs of Modern Greece,* for example, appeared to assume that Homer's creativity lived on in the spontaneous and naïve poetry of the Greek peasant. "Europeanness," for the Greek patriot Dora d'Istria, was a quality allotted to different ethnicities in hierarchical degrees: "the Serbs — even when Moslem by religion — are more European than the Turks, but the Greeks are the most European of all" (Herzfeld 1982:57). Whether the Greeks were embraced or excluded, what was never rejected was the standard of purity by which they were evaluated.[5]

But revolutionary Greece needed Europe just as much as Europe needed Greece. Freedom from the Ottoman Turks was impossible without European intervention, something dictated by both realpolitik (a balance of powers must be maintained on the continent) and ideology (the designated cradle of European identity must be protected from the infidel).[6] Turkey recognized the Greek state in 1829, but only in 1832 was Greece granted independence by the European powers. Europe's goal, according to Herzfeld, "was to form an entity made in their own image and upon their own terms" (1982:15). The new state's first monarch was a Bavarian prince, Otto I. The confusion of identity suggested by this graft of a German ruler upon a Greek people is emblematic of the whole struggle for coherence faced by the incipient Hellenic nation.

Although Greece had relatively little say in its own political self-creation, cultural identity is another matter. Above all it was crucial that Greece equate itself with antiquity. Herzfeld has compared this gesture of affiliation to Theodore Herzl's theoretical conception of a Zionist state as an *Altneuland:* "Political Hellenism shared with political Zionism a preoccupation with the physical site of the nation's history and cultural evolution, and both faced the paradox . . . which Herzl's phrase so concisely suggests" (1982:158n6). Greece also straddles a border, at once geographical and historical, between East and West.[7] Herzfeld suggests (19) that the Greek struggle to fashion itself anew can be viewed along two perpendicular axes: temporal, from ancient to modern, and geographical, from West to East. As a result, Greece was caught between two distinctive cultural models. The more aristocratic *Hellenist* model, directed outward, toward Western Europe, tended to valorize classical culture and all connections with antiquity. What Herzfeld calls the *Romeic* model, on the other hand, in more populist fashion stressed the nation's roots in the Eastern Orthodox and Byzantine past. Few would disagree that the Hellenist model has triumphed and persists to this very day. One of its greatest advocates was the eighteenth-century

Greek philologist Adamantios Koraïs. Koraïs spent the greater part of his life
in Paris, which he called "the Athens of modern Europe," and dreamt of the
founding of a Greco-Gallic state (see Jeffreys 1985:382). Koraïs declares at one
point in the *Battle Hymn of the Greeks (Asma polemistirion):* "French and Greek
bound together, united in friendship, are not Greek or French but one nation,
Grecofrench, crying 'Let cursed slavery be abolished and wiped from the surface of the earth.' *Zito i eleftheria.* Long Live Freedom!" (Jeffreys 1985:47).
We have encountered this kind of hypothetical nation before: in Lemaire's *Gaul*
plus *Troye,* in du Bellay's *Gallogrecz.* What *Grafting Helen* has tried to show is
that Western literature is the continual effort to found such a nation.

Even the official language of the new Greek state, designed almost single-
handedly by Koraïs, is a grafted construct. In 1822 the Constitution of Epi-
daurus "was promulgated in a language so archaic that few Greeks could fully
understand it" (Herzfeld 1982:6). This is because the spoken language of the
Greek people, called the *demotic* or *romeiko,* had little to do with the official,
written language of Greece, or *katharevousa.* Such an artificial medium would
have been impossible were it not for the remarkable stability of the Greek language. Margaret Alexiou has noted, in "Diglossia in Greece," that "the historical evolution of the Greek language reveals a continuing identity which cannot
be paralleled in any other Indo-European language" (1977:176). (That linguistic continuity, we will see in a moment, is something the modern Greek poet
can powerfully exploit.) This linguistic split or diglossia persisted up to the recent past. It was only in the 1980s that demotic Greek replaced *katharevousa*
as the national language.

Katharevousa means "a pure flowing." It would be difficult to find a better
example of the trope of cultural continuity translated into linguistic terms. In
"Adamantios Koraïs: Language and Revolution," Michael Jeffreys suggests that
two major principles governed the design of *katharevousa*—the recuperation
of antique forms and the elimination of foreign elements: "A . . . significant reason for the 'purification' of the language was the existence of . . . hellenized
Turkish words. If the nation and its language have some essential link—a belief
. . . hardly challenged at the time—every time a Greek speaker uses a Turkish word, he shows his . . . lack of independence and the subservient status of
his people" (1985:52).[8] *Katharevousa,* an artificial language essentially grafted
into existence, was paradoxically conceived by its creator, and defended by its
partisans, as the restoration of the true Greek tongue. The people did not buy it.

Helen in Modern Greek Poetry:
"Binding with your name the bridges of the ages"

Neither did the poets. The career of Dionysios Solomos (1798–1857) is typical in this respect. Often regarded as the "father" of modern Greek poetry,

author of the "Hymn to Liberty" (now Greece's national anthem), Solomos was born in Zante, one of the Heptanesian Islands on the Ionian coast, which were under Venetian rule from 1482 until 1797. Solomos grew up speaking both Greek and Italian. It was in Italian, the language of education and culture, that he began writing poetry. But as the movement for independence gained momentum, Solomos renounced Italian and began writing poetry in Greek. Linos Politis recounts the event as a return to nature itself. Solomos was "seized by the idea of putting his thoughts into his mother tongue, the language that he had imbibed with his mother's milk. . . . while his Italian sonnets are mature and terse, the Greek poems . . . are simple and almost naïve. It is as if Solomos, when writing Greek, was adapting himself to the primitive stage at which Greek poetry then found itself" (1973:114–15). Aesthetic simplicity here is the guarantor of authenticity. When Solomos writes verse in Greek, his *mother tongue,* he has returned home, like a child to his mother. Sophistication, on the other hand, suggests foreign intrusion, an invasion from the outside.[9]

Modern Greek poets, in one way or another, are always engaged in this act of expelling the foreign and returning to the source. Their poetry tends to function as a *katharevousa,* a pure flowing of past into present. The premise of cultural continuity here is axiomatic.[10] The translators Edmund Keeley and Philip Sherrard have tried to explain that premise. Why, they ask, do classical allusions seem to "belong" in modern Greek poetry? To allude to the "ancient world" is only "natural," they argue, "in a country which . . . remains full of the . . . remnants of antiquity . . . 'Scattered drums of a Doric column / Razed to the ground / By unexpected earthquakes' as Sikelianos puts it . . . or to quote Seferis . . . : 'fragments of a life . . . once complete . . . close to us . . . and then mysterious and unapproachable as the lines of a stone licked smooth by the wave' " (Seferis 1981:vii). As a result, they argue, the Greek poet exploiting classical allusions "enjoys a large advantage over his . . . contemporaries in England or America: he can evoke characters and settings that have mythological overtones with less danger of being merely literary . . . less danger of arbitrarily imposing gods or heroes on an alien landscape" (viii). The story here is that nothing, really, has changed. Greece is a place of memories that simply come to mind; its history is a gentle and uninterrupted weathering, the lapping of waves on a stone. But within this vision of continuity, the passages cited from Sikelianos and Seferis suggest history as a very different process: a story of violent dislocations and protracted alienation. The columns are shattered, the weathered stone is unrecognizable. Keeley and Sherrard go on to describe how George Seferis introduces classical myth into contemporary settings: "the myth comes to life fully, the ancient and modern worlds meet in a metaphor without strain or contrivance as we find the legendary figures moving anachronistically onto the contemporary stage" (1981:viii). I have been trying, in *Grafting Helen,* to locate the lines of strain and contrivance that lie hidden in just these kinds of formulations. Here, as is so often the case, Keeley and Sherrard want to have it both ways. They suggest that the geographical coincidence of ancient and modern Greece offers the Greek poet a real advantage. This is not, however, because the characters and settings invoked are less literary or arbitrary, but because they *seem* to be so. Willis Barnstone, another translator, has struggled with the same contradiction. There are not "two Greeces," he asserts in "Translating from Ancient and Modern Greek," but rather "a continuum of many connecting Greeces, including Homeric, classical, Alexandrian, Byzantine, Turkish, modern" (1990:332). The premise of genealogical continuity is familiar; so is the advice that follows upon that premise. Like du Bellay in sixteenth-century France, Barnstone urges the translator to "plunder time in order to create illusions of oneness" (322). The ideal translator, in other words, is a counterfeiter and a thief.

A good thief, like a good translator, goes unnoticed. Modern Greek poets are everywhere plundering antiquity, but you would not know that to read their poetry. What they appear to be doing is simply remembering the past. What could be more innocent, more natural, more reflexive, than remembering? This gesture of innocent remembrance is an essential rhetorical act in modern Greek poetry. It is part of a strategy for retrieving the past, at whatever cost, but without betraying the enormous effort and expense required. I. M. Panayotopoulos's "Sunday of the Aegean" is a good example. The poem begins with an idyllic image of a ship at sea. Into this lyrical frame enters Homeric epic, and Helen: "Soon the trireme of Paris will drift across our vision /—and it will mount high / toward the land of Troy." The theme of memory is immediately introduced: "It is thus in all its body, shivering in the midst of summer / . . . that the Aegean remembers your passing feet, / that it remembers your beauty, / Helen!" (Panayotopoulos 1970, trans. Friar 1982). No one in particular has to do the remembering here; the sea itself can do it for us. What better emblem of cultural continuity than *a place that remembers itself?* The speaker remains unidentified, but the act of speaking is accomplished. Apostrophe resurrects its target, even where there is no target. Helen returns, simply by being invoked. This ritual remembrance is a covert form of grafting, a strategy of connection that conceals the lines of splicing. This simple formula is the basis for many poems in modern Greek. By remembering, we prove that we have recovered what we had lost. In "Sunday of the Aegean," both the process of retrieval and what has been retrieved are blurred, softened, euphemistic. Helen's abduction is a πέρασμα, a drifting or crossing.

Things are not so easy in Odysseus Elytis's "Ἑλένη" ("Helen"). Here, the act of retrieval is far more painful and protracted—although equally profitable for the poet. Elytis's poem suggests the extent to which the very notion of a modern Greek poetics is a paradox, spoken always by one who is simultaneously at

home and in exile: "It is the damp wind, the autumnal hour, the separation, /
The elbow's bitter prop on the memory / That awakens when night starts to cut
us off from the light / Behind the square window facing towards grief / Revealing nothing ... / Because it has already become / A poem, line succeeding line,
sound keeping pace with the rain, / tears and words — / Words not like others but
whose single goal is You." ['Εσένα]" (1979:27–28, trans. Keeley 1981:136).
The premise of exile gives the poet a privileged connection to that from which
he or she is disconnected. The poet is he or she who has something to mourn,
who has something to remember, who has somewhere to return *to*. To be an
exile, by definition, is to have a home.[11] What is it that this exile wants? Poetry, it
would appear: "Words not like others." The window is Elytis's figure for memory and for poetry: that which separates us from the past and that through which
we glimpse it. What we glimpse, however, is "nothing." Poetry itself is allied to
processes of natural continuity: sequence, emotion, weather. At the same time,
it is not clear if poetry ever reaches its goal, its addressee: "You," "'Εσένα"
But "'Εσένα" is too close to "Helen," "'Ελένη," not to remind us of her, especially in a poem named after her. Perhaps Elytis is suggesting that all Greek
poetry functions as an apostrophe to Helen. Perhaps Helen is modern Greece's
Transcendental Addressee, and its Transcendental Memory.

The scene in which the poet or the speaker "recognizes" Helen, and calls
out her name, is so recurrent in the work of modern Greek poets that it can
stand as an emblem of their entire poetic enterprise as a summoning or citation
(from the Latin *citare,* to summon) of the classical past. Thus the unidentified
speaker in Panayotopoulos's "Sunday of the Aegean," thus Teucer in Seferis's
"'Ελένη" ("Helen"), discussed in detail below, thus the "I" in Takis Sinopoulos's "Ποίημα γιὰ τὴν 'Ελένη" ("A Poem for Helen"): "You who are beautiful
[ὡραία ἐσύ], unseeable / within the poem's sky, searing religion, airy woman /
dressed in dawns, a star symbol [σύμβολο] / binding with your name the bridges
of the ages [μὲ τ' ὄνομά σου δένοντας τῶν ἐποχῶν τὶς γέφυρες]. / You who
are beautiful, / nocturnal of the endless, the superb plunder of death, / reborn
out of the dust of death. / I recognize you my Helen [Σ' ἀναγνωρίξω 'Ελένη
μου]" (Sinopoulos 1951). Sinopoulos's poem (from a collection entitled simply
'Ελένη, *Helen*), "for Helen," but also *to* Helen and *about* Helen, is a study in
the gestures of dedication and address, recognition and remembrance, that constitute the labor of the poet. These, we know, are forms of graft, mechanisms
for "binding" with a name "the bridges of the ages." This is what Sinopoulos
suggests they are. Helen "herself" is never anything but a "symbol," a "name"
or a pronoun. If Sinopoulos's "Poem for Helen" is a love poem, and it certainly
looks like one, then it is entirely about the lover. The beloved is an excuse, an
occasion, a convention. There is a certain degree to which this is true of all love
poems, but it is especially true of writings about Helen. Helen is an idol, an
idée fixe, the addressee always available, always ready to listen: "Shall we meet

one more time I wonder," Sinopoulos's lover concludes his plea, "I full of distance, / you full of stars / always incorruptible, virgin untouched, sublimated?" Helen is a virgin, again, because Sinopoulos wants her to be.

Distance here is the point. A name that bridges the ages is also one that reminds us how far we have left the past behind. If Helen is Greece's Transcendental Memory, she is also its Transcendental Amnesia. Helen tends to play both roles in the poetry of Kostis Palamas. In his *Iambs and Anapests,* for example, two Helens are conflated in a single poem: "Menelaus charges and attacks / sword in hand / offering death / to faithless Helen // But she, all serene / offers with her blossom hand / the soothing herb that wards off all anger / and all pain / And Menelaus drinks it, /and the sword falls from his hand, / and he offers Helen a kiss" (Palamas 1958). The "But she," "Ἀλλὰ ἐκείνη," bridges the space between the *Iliad* and the *Odyssey,* the gap that Helen's *pharmakon* nullifies as it extinguishes memory, or anaesthetizes it. In Palamas's "Πατρίδες" ("Countries"), from the work Ἡ ἀσάλευτη ζωή (Life immovable), an Odysseus-like figure encounters Helen on an imaginary voyage: "Voyager, on the sea without waves I discovered / Calypso, and Helen the beautiful" ("Ταξιδευτής, ηὗρα ... τὴν Καλυψώ, καὶ τὴν πεντάμορφη Ἑλένη" [1970:62]). Immediately following these lines, the speaker recalls "and the Lotus-Eaters gave me drink / the blessed oblivion of all" ("πῆγα καὶ μὲ πότισαν οἱ Λωτοφάγοι / τὴ λησμονιὰ τῶν ὅλων τὴ μακαρισμένη"). In Panayotopoulos's "Ἡ μιὰ δὲν εἶσαι. Εἶσαι ὁ καημός" ("You are not one, you are desire"), Helen resists identification: "You are not one. You are desire / with the myriad faces / with the myriad names / with the body that changes as a dress fits / phantom of desire" ("Ἡ μιὰ δὲν εἶσαι. Εἶσαι ὁ καημός / μὲ τὰ περίσσια πρόσωπα, / μὲ τὰ περίσσια ὀνόματα, / μὲ τὸ κορμὶ ποὺ ὡς φόρεμα τὴν ἁρμογή του ἀλλάζει, / φάσμα τοῦ πάθους" [1970]). Helen is the "Memory made of countless memories," "Μνήμη ἀπὸ μνῆμες καμωμένη ἀνάριθμες."

Helen has always been a way of moving back and forth between memory and amnesia. Epistemological uncertainty on the part of the remember-er goes hand in hand with ontological uncertainty as to what is remembered. This is the case in Yannis Ritsos's *Helen*—where Helen herself is the one doing the remembering and the forgetting (1989:269–89). Ontological multiplication, destabilization, evacuation, replenishment: these are the tropes that have always made Helen valuable as poetic currency, constituting what we might call the "now you see it, now you don't" school of poetry. Sinopoulos's collection *Helen* begins with an epigram from the French poet P. J. Jouve's "Hélène," "Que tu es belle maintenant que tu n'es plus." In the first poem in that collection, "Ἑλένη" ("Helen"), the speaker is "swept away" by memories of violence: "you were there, you were not [ἤσουν ἐκεῖ δὲν ἤσουν], leaving / for an imagined country, the diaphanous [διάφανη] / the beautiful the immaculate the inconceivable / the living Helen, / with the serene weight of an ancient body [παμπάλαιου σώματος]" (Friar 1979:84–85). Is Helen there or not? Is she diaphanous and impalpable, or something with the "weight of an ancient body"?

Epistemological and ontological uncertainty bring with them a kind of temporal instability. Poems about Helen seem to struggle with their historicity, fluctuating between contemporaneity and nostalgia. "Seem to" is the key phrase: anachronism is what the poet always wants, and what Helen always provides. "Helen no longer exists," Sinopoulos abruptly declares in "Helen"—"The megaphones have already told us this." In another love poem, "Canto VII," Paris remembers the destruction of Troy, and Helen's efforts to flee, when suddenly a taxi arrives to take her away (Friar 1979:33–35). In Nikos Pappas's "Demolition" (1964), the present is a recurrent destruction of a past that continues to haunt it: "The neighborhood mansions have been torn down / balconies and sentimental terraces / . . . the small rose bushes have been torn down / new houses laden with imperfections / the palaces of the Atridae have been torn down / the renown of beautiful Helen / . . . the boundaries of the age have been torn down / the schoolyards with their songs / our youth has been torn down/unprepared, ancient material / loaded on large mythical carriages / and now it fills the city with midnight" (trans. Friar 1982:156–67). Pappas's poem seems to expose history itself as a continual form of demolition, a trope we have glimpsed intermittently throughout *Grafting Helen*. And yet the wreckage of the past is there: "ancient material / loaded on large mythical carriages." Out of it, perhaps, the present seeks to build itself anew.

The Greek poet Nanos Valaoritis, in a prose poem written in English called "Helen of Troy," turns anachronism and amnesia into a kind of historical or pedagogical methodology. The poem appears to be approximating the results of a classroom exercise conducted in an insane asylum, responding to the question that is at the heart of *Grafting Helen:* "Who is Helen of Troy?" Here is the answer:

In reality Helen of Troy's name was Helen of Ploy. Not Play as some think. She was too stiff to be toyed with. She was, if it is permitted to say it, an idol. A matinee idol. Marilyn Monroe claimed her and came close to impersonating the fickle Goddess. But she was left behind by playwrighting. Sad story, she hanged herself from a tree in Rhodes. Did she deserve it? Her brothers recovered the statue when Theseus stole it. No fool Euripides when he claimed that's what Paris took. He took it to Rome with him but it was too soon for the British Empire to be born. Lord Chesterfield did that for him later. He invented the cigarette. Do we have to, by all means, define it in a sentence? (1990:17)

Who is Helen? The answer to that question would seem to be a way of telling the history of the world, even if it is a way that would appear to sabotage the order and coherence of that history. The answer, which is no answer, or many answers, is, it seems to me, essentially correct, and the one which *Grafting Helen* has tried to offer: Helen is an idol, both too stiff to be toyed with and infinitely pliable, writeable, reproducible. Most of the Helens we have encountered in this study are here: epic heroine, cult goddess, statue, diva, and damsel in distress. "Do we have to, by all means, define it in a sentence?" That question is a good one for the scholar to keep in mind, but it can work in at least two ways. Must we define it in a sentence? Or must we define it in every possible way and thus in every possible sentence?

"A Helen": Seferis's "Helen"

Teucer, in Seferis's "Ἑλένη" ("Helen"), from *Log Book III* (1953), cannot define it. Teucer has seen the face of Helen too many times, enough to undo his faith in memory, identity, and names themselves: "Platres; where is Platres? And this island: who knows it? I've lived my life hearing names I've never heard before" ("*Ποιές εἶναι οἱ Πλάτρες; ποιός τὸ γνωρίζει τοῦτο τὸ νησί; Ἔζησα τὴ ζωή μου ἀκούγοντας ὀνόματα πρωτάκουστα*" [Seferis 1967: 243–46, trans. Keeley and Sherrard 1981]).

"Where is truth?" ("*Ποῦ εἶν' ἡ ἀλήθεια*"), asks Teucer. Truth and all of its cognates in this poem—meaning, memory, and history—are things from which Teucer has been exiled. Like Euripides' *Helen*, to which Seferis's poem closely adheres (and from which it, too, is exiled), Seferis's poem begins with the motif of displacement and dispossession. "I am an exile" (l. 90, trans. Vellacott 1954), Euripides' Teucer declares. Menelaus identifies himself in similar terms: "a wretched castaway, / all my friends lost" (409–10). But both the play and the poem are stories of epistemological, more than physical, shipwreck.

Seferis's poem, haunted by the echoes of Euripides' play, is an attempt to return to it. This is the very position of the exile, for Seferis: to be haunted by memories of the past. Seferis's Teucer, who begins by wondering at a name he does not know, is besieged by the specters of names he knows all too well. The problem is that they are just that, names, torn now from that which they once named: "some Ajax" ("*κάποιος Αἴαντας*"), "some other Teucer" ("*κάποιος ἄλλος Τεῦκρος*"), "a Helen" ("*μιὰν Ἑλένη*"). (Compare Seferis's Teucer here with Ritsos's Helen: "Argos, Athens, Sparta, Corinth, Thebes, Sikion—shadows of names" [1989:280].)

Seferis's Teucer is the hero in what is, in effect, a Cratylean tragedy. Plato urges us in the *Cratylus* not to put too much trust in the name. The name is an imperfect likeness of that to which it refers. The example Plato gives applies remarkably well to Teucer's situation. Cratylus is asked to imagine "the existence of two objects. One . . . Cratylus . . . the other the image (εἰκών) of Cratylus." Next, Plato tells Cratylus, suppose "some god makes not only a representation . . . of your outward form and color, but also . . . infuses motion . . . soul, and mind, such as you have, and in a word copies all your qualities, and places them by you in another form." Would you say, Plato asks, that "this was Cratylus and the image of Cratylus," or "that there were two Cratyluses?" (432b4–13, trans. Jowett 1892). This is the question Teucer is forced to ask about Helen: how to tell the real Helen from the counterfeit, the name from the named, the body from "an empty tunic" ("ἕνα πουκάμισο ἀδειανό")?

Among his many fanciful etymologies in the *Cratylus,* Socrates argues (421a) that the word ὄνομα or "name" is the conflation of a sentence, "being for which there is a search." Teucer is engaged in just such a search for being, he is a hunter of authenticity. And when he finds it, he calls it *Helen,* in the ritual and exclamatory invocation of the name that we have seen in almost every poem discussed in this chapter: "who would have believed it?—Helen! / She whom we hunted so many years by the bank of the Scamander" ("ποιός θὰ τό 'λεγε— ἡ Ἑλένη! / Αὐτὴ ποὺ κυνηγούσαμε χρόνια στὸ Σκάμαντρο"). But Teucer is not so sure by the end of the poem.

In examples as diverse as Classical Greek lyric and French medieval poetry, we have seen the power of the classical topos or name to serve as a point of mythic or narrative interpolation. Names, we have seen, become anchors for a present that has drifted far from antiquity, historical lifelines or umbilical cords to the past.[12] Here on Cyprus, far from home, Teucer tells us, "I anchored alone with this fable." Readers of Seferis's "Helen" have tended to believe in the power of the name to cross "the bridges of the ages"—far more than Teucer does. Politis speaks of "the symbolical language of Seferis in which there is continuous correspondence between myth and actuality" (1973:235).[13] Byron Raizis points out that names like Cyprus and Salamis are still in use today, and posits a "mental bridge" permitting the mind of the poet "to travel to the past and back like an almost automatic reflex" (1977:109–10). Andreas Karandonis traces the genesis of the poem to a bout of insomnia during one of Seferis's real visits to Cyprus: "The nightingales won't let you sleep in Platres" ("Τ' ἀηδόνια δὲ σ' ἀφήνουνε νὰ κοιμηθεῖς στὶς Πλάτρες") is, after all, the refrain. While meditating on the current situation of the island, the poet is brought into contact with a voice from antiquity: "an ancient myth came into his mind" ("ἦρθε στὸ νοῦ του ἕνας ἀρχαῖος μύθος" [Karandonis 1976:193]). The result is a seamless work without lines or joints, "a skillful mixture," writes Raizis, "of echoes from Greece's cultural heritage" (1977:115–16). Katerina Krikos-Davis (1979) even offers an appendix listing, as separate categories, "Borrowings from ancient Greek sources" and "Blendings of ancient and modern elements." Borrowings and Blendings is one way of putting it; Thefts and Grafts would be another.

Teucer, however, has lost faith in the name. Thanks to Helen. For him, the names made famous at the catastrophe of Troy are not symbols. They are just names, and the information they impart is no longer to be trusted. Raizis is confident that names continue to mean as they always have: "All these references have specific . . . connotations which proliferate the meaning of the poem. These . . . are like the face value of coins: they may be cashed any time for a certain amount." Seferis's "correlative allusions" to classical texts, as Raizis calls them, "have objective face values. When properly comprehended they yield specific . . . enriching meanings" (1977:117). Teucer, again, might respectfully disagree. The "correlative," after all, presupposes a certain faith in a stable poetic economy, a continuously circulating currency. If Raizis's comments point to a system of exchange made possible by Aristotelian νόμος, he has tried to control it, to freeze it. But we know from Aristotle that such a system is by definition improper and based on convention, not objective value. The system works, says Raizis, "when properly comprehended." But how can we be sure that we have properly comprehended? The instability of meaning, always present, must be carefully suppressed. Teucer, beset by phantom Helens and artificial Salamises, knows better; he knows that the name has been compromised and counterfeited beyond all hope. Connotations, Raizis suggests, "are like the face value of coins." Raizis's own notion of poetic stability depends on a metaphor that is all too unstable: the unsettling beauty of the face of Helen of Troy.

Helen has no objective face value. We can read Seferis's poem, if we want, as an argument against war. The *eidolon* of Helen had been read, we know, as early as Stesichorus as a metaphor for the inanity of war. But the *eidolon,* alluring and indefinite — "a Helen," "μιὰν Ἑλένη" — is difficult to pin down. Helen gives herself up, as always, to the interpretive desire of the critic, and tells the story he wants her to tell. Seferis's poem, whatever else it may be about, is a cautionary tale about interpretive desire. In Euripides' play, Helen, upon seeing Menelaus, remarks, "O gods; for to recognize is a god" ("ὦ θεοί· θεὸς γὰρ καὶ τὸ γιγνώσκειν φίλους"). Seferis's Teucer similarly asks, "What is a god? What is not a god? And what is there in between them?" It is the same question with which we began this book, the question posed by the elders upon the walls of Troy in *Iliad* 3. By now we know the answer to Teucer's question: it is Helen. The question effectively reproduces the space that is constitutive of all metaphor. Helen is the name for that which mediates or negotiates that space. Helen, we know, is always the *in between.*

It is, finally, perfectly fitting that Teucer the Archer should be the one to discover this. "My fate," he confesses, "τὸ ριζικό μου," as he recalls his unsuccessful attempts to fell Hector with an arrow, is "that of a man who missed his target," "ἑνὸς ἀνθρώπου ποὺ ξαστόχησε." But it is the nature of all metaphor, we have seen, to be a target that is missed, to be *like,* never to *be.* Furthermore, *hamartia,* Aristotle's term from the *Poetics* often translated as "tragic flaw," is employed in archery to refer, more literally, to any form of misstep or miscalculation. O. B. Hardison suggests "missing the mark" (in Golden and Hardison 1981). Critics like Else and Oswald, Hardison notes, understand *hamartia* as "a tendency to err created by lack of knowledge." This ignorance is central to the tragic recognition scene, which, according to Aristotle, is a change from ignorance to knowledge. That change, we may recall, is precisely the effect of the metaphor-enthymeme. Teucer's misfortune is to *recognize* Helen, to find out who she is, and therefore understand the terrible *error* of Troy. He is the tragic hero of a poem about mistaking metaphor for the real thing, or taking the beauty of a face at face value. Finally, the moment of recognition, when Teucer or Menelaus or the belated critic gazes upon the face of Helen, is also the moment of recollection (like that imagined by Socrates in the *Phaedrus,* when the lover, gazing upon his beloved, sees the likeness of the divinity he once followed in the realm of the Forms). It is also the likeness of antiquity, then—and, more specifically, the memory of Euripides' *Helen,* that haunts Seferis's poem like a phantom. We *recognize* Euripides, we might say, in Seferis. Thus Seferis's invocation of the name, "Ἑλένη!"—like Panayotopulos's "Ἑλένη!" in "Sunday of the Aegean" and Elytis's "Ἐσένα" in his "Helen"—is the signal of a dramatic ritual: the moment when the riddle is solved, the syllogism completed, the metaphor negotiated, the face of Helen recognized.

Conclusion

Grafting Helen: Profit and Plunder

It seems fitting to conclude this book as tourists on a trip to Greece, returning, in a sense, to where we started. But only in a sense. (One cannot help but note how pervasive the gesture of continuity is in all forms of cultural discourse. Here my effort to make a neat segue from "Prosthesis" to "Conclusion" suggests how much we value seamlessness in our thinking and our writing.) After all, that is exactly what Western culture has always argued it was doing when it imitated classical literature: returning to where it started. That is one of the figures of speech *Grafting Helen* has tried to expose. We know, by now, that we can't go home again. We can, however, try to bring a few pieces with us.

As a tourist myself in Athens a number of years ago, I remember the following scene, one that will be familiar to anyone who has traveled in Greece: a Byzantine church at the center of a busy traffic intersection. The building was almost entirely submerged beneath the level of the street: centuries of sedimentation and resurfacing had eventually raised the ground almost above the roof. It seemed natural to turn that church into a symbol of cultural continuity. Here, it appeared, was history as a process of sedimentation, an apparently uninterrupted and gentle shift from rustic antiquity to urban modernity. In the center of the contemporary city stood a building from the distant past, unchanged and unconcerned. A closer look, however, suggested a different relationship between the past and the present. For this Byzantine church was almost entirely constructed out of borrowed fragments. Fragments that had been borrowed, that is, and never returned: pieces taken from Roman temples, perhaps dismantled for that very purpose, perhaps already in ruins. That the bric-à-brac of this Christian house of worship were pieces from the pagan past may have been irrelevant, or it may have been a way of adding classical prestige to it. Perhaps it is more likely that the Byzantine builders simply grafted their church out of whatever elements lay at hand. That, too, is an image of how history has always worked. A *New York Times* article by John Tauranac, "Lost New York, Found in Architecture's Crannies," points out the number of architectural landmarks in that city that have been recycled out of the detritus of structures no longer standing. During the nineteenth century, according to Tauranac, "a movement of architectural salvage took hold":

Odd bits and pieces of the older structures — gates, railings, sculpture panels, statues, columns, even whole walls — were saved from the wrecker's ball and incorporated in new designs, usually to preserve links with the past, but also frequently to save money. A result is a city rich in architectural salvage, with fragments of buildings grafted onto others or standing alone, offering a glimpse of what otherwise might have been lost to history. (1999)

Literary history, too, is a continual process of salvage and wreckage. For the authors discussed in this book, as for the architects who set out to rebuild New York, graft has always been a way to preserve links with the past *and* a way to save money. Why not profit from the past, after all, while one is busy saving it?

In short, *Grafting Helen* is a study of the way in which the present continually profits from, and remakes itself out of, the pieces of the past. This is not a process, to speak figuratively, that takes place openly, in the light of day. The mechanisms for recuperating the past are the rules and rituals of a vast underground economy. Those mechanisms of recuperation — rhetorical strategies, or tropes — are all forms of graft. Each chapter in this book has attempted to expose the operation of a particular species of graft, from mimesis to deixis, from idolatry to prostitution. Meanwhile the official business of culture is conducted as it has always been, by way of faith, really, in another series of powerful and inscrutable tropes: influence, reception, origination, tradition. These are the laws and limitations of the economy of continuity and classicism.

Classicism is the particular cultural system in which *Grafting Helen* is interested. It is the privileged rhetorical language for describing cultural origins in the West. How, then, to begin the task of describing that system, in fact a complex and protracted form of cultural embezzlement? By way of a particular species of currency. No coin in the realm has been more valuable, more circulated, more coveted, more counterfeited, than the one that bears the face of Helen of Troy. Helen is this study's emblem, then, for the past as something valuable: something to be stolen, appropriated, imitated, extorted, and, again, coveted. That we covet the past — and will do almost anything to make it ours — is the simple truth that this book tries to uncover. What do we covet? Anything we want, and anything we do not have. That is why Helen is such a powerful device for understanding cultural history: she reminds us that that history is a love story, a tale of desire, jealousy, abandonment, fidelity, abduction. Our relationship to the past, I am saying, is not *like* the act of coveting: it *is* an act of coveting. It relies on the same strategies, the same defenses, the same denials, the same delusions.

It will be noticed that it is impossible to describe what *graft* means without resorting to analogies: architectural thefts, erotic pursuits, covert financial dealings, gardening, genealogy, and medical experiments, to name just a few that figure prominently here. But it should also be stressed that these are not *just* metaphors: they are specific examples, in different cultural registers, of the literal mechanism of graft. As I point out in the preface, it is the nature of graft always to bridge the specific and the general, the literal and the metaphorical, because its structure both figures and maps out—literally—the operation of metaphor itself. Graft is a metaphor, but not only a metaphor, for metaphor. Is a metaphor for metaphor a metaphor? Yes and no. This contradiction helps to explain why graft has an almost unlimited range of applications without ever losing its specificity and hermeneutic power. It is a very simple concept, but one, I would argue, that radically alters the way we look at cultural identity and cultural productivity. With regard to literary studies, it is a concept pervasive and flexible enough to function as a truly interdisciplinary instrument, shedding light on issues of imitation and intertextuality in fields as disparate as ancient Greek and modern French poetry.

It should be obvious by now that in *Grafting Helen* I try to show that those fields are not as disparate as we may have thought. (The rhetorical maneuvers executed by Giraudoux in *La guerre de Troie n'aura pas lieu* may have something to teach us about Euripides' manipulation of Homeric motifs in the *Helen,* and vice versa.) Let me say a word about those fields. Part 1 focuses on Homeric epic and the post-Homeric lyrical and rhetorical tradition in Classical Greece. It is only fair to say that Homer, as much as Helen, is the privileged currency in this section. Part 1 is the attempt to trace the mechanisms for saving, stealing, or counterfeiting the Homeric. Homer is the great stock for Greek and Latin antiquity, endlessly transplanted, sutured, and cloned. It would be naïve, however, to assume that the Homeric texts themselves somehow precede these transactions and negotiations. Part 1 suggests that Helen in Homer and epic itself are already grafted composites. Indeed, the notion of meaning or identity as an essentially grafted hybrid challenges the very possibility of any simple origin, a moment prior to graft. These are all insights that, to some degree, classicists themselves have articulated. Recognizing this does not detract, I think, from what this section of *Grafting Helen* accomplishes. One of the things that part 1 tries to do is show that classicists interested in Homer and the survival of epic motifs in the post-Homeric world have long been practicing what is basically a theory of graft, without ever calling it that. Calling it that, however, has consequences: it leads us to the possibility that the relationship between Homer and the post-Homeric poets in the ancient world can serve as a model for a much larger and more pervasive cultural phenomenon.

Hence part 2 of *Grafting Helen.* Attacking the official economy of continuity, and specifically the rhetorical system of classicism that continues to dominate our culture today, meant looking at Helen as a currency transportable across cultural, linguistic, national, and historical boundaries. Thus in part 2 Greek antiquity itself becomes the new stock, endlessly appropriated, synthesized, embraced, or rejected by European vernacular literatures. France seemed an ideal setting on which to focus, since from the early medieval era it had always defined itself as the privileged scion of the Greco-Roman past. Every European nation, of course, at one time or another identified itself in these terms. It is clear, however, that in no European nation is the problem of cultural exile and imitation more intensely felt or more powerfully articulated. It certainly would have been possible to write a different book focusing, for example, on Helen in Germany, or England, or Modern Greece, or the United States—and most of these cultures do play a significant role in *Grafting Helen* (for example, see the discussion in chapter 11 on Helen in *Faust* II and the exchange value of Goethe's poem in France; meanwhile, "Prosthesis" only begins to suggest how much Modern Greek literature has to tell us about the rhetorical operations of graft). One wonders what kinds of literary economies these books would reveal. Would different types of graft emerge, different mechanisms for restoring or rejecting the past? It is certain that they would.

Given its more detailed and accessible historical content, what part 2 allows us to see that part 1 could not clearly show is the extent to which cultural identity, beyond any literary formulations of or contributions to that identity, is rooted, so to speak, in graft. Benoît de Sainte-Maure's *Le roman de Troie,* Ronsard's *Sonets pour Helene,* and Nerval's translation of Goethe's *Faust* are more than acts of poetic emulation or competition: they are political gestures and affirmations of national identity. The sixteenth-century humanist's fervent faith in imitation, the eighteenth-century folklorist's search for a pure cultural language, and the nineteenth-century xenophobe's fear of cultural miscegenation all depend, in different ways, on the rhetorical manipulation of graft. A study of eugenics in Nazi Germany in relation to the rhetorical strategies of graft and the cultural prestige attached to classicism might have a great deal to offer. More recent news of "ethnic cleansing" in Bosnia would seem to make such a study all the more urgent. One could argue that the model of cultural survival advanced in *Grafting Helen* is peculiarly relevant to our contemporary world.

Transplantations: Fantasies and Facts

More and more we are living in a grafted world, with grafted identities. One might look at the case of Clint Hallam of Australia, who appears to be the first man with a successfully transplanted hand. Hallam, who lost his right arm in an accident in 1989, received a new one from an anonymous donor in an operation that took place in France in 1998. In an article in the *New York Times* dated September 25 of that year ("Surgeons in France Try Hand Transplant"), Lawrence K. Altman reports that "it will be some time before they can say the operation is a success. If the grafted hand takes, weeks must pass before doctors can tell how well it functions. . . . Failure of nerves to regenerate sufficiently . . . would leave the grafted hand a useless body part." In the meantime Hallam will depend on antirejection drugs that "suppress the immune system, leaving him vulnerable to infection, disease and perhaps serious reactions to the drugs themselves, which must be taken indefinitely." In an inset box a "Primer" with an illustration of a cross-section of the wrist and the subtitle "A Tangled Web to Weave" informs us: "Attaching all the necessary nerves, blood vessels, tendons, muscles, skin and bones in the hand is a daunting task, but suppressing the body's possible rejection of the various tissues of the donated hand is the procedure's greatest difficulty." Both the subtitle and the lesson that follows begin to spell out the narrative or textual implications of the operation in question. The objective of grafting here is what it has always been: that of suturing a new and seamless identity out of hybrid elements. The fears, too, are by now familiar cultural anxieties: that the foreign will fail to assimilate, or be expelled from the body (politic or proper), or even corrupt and destroy it.

A followup piece by the same author "The Patient's New Hand Is Doing Well in France," (October 16, 1998) focuses less on the medical details and more on the "human interest" aspects of the operation. The fantasies and fears that remained submerged in the previous article are free now to rise to the surface. Those fears and fantasies have been, to a large extent, the subject of this book. Literature, I have tried to show by way of Helen, is the continual record of those fears and fantasies, and the continual effort to forget or disguise them. The new article on Hallam begins with a "hook" that leaves no doubt as to the real story here: the loss of human identity as something whole and coherent: "The world's only person with somebody else's fingerprints is expected to leave a French hospital today with the transplanted hand and forearm he received there three weeks ago." A few paragraphs later Altman returns to the same conceit: "Mr. Hallam, 48, now has two sets of fingerprints—one he was born with, the other from the anonymous donor. Asked how it felt to have someone else's arm, Mr. Hallam said, 'It's my arm, not someone else's arm.' When asked "if the new hand felt like his own," Mr. Hallam replies " 'of course it does.' " Clint Hallam's insistence on appropriating for himself what formerly belonged to someone else is understandable, but also culturally sanctioned.

The rest of the October 16 story dwells on the implications of the transplantation for law enforcement. It turns out that Mr. Hallam, introduced in the previous article simply as a "businessman," is facing criminal charges in Perth—for committing corporate fraud. What better candidate to receive the benefits of graft than a man who is guilty of practicing it? Details such as these make the urge to turn Clint Hallam's story into emblem or allegory irresistible. They are not simply coincidences, however. The fact is that the operations of graft are so culturally pervasive on every level that events themselves are always tied to them. Graft always precedes those events, structuring the way we think about them or have come even to know them. Allegory becomes inevitable, and, with it, irony. Thus five months after Clint Hallam's pioneer hand-transplant, a similar operation takes place for the first time in the United States. Matthew Scott, who lost his hand in an accident in 1985, receives a new hand in an operation in Louisville, Kentucky. What he did not know at the time of the operation, according to Ian Markham-Smith writing in London's *Independent,* is that "the previous owner murdered a man and killed himself" (February 1999). The man in question is Glenn Johnson, and he indeed appears to have served nine years in prison for shooting a man in a bar. Just in case the connection between fact and fantasy is not clear enough, a member of Johnson's family is quoted as remarking after the operation: "It's like that movie (*The Hand,* starring Michael Caine) where the murderer's hand goes around killing people." In the movie in question, the protagonist loses his hand in a traffic accident. But the errant appendage appears to have a mind of its own, or the mind of its previous owner, a psychopathic killer. Caine—or the hand, it is not clear which—embarks upon a series of grisly murders.

I have spoken of certain cultural fears and fantasies embedded in the story of Hallam's transplanted hand. That these are truly cultural fears and fantasies becomes clear when one considers the number of popular fictions and films that, long before Clint Hallam and Matthew Scott, imagined their operations in various nightmarish scenarios: *Body Parts* (1991, directed by Eric Red), *The Fly* (1986, directed by David Cronenberg), and *The Hand* (1981, directed by Oliver Stone), just to name a few recent films that come immediately to mind. All of them rely on the same central conceit: the foreign parasite invading or attaching itself to the body, fusing with the host, controlling it, consuming it, or becoming it. Imitation and graft are perhaps the dominating principles at work in the horror genre or the monster film. This is very clear in *The Thing* (1982, directed by John Carpenter). The Thing is a being—a foreign being, of course, extraterrestrial in origin—without an identity proper to itself. It is, instead, a perfect imitation of whatever organism it consumes. At critical moments the disguise is dropped, and The Thing shows itself. There is, however, no Thing-in-itself.

What we see when we do see The Thing is the grafted composite of all of its victims: the body of a woman, the face of a man, the head of a dog.

John Carpenter's *The Thing*—which is itself an imitation of a 1951 film with the same title directed by Christian Nyby and Howard Hawks—suggests the extent to which contemporary horror films have also become technological thrillers. Technology is, in one way or another, the central force in these films in terms of both subject matter (science is a force that simulates nature, or corrupts it) and production (movies are ultimately about their own special effects). The contemporary techno-thriller, in other words, is as much about graft as its performance. This is also one reason why so many recent techno-thrillers are themselves remakes of earlier models, or grafts of multiple models. The best example may be Cronenberg's remake of *The Fly*. In the original (1958, directed by Kurt Neumann), the unfortunate Vincent Price is split into two almost comically literal hybrids, a man with the head of a fly and, as we might expect, a fly with the head of a man. The new version takes advantage, in both its plot and its production, of new technologies. Jeff Goldblum is now the victim of an experiment in genetic splicing gone awry, a hybrid being, half man and half fly. Grafting occurs here on the molecular level, so that the very principle of identity itself is compromised. Graft here is represented, notably, as a disease, a progressive mutation or corruption of the body and the mind, something that suggests the national trauma of AIDS.

Much of the enormous popularity of the television show *The X-Files* rests on its exploitation of these contemporary anxieties. In the double episode aired February 7 and 14, 1999, scientists succeed in creating a human–alien hybrid (fused on the genetic level), the first of a new species that will survive the coming alien plague, the "Black Virus." We live, indeed, in the Age of Graft. Virology, parasitology, genetic splicing, cloning, transplantation, exobiology, artificial intelligence, and cybernetics have all begun to alter the way we think about human identity. The particular type of cell that can be isolated from the body and cloned is called a *stem cell*. The self has become defined as that which can be—or already is—grafted. (One of the most common motifs in the alien fantasy genre is the realization that we are the aliens.)

Some will have begun to feel that graft is by now in danger of losing whatever specificity it might have had to begin with. At the risk of repeating myself, I stress again that this view underestimates the peculiar structure and strength of graft as an interpretive instrument. That structure is, I have suggested, that of metaphor itself: the linkage of any term *a* to term *b*, or the transference of meaning from term *a* to term *b*, or the dissolving of term *a* into term *b* (or term *b* into term *a*), or the application of term *a* to term *b*. To say that graft can be *applied* to a particular object is simply to describe the mechanism of graft itself. To use *graft* is to graft it to something. An example of this principle can be found in William Safire's "On Language" column for the *New York Times Sunday Maga-*

zine, in an article on the terminology of cloning ("Clone, Clone, Clone, Clone," April 6, 1997). "Clone," Safire asserts, which comes from a word for "twig" and which originally meant any "group of cells or organisms produced asexually from a single sexually produced ancestor," has suffered a degree of inflation in its current usage. By now it has come to mean simply "imitation" (1997:18). That inflation, I have been suggesting, is typical of graft and words in the graft family. Thus Safire notes that the word *clone* "has already grafted its way into political metaphor" (and an illustration follows: "Britain's Tony Blair is a Bill Clinton *clone*"). That phrase itself is, of course, a metaphor, and an example of graft. But all metaphor, political or otherwise, is itself a form of graft. And when Safire concludes, "Asexual propagation or political metaphor: it's all the same thing," there is a sense in which it *is* the same thing, and in which saying that may allow us to see something significant.

Helen as Frankenstein's Monster

Science today, it would appear, is simply catching up to our favorite metaphors. An article by John Lichfield in London's *Independent* on Hallam's operation begins with a phrase that is itself a graft of two cultural icons: "In a hospital in Lyons on Wednesday, Frankenstein met the Bionic Man" (Lichfield 1999:5). Hallam, third in this series, is the new grafted man (and a graft of the first two). In order to say a word about Frankenstein and the Bionic Man in relation to Helen, I need to return for a moment to the figure of Zeuxis, the mythical artist who painted the likeness of Helen of Troy. Cicero, we remember, turned Zeuxis into a paradigm of the ideal artist inventing the beautiful by imitating, gathering, and conjoining what lies scattered in nature. The story of Zeuxis, we saw, is an *ars poetica,* and one that informs later statements of artistic method from the Renaissance humanists onward. Art, that story suggests, is something artificial masquerading as the real, something unnatural simulating nature.

But Cicero's Zeuxis finds perhaps his most devoted adept in the figure of Frankenstein. And Mary Shelley's *Frankenstein; or, The Modern Prometheus* is the most obvious and directly influential model for all of the fictionalizations of graft discussed above. Zeuxis epitomizes the work he is about to accomplish as "true beauty . . . transferred from the living model to the mute likeness" (Hubbell 1993:2.1–2). This mimetic transference from the living to the dead is the essential discovery of Frankenstein, who finds himself "capable of bestowing animation upon lifeless matter" (Shelley 1963:46). Zeuxis set out to paint the likeness not of any woman, but of Helen herself, "so that the portrait though silent and lifeless might embody the surpassing beauty of womanhood" (Hubbell 1993:2.1–2). Frankenstein decides to create not simply any creature, but man himself, and not any man, but a man of vast proportions, "of gigantic stature" (47). Zeuxis's Helen is fashioned out of the union of distinct elements, borrowed each from nature, each one beautiful in and of itself. Just so is Franken-stein's Monster fashioned. The crucial motif is that of collecting. Frankenstein begins his task "successfully collecting and arranging . . . materials" (47). "I pursued nature to her hiding-places," Frankenstein recalls, "I collected bones from charnel-houses and disturbed, with profane fingers, the tremendous se-crets of the human frame" (48). And just before the final infusion of life into "the lifeless thing," remembers Frankenstein, "I collected the instruments of life around me" (51).

The result of Frankenstein's labors is a creature of Zeuxian order:

> How can I delineate my emotions at this catastrophe, or how delineate the wretch whom with such infinite pains and care I had endeavored to form? His limbs were in propor-tion, and I had selected his features as beautiful. Beautiful!—Great God! His yellow skin scarcely covered the work of muscles and arteries beneath; his hair was of lustrous black, and flowing; his teeth of a pearly whiteness; but these luxuriances only formed a more horrid contrast with his watery eyes, that seemed of the same colour as the dun white sockets in which they were set, his shrivelled complexion and straight black lips. (51)

Frankenstein resorts, here, to the rhetoric of the *blason,* a description of the be-loved that moves, in list fashion, from one feature to the other. The inventory of the Monster contains, in fact, almost nothing but perfect elements, and yet the result of their union leaves the viewer speechless with terror. The nature of this terror, I think, has been misinterpreted. Frankenstein's horror before the sight of his creation represents the fear, not of the grotesque or the hideous, but of the sublime, of the too-beautiful. Frankenstein's exclamation "Beautiful!— Great God!" is not, perhaps, inspired by the ironic realization of the failure of his project, but by the understanding, also ironic, that he has succeeded all too well. Frankenstein's viewing of the Monster is an epiphany, the moment where he understands that *this is what the beautiful is.* The Monster is horrifying not because he is hideous, but because he is perfectly beautiful. The perfectly beautiful is, and has always been, the unnatural and the monstrous. (It is also the feminine. Shelley's Monster suggests an inversion of the traditional gen-der paradigm: a Pygmalion falling in love with a male simulacrum. My analy-sis here joins Sandra Gilbert and Susan Gubar's discussion of Shelley's novel in *The Madwoman in the Attic* as a Romantic reading of *Paradise Lost,* one that reveals "hell's creations as monstrous imitations of heaven's creations, and hellish femaleness as a grotesque parody of heavenly maleness" [1979:221]. In my discussion, however, it is not so much a parody as a perfect literalization of the beautiful that we witness in the Monster.) Frankenstein's horror before the vision of the Monster is comparable only to the terror of the Trojan elders before the perfect face of Helen as she appears on the walls of Troy in *Iliad* 3. If Frankenstein is the Modern Prometheus, than his Monster is the Modern Helen.

What is interesting about these fantastic and grotesque narratives of simulation, body-snatching, cannibalism, and graft that emulate (or steal from) the story of Frankenstein is that they are neither fantastic nor grotesque. They are simply literal representations of standard cultural mechanisms for keeping the past alive. They are allegories, crudely realized, of the covert violence constitutive of cultural imitation. That imitation is always a form of graft, the past embezzled and smuggled by the present. Derrida refers to the imitation as a *surjet,* a seam, an overlapping, an overgrowth. In this sense the monster is always a *surjet.* The monster in its mythic form is, more often than not, a graft: a chimera, a griffon, a sphinx, a centaur. It is in the nature of poetry, perhaps, to be monstrous, to be improper. This impropriety, like that of the monster, is always erotic in nature. All of the monsters listed above are also, explicitly or implicitly, sexual predators, seducing, embracing, consuming their victims. The most terrifying of all is Helen herself.

This book has been an effort to show that the story of this monster is the story of cultural survival itself. Thomas Greene has described the pathos of sixteenth-century humanism in its "veerings towards or away from understanding the paradoxical status of the model, at once alien and accessible, separated from the imitator by a cultural divide and yet capable of partial contact" (1982:171). The past as alien: it sounds like science fiction, but it is also simply history. The authors we have read all struggle, in one way or another, with this paradox, seeking both to return to the past and to surpass it, to repeat and reinvent it, preserve it, destroy it, banish it, replace it, be it. Is there not something monstrous about this process? The authors in this study are not just mad scientists; they are also lovers wavering between aggressive desire and chaste adoration, rejection and reverence, violence and idolatry, love and hatred. This hatred and this love are rarely spoken aloud, but are articulated indirectly, neurotically, in circumlocution, metaphor, myth, so many rhetorical ruses. *Grafting Helen* is a study of those rhetorical ruses.

Helen as Phantom

Transplantations. Prostheses. Heterografts, homografts, autografts, and xenografts. Alien–human hybrids. Cyborgs. Of course these are only metaphors for poetry. If culture, this book has been suggesting, is always wounded — mutilated, amputated, and incomplete — then poetry is the way culture seeks to mend or restore itself, over and over again. But the past cannot really be brought back to life. The damage has been done (it has always already been done). We remain incomplete, the past torn from us. The past we salvage and attempt to restore to ourselves is only a fiction, or a *phantom.* Here is Oliver Sacks's definition of that term in its neurological sense in *The Man Who Mistook His Wife for a Hat:*

A "phantom" . . . is a persistent image or memory of part of the body, usually a limb, for months or years after its loss. Known in antiquity, phantoms were described and explored in great detail by the American neurologist Silas Weir Mitchell, during and following the Civil War. Weir Mitchell described several *sorts* of phantom—some strangely ghost-like and unreal . . . some compellingly, even dangerously, life-like and real; some intensely painful, others (most) quite painless; some photographically foreshortened or distorted . . . as well as "negative phantoms" or "phantoms of absence." (1987: 66)

We return, in the end, to Helen as *eidolon.* All of the Helens we have encountered in this study have been phantoms of one kind or another, prostheses for something that we lost a long time ago.

Supplement

"The world's first recipient of a hand transplant has had the hand amputated at his request, the surgeon who performed both operations said. Clint Hallam, a 50-year-old New Zealander, received the new hand in an operation in September 1998.

"Today, the surgeon, Dr. Nadey Hakim of St. Mary's Hospital in London, said he had amputated Mr. Hallam's right hand in a 90-minute operation on Friday evening at an unidentified private hospital in London."

"Transplanted Hand Amputated," *New York Times,* February 4, 2001, Sunday

Notes
Bibliography
Acknowledgments
Index

Notes

Preface

1. In its emphasis upon imitation and the humanist tradition, *Grafting Helen* is indebted above all to Thomas Greene's *The Light in Troy* (1982) as well as other works in medieval and early modern studies: Thomas Cave's *The Cornucopian Text* (1979), Margaret Ferguson's *Trials of Desire* (1983), David Quint's *Origin and Originality* (1983).

2. In this respect *Grafting Helen* resembles a number of works that have followed specific mythic figures as recurrent tropes in humanist writings: John Hollander's *The Figure of Echo* (1981), Stephanie Jed's *Chaste Thinking: The Rape of Lucretia and the Birth of Humanism* (1989), and Leonard Barkan's *Transuming Passions: Ganymede and the Erotics of Humanism* (1991).

3. The historian, Hayden White has argued, "serves no one well by constructing a specious continuity between the present world and that which preceded it. . . . we require a history that will educate us to discontinuity" (1966:134). *Grafting Helen* tries to be such a history. As such it reopens Paul de Man's discussion of modernity as trope in *Blindness and Insight* (1971) and other works.

4. *Grafting Helen* seeks to participate in what Jonathan Arac calls the "most urgent agenda for contemporary literary theory," the forging of a "new literary history": "From Frederic Jameson's slogan, 'always historicize,' to Michel Foucault's 'genealogies,' to the critiques of traditional (teleological, periodizing, objectifying) historiography by Jacques Derrida, Paul de Man, and Hayden White, to British 'historical materialism' and American New Historicism, this is the message" (quoted in Hays 1992:82).

5. The *teichoskopia* is, as Norman Austin puts it, the "*locus classicus* for the traditional Helen portrait" (1994:17).

6. As in Clader 1976, Suzuki 1989, and Austin 1994.

7. One might compare these strategies to Harold Bloom's revisionary ratios in *The Anxiety of Influence* (1973), defenses against the inevitable priority of the past. Both suggest a vision of history as repressed and recurrent *agon*. For Bloom, however, that *agon* is a psychological affair, a struggle between poets, while I see it as a textual affair, a struggle between poems.

8. The stock is: "a living plant or portion of a plant (as a root) designed or prepared for union with a scion in grafting . . . the original (as a man, a race, or a language) from which others have descended . . . a race, subrace . . . a sum of money . . . capital for in-

vestment . . . principal as distinguished from interest . . . property that produces income" (Gove 1963).

9. A number of earlier studies have focused on the figure of Helen of Troy in antiquity: Funck–Brentano 1935, Clota 1957, Lindsay 1974, Becker 1894. Others are surveys of the myth from antiquity to modernity: Oswald 1905, Newman 1968.

10. Culler cites the same passage in *On Deconstruction* and remarks: "What would such a treatise describe? It would treat discourse as the product of various sorts of combinations or insertions. . . . The fact that one has only the vaguest ideas of how to organize a typology of grafts indicates the novelty of this perspective" (1982:135).

11. Thus *Grafting Helen* is what Barbara Johnson (1987:116) calls an *intertextuality study* as opposed to a *source study,* the former emphasizing misreadings and violations, the second speaking in terms of legal transfers and borrowings.

Chapter 1. Mimesis

1. On Helen's undecidability, see also Austin 1975, duBois 1978, and Zeitlin 1996.

2. On Homeric epic as an oral-performative tradition with progressively authoritative claims to panhellenic status, see Nagy 1979 and 1990.

3. Bespaloff 1947:69 says of the elders at the Skaian gates: "They cannot help finding her beautiful. And this beauty frightens them like a bad omen, a warning of death."

4. Liddell and Scott and Stuart Jones 1940. All definitions of Greek terms come from this edition, unless otherwise stated. On the notion of terror as essential to *ainos,* see Devereux 1982. On *ainos* as a form of encoded speech with polyvalent significance in Archaic lyric and epic, see Nagy 1990:427ff.

5. All translations of the *Iliad* are taken from this edition unless otherwise stated.

6. For example Bergren 1979. See also Samuel Butler's 1922 work *The Authoress of the Odyssey* (Butler 1967). Robert Graves, on the other hand, wrote a novel, *Homer's Daughter* (1955b), with the premise that the author of the *Odyssey* is Nausikaa.

7. See Clader 1976:6–11 on Helen as a weaving poet in *Iliad* 3, and Miller 1986 on images of spinning and weaving as displaced mechanisms of feminine writing. Helen is also spinning in *Odyssey* 4. On the connections between Helen and Artemis, a goddess associated with spinning, see Scott 1913b. Note that in Helen's encounter with Aphrodite (her divine patroness/nemesis) in *Iliad* 3, the goddess assumes the guise of a spinning woman. See also Reckford 1964.

8. Philomela's embroidery is one important example of writing coming to substitute for the voice which has been rendered silent (in this case by Tereus, who has brutally raped Philomela and torn out her tongue). For Philomela, as for Helen (and also Arachne and Penelope), weaving is a defense against erotic violence.

9. Critics of the *Iliad* have long pointed out the anachronistic awkwardness of having Helen identify enemies Priam has been facing for some nine years now. See Ameis and Hentze 1887:163–70, Scott 1913b, Bowra 1930:110–13, Vivante 1970:147–48, Kakridis 1971:32, Kirk 1978:18–40.

10. Auerbach on Homer here sounds remarkably like the critics of medieval poets and historians I discuss in chapters 7 and 8.

11. See, for example, Derrida 1972a:203.

12. See Bespaloff 1947:66: "The Helen the two armies are contending for will never

be Paris' any more than she has been Menelaus'; the Trojans cannot own her any more than the Greeks could. Beauty, captured, remains elusive."

13. See Lefkowitz 1990:24.

14. All translations from the *Catalogues* are taken from this edition unless otherwise stated.

15. We may also note that in the *teichoskopia* "proper," Priam and Helen discuss Agamemnon, Odysseus, and Aias, but never Menelaus. Helen speaks of Menelaus only as a figure from her former, Spartan existence, while the real Menelaus stands on the plains below, about to fight to retrieve that existence. Note that Helen's assignation with Paris has its own pre-texts, too. Owen 1966:35 suggests that it "pictures, as it were, the original seduction of Helen with the necessary adjustment to present circumstances."

16. Carson 1986:4–5 sees Aphrodite's threat as the very paradigm of erotic paradox.

17. Calhoun 1937:24 suggests that Homer gives Aphrodite such prominence in *Iliad* 3 "because she so admirably personifies the warring emotions that end in Helen's reluctant compliance with her paramour's desire." Much has been written on the mutually exchangeable roles played by Helen and Aphrodite. Calhoun again writes of the latter: "She is at once the divine entourage, the personification of the impulses that jar and clash in Helen's bosom, and an actor in the drama who follows her own purposes" (24). Vernant 1965:37 writes: "In the double of the woman loved, under the seductive mask of Aphrodite, it is the unobtainable Persephone who appears" ("Dans le double de la femme aimée [Helen] sous le masque séducteur d'Aphrodite, c'est l'insaisissable Perséphone qui transparaît").

18. On Helen's "first" abduction by Theseus, see Devereux 1982:37–38.

19. Wilcock 1976:41 argues: "It seems likely that Homer or a predecessor, choosing at random from the epic stock a name for the handmaid of Helen, chanced to hit on 'Aithra, daughter of Pittheus'; the explanatory legend then arose through attempts of poets and mythologists to integrate the awkward detail into the total picture." But there is no evidence ruling out the existence of competing myths regarding Helen's various abductions. Homeric epic tends to accommodate conflicting myths without eliminating them.

20. On the cult of Helen see Nilsson 1932, Clader 1976, and Burkert 1985.

21. All citations from Herodotus are taken from this translation, unless otherwise stated.

22. Bowra 1930:5, among others, points out Zeus's reference to this "first" siege of Troy by Heracles in *Odyssey* 25.

23. In support of this idea, Nagy 1979:25 cites the reference to the quarrel (*neîkos*) between Odysseus and Achilles in the song of Demodokus in *Odyssey* 8.72–82: "The reference to Achilles and Odysseus as the 'best of the Achaeans' at 8.78 may have served to reveal that the poetic repertory of Demodokus is in control of two distinct themes that permeate the *Iliad* and the *Odyssey*—themes that define the central hero of each epic."

24. This is the thesis of Austin 1994, the authoritative work on the tradition of the *eidolon:* "The Homer whose works we possess, and sometimes read, is but the *eidolon* that the gods fashioned to pass for the real Homer." That Homer is another Helen *eidolon* for Western culture is, in large measure, the central thesis of the present study.

25. See Page 1962:fr. 192. However, Lycophron (622.i.71 Scheer; paraphrased in West 1967:fr. 358) claims that Hesiod was the first to sing of Helen as *eidolon*.

26. All translations of the *Agamemnon* are taken from this edition unless otherwise stated.

27. A moment later, in their greeting to Agamemnon, the chorus chastises their king in these terms: "when you marshalled this armament / for Helen's sake, I will not hide it, / in ugly style you were written in my heart / for *steering aslant* the mind's course / to bring home by blood / sacrifice and dead men that wild spirit" (799–804; my italics).

28. It may also remind us of the Bloomian scenario of the sublime confrontation between critic and unmasterable text, as treated by Culler 1981:110. Indeed, I treat the Trojan elders of the *teichoskopia* as literary critics in chapter 10.

29. All translations of the *Odyssey* are taken from this edition unless otherwise stated.

30. The back-and-forth between the literal and the figural is a recurrent motif in this study. In chapter 9, for example, we will see that grafting as a genealogical metaphor is both a metaphorical ideal for the emergent state of Burgundy in the fifteenth and sixteenth centuries and a literal political practice; in chapter 10 we will see that much of Ronsard's poetics is based upon this confusion of the figural and the literal; in chapter 12 we will witness this same confusion/conflation in Camus.

31. Trans. Jowett 1892. All translations of the *Cratylus* are taken from this edition.

32. This is a subject explored as well in Greene 1918.

33. Or the melody of a song. Music is approached in Plato as an imitation possessing moral consequences for the listener contingent upon what is being imitated (*Laws* 2.655bff., 7.812c).

34. All translations of the *Republic* are taken from this edition unless otherwise stated.

35. All translations of the *Sophist* are taken from this edition unless otherwise stated.

36. See Derrida 1972a:212–13. In "La double scéance" Derrida does not try to reduce Plato's theory of mimesis to eliminate contradiction but emphasizes the extent to which contradiction is built into the definition of imitation itself. Focusing upon the *Philebus* but including the whole of Plato's work in his field, Derrida suggests that at least two irreconcilable but simultaneous descriptions need to be applied to the imitation—a structure reminiscent of the *on the one hand / on the other hand* antinomy that is central to our discussion of Helen: (1) as a simple double of its model, the imitation is nothing in itself; ethically speaking, it is good if its model is good, bad if its model is bad; (2) the imitation *is* something, it exists, it is a supplement to its model; inferior to its model, at the same time it can replace it and is thus potentially superior to it.

37. For example, Greene 1918:55.

38. Given his earlier plays on the Trojan saga, all of which present Helen in a much less favorable light, Euripides' *Helen* functions in the manner of a Stesichorean recantation.

39. "If one accepts . . . that syntagmatic narratives are part of the same system as paradigmatic tropes . . . then the possibility arises that temporal articulations, such as narratives or histories, are a correlative of rhetoric and not the reverse. One would then have to conceive of a rhetoric of history prior to attempting a history of rhetoric or of literature or of literary criticism" (de Man 1978:30).

40. With commentary by O. B. Hardison. All translations of the *Poetics* are taken from this edition, unless otherwise stated. Citations from the original are from Else 1957.

41. De Man shows that Locke draws an explicit likeness between rhetorical language (by which Locke means principally metaphorical language) and an "improper" woman:

"It is clear that rhetoric is something one can decorously indulge in as long as one knows where it belongs. Like a woman, which it resembles . . . it is a fine thing as long as it is kept in its proper place. Out of place, among the affairs of men . . . it is a disruptive scandal" (de Man 1978:15–16).

42. Trans. J. H. Freese 1926. All translations of the *Rhetoric* are taken from this edition, unless otherwise stated. References to the original are from Else 1957.

43. W. R. Roberts in McKeon 1941 omits chapter 3.2–12; similarly Else 1957 leaves out chapters 21–23 and 25 of the *Poetics.*

44. Support for this statement can be found in Montmollin 1951, cited by Else 1957: 131n21. Montmollin suggests that b16, "inferring," συλλογίζεσθαι, from the passage in question in the *Poetics,* "implies the invention of the syllogism." Else is not so sure.

Chapter 2. Anamnesis

1. See Whitman 1958:249–50 on the various ways in which Homeric syntax may be said to be fractured.

2. This felicitous phrase was coined by W. R. Roberts, in his translation in McKeon 1941 of a similar passage from the *Rhetoric* (1371b4–11), treated below in this chapter.

3. A passage from Aristotle's *Memory and Reminiscence* (450a27–451a17) provides an interesting analogy: "A picture painted on a panel is at once a picture and a likeness: that is, while one and the same, it is both of these, although the 'being' of both is not the same, and one may contemplate it either as a picture or as a likeness" (trans. J. I. Beare, in McKeon 1941).

4. There are also striking parallels to the Nausikaa–Artemis analogy at *Odyssey* 6.101–9. See Pavlock 1990 on the Artemis metaphor in Homer, Apollonius, and Virgil. The choice of Artemis in Helen's description in *Odyssey* 4.123 could be further discussed; is the choice of the virgin goddess ironic or suggestive of a rehabilitated Helen? Artemis is, of course, another spinning goddess, armed, like Helen, with the distaff. See Anderson 1963:75 on the Helen–Artemis connection.

5. See Murnaghan 1987 and Lefkowitz 1990:136.

6. On the parallels linking Helen, Odysseus, and Penelope, see Anderson 1963, Devereux 1982, and Murnaghan 1987.

7. Zeitlin 1996:406 makes the same observation.

8. Zeitlin, among others, compares Helen's preternatural powers here to those of the Delian maidens in the *Homeric Hymn to Apollo* (154–64), a choral group able to imitate (*mimeisthai*) any human language or voice (Zeitlin 1996:409n51).

9. On this issue see Alexiou 1985.

10. On this ambiguity see Derrida 1972a:69–197.

11. This recalls Egyptian details mentioned earlier when Helen first enters with her serving women: "and Phylo brought the silver workbasket which had been given / by Alkandre, the wife of Polybos, who lived in Egyptian / Thebes, where the greatest number of goods are stored in the houses" (125–27). See also Menelaus's descriptions, in the same book, of his travels in Egypt on his way home from Troy.

12. In the words of her Phrygian slave, ll. 1380–433: "It happened that I, in Phrygian style, was wafting the breeze past Helen's curls with a round feather-fan, stationed before her face; and she the while, as eastern ladies use, was twisting flax on her distaff

with her fingers, but letting her yarn fall on the floor, for she was minded to embroider purple raiment as an offering from the Trojan spoils, a gift for Clytemnestra at her tomb" (trans. Coleridge in Oates and O'Neill 1938:155–56). Here weaving takes on an exotic and mysterious air. And indeed, Helen's miraculous escape from Orestes' sword is interpreted as an effect of sorcery: "but lo! she had vanished from the room, passing right through the house by magic spells or wizards' arts or heavenly fraud" (ll. 1489–514). Note that even here the authenticity of Helen's magic is questioned—is it real or a fraud?

Chapter 3. Supplement

1. This is a point made by Norman Austin in *Helen of Troy and Her Shameless Phantom* (1994), the essential work on the figure of the *eidolon*. On the theme of the *eidolon*, see also Kannicht 1969:26–41 and Bassi 1993. All three authors provide extensive bibliographies on the subject.

2. On the speeches and style of Lysias (ca. 459–ca. 380), see Jebb 1962, 1:158–316. At least two characteristics of Lysias's style, as presented by Jebb, are relevant to our discussion of the *Phaedrus*. The first is artifice and concealment, for Lysias tends to write in the "plain style," argues Jebb; "the plain style may . . . employ the utmost efforts of art, but the art is concealed" (1:172). The second is rhetoric as aural and optical illusion: "Vividness, ἐνάργεια— 'the power of bringing under the senses what is narrated'—is an attribute of the style of Lysias. The dullest hearer cannot fail to have before his eyes the scene described, and to fancy himself actually in presence of the persons introduced as speaking." (172) These are exactly the effects Socrates most strongly fears in the *Republic*.

3. All citations and translations from the *Phaedrus* are from this edition. See also 227c2: "But when the one in love with speeches (*logoi*) asked him to speak, he put on a pose, as if not eager to speak."

4. Cf. Mackenzie 1982:66, "Running through the work is the motif of madness and possession."

5. Roberts's appreciation of this *apparently* tranquil landscape is typical: "There is in all Plato no dialogue of greater grace and loveliness than that in which Socrates makes his way along the Illisus towards the plane-tree" (1928:8).

6. These nymphs, seductive yet potentially dangerous (think of Hylas, drowned and abducted by amorous naiads), will continue to haunt the *Phaedrus;* later we will see Socrates himself possessed by them. At 238d Socrates says: "For the spot seems really to be a divine one, so that if perhaps I become possessed by nymphs as my speech proceeds, do not be surprised." Achelous, meanwhile, recalls the figure of the savage river-god who wrestled Heracles for the hand of Deianeira; a figure, like Proteus, of elusive identity, with the power to transform himself into multiple forms. For the Achelous myth, see Ovid, *Metamorphoses* 9.1–100.

7. See Rowe 1986 on b2ff.

8. Graves 1955a, 1:365. The ode on Helen from the *Agamemnon* associates, as we saw in chapter 1, the arrival of Helen at Troy with the onset of the west wind (l. 692).

9. See 231d2–4: "For they themselves agree that they are sick rather than in their right

mind [ὁμολογοῦσι νοσεῖν μᾶλλον ἢ σωφρονεῖν], and that they know that they are out of their mind [κακῶς φρονοῦσιν], but cannot control themselves."

10. Note Rowe's succinct commentary on d5: "The metaphors are not by any means as dead as in our use of ecstatic." *Ecstatic* comes from the verb ἐξίστημι to *put out of place,* to *de-range.*

11. Carson 1986:123 points out the rhetorical-erotic coincidences of the first half of the *Phaedrus:* "Phaedrus is in love with a text composed by the sophist Lysias. It is an 'erotic *logos*' (227c), the written version of a speech delivered by Lysias on the subject of love. Its thesis is a deliberately repugnant one. Lysias argues that a beautiful boy would do better to bestow his favors on a man who is *not* in love with him than on a man who is in love with him, and he enumerates the ways in which a nonlover is preferable to a lover as an erotic partner. Desire stirs Phaedrus when he gazes at the words of this text (*epethumei*, 228b), and visible joy animates him as he reads it aloud to Sokrates (234d). Phaedrus treats the text as if it were his *paidika* or beloved boy, Sokrates observes (236b), and uses it as a tool of seduction, to draw Sokrates beyond the city limits for an orgy of reading in the open countryside (230d–e; cf. 234d)." What is not pointed out in these passages, however, is the recurrent motif of violent eroticism, the interplay of rhetorical possession and erotic possession, the difficulty of separating persuasion, seduction, and abduction.

12. This conjunction of rhetorical persuasion and compulsion recurs in the *Phaedrus.* Later, before Socrates begins his second speech, Phaedrus informs him (243d8–10): "Once you have given your praise of the lover, there will be every necessity for Lysias to be compelled by me to write a speech in his turn on the same subject."

13. Indeed, the notion of play is a serious one here. Socrates is clearly making fun of Phaedrus on several occasions; his statements professing oracular inspiration are clearly ironic—and yet, it is far from clear that there is not something less frivolous beneath the surface of fun and games (as, for that matter, in Euripides' parodic *Helen*). Here is the passage that leads to the pun at 238c: "the irrational desire which has gained control over judgement which urges a man towards the right, borne towards pleasure in beauty, and which is forcefully reinforced by the desires related to it in its pursuit of bodily beauty, overcoming them in its course, and takes its name from its very force (*rhome*)—this is called love (*eros*)."

14. Rowe 1986 notes in regard to c9–d2 that Aristotle employs *numpholeptos* regularly as a term for possession or madness.

15. See Rowe 1986 on 241b4.

16. To love is thus to worship an idol, a metaphoric substitute for the real: "So each selects his love from the ranks of the beautiful according to his own disposition, and fashions and adorns him like a statue, as if he were himself his god, in order to honour him and celebrate his mystic rites" (252d5–253b7).

17. Hamilton 1951:20–21 compares the myth of the *Phaedrus* to Diotima's speech in the *Symposium,* where Plato makes love into a link between the sensible world and the world of the Forms.

18. "Now in the case of gods," Socrates informs us, "horses and charioteers are all both good and of good stock [ἀγαθοὶ καὶ ἐξ ἀγαθῶν, good and from the good]; whereas in the case of the rest there is a mixture [μέμεικται]" (246a8–b1).

19. Cf. 265c. Rowe 1986 comments extensively upon this ambiguity in his reading of *Phaedrus* c10–d6.

20. Trans. Page 1955b. All citations from Sappho are taken from this edition unless otherwise stated.

21. Hoerber 1958, like Carson 1986, tries to have it both ways, reading the *Phaedrus* as a dialogue about rhetoric and about eros.

22. See Jaeger 1944:188, whose paraphrases of Plato are helpful: "Ultimately, it consists in the ability to compare everything with everything else. . . . The process of proof used by rhetors is mainly the demonstration of resemblances. . . . To define anything, we must know what it is like and what it is not like."

23. 262d1–8: "What is more, by some chance — so it seems — the two speeches which were given do have in them an example of how someone who knows the truth can mislead his audience by making play in what he says [*logoi*]."

24. See Jaeger 1944:188–89: "Now, if we assume that the purpose of rhetoric is to deceive the audience — to lead them to false conclusions by resemblances alone — that makes it imperative for the orator to have exact knowledge of the dialectical method of classification."

25. Carson 1986:171 writes: "In any act of thinking, the mind must reach across this space between known and unknown, linking one to another but also keeping visible their difference. It is an erotic space. To reach across it is tricky; a kind of stereoscopy seems required."

26. See, for example, Roberts 1928:9; also Derrida 1972a:69–198.

27. Carson 1986:166 goes so far as to say: "The *Phaedrus* is a written dialogue that ends by discrediting written dialogues. This fact does not cease to charm its readers. Indeed, it is the fundamental erotic feature of this *erotikos logos.*"

28. Here is how Mackenzie 1982:65 expresses that antinomy in "Paradox in Plato's 'Phaedrus' ": "At 277e7 Socrates says 'No λόγος has ever been written, whether in verse or in prose,' which is worthy of great attention.' . . . 'Socrates' says it; but Plato writes it. If he writes to convince, he writes that writing should not convince us; if what he writes does convince us, it convinces us that it should not convince us." Mackenzie refers to the paradox of dialectic as "the irrational erotics of antilogic."

29. Here I am paraphrasing Roman Jakobson's *poetic principle,* which would thus appear to be a way of linking poetry to dialectic. See Jakobson 1987:71.

30. Burnett 1960:155 summarizes the current philosophical debates on the status of the image that served as backdrop to both Plato's dialogues and Euripides' drama. Regarding Helen and Menelaus's reunion, and specifically line 557 ("Who are you, whose face am I looking on," τίς εἶ; τίν' ὄψιν σήν [. . .] προσδέρκομαι), Burnett writes: "Not only have pathos and melodrama mixed in the scene, but with the double word *opsis,* which makes of Helen's face an apparition and suggests that the eye may report an illusion, the philosophical game is renewed." Segal 1986:225 also makes the Euripidean Helen an emblem of the philosophical debates in fifth-century Athens over the status of the real: "Helen is herself the symbol of this mysteriousness of reality, a quality that she retains from the *Odyssey* to the Euripidean drama in Hofmannsthal's *Ägyptische Helena* and Seferis' Ἑλένη."

31. Cf. Segal 1986:224 on the *Helen:* "The central irony of the *Helen* lies in its antitheses of appearance and reality."

32. Segal 1986:257 again suggests a philosophical context for the Cratylean treatment of the name in the *Helen:* "The Helen not only points back to the Sophistic dichotomies of *onoma* and *pragma* but also looks ahead to the Platonic attempt to distinguish appearance from reality in a deeper sense."

33. See Segal's elaborate model of the pervasive dualistic structure subtending the *Helen* in 1986:225ff.

34. The ideal of purity is most extensively represented in the ode in which the chorus invokes the Mountain Mother of the Gods (ll. 1301–68).

35. The words are these, as reported by the Messenger: "You poor pitiful Trojans and suffering Greeks, it was a trick of Hera's that sent you to your deaths on the banks of the Scamander. Paris did not possess Helen, as you thought. Now that I have stayed as long as I had to stay, I return, as Fate ordains, to the sky that formed me. The curses that men heap on the unhappy Helen are mistaken: she has done nothing wrong." Note Burnett's use of the term *scapegoat,* which repositions Helen in the center of the Derridean system linking *pharmakon* (medicine/poison), *pharmakeus* (scapegoat), and *pharmakos* (magician) (Derrida 1972a:69–198).

36. On purity and the "problem" of Helen in nineteenth- and twentieth-century French literature, see chapter 11.

37. See Austin 1975:2 on the modern critic approaching Homer as an *eidolon.*

38. See Segal 1986:230 on this motif of suspension.

39. See Segal 1986 on the Greek representation of Egypt as the exotic in his discussion of Euripides' *Helen.*

40. The passage in question is Herodotus 2.16: "If then my judgement on these matters be right, the Ionians are mistaken in what they say of Egypt. If, on the contrary, it is they who are right, then I undertake to show that neither the Ionians nor any of the other Greeks know how to count. For they all say that the earth is divided into three parts, Europe, Asia, and Libya, whereas they ought to add a fourth part, the Delta of Egypt, since they do not include it either in Asia or Libya. For is it not their theory that the Nile separates Asia from Libya? As the Nile therefore splits in two at the apex of the Delta, the Delta itself must be a separate country, not contained in either Asia or Libya."

Chapter 4. Speculation

1. Two examples from Pindar: *Pythian* 11.33: "the halls of the Trojans, who were visited by fire for the sake of Helen," ἀμφ' Ἑλένᾳ (trans. Sandys 1915:11.33–34); *Paean* 6.95: "Yet, for high-coifed Helen's sake [περὶ δ'ὑψικόμῳ Ἑλένᾳ], it was fated, in the end, that the flame of blazing fire should destroy the spacious city of Troy" (Sandys 1915:6.95–98).

2. See Smyth 1920:347.

3. All translations of the *Nicomachean Ethics* are taken from this edition.

4. Singer 1958 defines *chremastismos* as "money-getting business" (30), and agrees that *oikonomia* and *chremastismos* are, for Aristotle, polar opposites (45). Chrematistics, writes Shell (1978:92), "supports the unnatural illusion that 'wealth consists of a quantity of money' (*Politics* 1257b)."

5. The comparison is a longstanding one. By *oikonomia,* according to Shell, Aristotle "refers to the conventions (*nomoi*) of and distribution (*nemesis*) within the household

(*oikos*). . . . Literary economy concerns similar problems of production, distribution, and relations" (1978:89–91). This is a parallel, Shell himself points out, already explicit in the *Poetics* (90). Else 1957:404ff. points out that Aristotle uses the term *oikonomia* to describe the essential concerns of both aesthetics and political philosophy.

6. Note Shell 1978:93 on Aristotle's *On Memory and Recollection:* "In Aristotle's thought, sealing and minting, or the transformation of a natural object (for example, a metal as commodity) into a supposedly unnatural medium (for example, the same metal as money), is often a metaphor for the impression of the mind by a memory."

7. All citations are from this edition unless otherwise stated.

8. Singer 1958:37 calls it distribution, or apportioning, relating the term to legalistic notions of governance, management, or ordering.

9. See *Catalogue of Women,* 175.2, M–W. Hermione is the daughter of Helen and Menelaus. See *Odyssey* 4.12–14: "but the gods gave no more children to Helen / once she had borne her first and only child, the lovely / Hermione, with the beauty of Aphrodite the golden." The insertion of Helen as a threat to a genealogical line is discussed as a trope in late medieval and early modern French literature in chapter 9.

10. See duBois 1995:115–17 on the Trojan war as trade dispute.

11. See duBois 1978 on this subject.

12. As in Austin 1994.

13. On these references to *eris* in Archaic literature, see Nagy 1979:218–19.

14. Helen's rhetorical methods are the subject of chapter 5, "Epideixis."

15. Meanwhile Helen as an entirely cosmetic figure in early modern love poetry is the subject of chapter 10, "Cosmetics."

16. DuBois 1995:108 draws similar connections between Fr. 16 and the *Nicomachean Ethics.* She begins her chapter on Fr. 16 with the premise that the poem can be read as a piece of philosophy (99).

17. See duBois 1978:93: "Before the invention of coined money, men exchanged valuable things. The Homeric world is characterized by the exchange of gifts; women too are exchanged, as gifts, as valuable prizes of war. The Trojan war is caused by a violation of proper exchange, since Menelaos, the recipient of Helen, loses possession of her."

18. Burnett 1983 suggests that Fr. 16 inverts the traditional public/private hierarchy.

19. This is the essential thesis articulated by Rissman 1983.

20. Helen in the poetry of Valéry is the subject of chapter 11.

21. DuBois 1995:106, for example, argues that the poem makes a "move toward a new kind of thinking, toward the cultural production of subjectivity and individualism and reason."

Chapter 5. Epideixis

1. All translations of the *Metamorphoses* are taken from this edition.

2. See Howatson 1989:596 on the possible connections between *vertere* and *Vertumnus.*

3. See Curran 1978 on violence and rape in the *Metamorphoses.*

4. See "La mythologie blanche" in Derrida 1972a:247–324 on the trope of truth as solar metaphor.

5. Roberts 1928:24 defines the enthymeme, simply, as a "rhetorical syllogism," permitting reasoning by (1) "signs" and (2) "likelihoods." Seaton 1914 offers a more traditional definition of the enthymeme or *abductive syllogism* as "a syllogism of which one proposition is suppressed—major, minor, or conclusion" (113). Seaton is here paraphrasing De Quincey, in *Blackwood's Magazine,* December 1828.

6. Shorey 1924:1–19 suggests how Helen might function as a middle term in the enthymeme. Shorey focuses on a passage from the *Phaedo* as a candidate for the origins of the Aristotelian syllogism. In the passage concerned, Socrates is explaining the immortality of the soul based on its perception of divine beauty. Such perception suggests for Socrates that the soul must in some way partake of that notion which it can only dimly comprehend: "whatever else is beautiful apart from absolute beauty is beautiful because it partakes of that absolute beauty, and for no other reason. . . . the one thing that makes that object beautiful is the presence in it or association with it, in whatever way the relation comes about, of absolute beauty. . . . it is by beauty that beautiful things are beautiful" (trans. Tredennick 1954:100c–d). Implicit here, Shorey argues (1924:7–8), is the doctrine of causality that will become central to the Aristotelian syllogism; in both cases there is an "apparent confusion of the reason with the physical cause (*An. Post.* I.2.5)." According to that doctrine, the cause of all things "is the presence of the corresponding ideas. The cause, that is, of a quality predicated is the presence of the abstract now corresponding to the predicate" (9). I stress here that Socrates demonstrates causality—that which joins the universal or abstract to the specific—through the notion of *beauty.* Helen, then, is the visible demonstration of the causality of beauty: a confusion of the reason with the physical cause, abstract beauty joined to beauty perfectly predicated.

7. Van Hook 1945:54 writes, for example, in an introduction to Isocrates' *Encomium:* "*The Encomium on Helen* is an epideictic, or display, composition on a theme which subsequently became extremely popular in the schools of rhetoric."

8. George Kennedy's presentation of the basic organization of the rhetorical art in the classical world is standard; see Kennedy 1963:104ff. For a broad review of the basic principles of classical rhetoric as a system of persuasion, see Burke 1950:49–180.

9. This paraphrase of Aristotle's oratorical system as presented in *Rhetoric* 1 can be found in Roberts 1928:27.

10. That definition has potentially broader ramifications, given, as Roberts 1928:55 points out, that Aristotle's *Rhetoric* "seems to group all 'literature' under the third division of oratory, the epideictic."

11. This information, and all excerpts from the *Encomium* cited, are taken from Diels 1903:271–94. All translations are from Van Hook 1945 unless otherwise stated.

12. Note that Van Hook here is essentially paraphrasing Aristotle's own criticism of Gorgias in *Rhetoric* 1404a24–29, as well as that of Dionysus of Halicarnassus in *On Imitation* 2.8.

13. Roberts 1928:40 sees in him an early proponent of aestheticism, a sort of prophet of the philosophy of art for art's sake, "la parole pour la parole," or language for the sake of language.

14. See Colie 1966:27 on the issue of rhetorical and logical paradox with reference to Helen.

15. Note Segal 1962: "The speech itself, in fact, is as much an encomium on the power

of the *logos* as on Helen herself" (102). In fact, it is my point that these two goals are *necessarily* one and the same.

16. On the function of the *proemium* or *exordium* as part of the traditional τάξις or *dispositio* of the rhetorical speech, see Kennedy 1963:11.

17. All passages from Gorgias's *Encomium on Helen* are from these editions unless otherwise stated. Paragraph divisions are indicated first, followed by line numbers.

18. The same question is asked by Sappho in Fr. 16, as we will see in chapter 6.

19. See also Kennedy 1963:123.

20. All citations from *Trojan Women* are taken from this translation unless otherwise stated.

21. For Lloyd 1992, both speakers are "rhetorically expert" (100); see also Gregory 1991. Croally 1994:153 and 155–56 suggests that both speakers owe much to fifth-century Athenian sophistry. The influence on Euripides of this "new science" has long been noted. Webster 1967:23 writes of Protagoras: "His statement that there are two opposed arguments on every subject [Diels-Kranz B6a] is quoted by Euripides in the early Phonix (fr. 812 N2) . . . and probably the debates in all Euripidean plays show something of Protagoras' technique of argument."

22. See Scodel 1980:98: "Though Menelaus' judgement is correct, the sentence with which we sympathize will never be carried out"; and see Croally 1994:139n54 on the many critics who appear to take Helen's guilt for granted.

23. See for example Scodel 1980:93, 99, 103.

24. On the juridical form of the *agon,* see Romilly 1986:120 and Croally 1994:136–37. Kennedy 1963:36 mentions this debate in a discussion of pseudo-judicial speeches found in classical literary works.

25. See Croally 1994:138.

26. I follow Croally 1994:138 here.

27. Gregory 1991:158 sees this antithesis as a central theme of *Trojan Women.*

28. See Gellie 1986:117–18.

29. Here I am in agreement with Croally 1994:138–39.

30. For the long list of critics who have read the *agon* as a rhetorical Helen defeated by a rational Hecuba, see Croally 1994:155n74.

31. See for example Lloyd 1992:102–5.

32. On the importance of the Judgment in Helen's speech, see Scodel 1980:97–100.

33. See here Scodel 1980:98–99 and Croally 1994:140.

34. On Euripides' debt to Gorgias, see Lloyd 1992:100 and Lloyd 1994:155–56.

35. On the distinction between forensic and epideictic oratory, see Kennedy 1963:6, 36.

36. It is not difficult to find examples of critics employing a double standard to reach a verdict against Helen. For example, Hecuba condemns Helen for exploiting her beauty, a strategy she herself recommends to Andromache. But the critics—for example, Gregory 1991:172—are less willing to forgive Helen: "The situation of the two women is entirely different, for Andromache is an authentic, Helen a simulated victim of force." Here the critical response is itself undone by a recurrent contradiction. Helen's assertion that beauty is coercion is here discounted, while Hecuba's appropriation of the same assertion is left standing; if Hecuba is justified in borrowing Helen's argument, then we must assume that this argument is supposed to make sense.

37. See above all Croally 1994:130 on this point.

38. Thus Lloyd 1992:104, it seems to me, has it exactly wrong when he argues, echoing Hecuba (as the critic almost always does): "Helen's defence in *Troades* depends on the literal truth of the myth of the Judgement of Paris"; see also Lloyd 1992:112.

39. For a demonstration of this fact, see Helen's silent literary "début," her first appearance on the walls of Troy in the *teichoskopia.*

40. Here I disagree with Lloyd 1992.

41. Croally 1994:135 notes how many critics have had difficulty seeing the dramatic relevance of the *agon* in *Trojan Women.*

42. Lattimore 1958:124: "The trial scene of Helen is a bitter little comedy-within-tragedy, but its juridical refinements defeat themselves and turn preposterous, halting for a time the emotional force of the play."

43. Scodel 1980:99 writes that "beneath Helen's specious introduction of Aphrodite into her defense lies only her own corrupt nature and Paris' attractions. . . . Yet the defense of the power of appearance is offset by our complete lack of sympathy for Helen."

44. Vellacott 1954:20 asserts that Helen has long been regarded as a "shallow" character, and deservedly so.

45. A performance of *Trojan Women* at La Mama, an experimental theater in New York, offers a fitting coda. In this revival of a famous production from the 1970s, there was no dialogue; actors spoke gibberish, punctuated with cries and shouts. The effect was to reduce Euripides' play to the spectacle of body, movement, and voice: *logos* as *opsis.*

Chapter 6. Deixis

1. Most 1982:85 cites a chapter in Bruno Snell's *The Discovery of Mind* entitled "The Rise of Individualism in Early Greek Lyric." But, as Most notes, lyric poetry is clearly already mature in Homer's time, and references to lyric genres abound in the *Iliad.*

2. De Man would call this the *phenomenalization of voice* as opposed to the *rhetorical construction of voice.* See de Man 1985:55–72.

3. See Johnson 1991:171 "It is not enough to say that the lyric has always reflected the nature of the relations between the sexes in Western culture; the lyric has surely had a role in constructing those relations."

4. See chapter 4, n. 9.

5. According to Bowra 1936, Sappho's poetry "looks like ordinary speech" (246).

6. See Jakobson 1987

7. The reception of Sappho's verse is an important model for later critics' engagements with women poets. In his portrait of Marceline Desbordes-Valmore, Charles Baudelaire refers to her as "an untiring priestess of the Muse . . . who could not be silent, because she was always full of cries and songs which had to pour our of her" ("prêtresse infatigable de la Muse . . . qui ne savait pas se taire, parce qu'elle était toujours pleine de cris et de chants qui voulaient s'épancher" [1954:720]). For Baudelaire, this natural and artless cry from the heart is the very definition of the feminine. At the same time, as Johnson points out, lyric itself, especially in the romantic period, is traditionally gendered as feminine (1991). Sappho, read as archetypal female and archetypal lesbian,

stands, paradoxically, as a model of poetic inspiration for the male heterosexual poet. On this paradox see DeJean 1989.

8. Bowra 1936:187 calls her a "priest and a pedagogue."

9. Page continues in the biographical vein, discussing the same fragment: "The theme of this poem, then, was probably some personal matter, to which the allusion to the Atridae was subsidiary. Sappho needs the help of Hera, as the Atridae needed it in the famous story."

10. Fr. 1 begins: "Richly-enthroned immortal Aphrodite, daughter of Zeus, / weaver of wiles, I pray to you: break not my spirit, Lady, / with heartache or anguish; / But hither come, if ever in the past you heard my cry from / afar, and marked it, and came, leaving your father's / house" (trans. Page 1955b).

11. See Austin 1962:6–7: "The name is derived, of course, from 'perform,' the usual verb with the noun 'action': it indicates that the issuing of the utterance is the performing of an action—it is not normally thought of as just saying something."

12. Austin 1962:6 insists that to employ the performative is "not to describe my doing . . . or to state that I am doing it: it is to do it."

13. This is an ambiguity Johnson exploits in "Poetry and Performative Language: Mallarmé and Austin" (in Johnson 1980:52–66).

14. Cf. Derrida 1972b, pp. 365–90, on the signature in relation to Austin's theories of speech-acts.

15. The following is an example of this kind of "competitive rhetoric" in Alcman 1.1 will be referring to the poem sporadically in the course of the rest of this chapter: "But I sing / of Agido's light. I see her / like the sun who shines on us / by order of Agido. . . . // Our splendid / leader will not have us praise / or abuse her, for her brilliance / is as if among a herd of cattle / one had set a champion racehorse, / sinewy, strong, with thunder-ringing hooves, / a creature from a dream with wings. / Do you see? The horse is Venetian, / and the mane of our cousin / Hagesichora is a blossom / of the purest gold, / and below is her silver face. / Can I tell you this more clearly? / There you have Hagesi-chora. / In beauty she may be second to Agido / but she will run like a / Skythian horse against a Lydian racer. / For as we carry Orthria's plow / so the Pleiades of dawn will rise / and strive against us / like the burning star of Sirios / through the ambrosial night" (trans. Barnstone 1962:48).

16. As in Fr. 132: "I have a beautiful daughter, who looks like golden flowers, / Cleis my darling, whom I would not exchange for all / Lydia or lovely . . ."(132).

17. See Nagy 1990:363.

18. Bowra 1936:1981: "This poem is a poem of love. . . . What Sappho wants is the physical presence of Anactoria."

19. "And fluttered the heart of Argive Helen in her breast; / driven mad with passion by the man from Troy, the / traitor-guest, she followed him in his ship over the sea, / Leaving her child at home forsaken, and her husband's / richly-covered bed, since her heart persuaded her to give / way to love, through the daughter of Dione and Zeus; / . . . Many of his brothers the dark earth holds, laid low on the / Trojan plain for the sake of Helen; / And many chariots tumbled in the dust . . . and many dark- / eyed . . . were trampled, and . . . Achilles . . . the slaughter" (trans. Page 1955b).

20. Title of a work by Roland Barthes, translated in the English edition as *Fragments:*

A *Lover's Discourse* (1978). One of the conventional amorous tropes analyzed in that work is "The Absent One." Speaking as the hypothetical Lover, here is Barthes on that trope: "Endlessly I sustain the discourse of the beloved's absence; actually a preposterous situation; the other is absent as referent, present as allocutory" (1978:15). A familiar situation in Sappho's poetry, where departure from the Sapphic fold is a recurrent crisis, and where meditation upon the physical and temporal distance of separation is a recurrent source of melancholy and occasion for reminiscence.

21. For a detailed discussion of Helen as mythic exemplum in medieval French literature, see chapter 7.

22. Discussed in chapter 4.

23. Excerpts from Alcman 1 are quoted in n. 15 above.

24. Regarding the myth of Helen and the Leukippides, see Kannicht 1969, 2:381–82. Nagy 1990:346n42 also refers us to Calame 1977, 1:326–30, "who shows that the theme of radiant horses is a sacred symbol for the dawn, a cult topic shared by the figure of Helen with the Leukippides, who in turn are consorts of the Dioskouroi, brothers of Helen. . . . It is important to note that the chorus of Alcman PMG 1 seems to be worshipping a dawn goddess, Aotis (verse 87)."

25. Graves 1955a links the name *Helen* to the divinities Helle, Selene, and Cybele, and calls her a Spartan moon goddess.

26. An issue touched upon briefly in chapter 1.

27. See Nilsson 1932:68–79. Nilsson's view here is contingent upon his premise that the Dorian invaders radically transformed a Mycenaean mythic base already in place: "For us the rape of Kore by Pluto looms in the most sacred light of Greek cult legend and religion; the rape of Helen presents itself as a frivolous and scandalous and quite profane story; but this difference may be a result of a development under different conditions. The myth told that the old pre-Greek goddess Helen was carried off, but the invading Greeks did not seize the deep sense of the legend, only the feature so common in the heroic age, the feuds of which were caused by the theft either of cattle or of women, that a woman was carried off. When the familiar motif of the rape of a fair woman was given as the cause of the Trojan war, the woman was called by the name of the goddess of whose carrying off the Greeks had heard but whose cult had fallen into disuse in most places. Or perhaps it is better to say that Helen was in cult legend replaced by Kore, who always retained her dignified position, not being drawn, as was Helen, into the heroic mythology" (75–76). It should be added that the causal sequence here advanced is far from certain.

28. Nagy 1990:345 notes that in Theocritus 18, the chorus praises Helen "in terms that resemble strikingly the description of Hagesikhora in Alcman PMG 1."

29. The founding of Helen's cult by inscription and commemoration is a scene repeated, in varied forms, in the love sonnets of early modern France. I return to Theocritus's aetiology in my discussion of Ronsard's *Sonets pour Helene* in chapter 10.

30. This movement back and forth across interdisciplinary boundaries is itself a repetition, in a sense, of the metaphorical discourse that Helen continually generates. It is, therefore, a recurrent aspect of the methodology of this book, and of many of the texts this book examines. Chapter 9, "Genealogy," for example, exposes the way literary graft is acted out in a literal sense in the political power plays of early Renaissance France

and Burgundy. At the same time, graft is seen to function as a trope in the literature of the period. It is difficult, in such scenarios, to decide what is figurative and what is literal.

31. See Jebb 1962, 2:100–106 on Isocrates' *Encomium on Helen* in relation to a political Hellenism.

Chapter 7. Idolatry

1. On the historical figure of Raoul de Soissons, see Winkler 1914.

2. Exempla, we will see, have typically been approached only as devices for constructing analogies or hyperboles. This is the approach of Dragonetti 1960, as in the following passage: "One notes that a certain number of these exempla, Paris and Helen, Tristan and Iseut especially, are treated like hyperboles which suggest that the love of the poet is very great and surpasses by far that of the most famous lovers" ("On constate qu'un certain nombre de ces exempla, Pâris et Hélène, Tristan et Yseut surtout, sont traités comme des hyperboles qui donnent à entendre que l'amour du poète est très grand et passe de beaucoup celui des plus célèbres amants" [1960:199]).

3. Other authors argue that some kind of historical self-awareness is implicit in intertextual allusions. On the penchant of medieval authors for anachronism, G. Raynaud de Lage 1976:157, for example, maintains that "they were completely conscious of most of their transpositions" ("ils étaient parfaitement conscients de la plupart de leurs transpositions"). See also Sanford 1944.

4. On the early appearance of motifs such as *media tempora, media aetas,* and *medium aevum,* see G. S. Gordon 1927.

5. On the rise of courtly love poetry in the context of medieval poetry in general, see Frappier n.d. On the troubadours, see Jeanroy 1934, Roubaud 1971, Bec 1977, Gaunt and Kay 1999. For an introduction to the poetry of the trouvères, see Dragonetti 1960 and Rosenberg and Tischler 1981.

6. A standard assertion in critical writings on the courtly love tradition. See Goldin 1975:51–100, Vance 1975:49, Kristeva 1983, and Vance 1985:101.

7. Note the parallel in a *chanson de croisade* by Conon de Béthune ("Ahi! Amours, com dure departie") between the captivity of the lover/exile and that of the Holy Land impatient for its liberation (Baumgartner 1983:244). See also Nichols 1984:103 on Marcabru's "Al departir del brau tempier," which performs a reenactment of the Passion.

8. On the somewhat confusing relationship between Capellanus and the troubadours, see Cherchi 1994.

9. On Bernart de Ventadorn see Nichols 1962.

10. See *De doctrina Christiana* 2.11, 2.40.

11. See Marrou 1958:494 on the history of allegorical exegesis from the Stoics and Cynics reading Homer to Clement of Alexandria. On Augustine's attachment to the allegorical method, see Pépin 1958.

12. *Confessions* 9.10: "And while we spoke of the eternal Wisdom, longing for it and straining for it with all the strength of our hearts, for one fleeting instant we reached out and touched it. Then with a sigh . . . we returned to the sound of our own speech, in which each word has a beginning and an ending—far, far different from your Word, our Lord, who abides in himself for ever, yet never grows old and gives new life to all

things" (trans. Pine-Coffin 1961:197–98). See Chadwick 1991:xxi on the role of words as both essential conduit and inevitable impasse between God and fallen man. Chadwick also points to the influence here of Plotinus.

13. Thus Curtius 1953:74 argues that Augustine's interpretive methodology is essentially allegorical and is a continuation of Macrobius's strategy for reading Cicero and Virgil.

14. Of course it has hardly required the insights of structuralist and poststructuralist criticism to argue that the real star of the *chanson courtoise* is the poet, not the lover. More often than not, the troubadour makes that argument himself, and often explicitly. Goldin 1983:52 points out that the genre of the *gap*, or boasting song, is offered quite openly as a virtuoso *poetic* performance. When the singer of the *gap* exposes false lovers (*fals amadour*)—rivals, mockers, hypocrites, standard *dramatis personae* in the courtly performance—he is really, Goldin suggests, indicting rival poets.

15. Nichols (1989) refers to Guillaume's poetry as "the voice of the body," reminding us that the basic formal unit of verse in the *chant,* the stanza, is referred to as the *frons,* or head, at the beginning of the poem, and as *cauda,* or tail, at the end.

16. On the troubadour as social or historical figure, see Köhler 1964:27–51.

17. See Dronke 1977:20–21 on the distinction between these roles and their potential class connotations.

18. This portrait of Petrarch turns him into a proto-modernist, a poet whose conscious efforts to revive the classical past suggest, ironically, a break with the medieval past. This is what Mazzotta 1991:50, for example, argues: "If there's any radicality in Petrarch's epistemological break from the Dark Ages, it will be found in the retrieval of antiquity . . . as a systematic undertaking."

19. The Petrarchan ideal of the stolen sign is dramatized in Dante's description of Bolgia 7 in Canto 25 of the *Inferno:* the den of thieves. As the thief in life took what did not belong to him, now his body is no longer his own property. The scene is a nightmarish vision of grafting: "For suddenly, as I watched, I saw a lizard / come darting forward on six great taloned feet / and fasten itself to a sinner from crotch to gizzard. // Its middle feet sank in the sweat and grime / of the wretch's paunch, its forefeet clamped his arms, / its teeth bit through both cheeks. At the same time // its hind feet fastened on the sinner's thighs: / its tail thrust through his legs and closed its coil / over his loins. I saw it with my own eyes! // No ivy ever grew about a tree / as tightly as that monster wove itself / limb by limb about the sinner's body; // they fused like hot wax, and their colors ran / together until neither wretch nor monster / appeared what he had been when he began: // just so, before the running edge of the heat / on a burning page, a brown discoloration / changes to black as the white dies from the sheet. // The other two cried out as they looked on: / 'Alas! Alas! Agnello, how you change! / Already you are neither two nor one!' // The two heads had already blurred and blended; / now two new semblances appeared and faded, / one face where neither face began nor ended. // From the four upper limbs of man and beast / two arms were made, then members never seen / grew from the thighs and legs, belly and breast. // Their former likenesses mottled and sank / to something that was both of them and neither; / and so transformed, it slowly left our bank" (trans. Ciardi 1954:215–16). Dante's vision suggests the illicit and erotic work of imitation and points the way ahead to the discourse of hybrid monstrousness and transformation that is a central part of early modern discourse on literary imitation

and translation. This image of metamorphosis and fusion is itself a transformation and amalgam of various Ovidian scenes. But it also puts a "spin" on that familiar notion that, in a larger sense, Dante's work represents the ultimate medieval monument to synthesis, the effort to link pagan antiquity to Christian modernity, Latin to the vernacular, Provençal poetry to Italian lyric (see Curtius 1953:238, 351–56). Dante's meeting with Virgil in the *Inferno,* Curtius writes, "is the sealing of the bond which the Latin Middle Ages had made between the antique and the modern world" (358). But one could just as well suggest that Dante has kidnapped Virgil.

20. Nichols 1984:107 writes: "In other words, the strength of the canon established by the early troubadours lay in its doubly specular nature: to represent a tradition which could be seen as unvarying from the 12th to the 14th centuries—what Zumthor calls the *grand chant courtois*—while at the same time encouraging the expression of altered worldviews . . . from generation to generation. From this point of view, the founders of the tradition would necessarily be viewed ambiguously: recognition for their achievement, but acknowledgement of their difference as well." This is a nice statement of the more general problem of discontinuity that is the subject of this study, the problem that demands both the strategy of graft and the concealment of that strategy.

21. On "sources" and "influences" in the poetry of Thibaut de Champagne, see Wollensköld 1925.

22. On the general relationship of feudalism to the state and monarchical power, see Bloch 1961:156–63.

23. Bloch 1966:309 reminds us of the extent to which courtly love borrows the "vocabulary of vassal hommage."

24. Bloch 1961:66 agrees that there is never a true "natural economy" in feudal Europe; rather, there is a sustained "shortage of currency."

25. On the relationship of feudalism and the developing power of the monarchy in France, see Ganshof 1964. See also Pirenne 1925 on the rise of urban trade in the medieval city.

26. On the medieval use of historical/mythic figures as historical/moral exempla, see Hampton 1990 and Sanford 1944. The bibliography on the exemplum in medieval poetry is enormous, but see Dornseiff 1927:218 and Kornhardt 1936:14.

27. One could cite many more examples: see also Raimon Jordan's "Quan la neus chai e gibron li verjan" (Raimon Jordan 1922). On the importance of Helen as an exemplum in medieval literature in general, see Dernedde 1887:119ff.

28. Marie-Noëlle Toury 1987:47–48, for example, argues that figures such as Jason, Piramus, and Tristan are "evoked in an unusual and unexpected manner" ("évoqués d'une façon inhabituelle et inattendue"). Thibaut's manipulation of these figures proves, Toury argues, that he refuses to be "the slave of a tradition, the link in a chain just like all the others" ("l'esclave d'une tradition, le maillon d'une chaîne semblable à tous les autres" [48]). In fact just the opposite is true; exempla are the links that confirm the poet's place in the "tradition."

29. It is thus not enough to say, as Toury 1987:48 does, that a figure like Jason "serves only as a measuring device in order to appreciate the suffering of the poet" ("ne sert . . . que d'une sorte d'instrument de mesure pour faire apprécier la souffrance du poète"). Appreciation, yes (especially in the sense of inflating); but Jason is a way of measuring, not just the poet's suffering, but his distance from the past.

Chapter 8. Translation

1. See Tuve 1966 on allegorical imagery in the medieval period and the discussion in chapter 7 of this book, under "Courtly Love as Idolatrous Cult" (105–11).

2. See Seznec 1939:13–15 on euhemerism. Seznec suggests that the church fathers saw deified heroes like Hercules and Romulus as evidence for euhemerization.

3. An influential passage from a chapter of the medieval *Book of Wisdom,* "De Iside et Osiride," cited by Cook (1927:398), offers two scenarios to explain the origins of pagan idolatry. In the first, a father fashions a statue in memory of a dead child; in the second, a people set up the likeness of an absent king. In both cases, the reverence paid to a living being is transferred to an imitation.

4. On medieval metaphors for cultural recuperation, see the chapter entitled "Metaphorics" in Curtius 1953:128–44.

5. See Seznec 1939:16.

6. On the allegorical mode in medieval and early modern Europe, see Fletcher 1964, Tuve 1966, Bloomfield 1981, Greenblatt 1981, and Whitman 1986.

7. Later, Dante will present a grandiose example, in true medieval fashion, of this technique: it is arguably the essential structural principle of the *Divine Comedy.* In the *Purgatorio,* to cite one instance, Christian and pagan figures are "systematically coordinated" (Curtius 1953:363), David with Trajan, Lucifer and Nimrod with the Titans. In Petrarch, too, we find history often conceptualized as a pair of parallel tracks, one pagan, one Christian. Consider the counterpoint between Petrarch (the classical view) and Giovanni Colonna (the biblical view) wandering the streets of Rome in *Familiares* 2.6.2.55–60 (see Rossi and Bosso 1933–42 and Bernardo 1975).

8. On this sense of continuity in the medieval period, see Poole 1918 and Ware 1976.

9. For Kahane and Kahane 1990:199–205, the importance of terms with the prefix *re-* in Carolingian texts, such as *Renovatio Romani imperii* ("renewal of the Roman Empire"), which appears on Charlemagne's imperial bull of 803, suggests a historical vision that sees the past in terms of both rupture and relation: "The meaning of re- is elusive, somewhere on the continuum 'return'/'blending of then and now'/'new beginning'" (201).

10. Thus the Trojan saga operates in the manner of an alternative creation myth, one that is parallel, as we might expect, to the Judeo-Christian narrative. As Baumgartner puts it: "To tell the story of Troy . . . is in effect to tell the story of an absolute beginning, or almost: only the Bible, in the Judeo-Christian universe, begins *a principio*" ("Raconter l'histoire de Troie . . . c'est en effet raconter l'histoire d'un commencement absolu, ou presque: seule la Bible, dans l'univers judéo-chrétien, commence *a principio*" [1987:13]). See Curtius 1953:28–29 on the biblical-Christian justifications of *translatio imperii* and *translatio studii.* Curtius emphasizes Ecclesiasticus 10:8: "Because of unrighteous dealings, injuries, and riches got by deceit, the kingdom is transferred from one people to another" ("Regnum a gente in gentem transfertur proper injustitias et injurias et contumelias et diversos dolos" [28]).

11. Curtius 1953:29n28 argues that the *translatio studii* is ultimately modeled upon Horace's famous declaration in the *Epistles* 2.1.156: "Greece . . . transferred the arts to wild Latium" ("Graecia . . . artes / Intulit agresti Latio"). See also Kelly 1978 on the adaptation of the *translatio studii* in medieval France.

12. See Birns 1993:50: "The Trojan myth is an exemplary instance of the way in which medieval textual practice embodied the constitutive gap between the medieval present and the classical and Biblical pasts."

13. All citations from *Cligés* are taken from this edition.

14. See Thibaut 1888:161.

15. On the *Pergama flere uolo* as a model for later narrative on Troy, see Boutemy 1946.

16. Ehrhart 1987:61, however, demonstrates that this history is also heavily indebted to Dares, as well as Orosius's *Historia adversos paganos;* cf. Buchthal 1971:4–5 and Raynaud de Lage 1976:267.

17. Outside France, Troy is just as prominent. Wace's *Roman du Brut* (1155), to cite one obvious case, explains the founding of Britain by way of Brutus, a descendant of Aeneas. Later, the subject of Troy will produce, in the fourteenth century, the *Seege of Troy,* the *"Geste historiale" of the Destruction of Troy* (1375), the *Laud Troy Book* (1343–1400) and, in the fifteenth century, John Lydgate's *Troy Book* (1412–20) as well as William Caxton's *Recuyell of the Historyes of Troye* (1468–74), itself a translation of Raoul le Fèvres's *Receuil.*

18. All passages from *Le roman de Troie* are taken from this edition, unless otherwise stated.

19. See Huchet 1989:38.

20. On the evolution of the *roman d'antiquité* in general, see Raynaud de Lage 1976.

21. On Benoît's preference for Dares, see Ehrhart 1987:39.

22. Huppé 1990:176 classes Benoît among the "name-droppers, transcribers, or makers of quotations."

23. Other critics employ more violent images to characterize Benoît's technique. See for example Faral 1913:409–10: "And thus the authors of the great romances will dress their subject in the rags they tore from it, that of Aeneas combined with the narrative of the Judgment of Paris, that of Troy with a narrative of the love of Jason and Medea" ("Voici que les auteurs de grands romans vont parer leur sujet de lambeaux qu'ils lui arracheront, celui d'Eneas avec un récit du Jugement de Paris . . . celui de Troie avec un récit des amours de Jason et Médée").

24. See Ehrhart 1987:39–41 on these multiple sources—Greek, Roman, Celtic, and French—and the way Benoît's treatment of the Judgment of Paris points to the genre of the dream-vision.

25. This is a common motif in the romances of the period: in Chrétien de Troyes's *Erec et Enide,* to give just one example, Erec's contentment in wedlock leads to neglect of his chivalric duties and puts his reputation in jeopardy. See Foucher 1970:33–87.

26. On this subject see George Duby's *Medieval Marriage: Two Models from Twelfth-Century France* (1978).

27. Some of these are discussed in Faral 1913:180–84. On the roots of the amplification/brevity dichotomy in Quintilian, *De oratore* 8, see Plöbst 1911:3.

28. See n. 24

29. On the Southern version and its relationship to Guido's transcription, see Chesney 1942:46–49.

30. The manuscript in question here is *Bibliothèque impériale, manuscrit français,* n. 821.

31. On the relationship between Benoît and Guido, see Buchthal 1971:38.

32. On the popularity of the Troy saga in early modern Burgundy, see chapter 9 below; see also Ehrhart 1987:51–52.

33. On the relationship between Guido and Millet, see Häpke 1899:5. On sources in Benoît, Guido, and Millet, see Meybrinck 1886.

Chapter 9. Genealogy

1. All citations of Chrétien's text refer to Micha 1957. All translations are taken from Staines 1990.

2. Per Nykrog, in a class on medieval romance at Harvard, once referred to *"Cligés's* intertextual ping-pong match with *Tristan."*

3. The rhetoric of legitimacy and illegitimacy, purity and impurity, chastity and promiscuity, is a recurrent issue in this study. For the centrality of this rhetoric in early modern humanist and civic writings, see Stephanie H. Jed's *Chaste Thinking: The Rape of Lucretia and the Birth of Humanism* (1989). Jed points out, for example, that Coluccio Salutati uses the term *immaculatus* in his *Declamatio Lucretiae* (1375–1406) *both* for Lucretia's chastity and for Florentine independence.

4. For historical overviews of the rise to power of the Burgundian state, see Thibaut 1888, Vaughn 1962, and Favier 1984:339–72. Erasmus, it should be noted, condemns this kind of political marriage in *Institution du prince Chrétien* (1516) and *Complainte de la paix* (1517). He maintains that marriage is properly a private sacrament, not a matter of public affairs; when it becomes the latter, "the result is very often what happened to the Greeks because of Helen" ("on en arrive à produire très souvent ce qui est advenu aux Grecs de par Hélène" [Telle 1950:10]).

5. See Pirenne 1903, 2:227.

6. See de Lettenhove 1864, 6:11.

7. Doutrepont 1906 and Seznec 1939:6.

8. The *Recueil* will be translated by William Caxton as the *Recuyell of the Historyes of Troye* (1468–74), the first book printed in the English language.

9. Book 3 of manuscript B.N. Fr. 253 begins: "Here follows the last Book of this volume, formerly composed in Latin by master Guy de Colonne, and formerly translated into French by the command of M. le duc de Bourgogne" ("Cy après s'ensieut le derrenier Livre de ce volume, composé en latin jadis pas maistre Guy de Colompne, et nagaires translaté en françois par le commandement de mons. le duc de Bourgogne" [cited by Bayot 1908:24]).

10. See for example V. L. Saulnier 1964:635: "The poetic style tries to be erudite, enriched with allusions" ("Le style poétique se veut recherché, enrichi d'allusions").

11. For an elaborate discussion of the coincidence of the discourses of humanism, patriotism, and crusading in the work of the *rhétoriqueurs,* see Zumthor 1978, in particular the chapter "Le discours de la gloire" (56–77). "In the same period," Zumthor writes, "the euphoria of discourse reveals itself in the special emphasis marking the opposition Us/Them: what has been called, perhaps abusively, the 'patriotism' of the *rhétoriqueurs.* . . . P. Jodogne has shown how heavily the context of nationalist French reactions to the Italian conflicts under Louis XII weighs upon the work of Lemaire. Hence these long works exalting the ruling dynasty, works like the *Illustrations de Gaule* of Lemaire." ("A

la même époque, l'euphorie du discours se manifeste par l'emphase particulière marquant l'opposition Nous/Eux: ce qu'on a, peut-être abusivement, nommé le 'patriotisme' des rhétoriqueurs. . . . P. Jodogne a montré combien pèse sur l'oeuvre de Lemaire le contexte des réactions nationalistes françaises aux conflits italiens sous Louis XII. De là ces longs ouvrages exaltant la dynastie, les *Illustrations de Gaule* de Lemaire" [63]).

12. This rejection is echoed by the Salic law, which forbade any female descendant the right to the French crown.

13. On this literary history see Kem 1994. See also Rabelais's parody of biblical genealogy in the first chapter of *Gargantua,* "Of the Genealogy and Antiquity of Gargantua" ("De la genealogie et antiquité de Gargantua"). This is also a parody of *translatio studii* and *imperii:* "I think that many who today are emperors, kings . . . are descended from beggars . . . just as, in the contrary sense, many who today are rogues . . . are descended from the blood and lineage of great kings and emperors, given the astonishing transplantation of reigns and empires: from the Assyrians to the Medes, from the Medes to the Persians, from the Persians to the Macedonians, from the Macedonians to the Romans, from the Romans to the Greeks, from the Greeks to the French" ("Je pense que plusieurs sont aujourd'huy empereurs, roys, . . . lesquels sont descenduz de quelques porteurs de rogatons . . . comme, au rebours, plusieurs sont gueux de l'hostiaire . . . lesquelz sont descenduz de sang et ligne de grandz roys et empereurs, attendu l'admirable transport des regnes et empires: / des Assyriens es Medes, / des Medes es Perses, / des Perses es Macedones, / des Macedones es Romains, / des Romains es Grecz, / des Grecz es Francoys" [Rabelais 1968:47–48]). See Carla Freccero's *Father Figures: Genealogy and Narrative Structure in Rabelais* (1991).

14. More parallels with the biblical paradigm: it is upon eating the apple that Adam and Eve recognize each other's nakedness; the body emerges as seductive surface.

15. Lewis 1936:83 deals with this question of belief, noting that classical poetry contains almost no "aesthetic contemplation" of the gods: "No religion, so long as it is believed, can have that kind of beauty which we find in the gods of Titian, of Botticelli, or of our own romantic poets. . . . The gods must be . . . disinfected of belief."

16. See Frappier 1963:293.

17. Cf. Ovid's *Heroides* 17, the letter from Helen to Paris (trans. Showerman 1914:ll. 175–84): "You urge on me that opportunity freely offered should not be wasted, and that we should profit by the obliging ways of a simple husband. I both desire it and I am afraid. So far my will is not determined; my heart is wavering in doubt. Both my lord is away from me, and you are without companion for your sleep, and your beauty takes me, and mine in turn you; the nights, too, are long, and we already come together in speech, and you—wretched me!—are persuasive, and the same roof covers us. May I perish if all things do not invite me to my fall; and yet some fear still holds me back!"

Chapter 10. Cosmetics

1. Weber and Weber 1963. All citations in French of Ronsard are taken from this edition (hereafter referred to as Weber), unless otherwise stated. All translations of Ronsard are my own.

2. So do Terence Cave, Grahame Castor, and Henri Weber.

3. Other cosmogonies in the *Sonets pour Helene* include 1.22, 2.3, 2.11, 2.12, and 2.38.

4. Certainly *SpH* 1.4 appears to owe as much to Petrarch as *Amours* 32 does—almost every line can be tied to possible Petrarchan models; see Weber and Weber 1963.

5. For the motif of Helen as a copy without a model, see also *SpH* 1.22, 2.3, 2.11, and 2.12.

6. The proliferation of the name is a frequent theme in the *Sonets pour Helene;* cf. 2.12, 2.16, 2.31, 2.37, 2.38, and 2.47.

7. Cited by Harvey 1989:7–8.

8. Cave 1973:2 traces "the process by which the 'external' materials provided by contemporary culture and history are absorbed and transformed through the medium of poetry." The notions of *absorption* and *transformation,* again, are effective to the extent that they remain obscure.

9. One more example, from A. H. T. Levi's "The Role of Neoplatonism in Ronsard's Poetic Imagination": "The *inner coherence* of the work of a poet is not philosophical but imaginative" (1973.121). My italics.

10. Langer 1986:3 attempts the same "rehabilitation" of *inventio:* "In the Renaissance . . . the rhetorical sense of invention is conservative and hardly able to accommodate newness. Yet the empirical sense of invention, as something new in the experiential world, is found for example in the Renaissance conception of the *inventor* and his *inventum.*"

11. Jameson 1971:26 has argued that Benjamin's emphasis on technology is not "historical analysis" but "an exercise in allegorical meditation, in the locating of some fitting emblem."

12. Seznec 1939, cited in Weber 1956:25, calls humanism the "reintegration of an ancient subject in an ancient form" ("réintegration d'un sujet antique dans une forme antique").

13. For Weber 1956:11, humanism thus has a great deal in common with the Reformation, that other cultural revolution of the sixteenth century, "the one returning to the texts of ancient poetry and thought, the other to the fundamental texts of Christianity" ("l'un revenant aux textes de la poésie et de la pensée antique, l'autre aux textes fondamentaux du christianisme").

14. For Wolf 1994:101 the makeover is a baptismal ritual that confers a new identity; this "liminal moment" — "after the old make-up is removed, but before the new is applied" — is rarely seen on talk shows.

15. If there is something new here, it is Orlan's feminist appropriation of the old myths. Her advance is in reclaiming agency; she is work of art *and* artist, Helen *and* Zeuxis.

16. From *Le premier livre des poemes* (Laumonier 1914–75, 15:252).

17. This is *imitatio* as *contaminatio.* Moss 1984:119–20 suggests that Ronsard "imitates the editor of a commonplace book translating nature into a composite language of literary references," since "the language of flowers was the common metaphorical language for talking theoretically about poetry" (118). Greene 1982:199 calls Ronsard's method a "syncretism" influenced by Ficino and Horace. Cave 1979 locates the roots of that syncretism in Erasmus's *De copia.*

18. See McFarlane 1973 and Garapon 1981 on Ronsard's spontaneity.

19. Russell and Winterbottom 1972:375.

20. On the survival of this "masculine" rhetorical tradition into the Renaissance, see Kritzman 1991. Much could be made of the gendered implications of Quintilian's fig-

ures, which are complex and confusing: inside every woman, Quintilian would seem to be saying, there is a naked man trying to get out. That is a subject, however, for another study.

21. Ovid goes on to list a number of prescriptions: "I have seen one who pounded poppies moistened with cool water, and rubbed them on her tender cheeks" (99–100).

22. According to Highet 1949:144, the *Franciade* "was designed to be a plaster cast of the *Aeneid.*" See also Silver 1961, 1:420 and Leslie 1979:18.

23. Leslie 1979:98 argues that it is in the *epyllion* that Ronsard successfully emulates classical epic. Works such as "Au roy" (1555), "Ode de la paix" (1550), and "Hymne de France" (1549) all function, in effect, as mini-*Franciades.* Ronsard's "truest" epic would be the story of the Gigantomachy borrowed from Hesiod and narrated in the "Hymne de l'Hyver" (98).

24. Some critics try to have it both ways, treating the *Sonets pour Helene* as Ronsard's last attempt to do battle with his younger poetic rivals, above all Desportes. See Levi 1973:135.

25. See Austin 1994.

26. Euripides' Helen, again, is really the "standard" Helen rendered more explicitly. In the *agon* between Helen and Hecuba in *Trojan Women,* the latter directs her gravest condemnation to Helen's beautification: "And now you dare to come outside/ figure fastidiously arranged" (Lattimore 1958:ll. 1022–23). Helen's beauty, like her words, is a rhetorical weapon, a seductive mask (See my pp. 79–80).

27. On the role of the *eidolon* in Ronsard's poetry, see Quainton 1995.

28. A fashion much in vogue, it would appear, at the time when the *Sonets pour Helen* was composed. Weber 1956:xxxii writes that 1570–80 marks a veritable Petrarchan renaissance in France.

29. Durling 1976:94.

30. *The Light in Troy* (1982:197–219).

31. See *Rime sparse* 192 and *SpH* 2.3.

32. See *SpH* 2.2 and 2.37, which explicitly compare Helene and Laura.

33. Or a cult based purely on market value. According to Berger 1972:21, today's original is "defined as an object whose value depends upon its rarity. This value is affirmed and gauged by the price it fetches on the market." Thus works of art acquire a new "bogus religiosity"; they "are discussed and presented as though they were holy relics."

34. See for example Castor 1964:7, Foucault 1966:58, and Dubois 1989:180–81.

35. This returns us to our discussion of invention in the sixteenth century as a technological notion. According to Castor 1964:90, "the poet has not always been a creator. In the sixteenth century, and probably for some time afterwards as well, he was simply a maker, a *facteur.*" See also Kritzman 1991:101 on Clément Marot's *blason* on the *Beau tetin* [Beautiful breast], which, he argues, asserts "the triumph of craftsmanship over the natural."

36. Or elsewhere in Ronsard (e.g., *Amours* 1.88). See Pacteau 1994:24 on Renaissance portrait poems; for Benjamin 1968:224 the cult function of art is sustained and debased in the portrait.

37. See Dubois 1989:176–77.

38. Garapon 1981:10 cites Binet's judgment that Ronsard praises Cassandre as "Petrarch did Laura, in love only with a beautiful name" ("Pétrarque avait fait sa Laure, amoureux seulement de ce beau nom").

39. See especially *SpH* 2.12, 2.16, 2.31, 2.37, 2.38, and 2.47.

40. See *SpH* 2.9 for another extended treatment of Helen's name *qua* name.

41. The speaker is not the only one embracing idols. In *SpH* 1.42, the poet complains of Helen's penchant for Neoplatonism: "You say that the love of the body is polluted. / To speak so is nothing but fantasy, / Which embraces what is false as if it were something known: / It is to reenact the story of Ixion, / Who feasted on the wind, and loved only clouds" ("Vous dites que des corps les amours sont pollues. / Tel dire n'est sinon qu'imagination, / Qui embrasse le faux pour les choses cognues: / Et c'est renouveler la fable d'Ixion, / Qui se paissoit de vent, & n'aimoit que des nues" [10–14]). For Helen, to refuse the body is, ironically, to embrace a fiction; her efforts to evade the claims of the body only reenact them in the realm of fantasy. Everyone here—lover and beloved, poet and reader—plays the role of a deluded Ixion making love to an imaginary Hera.

42. For an extended treatment of the optical fantasy, see Tyard 1950; Tyard and the Pléiade in general rely upon humanists like Bembo and Castiglione, who are themselves drawing upon Ficino's *De amore*. See also Gadoffre 1963:46–47.

43. See Kritzman 1991:98 on the sadism implicit in the *blasonneur*'s approach to the female body.

44. As in *SpH* 1.26, 1.45, 1.46, 1.60, 2.4, 2.24.

45. Dubois 1989:179–80 comments: "Helen is embodied, so to speak, only by the poem which celebrates her" ("Hélène ne prendra corps [si l'on peut dire] que par le poème qui la célèbre").

46. See Berg 1986:212 for a discussion of *SpH* 1.26. It is reported that Hélène herself sought to append a disclaimer to the sonnets, and that Ronsard's contemporary Du Perron offered this cruel response: "Instead of this letter, just put your portrait there" ("Au lieu de cest Epistre, il y fault seulement mettre vostre portraict" [*Perroniana* 1669 cited in Desonay 1959:219]). The Hélène as represented in the literature of the period is above all intelligent. Desonay 1959:203n3 cites Le Poulchre de la Motte-Messemé's *Le premier livre du passetemps* (1597): "I saw . . . in this divine company of nymphs who embellished our court, a Helene de Foncesques, highly esteemed by learned ones for her knowledge" ("J'ai veu . . . en ceste divine compagnie de nymphes qui embellisaient nostre cour, une Helene de Foncesques, fort estimée des doctes pour son sçavoir"). This would make Ronsard's Helen an anti-Helen and her sonnet cycle a mock-encomium.

47. See Silver 1969:43: "Mythology is by far the most pervasive element in Ronsard's poetry."

48. See Rigolot 1982:187–98 on the rhetoric of metamorphosis in the Renaissance: "In summary, the rhetoric of metamorphosis amounts, in the end, to a metamorphosis of rhetoric" ("En somme, la rhétorique de la métamorphose entraîne, pour ainsi dire, une métamorphose de la rhétorique" [198]).

49. In the *Sonets pour Helene*, the poet's desire is often represented in this way as a fantasized fusion with that desire, as in *SpH* 1.53: "I love with all my heart, I want to be loved. / Desire tied to desire in a tight knot" ("J'aime de tout mon coeur, je veux aussi qu'on m'aime. / Le desir au desir d'un noeud ferme lié").

50. Greene 1982:210.

51. As an alternative title for the *Metamorphoses,* one could consider *An Encyclopedia of Rape; or, How Plants Got Their Names.*

52. In *Metamorphoses* 1.553–59, Apollo's pursuit of Daphne is brought to an abrupt halt when the virgin nymph is transformed, at her own behest, into a tree. Apollo's desire, however, is not so easily deflected: "But even now in this new form Apollo loved her; and placing his hand upon the trunk, he felt the heart still fluttering beneath the bark. He embraced the branches as if human limbs, and pressed his lips upon the wood. But even the wood shrank from his kisses. And the god cried out to this: 'Since thou canst not be my bride, thou shalt at least be my tree. My hair, my lyre, my quiver shall always be entwined with thee, O laurel' " (trans. Miller 1916).

53. Derrida 1979 treats the figurative/literal implications of the author *living on (survivant)* through his or her writing.

54. Johnson 1987 connects the struggle for poetic originality in Mallarmé with the impotence of the son before a father whose very priority makes him unassailable: "Impotence is thus not a simple inability to write, but an inability to write *differently*" (120–21); "to seek to silence the father, to speak of his *not* having sung, is to run the risk of bringing the father back to life, since, if he does not sing, there is no proof that he is dead. In other words, the survival of the son is guaranteed by the way in which the son does *not* hear him" (122–23).

55. Here again, lyric poetry functions very much like hero cult in the way in which both diverge from epic. "The hero of cult," argues Nagy 1979:116, "must be local because it is a fundamental principle in Greek religion that his power is local. On the other hand, the *Iliad* and the *Odyssey* are Panhellenic."

56. Wells 1988:152n114 suggests that the poem "may possibly have to do with the connection of both Helen and the Ptolemies with Egyptian cults of Aphrodite."

57. See also *SpH* 2.51, the "Stances de la Fontaine d'Helene," in which two frustrated lovers come to lament the coldness of their mistresses at the Fountain of Helen; one proclaims: "Why could I not be abducted like the Argive child? / To avenge my death, I would like that / The shores, the sand, the meadows, and the river / Be called for ever after Helen, and my own name!" ("Que ne suis-je ravy comme l'enfant Argive? / Pour revencher ma mort, je ne voudrois sinon / Que le bord, le gravois, les herbes, & la rive / Fussent tousjours nommez d'Helene, & de mon nom!" [37–40]). For the poet, to be dead means more than to be remembered: to be dead is to be read.

58. The graffiti artist likes to believe, of course, that he is a revolutionary, that he is saying something new. Thus in the final epode to the 1550 *Ode* "A Madame Marguerite" (Laumonier 1914–75, 1:78, ll. 89–96), Ronsard promotes at one and the same time originality and erudition, *inventio* and *imitatio:* "let the Nymph see / That it was my lute, first / That showed the French how to play / And as if I were imprinting my path on the Attic and Roman field / with my own hands I unearthed / Callimachus, Pindar, Horace" ("que le Nymphe voie / Que mon luc premierement / Aus François montra la voie / De sonner si proprement: / Et comme imprimant ma trace / Au champ Attiq' & Romain, / Callimaq, Pindare, Horace, / Je deterrai de ma main"). Ronsard is at once a pioneer, taking the first steps on untrodden soil, and an archaeologist, exhuming the past that lies buried there.

Chapter 11. Miscegenation

1. This is the argument made by Gaudon 1985.

2. Honour 1968 is an invaluable study for anyone interested in the revival of the antique style in eighteenth-century France.

3. Nerval refers, for example, to the *Bibliothèque bleue.* For a survey of the evolution of the Faust legend in Europe from the Renaissance to the nineteenth century, see the introductions in Luke's translation of *Faust* (Goethe 1987:xiii–xiv) and Passage's translation (Goethe 1965:xiii–xxiv).

4. See Hugo 1966:246 on the divine/demonic power of the printed word: "Architecture is dethroned. The stone letters of Orpheus will be replaced by the lead letters of Gutenberg. The book will kill the building. The invention of the press is the greatest event in history. It is the mother of all revolutions" ("L'architecture est détrônée. Aux lettres de pierre d'Orphée vont succéder les lettres de plomb de Gutenberg. *Le livre va tuer l'édifice.* L'invention de l'imprimerie est le plus grand événement de l'histoire. C'est la révolution mère").

5. *Faust* II was, as noted, first published in its present form in 1832, under the title *Faust, Der Tragödie zweiter Teil in fünf Akten.* But as early as 1800, Goethe had composed a fragment called "Helena." It is upon that fragment that Goethe built *Faust* II, in 1827 publishing *Helena, Klassische-Romantische Phantasmagorie, Zwischenspiel zu Faust.* See Goethe 1965:liii for bibliographic information. All translations from *Faust* II are based on this edition.

6. On Helen's role in *Faust* II in general, see von Weise 1947.

7. See Friedman 1989:429 on the enduring mythic status of modern Jerusalem: "Itzik Yaacoby . . . noticed that most Christian tourists he showed around the city felt as though they were walking through the pages of the Bible." We will see another example of this *intertextual tourism* in the next chapter: in Flaubert's *La tentation de Saint Antoine,* Helen's phantom is part of the sightseeing.

8. Note the resemblance between this Antaeus-like image ("So steh' ich, ein Antäus an Gemüte"[7077]), which describes Faust awakening upon contact with the soil of classical culture, and this passage from Goethe's *Römische Elegien:* "Here on classical soil now I stand, inspired and elated: / Past and present speak plain, charm me as never before" ("Froh empfind ich mich nun auf klassischem Boden begeistert; / Vor- und Mitwelt spricht lauter und reizender mir" [Goethe 1977, ll. 1–2]).

9. Chénier 1950:viii: "The 'nursling of France' who wandered as far as the shores of the Bosphorus, where he made a match the fruit of which would prove to be one of the most beautiful ornaments of the orchard of French poetry, was named Louis de Chénier" ("Le 'nourrison de la France' qui se hasarda jusqu'aux rives du Bosphore pour y contracter une union dont le fruit allait se révéler un des plus beaux ornements du verger de la poésie française, s'appelait Louis de Chénier").

10. On Chénier's formative years, see also Fabre 1965.

11. This is the ideal behind Sainte-Beuve's comments on Theocritus in *Mes poisons* (1926): "These are the true classics; in reading them, it seems as if one retrieves one's soul from long ago, one remembers oneself" ("Voilà les vrais classiques; en les lisant, il semble qu'on retrouve son âme d'autrefois, on se ressouvient"). On the cultural myth

of poetry as a maternal or natural language, an idea that is of especial significance in the romantic period, see de Man 1971:166–86. This essay is particularly relevant because in it de Man explores the paradox that while modern poetry is valorized as a primordial, natural language (in opposition to prose), it is in and through that same poetry that modern culture locates its "modernity."

12. Starobinski 1978:48–49 says that this poem suggests "Chénier's attempt to come closer to the world's own youth, whether by giving shape to the essence of Poetry or by envisioning the appearance of the unsurpassable first poet—unsurpassable precisely because he remains so close to the origins of poetry. And this nostalgic gaze towards a world ideally and historically 'first'—toward, in short, a lost poetry—characterizes an age which was conscious of its own creative inferiority and wanted to transcend it. Out of this neoclassic regret, in fact, along with the self-generated reaction to it, was born that romantic and modern affirmation in which the imagination itself becomes the very origin at the heart of all of us, here and now."

13. For the circumstances of Chénier's arrest and execution, see Fabre 1965 and Scarfe 1965.

14. The conference-goer, generally, capitalizes upon this repetition. Emilie Noulet-Carner opens a conference commemorating the twentieth anniversary of the poet's death (September 2–11, 1965) at Cérisy by recollecting a previous gathering at Pontigny. "A new Valéry appears to us, the Valéry of the Cahiers," she suggests ("un nouveau Valéry se présente à nous, le Valéry des Cahiers"). At the same time she assures us that "Valéry will remain, despite the Cahiers, the poet who inhabits our memory by way of so many beautiful verses retained there" ("Valéry restera, malgré les Cahiers, le poète qui habite notre mémoire par tant de beaux vers retenus"). "Présentation de la décade 'Paul Valéry'" in Noulet-Carner 1968:8.

15. A fear that surfaces in images of hauntings and doubled identities, as in an address by Valéry at a conference in Brussels on January 9, 1942 (1947:7): "I turn myself, in this scene, into something like a ghost . . . because I must return, this evening, to the subject of myself and, in short, wander about like a real ghost through the memoirs of an already long life. At a certain age, you end up looking at your life as if it's someone else's" ("Je me fais, sur cette scène, un peu l'effet d'un revenant . . . parce que je dois revenir, ce soir, sur moi-même, et en somme errer comme un véritable revenant dans les souvenirs d'une vie déjà longue. A un certain âge, on finit par regarder sa vie comme la vie d'un autre"). See *Souvenirs poétiques, recueillis par un auditeur au cours d'une conférence prononcée à Bruxelles le 9 Janvier 1942.*

16. Hofmann acknowledged this betrayal at the 1965 Cérisy gathering: "And so we bring the soul of Valéry back to earth. . . . But this is to force the man out of that sanctuary where . . . he was so happy to be, 'outside of everything,' it is to pull him out of his shell. . . . In *Propos me concernant,* in effect, he multiplies his objections: 'I don't like memories which are to me images already carried away. . . . Don't expect me to go in search of lost time.'" ("Ainsi ramenons sur terre l'âme de Valéry. . . . Mais c'est faire sortir notre homme de cet asile où . . . il était si bien 'en dehors de toutes choses,' c'est le tirer de sa coquille. . . . Dans *Propos me concernant,* en effet, il mutiplie les protestations: 'je n'aime pas les souvenirs qui me sont des images déjà portées. . . . Ce n'est pas moi qui rechercherais le temps perdu!'" [in Noulet-Carner 1968:136]).

17. Given the essential role of the reader, the autonomy reserved by Valéry for the ideal poetic work can only be provisional. A "completed sonnet" is for Valéry an "abandoned sonnet," Genette notes. "The completed work is the work (being) read" (1979: 379).

18. Bloom 1973:95: "Influence is Influenza—an astral disease. If influence were health, who would write a poem? Health is stasis."

19. The doctor in *L'idee fixe* (1933) laments: "I have the sickness of activity! I do not know how to do nothing. . . . To remain two minutes without ideas, without words, without useful actions!" ("J'ai le mal de l'activité! . . . je ne sais ne rien faire. . . . Demeurez deux minutes sans idées, sans paroles, sans actes utiles!" [3].) Thought itself threatens the autonomy of the self, infects it: "A thought which tortures a man escapes the conditions of thought; it becomes an Other, a parasite" ("Une pensée qui torture un homme échappe aux conditions de la pensée; devient un autre, un parasite" [xv]). Cognition as infection is a frequent motif in Valéry's writings: "There are persons, who sense that their senses separate them from the real, from being. This sense in them infects their other senses" ("Il y a des personnages, qui sentent que leur sens les séparent du réel, de l'être. Ce sens en eux infecte leurs autres sens" ["Extraits du log-book de Monsieur Teste" in Valéry 1931:71]).

20. His apartment is a "pure and banal place" ("lieu pur et banal" [Valéry 1957:23]). It is because philosophy tries to say something—because it calls itself utilitarian—that Valéry rejects it "with Impure Things" ("parmi les Choses Impures" [12]). Teste is Valéry's antiphilosopher. Bouveresse 1995 argues that philosophy, for Valéry, obstinately treats language as a means (to knowledge, to nonlanguage); poetry, on the other hand, is the art of language as an end. Hence Valéry's admiration for mathematics, a pure language leading directly to nonlanguage: power and action.

21. "Les Fleurs du Mal Armé: Some Reflections on Intertextuality" in Johnson 1987: 116.

22. All citations from Valéry's poetry, except where otherwise indicated, are from *Poésies* (1929).

23. Nash's reading is seconded by Walzer 1953:106: "Helen, Orpheus, the Birth of Venus are Parnassian pictures, but renewed in an original way" ("Hélène, Orphée, Naissance de Vénus sont des tableaux parnassiens, mais renouvelés d'une façon originale").

24. Frederick J. E. Raby, "Explication," in Alex Preminger, ed., *Princeton Encyclopedia of Poetry and Poetics* (1956).

25. J. R. Lawler 1956:60 offers a reading of "Orphée" that is similarly orthodox, insisting on the coincidence of form and content ("Thus Orpheus-Amphion playing the lyre and building a temple is none other . . . than the very form of the sonnet made manifest"), and emphasizing the poem's "organicism" and "harmoniousness" by way of recurrent formal elements ("*Or,* apart from being a favourite 'ideal' word in Valéry, constitutes part of the fundamental harmony of *Orphée* and is organically justified . . . cf. the previous *or . . . bord . . . Orphée . . . essor . . . s'ordonne*").

26. As does Lawler 1956:61–62 with respect to Orpheus, a figure, for him, mediating between order and disorder. As in my New Critical reading of "Hélène," Lawler sees "Orphée" organized as a recurrent "act and response," a self-enclosed structure both "progressive and circular."

27. Leconte de Lisle 1969:33.

28. This is the argument of Kennedy 1989:19. Kennedy notes that in a short lyric addressed to Sand in 1839, de Lisle calls her a "mystic Helen."

29. See also Bourgeois 1969:92–100 on the relationship between Goethe's and Sand's respective Fausts.

30. Valéry 1944:100 depicts a perverted genealogy: an author confronted with a text he no longer recognizes as his own.

31. Walzer 1953:103 criticizes the *Album* precisely because "you can detect epochs and influences in it" ("On y sent les époques et les influences").

32. The self "receiving" the word, by whatever means, is a house divided: "It is impossible to receive the 'truth' from oneself. When one senses it forming . . . one forms, in the very same moment, another, unusual self . . . of which one is proud,—of which one is jealous. . . . (It is the crisis of internal politics.)" ("Il est impossible de recevoir la 'vérité' de soi-même. Quand on la sent se former . . . on forme du même coup un autre soi inaccoutumé. . . dont on est fier,—dont on est jaloux. . . . [C'est un comble de politique interne."]) (Valéry, "Extraits du log-book de Monsieur Teste," 73.)

33. An unsent letter (dated October 30, 1890) in which Valéry requests a copy of "Hérodiade," stages the potential relationship between the two poets as a Narcissus scenario (itself the subject of Mallarmé's poem): "A few pieces of Your Work . . . made me thirsty beyond all remedy. I compare with love these prodigious lines to priceless elixirs which, dropping pearl by pearl upon an educated tongue, awaken infinite joys. . . . I am bold to importune you thus—but Your Soul fascinates me like this mirror. I appeared in you like a distant shadow." ("Quelques bribes de Votre Oeuvre . . . m'ont assoiffé irrémédiablement. Je compare avec amour ces prodigieux vers à d'inestimables liqueurs qui, tombant perle à perle sur une langue experte éveillent d'infinies jouissances. . . . Je suis hardi de vous importuner ainsi—mais Votre Ame me fascine comme ce miroir. Je m'apparus en toi comme une ombre lointaine.") Cited in Austin, 1972:40–41.

34. Pommier 1946:9–10 acknowledges this fear in his address: "Nothing equals the lure of introspection, unless it is its danger: it is a game of Narcissus, who is in danger of drying up the spring by gazing at it. This heroic game, Valéry pursued it, with a bitter clairvoyance" ("Rien n'égale l'attrait de l'introspection, si ce n'est son danger: c'est un jeu du Narcisse, qui risque de tarir la source en s'y mirant. Valéry l'a poursuivi, ce jeu héroïque, avec une âpre clairvoyance").

35. On Mallarmé's place in Valéry's work, see Mondor, *L'heureuse rencontre de Valéry et Mallarmé* (1947), and Lawler 1956, as well as Nash 1983. Mallarmé's influence is matter for psychobiographical genealogies. Wilson 1943:64 is an example: "Paul Valéry first met Mallarmé in 1893, when Valéry was twenty-one: he became thereafter one of the most faithful of Mallarmé's disciples." Wilson describes this discipleship in the following predictable if incomprehensible terms: "Valéry, like his master, is 'haunted' by the 'azure'; but that azure is less a pure blue realm and more a rarefied upper air."

36. See Riffaterre 1983:30–31 for a discussion of "L'azur."

37. These are, according to Nash 1983:21–51 the essential strategies employed by Valéry for repelling anteriority.

38. This does not prevent critics from calculating origins and influences in precisely the way in which Mallarmé's poem laments; the critic thus makes the nightmare of "L'azur" come true. Noulet-Carner, for example, in the notes to the poem in Mallarmé

1945:1432: "The quadruple repetition within the same line . . . was suggested to Mallarmé, perhaps, by Edgar Poe's poem *The Bells*" ("La quadruple répétition à l'intérieur du même vers . . . fut peut-être suggéré à Mallarmé par le poëme d'Edgar Poe: *Les Cloches*").

39. According to Johnson 1987:120, "The fact that the word is repeated four times at the end of the poem would seem to indicate that what haunts Mallarmé is not simply some ideal symbolized by azure but the very word *azur* itself. Even a casual glance at nineteenth-century French poetry reveals that the word is par excellence a 'poetic' word—a sign that what one is reading is a poem."

40. On this haunting, see Dabezies 1991 and especially Blüher 1991.

41. There are, naturally, other voices to which Valéry's Faust refers. Bémol 1960:9 points to Valéry's first encounter with Faust by way of Nerval's translation in 1887 as the source of Valéry's idea. On possible sources or influences at work in Valéry's *Faust,* see Richthofen 1961, Fähnrich 1969:192ff and Wais n.d.:555–79.

42. On the implications of the word *lust* in the title of Valéry's work, see Lorenz 1971:178ff.

Chapter 12. Prostitution

1. So Fagles 1990 renders "κυνώπιδος" or "dog-faced"; Lattimore 1951 has "slut"; either way, the term is certainly meant to suggest a form of sexual depravity.

2. On Theseus, see *Cypria* (Allen 1912:fr. 1.5); Plutarch, *Theseus;* and *Iliad* 3.144; on Deiphobus, *Little Iliad* (Allen 1912, vol. 1); Euripides, *Trojan Women* 955–60, and *Odyssey* 4.276; on Achilles (whose marriage with Helen would take place after death, on the Isle of the Blest), Pausanius 3.19.11.

3. On the rise of this statistical genre in France, see Chevalier 1973.

4. On the principle of causality in Zola's naturalism, see James 1903:206, Hamon 1967:139–48, and Borie 1971.

5. "Paphnuce began to think of Thäis. . . . After a few hours of meditation, her image appeared to him with extreme clarity. He saw her again, just as he had seen her when she had tempted him, in all the beauty of her flesh. She appeared . . . like a Leda" ("Paphnuce se prit à songer à Thaïs. . . . Après quelques heures de méditation, l'image de Thaïs lui apparut avec une extrême netteté. Il la revit telle qu'il avait vue lors de la tentation, belle selon la chair. Elle se montra . . . comme une Léda" [France 1984:726]).

6. In this scene Thaïs is absorbed in her reflection in a mirror, a motif that is part of the conventional Helen repertory: "she was looking in the mirror for the first signs of the decline of her beauty and was thinking with horror that the time would come when there would be white hairs and wrinkles" ("elle épiait dans son miroir les premiers déclins de sa beauté et pensait avec épouvante que le temps viendrait enfin des cheveux blancs et des rides" [France 1984:777]). This is the same scene Ronsard prophesies in *SpH* 2.24, "Quand vous serez bien vieille."

7. This makes *La tentation,* Flaubert's first novel, very much like *Bouvard et Pécuchet,* his last. Donato 1979:215 cites Foucault's recognition of this congruence in "The Museum's Furnace: Notes toward a Contextual Reading of *Bouvard and Pécuchet*": "the *Temptation,* but also implicitly *Bouvard and Pécuchet,* 'is not only a book that Flaubert had long dreamed of writing; it is the dream of other books: all those other dreaming

and dreamt-of books—fragmented, taken up again, displaced, combined, distanced by the dream but also brought back by it to the imaginary and scintillating satisfaction of desire' "; Bouvard and Pécuchet " 'are tempted by books' " (Foucault 1967:11). If Bouvard and Pécuchet are readers, Antoine is an unreader: a reader seeking to exorcise the memory of all that he has read. On *La tentation* in relation to Flaubert's other novels, see Brombert 1973.

   8. I am here borrowing a distinction drawn by Barbara Johnson: see Johnson 1987: 129.

   9. Paul Claudel's *Protée* is a turn-of-the-century fantasy on Helen in the comic style of Offenbach. Jean-Louis Backès calls it a "farce" and a "bouffonnerie" (1984:124). But in its revisionary approach to myth it is very serious indeed and points the way to Giraudoux. The plot centers on an enterprising nymph named Brindosier who, with the arrival of the shipwrecked Menelaus and Helen upon Proteus's island, finds an opportunity to escape the clutches of the old sea-god. "Since we arrived," Menelaus complains, "She is so full of pride that / the only thing we can get out of her is: 'I am Helen'!" ("Depuis ce qui est arrivé, / Elle est si tellement pleine d'orgueil qu'on / ne peut rien en tirer / Hors 'Je suis Hélène'!" [Claudel 1965, 1:316]). Identity in this play—the real, the true, the singular—is a fragile and elusive thing when Helen is around. When Brindosier informs Proteus that Helen has arrived, Proteus exclaims: "I would like to see her" ("Ah, je voudrais la voir"). Brindosier asks: "You would like to have her?" ("Vous voudriez l'avoir?"). Proteus clarifies: "I'm saying I would like to look at her" ("Je dis que je voudrais la regarder" [329]). Claudel's word-play suggests that what lies behind the admiration of beauty is the will to possess it. As for Helen's *eidolon,* Proteus tells us it is a little joke he invented for his own amusement. In the end, however, it is Proteus who is deceived by his own creation. Brindosier's plan—to assume the appearance of Helen while Proteus persuades Menelaus that Brindosier *is* Helen, taking the real Helen for himself—leaves Proteus with nothing. In the end Brindosier sails off with Menelaus to Burgundy, and Helen is carried off by Iris to Olympus. The scene where Brindosier confronts Helen owes as much to Euripides as to Offenbach. There are now two Helens, instead of one. They are, however, differently dressed. Helen and Brindosier exchange ideas for styles and brand-names: why not *"La Troyenne"*? Or *"L'Hélénide"*? (2:348). And this is really Claudel's point: *Helen is a fashion* (think of poor Faust, left with only Helen's veil in his hands). When Helen and Brindosier exchange what they are wearing, they have effectively exchanged identities. On Claudel's theater in general, see Humes 1978.

   10. "You came, with soft steps, walking by there / Dear girl; and here is how one of them spoke: / 'I cannot help it, seeing her pass by, supernatural / And fair, I cannot be incensed that / The Greeks and the Trojans, for ten years now / Wounded, but not exhausted, suffer so many agonizing pains for her; / For she is as beautiful as a young goddess.' / And I did not find these words without wisdom" ("Tu vins, à pas légers, te promener par là, / Chère fille; et voici comment l'un d'eux parla: / 'J'ai beau faire; à la voir passer, surnaturelle / Et douce, je ne puis m'indigner que, pour elle, / Les Grecs et les Troyens, depuis bientôt dix ans, / Meurtris, mais non lassés, souffrent des maux cuissants: / Car elle est belle ainsi qu'une jeune déesse.' / Et je n'ai point trouvé ce propos sans sagesse" [Lemaître 1896, 1:9]).

   11. The scenario of adoration turned into aesthetic appreciation is a motif in *Contre*

Sainte-Beuve. It recurs, for example, in "La mort des cathédrales," in a description of the Catholic mass as witnessed by a nonbeliever. For the Proustian connoisseur is someone who does not need to believe in what he sees to enjoy it.

12. Beauty as repetition, as the return of the second-hand, is the subject, too, of Emile Verhaeren's 1912 tragedy *Hélène de Sparte*. Here the consequences are more destructive. Helen is a disease for which there is no cure and to which no one is immune. Repetition here becomes tantamount to contagion: an equation that is central to the fascination with the figure of the prostitute. A young man remembers his father, who "died, one evening, pronouncing her [Helen's] name" ("mourut, un soir, en prononçant son nom" [1912:29]). Castor is literally sick with love: "I find myself carried away by fever" ("Je me vois emporté par ma fièvre"). He is mad with delusions he cannot escape: "I am haunted. Helen is there, here, everywhere" ("Je suis hanté. Hélène est là, ici, partout" [74]). In this play Helen, emblem of individual desire, and yet symbol of collective catastrophe, is an always-contested piece of property. Castor, ruling in Menelaus's absence, declares: "She belongs to the world before belonging to anyone. . . . she belongs to whoever abducts her and possesses her and loves her / Especially to whoever keeps her and protects her" ("Elle appartient au monde avant d'être à personne /. . . . Elle est à qui l'enlève et la possède et l'aime; / Surtout à qui la garde et peut la protéger" [32]). Finders are keepers when it comes to Helen, but the keepers never keep her. The cycle of possession and dispossession is played out violently in Verhaeren's play: Castor resolves to abduct Helen, and assassinates Menelaus, who had just returned to claim his bride. But Castor is killed, in turn, by Electra, who has also fallen in love with Helen. (Electra's confession elicits this response from Helen: "Again! Again!" ("Encore! Encore!" [45]). It elicits a different reaction from a critic in the *Gaulois,* who, referring to both Castor and Electra, "bridles at a work where there are intimations of incest and homosexuality" ("s'affarouche d'une oeuvre où l'on frôle l'inceste et l'homosexualité" [May 7, 1912, in Trousson 1984:102]). When Pollux, taking up the reins of state, praises Helen in another *teichoskopia*-like ceremony, satyrs, naiads, and bacchants intrude, calling out their longing for Helen. The scene grows increasingly surrealistic. Earth and sea appear to reach out for her, and the air is filled with voices of desire calling out: "Hélène! Hélène! Hélène!" (100). Helen herself longs for annihilation to escape the *fatalité* of her own myth. To no avail: the play ends as Helen is abducted, this time by Zeus himself, and carried off to Olympus. Where, it seems clear, things will be no different than they were at Sparta.

13. See "Sappho, Fr. 16: Revisited" in chapter 6.

Prosthesis

1. Modern Greek poets, as we will see in the next section, not only write obsessively about Helen; they rarely resist the impulse to invoke or apostrophize her. Compare Sikelianos's "Σου" and "Σέ" with Elytis's "Εσένα" in his poem "Ελένη," "Helen" (discussed below).

2. On the role of rhetoric in nation building in general, see Benedict Anderson's *Imagined Communities: Reflections on the Origin and Spread of Nationalism* (1991).

3. It also explains the rise of the philhellenic movement in France in the early nineteenth century, which included volunteer groups like the Philanthropic Society for the

Assistance of the Greeks and pamphlets such as Chateaubriand's "Appeal to the Christian Nations: Considerations on the Greeks and the Turks." In 1827 the Académie Française chose "The Independence of Greece" as the subject for its poetry prize. On philhellenism, see Bikélas 1891 and Longnon 1921.

4. Racial essentialists like Jakob Philipp Fallmerayer and Arthur Comte de Gobineau saw little "Greekness" left in the contemporary Greek people. In the racial system the latter developed in the 1850s, black, yellow, and white peoples are distinguished as separate species, and the Greeks are characterized as an originally White Aryan people corrupted by black, Semitic, and Phoenician grafts (Herzfeld 1982:8 and Bernal 1987:360).

5. This is not just a feature of nineteenth-century thought. A *Wall Street Journal* column by Robert Kaplan (1989) contains the following assertion: "Greece in recent years has been an embarrassing sideshow of European politics — a low entertainment born of corruptive Byzantine and Ottoman influences." This is not all that far from the Greece described by Gobineau, Fallmerayer, and the European philhellenists, an unhealthy graft of Eastern and Western elements.

6. Isambert 1900:4 defends the role played by Europe in the liberation of Greece, which would appear to violate the law of noninterference in the interior affairs of sovereign nations, by arguing that Turkey is not a sovereign nation: "Turkey was not formed along the lines of the homogeneous and historical development of a nation: it is the reunion, held together by the sabre of a conquering army, of several nationalities successively subjugated, The sultans never encouraged the defeated populations to mix with the victorious race: there was a juxtaposition of diverse and contrasting elements, not the coherent formation of a state." (4) "La Turquie n'est pas formée par le développement homogène et historique d'une nation: c'est la réunion, sous le sabre d'une armée conquérante, de plusieurs nationalités successivemement soumises. Les sultanes n'ont jamais encouragé les populations vaincues à se fondre avec la race victorieuse: il y a eu juxtaposition d'éléments divers et contaires, et non formation cohérente d'un état" (4). The prohibition of miscegenation in the Ottoman state allows the historian to portray the empire as an artificial graft of occupier and occupied held together only by force: the Turkish people, Isambert claims, are "a barbarian encampment established temporarily in Europe"(12–13) "un camp barbare provisoirement établi en Europe" (12–13). Isambert can then affirm the autonomy and purity of the Greek race, uncorrupted by "Oriental" blood.

7. Van Coufoudakis 1988:56 summarizes the dilemma: "Since . . . independence from Turkish rule . . . Greece has sought an identity that would reconcile its competing ties to its Western heritage and its oriental experience. Greek elites . . . opted for the Western orientation. Furthermore, intervention by Greece's Western protectors . . . maintained this orientation."

8. Pei 1949:346 characterizes the two languages in a way that confirms Jeffrey's analysis: "After the liberation of Greece from Turkish rule . . . the spoken Greek tongue regained a small measure of its former splendor. The modern . . . language . . . has two forms: one, used in literary composition, called *katharevusa* . . . very close to the ancient tongue of Homer . . . the other a popular spoken tongue called *demotike,* which has borrowed considerably from foreign sources, particularly Turkish, and shows a certain measure of simplification of some of the old grammatical forms." Note that *katharevousa* is implicitly favored over demotic, which Pei understands as a corrupt hybrid.

9. The intrusion of the alien is the subject of Solomos's most celebrated poem. An incomplete series of fragments begun in 1826, *The Free Besieged* recounts the siege of Missolonghi and the massacre of its inhabitants. In Solomos's work the event becomes an allegory of purity and violation. The poem alternates between a narration of the siege itself and the lament of the Greeks trapped inside the city. Soldiers invoke the Greek Muse and curse the foreigners who have trespassed upon their sacred homeland.

10. On the politics of continuity and its role in the poetry of modern Greece, see Lambropoulos 1988.

11. On exile as a privileged rhetorical position for the vernacular poet, see Melara 1992:5 on *Les regrets:* "for du Bellay, literary excellence . . . is attainable through a series of 'exiles' . . . that is, literary success seems only to be possible if the poet is always, already 'in exile.' "

12. The argument has a particular resonance in Greece today. In a 1989 *Boston Globe* article entitled "In Greece, Myths Appear to Come Alive," we find the following. "Heroes I'd always thought were fictional are spoken of as once-living characters by guides at museums and ancient sites. Odysseus, Medusa, Hercules, Atlas and Medea are some of the ones they mention as having really existed. 'Achilles, Adonis!' calls a mother to two little boys playing ball in the stadium at Olympia" (Ibrovac 1989). The name here is accepted as a mysterious link, a miraculous bridge between modernity and antiquity. Compare the more cynical judgment of Seferis's revolutionary leader General Makryiannis, as he addresses his comrades: "You put a new leader in the fortress of Corinth, . . . and his name was Achilles. And hearing the name of Achilles, you imagined that this was the great Achilles, and you let the name fight the Turks. But fighting is not done by a name; what does the fighting is gallantry, patriotism, courage. And your Achilles of Corinth was a fine figure. And he had in the fortress everything necessary for fighting, and he had a great army. He saw in the distance the Turks of Dramali . . . and at the very first sight Achilles left the fort and fled without striking a blow" (Seferis 1966:34). Better the good Christian soldier, Makryiannis argues, than the good classical name: "Now if Nikitas had been there, would he have done that? Would Hadjichristo and the rest have done that? Of course not. Because they fought Dramali in the plain and routed him." Note that Makryiannis here in effect is advancing the Romeic, as opposed to the Hellenic, model of Greek culture. But the argument still relies on the mechanism of graft: his ideal Greek is not Achilles, but Hadjichristo, a name half-Turkish and half-Greek Orthodox.

13. Similarly, Krikos-Davis 1979:69n23 remarks that "the indefinite article applied to the phantom of Helen makes it a symbol."

Bibliography

Addison, J. 1905. *Classic Myths in Art.* London.

Ahl, F. 1985. *Metaformations: Soundplay and Wordplay in Ovid and Other Classical Poets.* Ithaca.

Alexiou, M. 1977. "Diglossia in Greece." In *Standard Languages: Spoken and Written.* Ed. W. Haas, 156–92. Manchester.

Alexiou, M. 1985. "C. P. Cavafy's 'Dangerous' Drugs: Poetry, Eros, and the Dissemination of Images." In *The Text and Its Margins.* Ed. M. Alexiou and V. Lambropoulos, 157–96. New York.

Allen, T. W., ed. 1912. *Homeri opera,* vol. 5. Oxford.

Altman, L. K. 1998. "The Patient's New Hand Is Doing Well in France." *New York Times,* October 16.

Ameis, K. F., and C. Hentze. 1877. *Anhang zu Homers Ilias.* Leipzig.

Anderson, B. 1991. *Imagined Communities: Reflections on the Origin and Spread of Nationalism.* New York.

Anderson, P. 1979. *Lineages of the Absolutist State.* London.

Anderson, W. S. 1963. "Calypso and Elysium." In *Essays on the Odyssey.* Ed. C. H. Taylor, Jr., 73–86. Bloomington.

Arnaut, D. 1978. *Le canzoni di Arnaut Daniel.* Ed. M. Perugi. 2 vols. Milan and Naples.

Auerbach, E. 1953. "Odysseus' Scar." In *Mimesis: The Representation of Reality in Western Literature.* Trans. W. R. Trask, 3–23. Princeton.

Austin, J. L. 1962. *How to Do Things with Words.* Oxford.

Austin, L. J. 1972. "Les premiers rapports entre Valéry et Mallarmé." In *Entretiens sur Paul Valéry: Actes du colloque de Montpellier des 16 et 17 octobre 1971.* Ed. D. Moutote. Paris.

Austin, N. 1975. *Archery at the Dark of the Moon: Poetic Problems in Homer's Odyssey.* Berkeley.

Austin, N. 1994. *Helen of Troy and Her Shameless Phantom.* Ithaca.

Backès, J.-L. 1984. *Le mythe d'Hélène.* Clermont-Ferrand.

Barkan, L. 1991. *Transuming Passions: Ganymede and the Erotics of Humanism.* Stanford.

Barnard, M., trans. 1958. *Sappho: A New Translation.* Berkeley.

Barnstone, W. 1990. "Translating from Ancient and Modern Greek." *Journal of Modern Greek Studies* 8:317–23.

300

Barnstone, W., trans. 1962. *Greek Lyric Poetry.* New York.

Barthes, R. 1957. *Mythologies.* Paris.

Barthes, R. 1970. *S/Z.* Paris.

Barthes, R. 1973. *Le plaisir du texte.* Paris.

Barthes, R. 1978. *A Lover's Discourse: Fragments.* Trans. R. Howard. New York.

Barthes, R. 1982. *Empire of Signs.* Trans. R. Howard. New York.

Bassi, K. 1993. "Helen and the Discourse of Denial in Stesichorus' Palinode." *Arethusa* 26:51–76.

Baudelaire, C. 1954. *Oeuvres.* Paris.

Baudrillard, J. 1983. *Simulations.* Trans. P. Foss, P. Patton, P. Beitchman. New York.

Baumgartner, E., ed. 1987. *Le Roman de Troie de Benoît de Sainte-Maure.* With modern French translation. Paris.

Baumgartner, E., and F. Ferrand, eds. 1983. *Poèmes d'amour des XIIe et XIIIe siècles.* With modern French translation. Paris.

Bayot, A. 1908. "La légende de Troie à la cour de Bourgogne." *Société d'emulation de Bruges: Mélanges* 1:3–50.

Beaton, R. 1976. "Dionysios Solomos: The Tree of Poetry." *Byzantine and Modern Greek Studies* 2:161–82.

Bec, P. 1977. *La lyrique française au moyen age (XIIe–XIIIe siècles): Contribution à une typologie des genres poétiques médiévaux,* vol. 1: *Etudes.* Paris.

Becker, F. 1894. *Die griechische Helena in Mythos und Epos.* Magdeburg.

Becker, P. A. 1893. *Jean Lemaire, der erste humanistische Dichter Frankreichs.* Strassburg.

Bellenger, Y., and D. Queruel, eds. *Thibaut de Champagne: Prince et poète au XIIIe siècle.* Lyon.

Bémol, M. 1960. "Le jeune Valéry et Goethe: Etude de genèse réciproque." *Revue de littérature comparée* 34:5–36.

Benjamin, W. 1968. "The Work of Art in the Age of Mechanical Reproduction." In *Illuminations.* Ed. H. Arendt and trans. H. Zohn, 217–51. New York.

Bennett, C. E., ed. 1914. Horace. *Odes and Epodes.* With translation. Cambridge, Mass.

Benveniste, E. 1974. *Problèmes de linguistique générale.* 2 vols. Paris.

Berg, E. 1986. "Iconoclastic Moments: Reading the Sonnets for Hélène, Writing the Portuguese Letters." In *The Poetics of Gender.* Ed. N. K. Miller, 208–21. New York.

Berger, J. 1972. *Ways of Seeing.* London.

Bergren, A. 1979. "Helen's Web: Time and Tableau in the *Iliad.*" *Helios* 7:19–34.

Bernal, M. 1987. *Black Athena: The Afroasiatic Roots of Classical Civilization,* vol. 1: *The Fabrication of Ancient Greece, 1785–1985.* New Brunswick.

Bernardo, A.S., trans. 1975. Petrarch. *Rerum familiarium libri* I–VIII. Albany.

Bernardo, A. S., and S. Levin, eds. 1990. *The Classics in the Middle Ages.* Binghamton.

Bernart de Ventadorn. 1966. *Chansons d'amour.* Ed. M. Lazar. Paris.

Bernheimer, C. 1989a. *Figures of Ill Repute: Representing Prostitution in Nineteenth-Century France.* Cambridge, Mass.

Bernheimer, C. 1989b. "Forty-five Thousand Copies of Emile Zola's *Nana* Are Sold on Its Publication Day: Prostitution in the Novel." In *A New History of French Literature.* Ed. D. Hollier, 780–85. Cambridge, Mass.

Berry, P. 1982. *Echo's Subtle Body: Contributions to an Archetypal Psychology.* Dallas.

Bespaloff, R. 1947. *On the Iliad.* Trans. Mary McCarthy. New York.

Bezucha, R. 1989. "Discourses on Misery." In *A New History of French Literature.* Ed. D. Hollier, 687–92. Cambridge, Mass.

Biehl, W., ed. 1970. Euripides. *Troades.* Lepizig.

Bikélas, D. 1891. "Le philhellénisme en France." *Revue d'histoire diplomatique* 5:346–65.

Binet, C. 1586, 1587, 1597. *Critical Edition of the Discours de la vie de Pierre de Ronsard par Claude Binet.* Ed. H. M. Evers. Philadelphia.

Birns, N. 1993. "The Trojan Myth: Postmodern Reverberations." *Exemplaria* 5:45–78.

Bloch, M. 1961. *Feudal Society.* Trans. L. A. Manyon. London.

Bloch, R. H. 1983. *Etymologies and Genealogies: A Literary Anthropology of the French Middle Ages.* Chicago.

Bloom, H. 1973. *The Anxiety of Influence.* New York.

Bloom, H. 1976. *Poetry and Repression.* New Haven.

Bloom, H. 1978. "Freud and the Poetic Sublime." *Antaeus* 30/31:355–76.

Bloomfield, M. W., ed. 1981. *Allegory, Myth, and Symbol.* Harvard English Studies 9. Cambridge, Mass.

Blüher, K. A. 1991. "Le statut intertextuel du *Faust* de Valéry." In *Paul Valéry: Le cycle de 'Mon Faust' devant la sémiotique théâtrale et l'analyse textuelle.* Ed. K. A. Blüher and J. Schmidt-Radefeldt, 55–70. Tübingen.

Body, J. 1975. *Giraudoux et l'Allemagne.* Paris.

Borie, J. 1971. *Zola et les mythes, ou: De la nausée au salut.* Paris.

Bourdeille, P. de., seigneur de Brantôme. 1876. *Oeuvres complètes,* vol. 9. Ed. L. Lalannne. Paris.

Bourgeois, R. 1969. "Les deux cordes de la lyre, ou Goethe jugé par George Sand." In *Hommage à George Sand.* Ed. L. Cellier, 92–100. Paris.

Boutemy, A. 1946. "Le poème *Pergama Flere Volo* et ses imitateurs du XIIe siècle." *Latomus* 5:240–41.

Bouveresse, J. 1995. "Philosophy from an Antiphilosopher: Paul Valéry." Trans. C. Fournier and S. Langier. *Critical Inquiry* 21:354–81.

Bowra, C. M. 1930. *Tradition and Design in the Iliad.* Oxford.

Bowra, C. M. 1936. *Greek Lyric Poetry.* Oxford.

Bowra, C. M. 1952. *Heroic Poetry.* London.

Brahney, K. J. 1998. *The Lyrics of Thibaut de Champagne.* New York.

Brasillach, R. 1963–64. *Oeuvres complètes.* Ed. M. Bardèche. 12 vols. Paris.

Brombert, V. 1973. *The Novels of Flaubert.* Princeton.

Brown, P. 1967. *Augustine of Hippo: A Biography.* Berkeley.

Browning, R. 1969. *Medieval and Modern Greek.* Cambridge.

Brownlee, M. S., K. Brownlee, and S. G. Nichols, eds. 1991. *The New Medievalism.* Baltimore.

Buchthal, H. 1971. *Historia Troiana: Studies in the History of Mediaeval Secular Illustration.* London.

Bundy, E. L. 1986. *Studia Pindarica.* Berkeley.

Burke, K. 1950. *A Rhetoric of Motives.* Berkeley.

Burkert, W. 1985. *Greek Religion.* Trans. John Raffan. Cambridge, Mass.

Burn, A. R. 1960. *The Lyric Age of Greece.* New York.

Burnett, A. P. 1960. "Euripides' *Helen:* A Comedy of Ideas." *Classical Philology* 55:51–64.

Burnett, A. P. 1983. *Three Archaic Poets.* Cambridge.

Butcher, S. H. 1932. *Aristotle's Theory of Poetry and the Fine Arts.* London.

Butler, H. E., ed. 1979. Quintilian. *Institutio oratoria.* 4 vols. With translation. Cambridge, Mass.

Butler, S. 1967. *The Authoress of the Odyssey.* Chicago.

Calame, C. 1977. *Les choeurs de jeunes filles en Grèce archaïque,* vol. 1: *Morphologie, fonction religieuse et sociale.* Rome.

Calhoun, G. M. 1937. "Homer's Gods—Prolegomena." *TAPA* 68:24–25.

Calmette. J. 1949. *Les grands ducs de Bourgogne.* Paris.

Camille, M. 1989. *The Gothic Idol.* Cambridge.

Campbell, D. A., ed. 1967. *Greek Lyric Poetry.* Bristol.

Camus, A. 1954. "L'exil d'Hélène." In *L'été,* 108–19. Paris.

Carson, A. 1986. *Eros the Bittersweet.* Princeton.

Castor, G. 1964. *Pléiade Poetics: A Study in Sixteenth-Century Thought and Terminology.* Cambridge.

Castor, G. 1971. "The Theme of Illusion in Ronsard's *Sonnets pour Hélène* and in the Variants of the 1552 *Amours." Forum for Modern Language Studies* 7:361–73.

Castor. G. 1973. "Petrarchism and the Quest for Beauty in the Amours of Cassandre and the Sonnets for Hélène." In *Ronsard the Poet.* Ed. T. Cave, 79–120. London.

Cave, T. 1973. "Ronsard's Mythological Universe." In *Ronsard the Poet.* Ed. T. Cave, 159–209. London.

Cave, T. 1979. *The Cornucopian Text: Problems of Writing in the French Renaissance.* Oxford.

CBS. 1993. Transcript, *Eye to Eye with Connie Chung,* December 23.

Cerquiglini, B. 1989. *Eloge de la variante.* Paris.

Chadwick, C. 1954. "The Composition of the Sonnets pour Hélène." *French Studies* 5:326–32.

Chadwick, H., trans. 1991. Saint Augustine. *Confessions.* With introduction. New York.

Chamard, H., ed. 1948. Joachim du Bellay. *La deffence et illustration de la langue françoyse.* With notes and the *Quintil Horatian* of Barthélemy Aneau. Paris.

Champion, P. 1925. *Ronsard et son temps.* Paris.

Chantraine, P. 1968. *Dictionnaire étymologique de la langue grecque.* 4 vols. Paris.

Chastel, A., ed. 1959. *Trésors de la poésie médiévale.* Paris.

Chénier, A. 1950. *Oeuvres complètes.* Ed. G. Walter. Paris.

Cherchi, P. 1994. *Andreas and the Ambiguity of Courtly Love.* Toronto.

Chesney, K. 1942. "A Neglected Prose Version of the *Roman de Troie." Medium Aevum* 11:46–49.

Chevalier, L. 1973. *Laboring Classes and Dangerous Classes.* Trans. Frank Jellinek. New York.

Ciardi, J., trans. 1954. Dante. *The Inferno.* New York.

Clader, L. L. 1976. *Helen: The Evolution from Divine to Heroic in Greek Epic Tradition.* Leiden.

Claudel, P. 1965. *Protée.* In *Théâtre.* Paris.

Clota, J. A. 1957. "Helena de Troya: Historia de un Mito." *Helmantica* 8:373–94.

Cohen, G., ed. 1950. Ronsard. *Oeuvres complètes.* 2 vols. Paris.

Coleman, R. 1971. "Structure and Intention in the *Metamorphoses.*" *Classical Quarterly* 65:461–76.

Colie, R. 1966. *Paradoxia Epidemica.* Princeton.

Cook, J. D. 1927. "Euhemerism, a Medieval Interpretation of Classical Paganism." *Speculum* 21:396–440.

Cooper, L., trans. 1938. *Phaedrus, Ion, Gorgias, and Symposium.* Ithaca.

Cornford, F. M., trans. 1931. *Plato's Theory of Knowledge: The Theaetetus and the Sophist.* Oxford.

Coufoudakis, V. 1988. "Greek Foreign Policy since 1974: Quest for Independence." *Journal of Modern Greek Studies* 6:55–79.

Croally, N. T. 1994. *Euripidean Polemic: The Trojan Women and the Function of Tragedy.* Cambridge.

Culler, J. 1981. *The Pursuit of Signs: Semiotics, Literature, and Deconstruction.* Ithaca.

Culler, J. 1982. *On Deconstruction: Theory and Criticism after Structuralism.* Ithaca.

Curran, L. 1978. "Rape and Rape Victims in the *Metamorphoses.*" *Arethusa* 11:213–41.

Curtius, E. R. 1953. *European Literature and the Latin Middle Ages.* Trans. W. R. Trask. Princeton.

Dabezies, A. 1991. "*Mon Faust* et la tradition du *Faust* allemand." In *Paul Valéry: Le cycle de 'Mon Faust' devant la sémiotique théâtrale et l'analyse textuelle.* Ed. K. A. Blüher and J. Schmidt-Radefeldt, 37–52. Tübingen.

Dahlberg, C., trans. 1995. *The Romance of the Rose by Guillaume de Lorris and Jean de Meun.* 3d ed. Princeton.

Dale, A. M., ed. 1967. Euripides. *Helen.* With introduction and commentary. Oxford.

DeJean, J. 1989. *Fictions of Sappho, 1546–1937.* Chicago.

de Lettenhove, K., ed. 1864. *Oeuvres de Georges Chastellain.* Brussels.

de Lisle, L. 1852. *Poèmes antiques.* Paris.

de Lisle, L. 1928. *Poésies complètes de Leconte de Lisle.* Paris.

de Lisle, L. 1929. *Oeuvres,* vol. 4: *Poèmes antiques.* Paris.

de Lisle, L. 1969. *Choix de poèmes de Leconte de Lisle.* Ed. P. Gallissaires. Paris.

de Man, P. 1971. *Blindness and Insight.* Minneapolis.

de Man, P. 1978. "The Epistemology of Metaphor." *Critical Inquiry* 5:13–30.

de Man, P. 1983. "*Appendix A: A Review of Harold Bloom's* Anxiety of Influence." In *Blindness and Insight: Essays in the Rhetoric of Contemporary Criticism.* Rev. ed., 267–76. Minneapolis.

de Man, P. 1984. *The Rhetoric of Romanticism.* New York.

de Man, P. 1985. "Lyrical Voice in Contemporary Theory: Riffaterre and Jauss." In *Lyric Poetry: Beyond New Criticism.* Ed. C. Hosek and P. Parker, 55–72. Ithaca.

Demats, Paule. 1973. *Fabula: Trois études de mythologie antique et médiévale.* Geneva.

Demerson, G. 1972. *La mythologie classique dans l'oeuvre lyrique de la "Pléiade."* Geneva.

Denniston, J. D., and D. Page. 1957. *Agamemnon.* Oxford.

Dernedde, R. 1887. *Über die den altfranzösischen Dichtern bekannten epischen Stoffe aus dem Altertum.* Erlangen.

Derrida, J. 1967. *De la grammatologie.* Paris. = *Of Grammatology.* Trans. and intro. G. C. Spivak. Baltimore. 1976.

Derrida, J. 1972a. *La dissémination*. Paris. = *Dissemination*. Trans. B. Johnson. Chicago. 1981.

Derrida, J. 1972b. *Marges de la philosophie*. Paris.

Derrida, J. 1974. *Glas*. Paris.

Derrida, J. 1977. "Qual quelle: Les sources de Valéry." In *Marges de la philosophie*, 325–63. Paris.

Derrida, J. 1979. "Living On. Border Lines." Trans. J. Hulbert. In *Deconstruction and Criticism*. Ed. H. Bloom et al., 75–176. New York.

Derrida, J. 1984. *Signéponge*. With translation by R. Rand. New York.

Deschamps, G. 1898. "Victor Hugo et le philhellénisme." *Revue des cours et conférences* (June 23):693–706.

Desonay, F. 1959. *Ronsard poète de l'amour*. Brussels.

Detienne, Marcel. 1973. *Les maîtres de vérité dans la Grèce archaïque*. 2d ed. Paris.

Devereux, G. 1982. *Femme et mythe*. Paris.

De Vries, G. J. 1969. *A Commentary on the Phaedrus of Plato*. Amsterdam.

Diderot, D. 1976. *Parodoxe sur le comédien*. Paris.

Diels, H., and W. Kranz, eds. 1903. *Die Fragmente der Vorsokratiker*. Berlin.

Diez, F. 1845. *La poésie des troubadours*. Trans. F. de Rosin. Paris.

Donato, E. 1979. "The Museum's Furnace: Notes toward a Contextual Reading of *Bouvard and Pécuchet*. In *Textual Strategies: Perspectives in Post-Structuralist Criticism*. Ed. J. V. Harari, 213–38. Ithaca.

Dornseiff, F. 1927. *Vorträge der Bibliothek Warburg 1924–25*. Leipzig.

Doutrepont, G. 1906. *Inventaire de la "Librairie" de Phillipe le Bon (1420)*. Brussels.

Doutrepont, G. 1934. *Jean Lemaire de Belges et la Renaissance*. Brussels.

Dragonetti, R. 1960. *La technique poétique des trouvères dans la chanson courtoise*. Brugge.

Dronke, P. 1977. *The Medieval Lyric*. 2d ed. New York.

Dubois, C.-G. 1989. "Autour du nom d'Hélène: Doubles et couples, similitudes et simularcres." In *Études Ronsardiennes II: Ronsard et son 14e centenaire*. Ed. Y. Bellenger, J. Cedard, D. Menanger, and M. Simonin, 173–81. Geneva.

duBois, P. 1978. "Sappho and Helen." *Arethusa* 11:89–100.

duBois, P. 1995. *Sappho Is Burning*. Chicago.

Duby, G. 1978. *Medieval Marriage: Two Models from Twelfth-Century France*. Trans. E. Forster. Baltimore.

Durling, R. M., ed. 1976. *Petrarch's Lyric Poems: The Rime Sparse and Other Lyrics*. With translation and introduction. Cambridge, Mass.

Ehrhart, M. J. 1987. *The Judgment of the Trojan Prince Paris in Medieval Literature*. Philadelphia.

Else, G. F., ed. 1957. *Aristotle's Poetics: The Argument*. With translation and commentary. Cambridge, Mass.

Elytis, O. 1979. *Ἐκλογή 1935–1977*. Athens.

Engels, J. 1945. *Études sur l'"Ovide moralisé*. Groningen.

Erbse, H., ed. 1969. *Scholia Graeca in Homeri Iliadem*, vol. 1. Berlin.

Evelyn-White, H., ed. 1914. *Hesiod, the Homeric Hymns, and Homerica*. With translation. Cambridge, Mass.

Fabre, J. 1965. *Chénier*. Paris.

Fagles, R., trans. 1990. Homer. *The Iliad.* New York.

Fähnrich, H. 1969. *Paul Valéry und Goethe.* Weimar.

Fairclough, H. R., ed. 1926. Horace. *Satires, Epistles, and Ars Poetica.* With translation. Cambridge, Mass.

Fairclough, H. R., ed. 1999. *Virgil.* With translation. Cambridge, Mass.

Faral, E. 1913. *Recherches sur les sources des contes et romans courtois du moyen âge.* Paris.

Favier, J. 1984. *Le temps des principautés.* Paris.

Ferguson, M. 1983. *Trials of Desire: Renaissance Defenses of Poetry.* New Haven.

Ferguson, M. 1989. "Joachim Du Bellay Publishes *La défense et illustration de la langue française:* An Offensive Defense for a New Intellectual Elite." In *A New History of French Literature.* Ed. D. Hollier, 194–98. Cambridge, Mass.

Flaubert, G. 1968. *La tentation de Saint Antoine.* Edited and with an introduction by E. Maynial. Paris.

Fletcher, Angus. 1964. *Allegory: The Theory of a Symbolic Mode.* Ithaca.

Ford, A. L. 1985. "The Seal of Theognis: The Politics of Authorship in Archaic Greece." In *Theognis of Megara: Poetry and the Polis.* Ed. T. J. Figueira and G. Nagy, 82–95. Baltimore.

Foucault, M. 1966. *Les mot et les choses.* Paris.

Foucault, M. 1967. "La bibliothèque fantastique." Introduction to Flaubert, *La tentation de Saint Antoine.* Ed. Henri Ronse. Paris.

Foucault, M. 1990. *The History of Sexuality I: An Introduction.* Trans. R. Hurley. New York.

Foucher, J.-P., ed. 1970. *Chrétien de Troyes: Romans de la table ronde.* With translation. Paris.

Fowler, H. W., and F. G. Fowler, trans. 1905. *The Works of Lucian of Samosota,* vol. 1. Oxford.

France, A. 1984. *Thaïs.* In *Oeuvres.* Paris.

Frappier, J. 1963. "L'humanisme de Jean de Belges." *Bibliothèque d'humanisme et Renaissance* 25:289–306.

Frappier, J. N.d. *La poésie lyrique en France aux XIIe et XIIIe siècles.* Paris.

Frappier, J., ed. 1947. *Jean Lemaire de Belges: La concorde des deux langages.* With notes. Paris.

Freccero, C. 1991. *Father Figures: Genealogy and Narrative Structure in Rabelais.* Ithaca.

Freccero, J. 1975. "The Fig Tree and the Laurel: Petrarch's Poetics." *Diacritics* 5:34–40.

Freeman, K., ed. 1966. *Ancilla to the Pre-Socratic Philosophers: A Complete Translation of the Fragments in Diels, Fragmente der Vorsokratiker.* Cambridge, Mass.

Freese, J. H., ed. 1926. Aristotle. *The "Art" of Rhetoric.* With translation. Cambridge, Mass.

Freud, S. 1954. *The Standard Edition of the Complete Psychological Works of Sigmund Freud.* 24 vols. Ed. and trans. J. Strachey. London.

Freud, S. 1957. *A General Selection from the Works of Sigmund Freud.* Ed. J. Rickman. New York.

Freud, S. 1965. *The Interpretation of Dreams.* Trans. J. Strachey. New York.

Friar, K., ed. 1982. *Modern Greek Poetry.* With translation. Athens.

Friedman, T. L. 1989. *From Beirut to Jerusalem.* New York.

Funck-Brentano, F. 1935. *La belle Hélène, reine de Sparte.* Paris.

Gadoffre, G. 1960. *Ronsard par lui-même.* Paris.

Gadoffre, G. 1963. "Ronsard et la pensée ficinienne." *Archives de philosophie* 26:45–58.

Galinsky, G. K. 1975. *Ovid's Metamorphoses: An Introduction to Its Basic Aspects.* Berkeley.

Ganshof, F. L. 1964. *Feudalism.* Trans. P. Grierson. London.

Garapon, R. 1981. *Ronsard, chantre de Marie et d'Hélène.* Paris.

Gaudon, J. 1985. *Victor Hugo et le théâtre: Stratégie et dramaturgie.* Paris.

Gaunt, S., and S. Kay, eds. 1999. *The Troubadours: An Introduction.* New York.

Gautier, T. 1966. *Mademoiselle de Maupin.* Paris.

Gellie, G. 1986. "Helen in *The Trojan Women.*" In *Studies in Honour of T. B. L. Webster.* Ed. J. H. Betts, J. T. Hooker, J. R. Green, 114–21. Bristol.

Genette, G. 1979. "Valéry and the Poetics of Language." In *Textual Strategies.* Ed. J. Haran, 359–73. Ithaca.

Ghali-Kahil, L. 1955. *Les enlèvements et le retour d'Hélène dans les textes et les documents figurés.* Paris.

Ghali-Kahil, L. 1981–90. "Helene." In *Lexicon iconographicum mythologiae classicae.* 4 vols. Zurich.

Gilbert, S., and S. Gubar. 1979. *The Madwoman in the Attic.* New Haven.

Gilson, E. 1932. *Les idées et les lettres.* Paris.

Giraudoux, J. 1935. *La guerre de Troie n'aura pas lieu.* Paris.

Giraudoux, J. 1949. *Siegfried.* Paris.

Giraudoux, J. 1982. *Théâtre complet.* Paris.

Goethe, J. W. 1950. *Faust,* vol. 1. Ed. R.-M. S. Heffner, H. Rehder, W. F. Twaddell. Madison.

Goethe, J. W. 1961. *Faust: Eine Tragödie.* Ed. E. Trunz. Hamburg.

Goethe, J. W. 1965. *Faust.* 2 vols. Trans. D. E. Passage. New York.

Goethe, J. W. 1977. *Roman Elegies.* Trans. D. Luke. New York.

Goethe, J. W. 1987. *Faust,* vol. 1. Trans. D. Luke. Oxford.

Golden, L., and O. B. Hardison, Jr., eds. 1981. *Aristotle's Poetics.* With translation by L. Golden and commentary by O. B. Hardison, Jr. Tallahassee.

Goldin, F. 1967. *The Mirror of Narcissus in the Courtly Love Lyric.* Ithaca.

Goldin, F. 1975. "An Array of Perspectives in the Early Courtly Love Lyric." In *The Pursuit of Perfection: Courtly Love in Medieval Literature.* Ed. Joan M. Ferrante and George Economou, 51–100. Port Washington, N.Y.

Goldin, F., ed. 1983. *Lyrics of the Troubadours and Trouvères: An Anthology and a History.* With translation. Gloucester, Mass.

Goodman, J. 1992. Rev. of *The Medieval Translator: The Theory and Practices of Translation in the Middle Ages.* Ed. R. Ellis. *Allegorica* 13:89–95.

Goold, G. P., ed. 1990. *Propertius: Elegies.* With translation. Cambridge, Mass.

Gordon, C. H. 1962. *Before the Bible.* New York.

Gordon, G. S. 1927. *Medium Aevum and the Middle Ages.* Tract 19. Oxford.

Gottlieb, R. 1990. "Why We Can't 'Do without' Camille." In Bernardo and Levin, 153–64.

Gove, P. B., ed. 1963. *Webster's Third New International Dictionary of the English Language*. Springfield, Mass.

Graves, R. 1955a. *Greek Myths*. 2 vols. London.

Graves, R. 1955b. *Homer's Daughter*. Garden City.

Greenblatt, S. J., ed. 1981. *Allegory and Representation*. Selected Papers from the English Institute, 1979–80. Baltimore.

Greene, R. 1991. *Post-Petrarchism*. Princeton.

Greene, T. 1982. *The Light in Troy: Imitation and Discovery in Renaissance Poetry*. New Haven.

Greene, W. C. 1918. "Plato's View of Poetry." *HSCP* 29:1–76.

Greene, W. M., trans. 1963. Saint Augustine. *The City of God against the Pagans,* vol. 2. Cambridge, Mass.

Gregory, J. 1991. *Euripides and the Instruction of the Athenians*. Ann Arbor.

Greico, S. F. M. 1991. *Ange ou diablesse: La représentation de la femme au XVIe siècle*. Paris.

Grube, G. M. A. 1965. *The Greek and Roman Critics*. London.

Gummere, R. M., ed. 1970. Seneca. *Ad Lucilium epistulae morales*. 3 vols. With translation. Cambridge, Mass.

Hackforth, R., trans. 1945. *Plato's Examination of Pleasure: A Translation of the Philebus*. With introduction and commentary. New York.

Hadas, M., and J. McLean, trans. 1960. *Ten Plays by Euripides*. New York.

Halévy, L., and H. Meilhac, N.d. *La Belle Hélène*. In *Théâtre*. With a preface by P. Carton. Paris.

Hamilton, W., trans. 1951. Plato. *The Symposium*. London.

Hamon, P. 1967. "A propos de l'impressionisme de Zola." *Les cahiers naturalistes* 34: 139–48.

Hampton, T. 1990. *Writing for History: The Rhetoric of Exemplarity in Renaissance Literature*. Ithaca.

Häpke, G. 1899. *Kritische Beiträge zu Jacques Milets dramatischer Istoire de la Destruction de Troye la Grant*. Marburg.

Harvey, D. 1990. *The Condition of Postmodernity*. Cambridge, Mass.

Hays, M., ed. 1992. *Critical Conditions: Regarding the Historical Moment*. Minneapolis.

Herzfeld, M. 1982. *Ours Once More: Folklore, Ideology, and the Making of Modern Greece*. Austin.

Highet, G. 1949. *The Classical Tradition: Greek and Roman Influences on Western Literature*. New York.

Hoerber, R. G. 1958. "Love or Rhetoric in Plato's *Phaedrus?*" *Classical Bulletin* 34:33–34.

Hofmann, C. 1968. "De quelques sources à Paul Valéry." In Noulet-Carner, ed., 135–61.

Hofmannsthal, H. von. 1928. *Die Ägyptische Helena*. Music by Richard Strauss. With introduction and translation by S. Kohler. Detroit Symphony Orchestra.

Hollander, J. 1981. *The Figure of Echo*. Berkeley.

Hollier, D. 1989. "On Schools, Churches, and Museums." In *A New History of French Literature*. Ed. D. Hollier, 830–36. Cambridge, Mass.

Hollier, D., ed. 1989. *A New History of French Literature*. Cambridge, Mass.

Honour, H. 1968. *Neo-Classicism*. London.

Hosek, C., and P. Parker, eds. 1985. *Lyric Poetry: Beyond New Criticism.* Ithaca.

Howatson, M. C., ed. 1989. *The Oxford Companion to Classical Literature.* New York.

Hubbell, H. M., trans. 1993. Cicero. *De inventione; De optimo genere oratorum; Topica.* Cambridge, Mass.

Huchet, J.-C. 1989. "The Romances of Antiquity." In *A New History of French Literature.* Ed. D. Hollier, 36–40. Cambridge, Mass.

Huet, G., ed. 1912. *Chansons et descorts de Gautier de Dargies.* Paris

Hugo, V. 1964. *Oeuvres poétiques,* vol. 1. Paris.

Hugo, V. 1966. *Notre-Dame de Paris.* Paris.

Hugo, V. 1968. *Odes et ballades; Les orientales.* With introduction by Jean Gaudon. Paris.

Huizinga, J. 1937. *The Waning of the Middle Ages.* London.

Hult, D. F. 1989. "Jean de Meun's Continuation of *Le roman de la rose.*" In *A New History of French Literature.* Ed. D. Hollier, 97–103. Cambridge, Mass.

Humes, J. N. 1978. *Two against Time: A Study of the Very Present Worlds of Paul Claudel and Charles Péguy.* Chapel Hill.

Huppé, B. 1990. "Aeneas' Journey to the New Troy." In Bernardo and Levin, 175–87.

Ibrovac, M. 1966. *Claude Fauriel et la fortune européenne des poésies populaires grecque et serbe.* Paris.

Ibrovac, M. 1989. "In Greece, Myths Appear to Come Alive." *Boston Globe,* March 19.

Isambert, G. 1900. *L'indépendence grecque et l'Europe.* Paris.

Jacobus, M. 1985. "Apostrophe and Lyric Voice in the Prelude." In *Lyric Poetry: Beyond New Criticism.* Ed. C. Hosek and P. Parker, 167–81. Ithaca.

Jaeger, W. 1944. *Paideia: The Ideals of Greek Culture,* vol. 3. Trans. G. Highet. New York.

Jakobson, R. 1987. "Linguistics and Poetics." In *Language in Literature.* Ed. K. Pomorska and S. Rudy, 62–94. Cambridge, Mass.

James, H. 1903. "Emile Zola." *Atlantic Monthly* 92:193–210.

Jameson, F. 1971. *Marxism and Form.* Princeton.

Jeanroy, A. 1869–99. *Histoire de la langue et de la littérature française des origines à 1900,* vol. 1. Ed. L. Petit de Julleville. 8 vols. Paris.

Jeanroy, A. 1934. *La poésie lyrique des troubadours.* Toulouse.

Jebb, R. C. 1962. *Attic Orators from Antiphon to Isaeos.* 2 vols. New York.

Jed, S. 1989. *Chaste Thinking: The Rape of Lucretia and the Birth of Humanism.* Bloomington.

Jeffrey, M. 1985. "Adamantios Koraïs: Language and Revolution." In *Culture and Nationalism in Nineteenth-Century Eastern Europe.* Ed. R. Sussex and J. C. Eade, 42–55. Columbus, Ohio.

Jenkinson, A. J. 1941. "Prior Analytics." In McKeon, ed.

Jodogne, P. 1970. " 'Les rhétoriqueurs' et l'humanisme: Problème d'histoire littéraire." In *Humanism in France at the End of the Middle Ages and in the Early Renaissance.* Ed. A. H. T. Levi, 150–75. New York.

Johnson, B. 1978. "The Frame of Reference: Poe, Lacan, Derrida." In *Psychoanalysis and the Question of the Text.* Ed. G. Hartman, 149–71. Baltimore.

Johnson, B. 1980. "Poetry and Performative Language: Mallarmé and Austin." In *The Critical Difference: Essays in the Contemporary Rhetoric of Reading,* 52–66. Baltimore.

Johnson, B. 1987. "Les Fleurs du Mal Armé: Some Reflections on Intertextuality." In *A World of Difference*, 116–33. Baltimore.

Johnson, B. 1989. "The Lady in the Lake." In *A New History of French Literature*. Ed. D. Hollier, 627–32. Cambridge, Mass.

Johnson, B. 1991. "Gender and Poetry: Charles Baudelaire and Marceline Desbordes-Valmore." In *Displacements: Women, Tradition, Literatures in French*. Ed. J. DeJean and N. K. Miller, 163–81. Baltimore.

Joly, A. 1870. *Benoît de Sainte-More et Le roman de Troie, ou: Les métamorphoses d'Homère et de l'épopée gréco-latine au moyen-age*. Paris.

Jones, J. 1962. *On Aristotle and Greek Tragedy*. Stanford.

Jourda, P., ed. 1962. Rabelais. *Oeuvres complètes*, vol. 1. With introduction and notes. Paris.

Jowett, B., trans. 1892. *The Dialogues of Plato*. With commentary. Oxford.

Joyce, J. 1916. *Portrait of the Artist as a Young Man*. New York.

Joyce, M., trans. 1935. *Plato's Symposium, or: The Drinking Party*. New York.

Kahane, H. and R. Kahane. 1990. "Language: Vehicule of Classical Heritage." In Bernardo and Levin, 199–205.

Kakridis, J. Th. 1971. *Homer Revisited*. Lund.

Kannicht, R. 1969. *Euripides, Helena. Hrsg. u. eklärt von Richard Kannicht*. 2 vols. Heidelberg.

Kaplan, A. Y. 1989. "Literature and Collaboration." In *A New History of French Literature*. Ed. D. Hollier, 966–71. Cambridge, Mass.

Kaplan, R. D. 1989. "Understanding Mr. Papandreou's Final Insult to Greece." *Wall Street Journal*, August 7.

Karandonis, A. 1976. Ὁ ποιητὴς Γιῶργος Σεφέρης. Athens.

Kaufmann, V. 1989. "I Cannot Abide Stupidity." In *A History of French Literature*. Ed. D. Hollier, 876–81. Cambridge, Mass.

Keeley, E., and P. Sherrard, trans. 1981. *Voices of Modern Greece*. Princeton.

Kelly, D. 1978. "'Translatio studii': Translation, Adaptation, and Allegory in Medieval French Literature." *Philological Quarterly* 57:287–310.

Kem, J. 1994. *Jean Lemaire de Belges' Les Illustrations de Gaule et Singularitez de Troye: The Trojan Legend in the Late Middle Ages and Early Renaissance*. New York.

Kennedy, G. 1958. "Isocrates' *Encomium of Helen*: A Panhellenic Document." *TAPA* 89:77–83.

Kennedy, G. 1963. *The Art of Persuasion in Greece*. Princeton.

Kennedy, G. A. 1989, trans. George Sand. *A Woman's Version of the Faust Legend: The Seven Strings of the Lyre*. With introduction by trans. Chapel Hill.

Kennedy, W. J. 1978. *Rhetorical Norms in Renaissance Literature*. New Haven.

Kirk, G. S. 1966. *The Presocratic Philosophers*. Cambridge.

Kirk, G. S. 1978. "The Formal Duels in Books 3 and 7 of the *Iliad*." In *Homer, Tradition, and Invention*. Ed. B. C. Fenik, 18–40. Leiden.

Kitto, H. D. 1961. *Greek Tragedy*. London.

Klein, R. 1970. "Straight Lines and Arabesques: Metaphors of Metaphor." *Yale French Studies* 45:64–86.

Knott, B. I., ed. 1978. *Erasmus' Copia: On the Foundations of the Abundant Style* [*De duplici copia verborum ac rerum*]. With translation. Vol. 2 of *Collected Works of Erasmus*. Toronto.

Köhler, E. 1964. "Observations historiques et sociologiques sur la poésie des troubadours." *Cahiers de civilisation médiévale* 7:27–51.

Kornhardt, H. 1936. "Exemplum: Eine bedeutungsgeschichtliche Studie." Ph.D. dissertation. Göttingen.

Kretschmer, F. A. 1975. "The 'Res/Verba' Dichotomy and 'Copia' in Renaissance Translating." *Renaissance and Reformation* 11:24–29.

Krikos-Davis, K. 1979. "On Seferis' 'Helen.'" *Byzantine and Modern Greek Studies* 5:57–76.

Kristeva, J. 1969. *Semiotiké*. Paris.

Kristeva, J. 1983. "Les troubadours: Du 'grant chant courtois' au récit allégorique." In *Histoires d'amour,* 263–76. Paris.

Kritzman, L. 1991. *The Rhetoric of Sexuality and the Literature of the French Rensissance*. Cambridge.

Lambropoulos, V. 1988. *Literature as National Institution: Studies in the Politics of Modern Greek Criticism*. Princeton.

Langer, U. 1986. *Invention, Death, and Self-Definition in the Poetry of Pierre de Ronsard*. Stanford.

Langlois, E., ed. 1914–24. *Le Roman de la rose*. 5 vols. Paris.

Laroche, E. 1949. *Histoire de la racine 'nem-' en grec ancien*. Paris.

Lattimore, R., trans. 1947. *Aeschylus I: Oresteia*. Chicago.

Lattimore, R., trans. 1951. *The Iliad of Homer*. Chicago.

Lattimore, R., trans. 1958. *Trojan Women*. In *Euripides III*. Ed. D. Grene and R. Lattimore. Chicago.

Lattimore, R., trans. 1965. *The Odyssey of Homer*. New York.

Laumonier, P., ed. 1914–75. Ronsard. *Oeuvres complètes*. 20 vols. Paris.

Lawler, J. R. 1956. "The Technique of Valéry's *Orphée*." *Journal of the Australian Universities' Modern Language Association* 5:54–64.

Ledwidge, B. 1987. *Sappho: La première voix d'une femme*. Paris.

Lefkowitz, M. R. 1981. *Heroines and Hysterics*. Baltimore.

Lefkowitz, M. R. 1990. *Women in Greek Myth*. Baltimore.

Lemaître, J. 1896. *La Bonne Hélène*. Paris.

Leslie, B. R. 1979. *Ronsard's Successful Epic Venture: The Epyllion*. Lexington, Ky.

Levi, A. H. T. 1973. "The Role of Neoplatonism in Ronsard's Poetic Imagination." In *Ronsard the Poet*. Ed. T. Cave, 121–58. London.

Lewis, C. S. 1936. *The Allegory of Love*. Oxford.

Lichfield, J. 1999. "Doctors Transplant Hand; Medical Frontier: 'Frankenstein' Operation Takes Science into New Moral Territory." London *Independent,* February 8, 5.

Liddell, H. G., R. Scott, and H. Stuart Jones, eds. 1940. *Greek-English Lexicon*. Oxford.

Lindsay, J. 1974. *Helen of Troy: Woman and Goddess*. Totowa, N.J.

Lloyd, M. 1992. *The Agon in Euripides*. Oxford.

Lobel, E., and D. Page, eds. 1955. *Poetarum lesbiorum fragmenta*. Oxford.

Longnon, J. 1921. "Quatre siècles de philhellénisme français." *Revue de France* 1:512–42.

Longon, H. 1950. "Les déboires de Ronsard à la cour." *Bibliothèque d'humanisme et Renaissance* 2:60–80.

Lord, G. deF, ed. 1984 *Andrew Morrell: The Complete Poems.* London.

Lorenz, E. 1971. "Der Name *Lust* in Paul Valéry's erstem Faustfragment." *Romanistisches Jahrbuch* 22:178–90.

Lubow, A. 1993. "What's Killing the Grapevines of Napa?" *New York Times Sunday Magazine,* October 17, 26.

Mackenzie, M. M. 1982. "Paradox in Plato's 'Phaedrus.' " *Proceedings of the Cambridge Philological Society* 208:64–76.

Mallarmé, S. 1945. *Oeuvres complètes.* Ed. H. Mondor and G. Jen-Aubry. Paris.

Mandelbaum, A., trans. 1961. *The Aeneid of Virgil.* New York.

Marcus, G. 1989. *Lipstick Traces.* Cambridge, Mass.

Marrou, H. I. 1958. *St. Augustin et la fin de la culture antique.* 4th ed. Paris.

Mastrodimitris, P. D. 1964. Ἡ ἀρχαία παράδοσις εἰς τὴν ποίησιν τοῦ Σεφέρη. Athens.

Mazzotta, G. 1991. "Antiquity and the New Arts in Petrarch." In *The New Medievalism.* Ed. M. S. Brownlee, K. Brownlee, and S. G. Nichols, 46–69. Baltimore.

McCracken, P. 1998. *The Romance of Adultery: Queenship and Sexual Transgression in Old French Literature.* Philadelphia.

McFarlane, I. D. 1973. "Aspects of Ronsard's Poetic Vision." In *Ronsard the Poet.* Ed. T. Cave, 13–78. London.

McKeon, R. 1936. "Literary Criticism and the Concept of Imitation in Antiquity." *Modern Philology* 34:3–35.

McKeon, R., ed. 1941. Aristotle. *The Basic Works of Aristotle.* New York.

Melara, M. 1992. "Du Bellay and the Inscription of Exile." *Renaissance and Reformation* 28:5–19.

Mentelin, J. 1473. *[Vincent of Beauvais]. Speculum historiale.* Strassburg.

Merrimé, P. 1951. "La Vénus d'Ille." In *Romans et nouvelles.* Paris.

Meybrinck, E. 1886. *Die Auffassung der Antike bei Jacques Milet, Guido de Columna und Benoît de Ste-More.* Marburg.

Meyer, P. 1885. "Les premières compilations françaises d'histoire ancienne." *Romania* 4:63–81.

Micha, A., ed. 1982. *Les romans de Chrétien de Troyes,* vol. 2: *Cligés.* Paris.

Miller, F. J., ed. 1916. *Ovid,* vol. 4: *Metamorphoses.* With translation. Cambridge, Mass.

Miller, N. K. 1986. "Arachnologies: The Woman, the Text, and the Critic." In *The Poetics of Gender.* Ed. N. K. Miller, 270–95. New York.

Mondor, H. 1947. *L'heureuse rencontre de Valéry et Mallarmé.* Paris.

Monro, D. 1901. *Homer's Odyssey,* vol. 2: *Books 13–24.* Oxford.

Montmollin, D. 1951. *La poétique d'Aristote: Texte primitif et additions ultérieures.* Neuchatel.

Morris, M. 1993. "Things to Do with Shopping Centres." In *The Cultural Studies Reader.* Ed. S. During, 295–319. London.

Moss, A. 1984. *Poetry and Fable: Studies in Mythological Narrative in Sixteenth-Century France.* Cambridge.

Most, G. W. 1982. "Greek Lyric Poets." In *Ancient Writers.* Ed. T. J. Luce, 75–98. New York.

Mozley, J. H., ed. 1929. *Ovid,* vol. 2: *The Art of Love and Other Poems.* With translation. Cambridge, Mass.

Mulhauser, R. E. 1969. *Sainte-Beuve and Greco-Roman Antiquity.* Cleveland.

Murnaghan, S. 1987. *Disguises and Recognition in the Odyssey.* Princeton.

Musset, A. de. 1973. "Lettre de Dupuis et Cotonet." In *Poésies.* Ed. B. Lalande, 124–37. Paris.

Nagy, G. 1974. *Comparative Studies in Greek and Indic Meter.* Cambridge, Mass.

Nagy, G. 1979. *The Best of the Achaeans: Concepts of the Hero in Archaic Greek Poetry.* Baltimore.

Nagy, G. 1990. *Pindar's Homer: The Lyric Possession of an Epic Past.* Baltimore.

Nagy, G. 1996. "The Homeric Nightingale and the Poetics of Variation in the Art of the Troubadour." In *Poetry as Performance: Homer and Beyond,* 7–38. Cambridge.

Nash, S. 1983. *Paul Valéry's* Album de vers anciens: *A Past Transfigured.* Princeton.

Nelli, R. 1963. *L'erotique des troubadours.* Toulouse.

Nerval, G. de. 1961. *Oeuvres,* vol. 1. Paris.

Newman, P. 1968. *Hélène de Sparte: La fortune du mythe en France.* Paris.

Nichols, S. G. 1984. "The Promise of Performance: Discourse and Desire in Early Troubadour Lyric." In *The Dialectic of Discovery.* Ed. J. D. Lyons and N. J. Vickers, 93–108. Lexington, Ky.

Nichols, S. G. 1989. "The Old Provençal Lyric." In *A New History of French Literature.* Ed. D. Hollier, 30–35. Cambridge, Mass.

Nichols, S. G. 1991. "An Intellectual Anthropology of Marriage in the Middle Ages." In Brownlee, 70–95.

Nichols, S. G., ed. 1962. *The Songs of Bernart de Ventadorn.* Chapel Hill.

Nilsson, M. P. 1932. *The Mycenaean Origin of Greek Mythology.* Berkeley.

Nilsson, M. P. 1971. *Minoan-Mycenaean Religion and Its Survival in Greek Religion.* New York.

Norton, G. P. 1981. "Humanist Foundations of Translation Theory (1400–1450): A Study in the Dynamics of Word." *Canadian Review of Comparative Literature* (spring): 173–203.

Norton, G. P. 1984. *The Ideology and Language of Translation in Renaissance France and Their Humanist Antecedents.* Geneva.

Norton, G. P. 1989. "Jacques Peletier Translates Horace's *Ars Poetica.*" In *A New History of French Literature.* Ed. D. Hollier, 180–84. Cambridge, Mass.

Noulet-Carner, E. 1968. "Présentation de la décade 'Paul Valéry.'" In Noulet-Carner, ed., 7–8.

Noulet-Carner, E., ed. 1968. *Entretiens sur Paul Valéry.* Paris.

Oates, W. J., and E. O'Neill, Jr., eds. 1938. *The Complete Greek Drama II.* With translations. New York.

Oswald, E. 1905. *The Legend of Fair Helen as Told by Homer, Goethe, and Others.* London.

Owen, E. T. 1966. *The Story of the Iliad.* Ann Arbor.

Owen, S. 1989. *Mi-Lou: Poetry and the Labyrinth of Desire.* Cambridge, Mass.

Pacteau, F. 1994. *The Symptom of Beauty.* Cambridge.

Page, D. 1955a. *The Homeric Odyssey.* Oxford.

Page, D. 1955b. *Sappho and Alcaeus.* With translation and commentary. Oxford.

Page, D., ed. 1962. *Poetae melici Graeci.* Oxford.

Palamas, K. 1958. *Ο Τάφος με τους Ιάμβους καὶ Αναπαίστους.* Athens.

Palamas, K. 1970. *Anthology.* Athens

Panayotopoulos, I. M. 1970. *Poems.* Athens.

Panofsky, E. 1954. *Galileo as a Critic of the Arts.* The Hague.

Parent-Duchâtelet, A. 1836. *De la prostitution dans la ville de Paris.* Abridged as *La prostitution à Paris au XIXe siècle.* Ed. Alain Corbin. Paris, 1981.

Parry, J. J., trans. 1990. *Andreas Cappellanus: The Art of Courtly Love.* New York.

Pasquier, A. 1985. *La Vénus de Milo et les Aphrodites du Louvre.* Paris.

Pavlock, B. 1990. *Eros, Imitation, and the Epic Tradition.* Ithaca.

Pei, M. 1949. *The Story of Language.* Philadelphia.

Pelan, M. 1953. "Ronsard's 'amour d'automne.' " *French Studies* 7:214–22.

Peletier du Mans, J. 1970 [1545; facsimile ed.]. *L'art poétique d'Horace traduit en vers français par Jacques Peletier du Mans, recognu par l'auteur depuis la première impression.* Paris.

Pépin, J. 1958. *Mythe et allégorie: Les origines grecques et les contestations judéo-chrétiennes.* Paris.

Pigman, G. W., III. 1980. "Versions of Imitation in the Renaissance." *Renaissance Quarterly* 33:1–32.

Pine-Coffin, R. S., trans. 1961. Saint Augustine. *Confessions.* Baltimore.

Pirenne, H. 1903. *Histoire de Belgique,* vol. 2. Brussels.

Pirenne, H. 1925. *Medieval Cities.* Trans. F. D. Halsey. Princeton.

Pirenne, H. 1937. *Economic and Social History of Medieval Europe.* New York.

Plöbst, W. 1911. *Die Auxeris.* Munich.

Polites, N. G. 1965. *Παραδόσεις,* vol. 1. Athens.

Politis, L. 1973. *A History of Modern Greek Literature.* Oxford.

Pollan, M. *Second Nature: A Gardener's Education.* New York.

Pommier, J. 1946. "Leçon d'ouverture prononcée au Collège de France." In *Paul Valéry et la création littéraire.* Paris.

Poole, R. L. 1918. *Medieval Reckonings of Time.* London.

Post, L. A., trans. 1925. *Thirteen Epistles of Plato.* Oxford.

Proust, M. 1954. *A la recherche du temps perdu.* 3 vols. Paris.

Proust, M. 1971. *Contre Sainte-Beuve, précédé de pastiches et mélanges.* Ed. Pierre Clarac. Paris.

Pucciani, O. F. 1954. *The French Theater since 1930.* Boston.

Quainton, M. 1995. "Ronsard's *Sonnets pour Hélène* and the Alternative Helen Myth." *Michigan Romance Studies* 15:77–112.

Quint, D. 1983. *Origin and Originality in Renaissance Literature: Versions of the Source.* New Haven.

Raby, F. J. E. 1956. "Explication." In *Princeton Encyclopedia of Poetry and Poetics.* Ed. A. Preminger. Princeton.

Race, W. 1982. *The Classical Priamel from Homer to Boethius.* Leiden.

Raimon Jordan. 1922. *Le troubadour Raimon Jordan.* Ed. H. Kjellman. Uppsala.

Raizis, M. B. 1977. "The Poetic Manner of George Seferis." *Folia neohellenica* 2:105–26.

Rawlinson, G., trans. 1942. *The Persian Wars by Herodotus.* New York.

Raymond, A. G. 1966. *Jean Giraudoux: The Theater of Victory and Defeat.* Amherst, Mass.

Raynaud de Lage, Guy. 1976. *Les premiers romans français.* Geneva.

Reckford, K. J. 1964. "Helen in the *Iliad.*" *Greek, Roman, and Byzantine Studies* 5:5–20.

Reckford, K. J. 1981. "Helen in *Aeneid* 2 and 6." *Arethusa* 14:85–99.

Richard, J.-P. 1970. *Etudes sur le romantisme.* Paris.

Richthofen, E. von. 1961. *Commentaire sur* Mon Faust *de Paul Valéry.* Paris.

Riffaterre, M. 1978. *Semiotics of Poetry.* Bloomington.

Riffaterre, M. 1983. *Text Production.* Trans. Terese Lyons. New York.

Rigolot, F. 1982. *Le texte de la renaissance des rhétoriqueurs à Montaigne.* Geneva.

Rigolot, F. 1989. "Charles Augustin Sainte-Beuve Misses the Deadline for the Submission of His Essay on 16th-Century Literature to the Académie Française: The Invention of the Renaissance." In *A New History of French Literature.* Ed. D. Hollier, 638–44. Cambridge, Mass.

Rimbaud, A. 1972. *Oeuvres complètes.* Paris.

Rissman, L. 1983. *Love as War: Homeric Allusion in the Poetry of Sappho.* Beiträge zur Klassischen Philologie 157. Königstein.

Ritsos, Yannis. 1989. *Selected Poems 1938–1988.* Trans. K. Friar and K. Myrsiades. Brockport, New York.

Roberts, W. R. 1928. *Greek Rhetoric and Literary Criticism.* London.

Roberts, W. R., trans. 1941. *Rhetorica.* In McKeon, ed.

Romilly, Jaqueline de. 1986. *La modernité d'Euripide.* Paris.

Rosenberg, S. N., and H. Tischler, eds. 1981. *Chanter m'estuet: Songs of the trouvères.* London and Boston.

Ross, D. J. A. 1952. "Some Notes on the Old French Alexander Romance in Prose." *French Studies* 6:135–47.

Ross, W. D., trans. 1941. *Nicomachean Ethics.* In McKeon, ed.

Rossi, V., and U. Bosso, eds. 1933–42. Petrarch. *Le familiari,* 4 vols. Florence.

Roubaud, J. 1971. *Les troubadours.* Paris.

Rowe, C. J., ed. 1986. Plato. *Phaedrus.* With introduction and translation. Wiltshire, England.

Russell, D. A., and M. Winterbottom, eds. 1972. *The Rhetoric of Sexuality and the Literature of the French Renaissance.* Cambridge.

Sacks, O. 1987. *The Man Who Mistook His Wife for a Hat.* New York.

Safire, W. 1997. "On Language; Clone, Clone, Clone, Clone." *New York Times Sunday Magazine,* April 6, 18–20.

Said, E. 1979. *Orientalism.* New York.

Sainte-Beuve, C. A. 1881. *Portraits contemporains.* 5 vols. Paris.

Sainte-Beuve, C. A. 1926. *Mes poisons.* Paris.

Sainte-Beuve, C. A. 1930. *Les grands ecrivains français.* Paris.

Sainte-Beuve, C. A. 1953. *Causeries du lundi.* 2 vols. Paris.

Sainte-Beuve, C. A. 1960. *Oeuvres.* 2 vols. Paris.

Sainte-Beuve, C. A. 1963. *Tableau historique et critique de la poésie française au XVIe siècle.* With commentary by Marcel Françon. Cambridge, Mass.

Sand, G. 1869. *Les sept cordes de la lyre.* Paris.

Sandys, J. E., ed. 1915. *Pindar.* With translation. Cambridge, Mass.

Sanford, E. M. 1944. "The Study of Ancient History in the Middle Ages." *Journal of the History of Ideas* 5:21–43.

Sartre, J.-P. 1947. *Situations,* vol. 1. Paris.

Saulnier, V. L. 1964. "Rhétoriqueurs." In *Dictionnaire des lettres françaises,* vol. 1. Ed. V.-L. Fayard. Paris.

Saussure, F. de. 1985. *Cours de linguistique générale.* Ed. T. de Mauro. Paris.

Scarfe, F. 1965. *André Chénier.* Oxford.

Scodel, R. 1980. *The Trojan Trilogy of Euripides.* Göttingen.

Scott, J. A. 1913a. "Paris and Hector in Tradition and in Homer." *Classical Philology* 8:163–71.

Scott, J. A. 1913b. "The Assumed Duration of the War of the *Iliad.*" *Classical Philology* 8:445–56.

Scott-Kilvert, I., trans. 1960. Plutarch. *The Rise and Fall of Athens: Nine Greek Lives.* London.

Seaton, R. C. 1914. "The Aristotelian Enthymeme." *Classical Review* 28:113–19.

Séché, L., ed. 1903. Du Bellay. *Oeuvres complètes,* vol. 1. Paris.

Seferis, G. 1963. *Discours de Stockholm.* Paris.

Seferis, G. 1966. *On the Greek Style.* Trans. R. Warner and T. D. Frangopoulos. Athens.

Seferis, G. 1967. *Poemeta.* Athens.

Seferis, G. 1981. *Collected Poems.* Trans. and intro. E. Keeley and P. Sherrard. Princeton.

Seferis, G. 1989. *Orpheus: The Myth of the Poet.* Baltimore.

Segal, C. 1962. "Gorgias and the Psychology of the Logos." *HSCP* 66:99–155.

Segal, C. 1986. *Interpreting Greek Tragedy: Myth, Poetry, Text.* Ithaca.

Sélincourt, A. de, trans. 1954. *Herodotus: The Histories.* London.

Seznec, J. 1939. *La survivance des dieux antiques.* London.

Sheed, F. J., trans. 1993. Augustine. *Confessions: Books 1–13.* With introduction by Peter Brown. Rev. ed. Indianapolis.

Shell, M. 1978. *The Economy of Literature.* Baltimore.

Sheridan, S., ed. 1988. *Grafts: Feminist Cultural Criticism.* London.

Shorey, P. 1924. "The Origin of the Syllogism." *Classical Philology* 19:1–19.

Shorey, P., ed. 1930 [1953]. Plato. *The Republic.* With translation. Cambridge, Mass.

Showalter, E. 1986. "Piecing and Writing." In *The Poetics of Gender.* Ed. N. K. Miller, 222–47. New York.

Showerman, G., ed. 1914. *Ovid,* vol. 1: *Heroides and Amores.* With translation. Cambridge, Mass.

Sifakis, G. M. 1986. "Learning from Art and Pleasure in Learning: An Interpretation of Aristotle Poetics 4.1448b8–19." In *Studies in Honour of T. B. L. Webster.* Ed. J. H. Betts, J. T. Hooker, J. R. Green, 211–22. Bristol.

Sikelianos, A. 1951. *Apanta III.* Athens.

Silver, I. 1961. *Ronsard and the Hellenic Renaissance in France,* vol. 1: *Ronsard and the Greek Epic.* Paris.

Silver, I. 1969. *The Intellectual Evolution of Ronsard,* vol. 1: *The Formative Influences.* St. Louis.

Silver, I. 1987. *Ronsard and the Hellenic Renaissance in France,* vol. 2: *Ronsard and the Grecian Lyre.* Geneva.

Silverman, K. 1983. *The Subject of Semiotics.* New York.

Simpson, J. A., and E. S. C. Weiner, eds. 1989. *The Oxford English Dictionary*. Oxford.

Singer, K. 1958. "Oikonomia: An Inquiry into Beginnings of Economic Thought and Language." *Kyklos* 2:29–55.

Sinopoulos, T. 1951. *Landscape of Death*. Trans. K. Friar. Columbus, Ohio.

Smith, G. M., J. B. Overton, et al. 1928. *A Textbook of General Botany*. New York.

Smock, A. 1986. *Double Dealing*. Lincoln.

Smock, A. 1989. "Jean Giraudoux's First Play, *Siegfried*, Is Staged by Louis Jouvet at the Comédie des Champs-Elysées in Paris: Amnesias." In *A New History of French Literature*. Ed. D. Hollier, 881–87. Cambridge, Mass.

Smyth, H. W. 1920. *Greek Grammar*. Cambridge, Mass.

Staines, D., trans. 1990. *The Complete Romances of Chrétien de Troyes*. Bloomington.

Starobinski, J. 1978. "André Chénier and the Allegory of Poetry." Trans. W. Walling. In *Images of Romanticism: Verbal and Visual Affinities*. Ed. K. Kroeber and W. Walling, 39–60. New Haven.

Stecher, J., ed. 1885. *Oeuvres de Jean Lemaire de Belges*. 3 vols. Louvain.

Steiner, G. 1975. *After Babel: Aspects of Language and Translation*. New York.

Stone, D., Jr., 1966. *Ronsard's Sonnet Cycles: A Study in Tone and Vision*. New Haven.

Struever, N. S. 1970. *The Language of History in the Renaissance: Rhetorical and Historical Consciousness in Florentine Humanism*. Princeton.

Suzuki, M. 1989. *Metamorphoses of Helen: Authority, Difference and the Epic*. Ithaca.

Tauranac, J. 1999. "Lost New York, Found in Architecture's Crannies." *New York Times*, February 12.

Taylor, C. H., ed. 1963. *Essays on the Odyssey*. Bloomington.

Telle, E. V. 1950. "Erasme et les mariages dynastiques." *Bibliothèque d'humanisme et Renaissance* 12:7–13.

Thibaut, F. 1888. *Marguerite d'Autriche et Jehan Lemaire de Belges*. Paris.

Tieghem, P. V. 1923. *Le mouvement romantique*. Paris.

Tredennick, H., trans. 1954. *The Last Days of Socrates*. Harmondsworth, Middlesex.

Troeltsch, E. 1922. *Der Historismus und seine Überwindung*. Berlin.

Trojel, E., ed. 1892. *Andrea Capellani regii Francorum De amore libri tres*. Havniae.

Trousson, R. 1984. "L'accueil fait au théâtre de Verhaeren." In *Emile Verhaeren*. Ed. P.-E. Knabe, 93–106. Brussels.

Tuve, R. 1966. *Allegorical Imagery: Some Mediaeval Books and Their Posterity*. Princeton.

Tyard, P. de. 1950. *Oeuvres: Le solitaire premier*. Geneva.

Valatoritis, N. 1990. *My Afterlife Guaranteed*. San Francisco.

Valéry, P. 1929. *Poésies*. Paris.

Valéry, P. 1931. "Extraits du log-book de Monsieur Teste." In *Oeuvres de Paul Valéry*. Paris.

Valéry, P. 1933. *L'idée fixe*. Paris.

Valéry, P. 1944. *Variété V*. Paris.

Valéry, P. 1946. *Mon Faust (Ebauches)*. Paris.

Valéry, P. 1947. *Souvenirs poétiques, receuillis par un auditeur au cours d'une conférence prononcée à Bruxelles le 9 janvier 1942*. Paris.

Valéry, P. 1952. *Lettres à quelques-uns*. Paris.

Valéry, P. 1957. *Oeuvres*. 2 vols. Ed. J. Hytier. Paris.

Valéry, P. 1957–61. *Cahiers.* 29 vols. Paris.

Valesio, P. 1976. "The Virtues of Traducement: Sketch of a Theory of Translation." *Semiotica* 18:1–96.

Vance, E. 1975. "Love's Concordance: The Poetics of Desire and the Joy of the Text." *Diacritics* (spring):40–52.

Vance, E. 1985. "Greimas, Freud, and the Story of Trouvère Lyric." In Hosek and Parker, eds., 93–105.

Van Hook, L. 1923. *Greek Life and Thought.* New York.

Van Hook, L., ed. 1945. *Isocrates,* vol. 3. With translation. Cambridge, Mass.

Vaughn, R. 1962. *Philip the Bold: The Formation of the Burgundian State.* Cambridge, Mass.

Vellacott, P., trans. 1954. Euripides. *The Bacchae and Other Plays.* London.

Verhaeren, E. 1912. *Hélène de Sparte.* Paris.

Vernant, J. P. 1965. *Mythe et pensée chez les Grecs: Études de psychologie historique.* Paris.

Vianey, J. 1909. *Le Petrarquisme en France au XVIe siècle.* Montpellier.

Vinge, L. 1967. *The Narcissus Theme in Western European Literature up to the Early Nineteenth Century.* Trans. R. Dewsnap, N. Reeves, et al. Lund.

Vivante, P. 1970. *The Homeric Imagination: A Study of Homer's Poetic Perception of Reality.* Bloomington.

von Weise, B. 1947. *Die Helena-Tragödie in Goethe's Faust.* Essen.

Wais, K. N.d. "Goethe und Valéry's 'Faust.' " In *Mélanges de littérature comparée et de philologie offerts à Mieczyslaw Brahmer,* 555–79. Warsaw.

Wall, K. 1988. *The Callisto Myth from Ovid to Atwood: Initiation and Rape in Literature.* Kingston, Ontario.

Walsh, P. G., ed. 1982. *De amore et amoris remedio.* With introduction. London.

Walzer, P.-O. 1953. *La poésie de Valéry.* Geneva.

Ware, R. D. 1976. "Medieval Chronology." In *Medieval Studies: An Introduction.* Ed. J. M. Powell, 213–37. Syracuse.

Warren, F. M. 1901. "On the Latin Sources of Thèbes and Enéas." *PMLA* 16:3885.

Watts, W., ed. 1912. *St. Augustine's Confessions.* London.

Way, A. S., ed. 1912. *Euripides,* vol. 1. With translation. Cambridge, Mass.

Weber, H. 1956. *La création poétique au XVIe siècle en France.* Paris.

Weber, H., and C. Weber, eds. 1963. *Pierre de Ronsard: Les amours.* With introduction and notes. Paris.

Webster, T. B. L. 1967. *The Tragedies of Euripides.* London.

Weinberg, B. 1950. *Critical Prefaces of the Renaissance.* Evanston, Ill.

Weinberg, K. 1976. *The Figure of Faust in Valéry and Goethe: An Exegesis of Mon Faust.* Princeton.

Wells, R., trans. 1988. Theocritus. *The Idylls.* London.

Welter, J. T. 1927. *L'exemplum dans la littérature du moyen âge.* Paris.

West, M. 1967. *Fragmenta Hesiodea.* Oxford.

West, M. 1970. "Burning Sappho." *Maia* 22:307–30.

White, H. 1966. "The Burden of History." *History and Theory* 5:111–34.

Whitman, C. H. 1958. *Homer and the Heroic Tradition.* Cambridge.

Whitman, J. 1986. *Allegory.* Cambridge, Mass.

Wilamowitz-Moellendorff, U. von. 1913. *Sappho und Simonides.* Berlin.

Wilcock, M. 1976. *A Companion to the Iliad.* Chicago.

Will, E. 1954. "De l'aspect éthique des origines grecques de la monnaie." *Revue historique* 212:209–31.

Wilson, E. 1943. *Axel's Castle: A Study in the Imaginative Literature of 1870–1930.* New York.

Wimsatt, W. K., and M. C. Beardsley. 1981. "The Intentional Fallacy." In *Critical Theory since Plato.* Ed. H. Adams, 1014–23. New York.

Winkler, E. 1914. *Die Lieder Raouls von Soissons.* Niemeyer.

Wolf, N. 1994. *The Beauty Myth: How Images of Beauty Are Used against Women.* New York.

Wollensköld, A., ed. 1925. *Thibaut de Champagne.* Paris.

Zeitlin, F. I. 1996. *Playing the Other: Gender and Society in Classical Greek Literature.* Chicago.

Zola, E. 1885. *Nana.* Paris.

Zola, E. 1971. *Le roman expérimental.* Paris.

Zumthor, P. 1972. *Essai de poétique médiévale.* Paris.

Zumthor, P. 1987. *La lettre et la voix: De la "littérature" médiévale.* Paris.

Zumthor, P., ed. 1978. *Anthologie des grands rhétoriqueurs.* Paris.

Zumthor, P. and L. Vocina-Pusca. 1974. "Le *je* de la chanson et le *moi* du poéte chez les premiers trouvères 1180–1220." *Canadian Review of Comparative Literature* 1:9–21.

Acknowledgments

This book has survived only by way of tiny cataclysms and comic catastrophes, much like its eponymous heroine, and through the kindness of many strangers and friends, whose gifts—so generously were they offered, so shamelessly were they accepted—have by now become thefts. I am, in other words, seriously in debt. One of the suggestions of this book is that there is no way to repay a debt, but that saying thank you seems to make those who owe, and those who are owed, feel a little bit better. Thank you, then:

To Marjorie Garber, Per Nykrog, Stephen Owen, Susan Suleiman, Jan Ziolkowski, and all of my teachers and mentors and colleagues at the Department of Comparative Literature and the Literature Concentration at Harvard University, where much of this book was written as a doctoral dissertation; but especially to my dissertation advisers, Margaret Alexiou, Barbara Johnson, and Gregory Nagy, a most enviable triumvirate. This book and, in fact, my entire academic career owes more to Barbara, perhaps, than to anyone else as simply the best teacher I ever had.

To Chris Braider, Margaret Ferguson, Paul Gordon, Ralph Hexter, Vernon Minor, the Department of Humanities and Comparative Literature, and the participants in the College Interdisciplinary Seminar in the Humanities on "Discourses of History," all at the University of Colorado at Boulder; and to Keith Cohen, Heather Evans, Katherine Lydon, Mary Lydon, Sylvia Montiglio, and Jane Tylus at the University of Wisconsin–Madison. All of them in various ways helped to rescue Helen from the overgrown and entangled forest that was my manuscript.

To the Office of the Provost at Bilkent University in Ankara, Turkey, for a research grant that allowed me to meet with my editors at the University of Wisconsin Press and to hand over to them, safe and sound, a new and improved Helen, complete with make-over and considerably slimmer.

To Carla Aspelmeier, Jane Barry, Amalia Culp, Sheila McMahon, and Alison Ruch, who all worked very hard at the University of Wisconsin Press and demonstrated patience of heroic proportions in dealing with a difficult and unwieldy text; especially to Raphael Kadushin, without whom this book might not have been published—at least not yet.

Last but most certainly not least, to all of those friends who, through the years, kept vigil over Helen and, on a number of occasions, resuscitated her (or was it me?) when she (I) was on the point of expiring: Patricia Barbeitos, Alessandra Benedicty, Florence Bernault, Ksenija Bilbija, Elena Coda, Laura Deluca, Karl-Heinz Finken, Nina Gellert, Sarah Gore, Richard Halpern, Gillian Johnson, Svetlana Karpe, Gerhard Richter, Patrick and Graziella Rumble, and Monique Tschofen; but above all to Christopher Calderhead, Vangelis Calotychos, José Manuel Delpino, Rhonda Garelick, and Tania November; and to my parents Esther and Gary, and my brother, Eric.

A special thank you must go, finally, to Elizabeth Amann, whose unrelenting and unforgiving critical intelligence, and simple common sense, transformed this book from something pretty bad into something, well, maybe not so bad.

Index

abduction: Helen's, xi, xiv, 4, 9, 10, 21, 23;
  Clotilde's, 157–58; Kore's, 9–10, 279*n27*;
  in *Phaedrus,* 45; repetition and, 9, 10; syllogism as, 23, 50, 71, 275*n5;* in *Theseus,*
  295*n2*
Achelous, 45–46, 270*n6*
Achilles: in *La Belle Hélène,* 226, 275; and
  figure of tomb, 188, 189; as Helen's husband,
  7, 12, 58, 218, 295*n2;* in *Iliad,* 5, 25, 37,
  64, 188; in modern Greece, 299*n12;* and
  Odysseus, 267*n23;* in *Le roman de Troie,*
  133, 134, 135
Adam. *See* Eve
Adonis, 226, 299*n12*
adynaton (impossibility), 117
Aeneas: and Benoît de Sainte-Maure, 284*n23*
Aeschylus, 12–13, 270*n8*
—work of: *Agamemnon,* 12–13, 268*n27*
Agamemnon: in *Agamemnon,* 12–13, 268*n27;*
  in *La Belle Hélène,* 225, 226; in *Iliad,* 5, 9,
  64, 267*n15;* in *teichoskopia,* 267*n15*
Agido, 91, 95, 278*n15*
Agnello, 281*n19*
agon: Harold Bloom on, 266*n7;* juridical form
  of, 276*n24;* Trojan war as, 79; in *Trojan
  Women,* 39, 71, 76–81, 276*n30,* 277*n41,*
  288*n26*
Aias. *See* Ajax
ainos (enigma), 4, 266*n4*
Aithra (Aethra), handmaiden of Helen, 7, 9,
  267*n19*
Ajax, 58, 226, 247, 267*n15*
Albertus (father of Helen in George Sand's *Les
  sept cordes de la lyre*), 207
Alcaeus, 84, 87, 92, 93, 278*n19*
Alcimus Avitus, 125
Alcman, 84, 86, 91, 278*n15,* 279*nn23, 24, 28*

Alexandre (heir to throne of Constantinople in
  Cligés), 143
Alexandros. *See* Paris
Alexiou, Margaret, 241, 269*n9*
Alis, king of Constantinople, 143
Alkandre, wife of Polybos, 269*n11*
allegory of cave, 14–17; as *teichoskopia,* 16–17
Altman, Lawrence K., 255–56
Altneuland: Greece as, 239, 240
Ameis, K. F., 266*n9*
Amour: as artisan in Ronsard's poetry, 180
Amphion, 293*n25*
amplificatio: brevity and, 284*n27;* in *Illustra-
  tions de Gaule et singularitez de Troye,* 156;
  in *Le roman de Troie,* 137–38
anachronism, 5–6, 7, 225–26; in *A la recher-
  che du temps perdu,* 236–37; Auerbach on,
  6; exemplum and, 102; in *Iliad,* 5–6, 266*n9;*
  in medieval authors, 280*n3;* in *Le roman de
  Troie,* 133–35; in *teichoskopia,* 5
Anactoria, 65, 66, 67, 92, 93, 94, 95; as choral
  leader, 95; Helen as foil to, 67; missed by
  Sappho, 278*n18*
anagnorismos (recognition): Aristotle on, 27,
  32–33
anax (master): and Anactoria 95; and Dioscuri,
  95
Anderson, Benedict, 295*n2*
Anderson, W. S., 269*n4*
Andromaque: in *La guerre de Troie n'aura
  pas lieu,* 229, 230, 231; in *Trojan Women,*
  276*n36*
Anne de Bretagne, patron of Jean Lemaire de
  Belges, 158, 159
Annius de Viterbe, 152
Antaeus: Goethe's Faust as, 291*n8*
Antenor: as Judas in *Le roman de Troie,* 133